Deliberative Theory and Deconstruction

Deliberative Theory and Deconstruction
A Democratic Venture

Steven Gormley

EDINBURGH
University Press

Edinburgh University Press is one of the leading university presses in the UK. We publish academic books and journals in our selected subject areas across the humanities and social sciences, combining cutting-edge scholarship with high editorial and production values to produce academic works of lasting importance. For more information visit our website: edinburghuniversitypress.com

© Steven Gormley, 2020, 2022

Edinburgh University Press Ltd
The Tun – Holyrood Road
12(2f) Jackson's Entry
Edinburgh EH8 8PJ

First published in hardback by Edinburgh University Press 2020

Typeset in 10/12 Bembo by
Servis Filmsetting Ltd, Stockport, Cheshire

A CIP record for this book is available from the British Library

ISBN 978 1 4744 7528 0 (hardback)
ISBN 978 1 4744 7529 7 (paperback)
ISBN 978 1 4744 7530 3 (webready PDF)
ISBN 978 1 4744 7531 0 (epub)

The right of Steven Gormley to be identified as the author of this work has been asserted in accordance with the Copyright, Designs and Patents Act 1988, and the Copyright and Related Rights Regulations 2003 (SI No. 2498).

Contents

Acknowledgements	vi
List of Abbreviations	viii
Introduction: Doing Justice to the Other	1
1. Blind Spots and Insights: Between Deliberation and Agonism	12
2. A More Expansive Conception of Deliberation	62
3. Arguments and Hearing Something New	102
4. The Possibility of Political Thought and the Experience of Undecidability	144
5. The Demands of Deconstruction	189
6. The Democratic Venture	231
Bibliography	275
Index	299

Acknowledgements

This book started out as a PhD thesis. It was a huge stroke of luck to have David McNeill assigned as a supervisor. The debt I owe David, not only for his supervision but for his guidance and friendship, is immeasurable. I am equally grateful for not only having had Dan Watts on my PhD boards, but to now have him as a colleague and friend. I would also like to thank Peter Dews for meeting up to discuss my work in its early stages, Fabian Freyenhagen for feedback on earlier pieces, and Alexandra Popescu for her feedback on the manuscript and for all her work on the index. I am grateful to colleagues in the philosophy department at Essex for the numerous ways in which they have supported me (whether it's conversations about my work, bringing emergency supplies around when I was in bunker mode during the last stages of writing, or stepping in to cover my admin duties at very short notice so I could focus on getting the manuscript finished). Many thanks to the FLSC for much-needed laughter. I would also like to thank two anonymous reviewers for their helpful comments, Carol Macdonald and James Dale at Edinburgh University Press for all their help, and Cathy Falconer for her meticulous copy-editing. The IDA programme at Essex has been a hospitable environment over the years. Special thanks to Jason Glynos, David Howarth and Aletta Norval who have all been supportive and generous with their time. I am particularly fortunate to have met Savvas Voutryas there. His critical voice and sense of humour have been a constant source of encouragement. This book is part of the conversation we began in Thessaloniki back in 2008.

My debt to my partner, Alexandra, is incalculable. She continues to teach me every day what doing justice to the other looks like.

Material from Chapter 2 was published in 'Deliberation, Unjust Exclusion, and the Rhetorical Turn', *Contemporary Political Theory*, 18:2 (2019), 202–26. Material from Chapters 4 and 5 was published in 'Rearticulating the Concept of Experience, Rethinking the Demands of Deconstruction', *Research in Phenomenology*, 42:3 (2012), 374–407.

Abbreviations

Works by Jacques Derrida

AD   *Adieu to Emmanuel Levinas*, trans. Pascale-Anne Brault and Michael Naas (Stanford: Stanford University Press, 1999).

AP   *Aporias*, trans. Thomas Dutoit (Stanford: Stanford University Press, 1993).

ARSS   'Autoimmunity: Real and Symbolic Suicides', in Giovanni Borradori (ed.), *Philosophy in a Time of Terror* (Chicago: University of Chicago Press, 2003), 85–136.

DE   *Deconstruction Engaged: The Sydney Seminars*, ed. Paul Patton (Sydney: Power Publications, 2001).

FL   'Force of Law: The "Mystical Foundation of Authority"', in Drucilla Cornell, Michael Rosenfeld and David Gray Carlson (eds), *Deconstruction and the Possibility of Justice* (London: Routledge, 1992), 3–67.

FWT   *For What Tomorrow Brings*, with Elisabeth Roudinesco, trans. Jeff Fort (Stanford: Stanford University Press, 2004).

GD   *The Gift of Death*, trans. David Wills (Chicago: University of Chicago Press, 1996).

IOG   *Edmund Husserl's Origin of Geometry: An Introduction* (Lincoln: University of Nebraska Press, 1989).

LI   *Limited Inc* (Evanston: Northwestern University Press, 1988).

LR   'The Laws of Reflection: For Nelson Mandela', in Jacques Derrida and Mustapha Tili (eds), *For Nelson Mandela* (New York: Seaver Books, 1987), 13–42.

M	*Margins of Philosophy*, trans. Alan Bass (Brighton: Harvester Press, 1982).
N	*Negotiations: Interventions and Interviews, 1971–2001*, ed. Elizabeth Rottenberg (Stanford: Stanford University Press, 2002).
OG	*Of Grammatology*, trans. Gayatri Chakravorty Spivak (Baltimore: Johns Hopkins University Press, 1976).
OH	*Of Hospitality*, trans. Rachel Bowlby (Stanford: Stanford University Press, 2000).
PF	*Politics of Friendship*, trans. George Collins (London: Verso, 1997).
PM	*Paper Machine*, trans. Rachel Bowlby (Stanford: Stanford University Press, 2005).
PS	*Points . . . Interviews 1974–1994*, ed. Elisabeth Weber (Stanford: Stanford University Press, 1995).
PSY	*Psyche: Inventions of the Other, Volume I*, ed. Peggy Kamuf and Elizabeth Rottenberg (Stanford: Stanford University Press, 2007).
RDP	'Remarks on Deconstruction and Pragmatism', in Chantal Mouffe (ed.), *Deconstruction and Pragmatism* (London: Routledge, 1996), 78–90.
ROD	*Responsibilities of Deconstruction*, ed. Jonathan Dronsfield and Nick Midgley, *PLI: Warwick Journal of Philosophy*, 6 (Summer 1997).
RS	*Rogues: Two Essays on Reason*, trans. Pascale-Anne Brault and Michael Naas (Stanford: Stanford University Press, 2005).
SM	*Spectres of Marx*, trans. Peggy Kamuf (London: Routledge, 1994).
SP	*Speech and Phenomena*, trans. David B. Alison (Evanston: Northwestern University Press, 1973).
TOH	*The Other Heading*, trans. Pascale-Anne Brault and Michael Naas (Bloomington: Indiana University Press, 1992).
VM	'Violence and Metaphysics', in *Writing and Difference*, trans. Alan Bass, (London: Routledge, 1978), 97–192.
VR	'The Villanova Roundtable', in John Caputo (ed.), *Deconstruction in a Nutshell* (New York: Fordham University Press, 1997), 3–28.

WA   *Without Alibi*, trans. Peggy Kamuf (Stanford: Stanford University Press, 2002).

Works by Jürgen Habermas

BFN   *Between Facts and Norms: A Contribution to a Discourse Theory of Law and Democracy*, trans. William Rehg (Cambridge: Polity Press, 1996).
CD   'Constitutional Democracy: A Paradoxical Union of Contradictory Principles?', *Political Theory*, 29:6 (2001), 766–81.
E   *Europe: The Faltering Project*, trans. Ciaran Cronin (Cambridge: Polity Press, 2009).
IO   *The Inclusion of the Other: Studies in Political Theory*, trans. Ciaran Cronin (Cambridge, MA: MIT Press, 1999).

Works by Others

A   Chantal Mouffe, *Agonistics: Thinking the World Politically* (London: Verso, 2013).
CIS   Richard Rorty, *Contingency, Irony, Solidarity* (Cambridge: Cambridge University Press, 1989).
CP   Richard Rorty, *Consequences of Pragmatism* (Brighton: Harvester Press, 1982).
DDB   John S. Dryzek, *Deliberative Democracy and Beyond: Liberals, Critics, Contestations* (Oxford: Oxford University Press, 2002).
DP   Chantal Mouffe, *The Democratic Paradox* (London: Verso, 2000).
EHO   Richard Rorty, *Essays on Heidegger and Others: Philosophical Papers, Volume 2* (Cambridge: Cambridge University Press, 1991).
IDT   Richard Rorty, 'Is Derrida a Transcendental Philosopher?', in Gary B. Madison (ed.), *Working Through Derrida* (Evanston: Northwestern University Press, 1993), 137–46.
LD   Thomas McCarthy, 'Legitimacy and Diversity: A Dialectical Reflection on Analytic Distinctions', *Cardozo Law Review*, 17 (1995), 1082–125.

ABBREVIATIONS

OP Chantal Mouffe, *On the Political* (Oxford: Routledge, 2005).
PD James Bohman, *Public Deliberation: Pluralism, Complexity, and Democracy* (Cambridge, MA: MIT Press, 1996).
PI Thomas McCarthy, 'The Politics of the Ineffable: Derrida's Deconstructionism', in *Ideals and Illusions: On Reconstruction and Deconstruction in Critical Theory* (Cambridge, MA: MIT Press, 1991), 97–119.
R Aristotle, *Rhetoric*, trans. Joe Sachs (Newburyport, MA: Focus Publishing, 2009).
RP Chantal Mouffe, *The Return of the Political* (London: Verso, 1998).
TJ Ernesto Laclau, 'The Time Is Out of Joint', in *Emancipation(s)* (London: Verso, 1996), 66–86.
TP Richard Rorty, *Truth and Progress: Philosophical Papers, Volume 3* (Cambridge: Cambridge University Press, 1998).

To my mother for never uttering the phrase 'proper job' and for putting up with the professional student; to my brother for driving me all over the country and for giving me the shoes off his feet; to my sister for her 'education speech' and for showing me that things could be otherwise.

Introduction: Doing Justice to the Other

> The equal respect for everyone else demanded by a moral universalism sensitive to difference thus takes the form of a *nonleveling* and *nonappropriating* inclusion of the other *in his otherness*.
>
> Jürgen Habermas (IO, 40)

> Justice is not the same as rights; it exceeds and founds the rights of man ... It is the experience of the other as other, the fact that I let the other be other ...
>
> Jacques Derrida (N, 105)

In 2015 an article appeared in Britain's most widely read newspaper, *The Sun*, that opened with the following: 'No, I don't care. Show me pictures of coffins, show me bodies floating in water, play violins and show me skinny people looking sad. I still don't care.' The article went on to warn the reader to 'make no mistake, these migrants are like cockroaches', before proposing the solution: 'Bring on the gunships, force migrants back to their shores and burn the boats.'[1] That such an article was published is staggering; that its appearing is not entirely incomprehensible is disturbing. While we may not be living in truly dark times just yet (though some, no doubt, are), we are living in increasingly hostile times. And the horizons are darkening.

In 2012 Theresa May, then a Home Secretary who would become Prime Minister of the UK four years later, made the following statement: 'The aim is to create, here in Britain, a really hostile environment for illegal immigrants.'[2] That plan – far more ambitious than 'illegal' would suggest – has been a terrible success. Not only has May's policy created a hostile environment for pretty much anyone arriving on these shores,[3] but the spirit of May's poisonous statement has spread its way through society. Whether it's refugees, immigrants, foreigners, ethnic minorities, the unemployed, the poor, the homeless, those who have a disability, Jews, Muslims, Travellers or the LGBTQI community, hostility to constructed 'others' increasingly defines Britain in 2020.[4] Looking further afield – for example, Europe and the US – the sense that this hostility is threatening to engulf us all in truly dark times is difficult to resist.

I point to these problems not in order to propose a solution to them in the pages that follow (this would be a preposterous claim), but to signal the context in which the notion of doing justice to the other in their otherness is still very much 'a "central" – if not *the* central – theoretical/practical question of our time'.[5] Western liberal democracies have drifted along in the drowsy assurance that certain historical experiences were just that – historical experiences that have been overcome through struggles for justice. But it's increasingly clear that many of our seemingly dead rights have disturbingly live futures.[6]

In thinking about what doing justice to the other involves, this book turns to the work of Jürgen Habermas and Jacques Derrida, and the traditions of deliberative theory and deconstruction they have respectively inspired. The question of how to do justice to the other is central to their work. This is unsurprising given that the thought of both developed in the shadow of a murderous anti-Semitism. Recalling his experience as a teenager in Nazi Germany listening to the Nuremberg trials on the radio, Habermas describes being 'struck by the ghastliness' of the 'collectively realized inhumanity' revealed, an experience that constituted 'the first rupture, that still gapes'.[7] Growing up in Algeria, Derrida, 'a little black and very Arab Jew', experienced 'one of the earthquakes' of his life when he was expelled from school as a result of legislation reducing the percentage of Jews that could be admitted to Algerian classes.[8] Derrida described being 'deeply wounded by anti-Semitism', a wound that 'never completely healed' (FWT, 111). His teenage years were also marked by a pervasive racism:

I knew from experience that the daggers could be bared at any moment, as one left school, in the football stadium, in the midst of racist taunts that spared no one: the Arab, the Jew, the Spaniard, the Maltese, the Italian, the Corsican . . . It is an experience that leaves nothing intact, an atmosphere that one goes on breathing for ever. (PS, 120)

I mention these biographical details not to justify turning to these individual thinkers (as indicated, this book engages with broader traditions), but to remind ourselves of the darkening of horizons that motivates the central problem this book addresses, namely, what does it mean, and how can we respond to the demand, to do justice to the other? Habermas and Derrida, and the traditions they have inspired, not only put this question at the centre of their work; they provide compelling answers in response to this demand.

We can think about the difficulties generated by this demand as follows. Doing justice to the other implies a gesture towards an egalitarian universalism, understood in terms of equal respect and equal treatment for all. And this universalism requires abstracting away from the concrete singularity of the individual to the abstract features one shares with all others as a person. However, doing justice to the other in their otherness also demands that we remain sensitive to the concrete singularity of the other *as other*. And this requires a suspension of abstraction.[9] The problem, then, is that justice requires us to grasp the other as both the abstract bearer of universal characteristics and a singular, irreplaceable individual. This book addresses this aporia head on.

Deliberative theorists respond to the demand to do justice to the other by developing an account of inclusive processes of democratic deliberation. The thought is that through such processes one is able to generate universalisable norms that secure equality and ensure democratic legitimacy, without this being at the expense of the singularity of the individual. Inclusive, non-levelling and non-appropriating processes of deliberation thus become a central concern for deliberativists. The non-levelling requirement resists reducing social actors to the abstract determinations they share with all. The non-appropriating requirement resists imposing on unique individuals a specific form of identity and comportment as a condition for participating in deliberation.

Critics of deliberative theory remain sceptical. They maintain that the deliberative approach is modelled on restrictive conceptions of rational argument, impartiality and consensus. This, critics contend, leaves deliberative theory blind to the nature of political contestation and the ways in which it unjustly excludes certain voices from the deliberative stage. The other is included, but not *as other*. While critics raise important questions about the deliberative approach, I suggest that not only do these involve a misreading of Habermas in crucial respects, but they also fail to take into account the reworking of Habermas's account by successive generations of deliberative theorists.

Turning to the work of Derrida, I respond to misreadings from two directions. On the one hand, critics tend to read Derridean deconstruction as a totalising critique of reason that withdraws from the realm of politics. This leaves deconstruction, at best, with nothing substantial to say, and, at worst, in a normative paralysis that remains vulnerable to the worst. On the other hand, a number of thinkers sympathetic to Derrida's work maintain that Derrida does have substantial things to say, but his work is without any normative dimension and this is no bad thing.

If this book tasks itself with confronting the aporia of doing justice to the other as other, claiming that we need to draw on the insights of both deliberative theory and deconstruction might seem to be doubling our difficulties by generating a methodological problem. Such an approach will find itself caught in 'the time-honoured debate about conflict and consensus-orientated social and political thought'.[10] This debate – in relation to deliberativists and difference democrats (to use John Dryzek's term) – remains in an impasse. If we are to make progress on the substantive problem of doing justice to the other, then we need to make progress on the methodological problem. These two broad traditions of political thought need to do justice to each other.[11]

My strategy consists of two steps. Firstly, I argue for a more expansive conception of deliberation and a more minimal account of democratic legitimacy. I develop this through a critical engagement with critiques of Habermas and developments within contemporary deliberative theory. This reveals a deliberative theory far more open to difference and contestation than critics suggest. Secondly, I argue that Derridean deconstruction is neither a normatively impotent ethics of mere 'openness to the other' nor a politically disabling withdrawal from empirical inquiry into transcendental reflection. Challenging such readings, offered by both critical theorists and poststructuralists, I argue that Derridean deconstruction should be understood as orientated by the demand to maintain an ethos of interruption. Such an ethos commits one to a constitutional democracy and, far from withdrawing from the empirical, propels one into struggles to transform the contexts and institutions in which one finds oneself. Clearing away these mutual misunderstandings will, hopefully, reveal ground on which a more productive dialogue can develop.

Approaching this dialogue from the deconstructive end, I argue that Derrida has been engaged in a long-standing effort to develop a more expansive conception of reasoned argument that overlaps with recent work in deliberative theory. I also show that deconstruction points to, and engages in, a democratic form of politics and shares with deliberativists a dynamic understanding of constitutional democracy. From the deliberative end, I show how contemporary deliberativists are developing a more conflictual conception of democratic deliberation and are engaging in empirical work that suggests concrete ways of responding to the deconstructive demand to maintain an ethos of interruption.

The possibility of such a dialogue is not limited to correcting misunderstandings and revealing overlapping areas of concern. The dialogue that I am proposing seeks to include both approaches, but in a way that avoids simply levelling out the differences or appropriating one in the terms of the other. The aim is to open up the possibility of a *dialogue*. Drawing on the insights of each is crucial if this is to be productive for both. The deliberative approach is key for thinking through the procedures that can help maintain the very ethos of interruption that inspires the deconstructive approach. The deconstructive approach is crucial in revealing the unavoidable aporias generated by trying to do justice to the other and for identifying the forms and codes that serve to prevent certain voices from making it onto the deliberative stage.

While tensions between each approach remain, I suggest that these tensions can be productive.

In Chapter 1 I discuss Chantal Mouffe's critique of Habermas, focusing on two aspects of that critique: what I call the elimination of the passion argument and the antagonistic exclusion thesis. The former charges Habermas's approach with being blind to the affective dimension of democratic politics; the latter with failing to grasp the ineradicable nature of antagonistic exclusion. This results in a deliberative approach that not only unjustly excludes certain voices from the public sphere, but eliminates politics as such. I think Mouffe's critique misses its mark in crucial respects. A key reason for this is because Mouffe does not engage with Habermas's two-track model of democratic politics. Habermas's account of an 'anarchic' sphere of informal opinion-formation points to a conception of democratic politics that does not require the elimination of the passions and is not blind to collective identifications. While Habermas's account lacks a detailed analysis of both, this does not mean that deliberative theory requires the elimination of either. Where Mouffe's critique does hit its mark – in revealing tensions in Habermas's account of what entering practical discourse entails, and, specifically, in the demand for impartiality – I show that this has been addressed within deliberative theory. In the second half of the chapter I critically engage with Mouffe's agonistic approach. I argue that Mouffe's account of the affective dimension of collective identifications provides an insufficient theorisation of the role of the passions and fantasy in democratic life. I also suggest two problems with her account of antagonistic exclusion. First, her claim that a universal 'we' is a conceptual impossibility is insufficiently defended. Second, there is a continual slip between a possible and necessary antagonism that reveals an unresolved dilemma at the heart of her account.

In Chapter 2 I argue that contemporary deliberativists are rethinking deliberative theory in ways that meet the major criticisms made of Habermas's model. While these theorists differ in terms of the account of deliberation they favour, all are concerned to avoid the exclusionary implications of overly rationalistic conceptions of public reason and overly idealised demands of impartiality and consensus. This leads to more expansive conceptions of public deliberation and more minimal accounts of democratic legitimacy. I critically assess these developments by examining how they respond to the charge that deliberative theory unjustly excludes certain voices from public deliberation. I focus on two general responses: the supplementing and systemic approaches. While both open up deliberation in important ways, I argue that they each remain vulnerable to the unjust exclusion charge. In refusing to give up on a distinctly 'rational' conception of argumentation, one that remains untouched by 'supplementary' modes of communication (such as rhetoric), the supplementing approach presupposes the very picture that generates the unjust exclusion charge in the first place. In response, I turn to Aristotle's account of rhetoric to show that rhetorical forms of communication are constitutive of public deliberation, rather than mere supplements. While the systemic response radically opens up deliberation to various forms of political speech, it sacrifices core deliberative ideals – such as equality of deliberative standing – where there are perceived net benefits to the deliberative system. I argue that this violates citizens' deliberative freedom and unjustly accepts the political impoverishment of vulnerable actors. I suggest that deliberativists could productively draw on Aristotle's account of rhetoric as this opens up deliberation in a way that overcomes the problems associated with the supplementing approach, whilst avoiding some of the unwelcome consequences of the systemic approach. At the end of the chapter I suggest an unexpected crossing of paths between Bohman and Derrida that points the way to a deconstructive entry into the debate.

Chapter 3 develops that suggestion by arguing that Derrida's long-standing efforts to multiply the forms and codes of reasoned argument overlap with deliberative attempts to (in the words of Bohman) pluralise public reason. I develop this argument by responding to the recurring claim that Derrida's work does not engage in argumentation. In the first half of the chapter I respond to Richard Rorty's version of that claim. I show that Rorty's position rests on the kind of distinctions that Derrida's work seeks to complicate. Discussing the more general 'no argument' charge directed at deconstruction, the second half of the chapter sets out Derrida's attempt to develop a more differentiated, and thus more inclusive, conception of reasoned argument. Here Derrida and Bohman cross paths once again to reveal a deconstruction that has consistently engaged in what I call a politics of the stage and the work of resistance. The significance of this discussion thus goes beyond a 'Derrida and his critics' debate. What is at stake in this disagreement is the issue of what does and does not count as an argument and the kind of exclusions that follow from that determination. That is to say, this discussion is concerned with precisely those worries about restrictive, and potentially exclusionary, approaches to reason and argumentation that occupied us in the previous two chapters.

Chapters 4 and 5 seek to ground that politics of the stage and work of resistance in the theoretical commitments of Derridean deconstruction. Chapter 4 challenges two misreadings of Derrida's work that aim to show that no such grounding is possible: the withdrawal and mere openness readings. The former, offered by critical theorists such as Dews, Fraser, Habermas and McCarthy, argues that deconstruction rejects the empirical realm of politics as a matter of principle and withdraws into a politically disabling transcendental reflection. The latter reading, offered by thinkers sympathetic to deconstruction – I focus on Laclau and address Hägglund's version in Chapter 5 – argues that deconstructive undecidability reveals the contingency of political structures but points in no particular direction. Behind both arguments is the claim that no ethico-political injunction flows from deconstruction. After correcting both misreadings, I set out the positive thesis that the 'experience of undecidability', emphasised by Derrida, is normatively structured. My key claim is that the ordeal of undecidability is a constitutive aspect of doing justice to the other as other.

Chapter 5 extends this analysis by outlining the normative demands that flow from the ordeal of undecidability, which I summarise as the demand to maintain an ethos of interruption. I argue that the usual charge that deconstruction advocates a mere openness to the other that leaves us in a paralysing undecidability overlooks Derrida's insistence on the necessity of calculation, deliberation, knowledge and laws, as well as his claim that we need to identify and close off the arrival of certain others. Drawing on Freyenhagen's work on Adorno, I argue that the normativity of deconstruction should be understood as a form of epistemic and meta-ethical negativism.[12] The former is the view that we cannot know the good, the latter that the identification of a wrong is sufficient for normative judgements. In the second half of the chapter I discuss the ethico-political challenge maintaining an ethos of interruption presents. While I argue that this demand points to a democratic form of politics, I identify two problems. First, Derrida's characterisation of democracy in terms of *différance* is overly abstract and does not sufficiently theorise the kind of democratic practice this would involve. Here the 'politically disabling' worry re-emerges. Second, Derrida's account of democratic auto-immunity (that is, the denying of democracy in the name of democracy) not only identifies an essential pervertibility in democracy, but seems to abandon us to this pervertibility. Here the 'mere openness' worry returns. In response, I show that the demand driving deconstruction – to maintain an ethos of interruption – requires that we minimise that threat as much as possible and that, in turn, requires some account of the concrete practices that could contribute to that task.

In the final chapter I address these concerns by critically discussing deconstructive and deliberative approaches to the paradoxes of constitutional democracy. I begin by returning to the deconstructive account of democratic pervertibility to show that Derrida's account of democracy, and his own practice of deconstruction, presupposes constitutional safeguards. This, I argue, implies that pervertibility must, in principle, be checked. I support this theoretical point by analysing Derrida's intervention in the civil war in Algeria, which was sparked by the cancellation of the second-round elections in 1992 when it looked as if a nondemocratic party was going to gain power. Derrida's response is guided, in the name of democracy, by the deconstructive injunction of pursuing the least perverting perversion. I then bring deliberative and deconstructive accounts of constitution making into conversation with one another. While I show that they share a historical understanding of democratic legitimacy, I identify a key difference: the former understands this process as a dialectical story of self-correcting learning processes, while the latter emphasises the 'non-dialectizable' indeterminacy of this process. These two pictures present contrasting accounts of how to understand the legitimacy of our current practices. The former risks slipping into self-congratulation and missing the injustice of our current practices; the latter counsels an anxious vigilance concerning these ongoing injustices, without slipping into cynicism or despair. Despite this difference, I show that the two approaches overlap in their shared hope (rather than confidence) in the promise of democracy to open up the possibility of doing justice to the other. I end the chapter by pointing to current empirical research that provides encouragement not only for a more promising dialogue between these two approaches, but for our practical struggles to do justice to the other in their otherness.

In *Beyond Good and Evil* Nietzsche writes:

> It is comfortable for our eye to react to a particular object by producing again an image it has often produced before than by retaining what is new and different in the impression . . . To hear something new is hard and painful to the ear; we hear the music of foreigners badly. When we hear a foreign language we involuntarily attempt to form the sounds we hear into words which have a more familiar and homely ring.[13]

Elsewhere Nietzsche reminds us that we have to '*learn to hear* a figure and melody', that we need to exercise goodwill with its 'strangeness', patience with its 'appearance and expression', and kind-heartedness with its 'oddity'. In time the strange that we merely tolerated may come to be that for which we wait, that which we should miss were it absent. 'This', Nietzsche adds, 'is its *thanks* for our hospitality.'[14] I hope this book will contribute to our hearing the voices in this discussion differently and, through this, to our seeing one another more hospitably.

Notes

1. See Jewell, 'Katie Hopkins and *The Sun*', *The Conversation*, 20 April 2015.
2. Kirkup and Winnett, 'Theresa May Interview', *The Telegraph*, 25 May 2012.
3. See Gentleman, 'Revealed: Depth of Home Office failures on Windrush', *The Guardian*, 18 July 2018; Gentleman, 'Sajid Javid urged to act in immigration scandal "bigger than Windrush"', *The Guardian*, 23 April 2019; O'Carroll, 'EU citizens in UK at risk of Windrush-style catastrophe, say MPs', *The Guardian*, 30 May 2019.

4. Home Office figures indicate that between 2011 and 2018 recorded hate crimes have increased in the following categories as follows: transgender by 427%; religion by 415%; disability by 313%; sexual orientation by 168%; race by 98%. See Home Office, *Hate Crime, England and Wales, 2017–18*. While crimes against homeless people are not recorded under a specific category, investigations into police figures indicate that between 2014 and 2018 such attacks have increased by 155%. See Marsh and Greenfield, 'Recognise attacks on rough sleepers as hate crimes, say experts', *The Guardian*, 19 December 2018.
5. Bernstein, *The New Constellation*, 219.
6. Honig, 'Dead Rights, Live Futures'.
7. Bernstein, *The New Constellation*, 202.
8. Peeters, *Derrida: A Biography*, 19.
9. For an insightful account of this problem see Fritsch, 'Equality and Singularity in Justification and Application Discourses'.
10. Karagiannis and Wagner, 'Varieties of Agonism', 323.
11. On the specific Habermas-Derrida debate, see Thomassen, *The Derrida-Habermas Reader*. Bernstein's *The New Constellation* was very early on suggesting the potential for supplementing one with the other. Bernstein's book remains one of the most important works in this debate.
12. Freyenhagen, *Adorno's Practical Philosophy*.
13. Nietzsche, *Beyond Good and Evil*, aphorism 192.
14. Nietzsche, *The Gay Science*, aphorism 334.

1
Blind Spots and Insights: Between Deliberation and Agonism

Over the past few decades democratic theory has been reinvigorated by the idea of deliberative democracy. Emphasising engagement in public dialogue, the turn to deliberation promises to provide democratic theory with a renewed sense of legitimacy and critical potential. However, friends and critics alike worry that deliberative theory works with conceptions of deliberation that are too idealised or demanding, leading to the danger of democratic theory either losing touch with our everyday democratic practices, and thus having no real political purchase on our non-ideal world, or attaching so many conditions to deliberation that political discussion becomes unnecessarily constrained and exclusive. Theorists of agonistic democracy have emerged as some of the most vocal critics of the deliberative approach. Chantal Mouffe has been at the forefront of this approach, and it is her sustained critique of deliberative theory that has shaped much of the debate.[1] Discussing Mouffe's critique of Habermas will prove useful in setting out some of the key issues in the debate between consensus and conflict-orientated democratic theory and, through this, help us better understand, and respond to, the demand to do justice to the other as other.[2]

I shall focus on two aspects of Mouffe's critique of Habermas's deliberative theory. The first, informed by Freud's observations on affective libidinal bonds, I shall call the elimination of the passions argument. The second, drawing on Carl Schmitt's insistence on the irreducible political distinction of friend/enemy, I shall call the antagonistic exclusion thesis. While these are inextricably intertwined in Mouffe's approach, for analytic purposes I shall treat them separately in order to bring out the underlying issues more clearly.[3] While Mouffe's elimination of the passions argument yields important insights concerning collective forms of identification and the dangers that emerge if we do not take the affective dimension of politics seriously, I argue that her criticism of Habermas offers an overly narrow reading of what entering practical discourse entails, overlooks Habermas's two-track model of democracy, and provides an inadequate account of the role of the passions and fantasy in political life. Despite these shortcomings, Mouffe's critique does point to problems in Habermas's account, particularly the demand for impartiality and universality, and the lack of any detailed account of the role the passions play in democratic politics.

Turning to the antagonistic exclusion thesis, I show, firstly, that, *pace* Mouffe, Habermas is not blind to collective identities. I then identify a dilemma opened up by the problem of modal slippage in Mouffe's critique of the deliberative approach and her employment of the 'constitutive outside' thesis that she hopes will save her from Schmitt. I argue that the antagonistic exclusion thesis never fully works out the modal status of its claims and this leads to an unresolved dilemma: holding on to strong claims of a *necessary* antagonism in order to attack the deliberative approach leaves Mouffe in a Schmittian embrace, while deploying the 'constitutive outside' thesis to weaken antagonism to one political *possibility* among others, and thereby hold on to an agonistic pluralism of 'adversaries', means giving up the claims of necessity contained in the antagonistic exclusion thesis. Indeed, it is not clear in what sense antagonism is possible if we take seriously the impossibility of closure that the constitutive outside thesis reveals. Moreover, the key argument that any fully inclusive 'we' is a conceptual impossibility is not sufficiently defended. In the final section, I address the broader ongoing debate between these two approaches and suggest possibilities for a more productive dialogue.

I. Deliberation and Consensus

Although the term 'deliberative democracy' is of recent invention, the idea of democratic deliberation is not a contemporary innovation.[4] In this phrase one can hear Mill's claim that parliament is best understood as 'congress of opinions';[5] Marsilius of Padua's argument that '[t]he authority to make laws belongs ... to the whole body of citizens';[6] and Pericles's praise of the Athenians who 'are all personally involved either in political discussion or in deliberation about them' and who think 'that it is not words which thwart effective action but rather the failure to inform action with discussion in advance'.[7] The contemporary turn to deliberation is thus the revival of a much older idea of democracy. Indeed, as Elster notes, 'The idea of deliberative democracy ... is as old as democracy itself.'[8]

I say revival and not continuation, however, for the 'uncontrollable adventure of democracy', as Lefort aptly describes it, has rarely held to the deliberative course.[9] For much of the twentieth century, for example, the terrain was either dominated by Weber's gods and demons, fighting it out in a realm populated by Schumpeter's 'politically uninformed, apathetic, and manipulable' electorate,[10] or it was inhabited by 'the shadowy figure of *Homo economicus*, with his rational preference orderings and strangely unencumbered ... identity'.[11] The contemporary turn to deliberation seeks to replace these approaches to democracy, modelled on competing elites and the logic of the market, with one based on dialogue and consensus, where 'slogans and marching tunes'[12] would give way to forums and debate, and where mechanisms for aggregating individual preferences would be overtaken by institutions designed to respond to citizens' public deliberations about what is of common interest.

This attempt to move from the market to the forum can be seen in Habermas's model of deliberative democracy. Taking inspiration from Kant — albeit a detranscendentalised Kant fit for postmetaphysical problem solving — Habermas undertakes a communicative reconstruction of Kant's moral theory, in which 'the categorical imperative receives a discourse-theoretic interpretation' (IO, 33). Once it is appreciated that '[a]s historical and social beings we find ourselves always already in a linguistically structured life world',[13] the validity of norms for Habermas 'can only be realized under conditions of communication that ensure that *everyone* tests the acceptability of a norm' (IO, 33). Looking back through the lens of the linguistic turn, Habermas cannot start with 'Kant's lonely but clever subject' monologically generating universalisable maxims that could be validly ascribed to all.[14] Instead, he begins from an intersubjective relation, where the validity of one's claims is discursively put to the test. McCarthy summarises this shift well:

> The emphasis shifts from what each can will without contradiction to be a general law to what all can agree to as a general norm. Accordingly, 'rational will-formation' is not something that can be identified and certified privately; it is inextricably bound to communication processes in which agreements are both discovered and shaped.[15]

If the validity of any particular norm is based on intersubjective communication and agreement, then one of the tasks for deliberative theory is to specify those processes of communication in order to enable one to evaluate the kind of agreements that emerge. That is to say, one needs to differentiate a form of legitimate consensus from a mere agreement or *modus vivendi*. The seeds of this are already there in Habermas's reworking of Kant.

Habermas argues that although Kant's unhistorical way of thinking means that he fails to appreciate the traditions and practices within which identities are formed, and that 'reason is by its very nature incarnated in contexts of communicative action and in structures of the lifeworld',[16] there is no suggestion of 'falling back behind Kant' to Aristotle.[17] However, one cannot remain with Kant either. The categorical imperative may well be addressed to a second person singular, but as Habermas goes on to note:

> [T]he reflexive application of the universalization tests calls for a form of deliberation in which each participant is compelled to adopt the perspective of all others in order to examine whether a norm could be willed by all *from the perspective of each person*. This is the situation of a *rational discourse* orientated to reaching understanding in which all those concerned participate. (IO, 33)

Habermas holds on to the principle of universalisation behind the categorical imperative, but he recasts it in communicative terms. The former is spelt out with Habermas's principle of universalisation (U); the latter is captured by the discourse principle (D):

[U] For a norm to be valid, the consequences of the side effects that its *general* observance can be expected to have for the satisfaction of the particular interests of *each* person affected must be such that *all* affected can accept them freely.

[D] Only those norms can claim to be valid that meet (or could meet) with the approval of all affected in their capacity as participants in a practical discourse.[18]

By combining the two, this discourse-theoretical interpretation of the categorical imperative seeks to avoid the liberal reduction of the democratic process to the calculations of isolated individuals, whilst not succumbing to the 'ethical overload' of the republican model (IO, 239).

According to Habermas, this overload is generated by the attempt to tie democratic will-formation to a substantial ethical life in conditions of cultural and social pluralism, where any background consensus on moral norms has 'shattered' and any shared ethos 'disintegrated' (IO, 41). In the 'internally differentiated and pluralized lifeworlds' of postconventional societies (BFN, 26), the attempt to settle disputes through a shared ethical understanding is 'doomed to failure' (IO, 39). However, by anchoring the validity of any particular norm to the outcome of a rational deliberation that would be open to all concerned, where each participant adopts the moral point of view and puts forward claims equally in the interest of all with the aim of reaching a rationally motivated consensus, the Habermasian model seeks to hold on to the importance of a communicatively united citizenry, as well as the basic principles of the constitutional state that would be necessary for institutionalising the democratic processes of such deliberation (IO, 248). Habermas aims to steer a middle course between liberalism and republicanism in the hope of bringing together discourses on constitutionalism and democracy, justice and solidarity, in a way that takes into account the predicaments of postmetaphysical justification in a postconventional context.[19]

For a number of commentators, however, the Habermasian model has significant problems. Particular concerns emerge about the role played by rationality, impartiality and consensus. The fear is that despite the best intentions of Habermas and his followers, these key aspects of his account end up becoming devices of unjust exclusion. Such concerns emerge from a perspective that places contestation and disagreement at the heart of politics.

II. Mouffe's Critique of Habermas

Informed by Freud's account of affective libidinal investment, and drawing upon Carl Schmitt's insistence on the irreducible political distinction of friend/enemy, Chantal Mouffe's theorisation of agonistic politics seeks to bring to the fore the ineradicable dimensions of antagonism and contestation.[20] The idea that contestation is an unavoidable part of politics seems, given what deliberativists call the fact of pluralism, uncontroversial. However, the antagonism that Mouffe wishes to draw attention to, and which she charges the deliberative approach of failing to acknowledge, is not a form of contestation understood as an empirical obstacle that could be overcome through an idealised set of procedures. What Mouffe points to is an antagonism that is 'constitutive of human societies' as such. That is to say, it is an antagonism that goes all the way down, an 'ontological' (OP, 9, 16) condition that leaves one faced with 'the ineradicability of the conflictual dimension of social life' (DP, 20; cf. DP, 99, 101; OP, 4, 20, 119; RP, 140). In the next two sections I shall outline each aspect of Mouffe's critique.

Rationalism: The elimination of the passions

Drawing on Freud's observation that 'it is always possible to bind together a considerable number of people in love, so long as there are other people left over to receive the manifestations of their aggressiveness' (cited in OP, 26), Mouffe points to this affective dimension of identification as one of the blind spots of the Habermasian approach. 'The mistake of liberal rationalism', writes Mouffe, 'is to ignore the affective dimension mobilized by collective identifications' (OP, 26). By privileging rationality, such an approach fails to grasp 'the crucial role played by passions and affects' (DP, 95; OP, 24–8) and this leaves it incapable of delivering the kind of politics that can have 'a real purchase on people's desires and fantasies'. Not only does Habermas's approach ignore the role of the passions, but it seeks to 'eliminate passions in order to create a rational consensus'.[21] Such a move is not possible on the Mouffean picture because the passions are 'at the origin of collective forms of identification'. And given that 'to act politically people need to be able to identify with a collective identity' (OP, 24, 25), politics is rooted in the passions of collective identification (OP, 28).

This picture emerges from Mouffe's reading of Freud on the affective dimension of identification and Canetti's reflections on the drive to become one with the crowd. Although it is beyond the scope of this discussion to assess Mouffe's appropriation of these thinkers, Mouffe herself summarises it for us: 'The lesson to be drawn from Freud and Canetti is that . . . the need for collective identifications will never disappear since it is constitutive of the mode of existence of human beings' (OP, 28). To eliminate the passions, then, would be to eliminate the fundamental forms of collective identification that make political action possible.

From a Mouffean perspective, when Habermas ties legitimacy to a rational consensus that can be achieved only by adopting the moral point of view, a viewpoint in which participants 'look beyond what is good *for them* and examine what lies equally in the interest of all' (BFN, 102), the attempt is being made to circumscribe an impartial domain that eliminates the partisan passions of political identification, a domain where deliberators 'aim at the impartial evaluation of action conflicts' by adopting 'a perspective freed of all egocentrism or ethnocentrism' (BFN, 97). But given the psycho-anthropological picture Mouffe presents, the impartiality of the 'enlarged first person plural perspective of a community that does not exclude anyone' (IO, 30) posited by Habermas is seen as impossible. To imagine that it is possible to enter into practical discourse, such that one is moved not by partisan passions but 'only the compelling force of the better argument' (BFN, 10), is, for Mouffe, to misunderstand not only fundamental aspects of human modes of existence, but also the nature of political identity-formation. The agonistic politics that Mouffe advocates will not be a politics of impartial deliberation that aims to achieve a rational consensus, but a partisan politics of collective identifications that, rather than attempting to eliminate the passions, seeks to mobilise them.

Individualism: *The antagonistic exclusion thesis*

We have already touched on the second aspect of Mouffe's critique, what I call the antagonistic exclusion thesis. Here Mouffe draws on Carl Schmitt's conception of the political, insisting that the constitution of any political identity involves the formation of a frontier between 'us' and 'them'. This is the antagonistic moment of collective identification and exclusion described by Schmitt as friend/enemy.

For Mouffe, the friend/enemy distinction is 'one of Schmitt's central insights' for it brings out 'the relational nature of political identities' and reveals the inescapable moment of exclusion in the formation of political identity (OP, 14–15). This becomes clear, for Mouffe, if one considers the way in which Schmitt conceives of democracy. The fundamental starting point for democracy, according to Schmitt, is not the abstract equality of all persons as persons – that's liberal individualism – but the substantive equality of those who belong to the demos. That is to say, democratic equality requires the formation of a collective identity through the creation of a frontier between those who belong to the demos and those who remain exterior to it. And this, in turn, means that equality always entails inequality. As Schmitt puts it:

> Every actual democracy rests on the principle that not only are equals equal but unequals will not be treated equally. Democracy requires, therefore, first homogeneity and second – if the need arises – elimination and eradication.[22]

For Mouffe, this contains the crucial insight that the identity of a political community 'hinges on the possibility of drawing a frontier between "us" and "them"' and, as such, it 'always entails relations of inclusion-exclusion' (DP, 43). If the very possibility of constructing a political identity requires excluding some other group from the political order, then the possibility of a concrete antagonism, where 'one fighting collectivity confronts another', remains ever present.[23] This ever-present possibility of antagonism is precisely what Schmitt means to capture by the friend/enemy distinction, a distinction that is definitive for 'the political'.

Mouffe follows Schmitt in seeing this antagonistic frontier as a blind spot of the liberal approach. The latter, according to Schmitt, evades the political by refiguring the friend/enemy distinction in either economic or moral terms. In the former domain there are no enemies, 'only competitors'; in the latter, 'perhaps only debating adversaries'.[24] But Schmitt insists that the friend/enemy distinction is not to be understood in this metaphorical sense, but in its 'concrete and existential sense'.[25] That is to say, as the real possibility of conflict. The liberal transformation of the enemy into an economic competitor or debating adversary is seen as a thoroughly depoliticising vision that not only attempts to 'obliterate the whole dimension of power and antagonism', a dimension which remains ever present given the exclusions that necessarily take place in the constitution of political identity, but also neglects the 'predominant role of the passions' in the affective ties of political identification (RP, 140).

From this antagonistic account of passionate identification and exclusion, Mouffe rejects the very possibility of Habermas's model of democratic deliberation. If relations of inclusion-exclusion are inscribed within the very constitution of political identity, and if that constitution has an ineliminable affective dimension, then, for Mouffe, this implies 'the impossibility of a fully inclusive "rational" consensus' (OP, 11; DP, 43). Although one may aim for the elimination of this antagonism through the creation of a common 'we', this can never be fully inclusive for Mouffe because the possibility of constructing a 'we' requires identifying and excluding a 'they'. This exclusion of the other is the condition of possibility for any 'we' to emerge, and thus the attempt to achieve a rational consensus, free of antagonism, will always remain frustrated for *essential* reasons. The antagonistic frontier of friend/enemy, as revealed by Schmitt, is the second blind spot of the Habermasian approach (RP, 140).

While Habermas acknowledges 'the empirical evidence ... about permanent dissensus',[26] for Mouffe he fails to appreciate the more fundamental level of such dissensus. Mouffe's argument for this claim runs something like this. The condition of possibility of consensus depends on the formation of a 'we'. But a 'we' can only emerge through the identification and exclusion of an external 'they'. This is the relational logic of the friend/enemy distinction:

no identity without difference; no difference without exclusion. And it is precisely this identification and exclusion of a 'they' that renders any fully inclusive 'we', and by implication rational consensus, impossible. Consensus is always based on acts of exclusion that are made in the antagonistic realm of political identity-formation. As such, the anticipated rational consensus of the deliberative democrat, based on an impartial deliberation where each puts forward claims in the interests of all, is always politically (in the Mouffean sense), not rationally (in the Habermasian sense), constituted. To imagine that one could achieve a rational consensus, where, to quote Habermas, one has 'thrown off the shackles of any exclusionary community' (IO, 30), is to dream of a social order where there are no we/they groupings. Or, as Mouffe puts, 'it is to dream of a society without politics' (RP, 50).

While Habermas is applauded for trying to provide an alternative to the economic model, he is criticised for trying to replace it with a moral one. If Habermas thought settling disputes with reference to our ethical self-understanding was 'doomed to failure' (IO, 39), Mouffe's retort is that trying to negate antagonism through a rational deliberation aimed at a fully inclusive consensus is equally 'doomed to failure'.[27] Given Mouffe's account of identification through exclusion, the moral point of view that Habermas sees as the only way of achieving a rational consensus in the midst of empirical dissensus is itself rejected as a 'conceptual impossibility' (DP, 33).

III. The Elimination of the Passions Charge

Islands of discourse

In response to Mouffe's elimination of the passions charge, we can begin by noting that the idea of a rational consensus presupposes that one enters practical discourse and Habermas understands the latter as a particular type of communication. 'Discourses are islands in the sea of practice', as he puts it. One thing that this image seeks to capture is the rarity of practical discourse: it is the 'exception', 'improbable', 'fleeting'.[28] For the most part, it is within the sea of practice that democratic actors find themselves struggling. It is only when we are 'sucked into the whirlpool of problematization' (BFN, 97) – due to problems that are such that we cannot go on any longer – that we are temporarily washed ashore onto the islands of discourse. There is nothing in Habermas's account to suggest that the sea in which democratic actors find themselves most of the time is without any affective currents or passionate tides. There is no reason why the idea of being orientated towards a rational consensus in practical discourse necessarily disables one from acknowledging the role of the passions in democratic life more broadly.

A possible response here would be to say that even if Habermas does acknowledge passions in the surrounding sea of practice, once we set foot on the islands of practical discourse we must leave our passions behind. Although conflicting interests, needs and passions may *prompt* the move to practical discourse, *entering* such discourse requires, as Mouffe puts it, leaving 'all our particular interests aside' (DP, 48). And this is precisely what we flesh-and-blood actors cannot do.

But this is something that Habermas acknowledges. Entering practical discourse does not require that 'we take on unearthly forms' by transforming our 'real' characters into intelligible ones.[29] When one sets foot on an island of practical discourse, it is not the case that passions and interests must be left anchored off-shore. If this were the case, then there would be no issues for deliberators to try and reach agreement about. As Habermas emphasises:

> On the contrary, if actors do not bring with them, and into their discourse, *their* individual life-histories, *their* identities, *their* needs and wants, *their* traditions, memberships, and so forth, practical discourse would be at once robbed of all content.[30]

If we take Habermas's reference to 'identities', 'needs' and 'wants' seriously, then it is hard to see how one could admit these without also admitting an affective dimension. At the very least, there is nothing here that rules out the affects. That is to say, we are washed ashore with all our belongings. No doubt this picture lacks any detailed account of our passionate belongings and how they would function on shore, but it does not require their elimination.

Moreover, to insist on the exclusion of such contents would be to ignore Hegel's critique of Kant for his abstractness, a critique that Habermas tries to incorporate into his approach. It is precisely to avoid such problems that Habermas reformulates the principle of universalisation to include 'value orientations'. This, he explains, 'points to the role played by pragmatic and ethical reasons of individual participants in practical discourse' and is 'designed to prevent the marginalization of the self-understanding and worldviews of particular individuals or groups' (IO, 42, 225).[31] The rationality of consensus for Habermas is achieved not by the exclusion of 'interests', 'identities', 'wants', 'needs' or 'values', but by the equal inclusion of all participants.[32]

But this is where Mouffe's point can have more of a bite. If we return to the sea/island image, it now seems that they are not as separate as the image initially suggested. Habermas insists that our interests, needs, wants, values, identities, memberships and traditions are brought with us into practical discourse. And this, I have suggested, would bring with it (or at least not rule out) the affective dimension of the passions too. But Mouffe can now press her claim. If these contents are included, the issue, then, is whether we can ever adopt the impartial, moral point of view, even temporarily, for the sake of resolving those problems that have thrown us onto the shores of discourse. While the critique of Habermas for attempting to eliminate the passions misses its mark here, Mouffe does raise a serious question about the possibility of adopting the impartial standpoint required in practical discourse.

This is a serious problem and one to which I shall return. For now, we can note that it does not clinch the elimination of the passions charge. It would only do so if engaging in rational argumentation required the eradication of the passions. But there is nothing in principle to say that deliberators could not articulate their needs, wants, values and interests in a passionate way. Mouffe's account seems to attribute to Habermas the view that all passions are coercive and therefore deliberation must be dispassionate. But if we view Habermas's account of rational argumentation negatively – as refraining from coercive acts – then room opens up for a more passionate understanding of deliberation. This would mean that the inclusive 'we' that Habermas refers to would 'resist all substantial determinations' and 'would constitute itself *solely by the negative idea* of abolishing discrimination and harm' (IO, xxxvi, my emphasis). As Patchen Markell has suggested, understood in this way, being orientated towards agreement through rational argumentation would require 'forswearing of the mechanism of coercion . . . in the pursuit of one's goals and a corresponding commitment to provide reasons for one's claims if they are challenged'.[33] So understood, rational argumentation would be part of a non-coercive public sphere of challenge and contestation, rather than a procedure for discovering 'the grounds of bliss or path to eternity'.[34] Thus the deliberative democrat need not posit the end state of reconciled rational utopia nor the 'dream of perfect harmony or transparency', as Mouffe suggests.[35] Indeed, Habermas is quite explicit about this:

> Nothing makes me more nervous than the imputation that [the theory of communicative action] proposes, or at least suggests, a rationalistic utopian society. I do not regard the fully transparent society as an ideal, nor do I wish to suggest *any* other ideal.[36]

On this negative construal, then, we can think of reason in Habermas as being far more open to challenge, contestation and passionate disagreement than Mouffe allows.[37] As Daniel Halin puts it: 'Reason . . . is not opposed to passion, but to tradition . . . authority . . . coercion.'[38]

A 'wild' public sphere

Even if one accepts Mouffe's account of what entering practical discourse entails, her broader claim that Habermas's deliberative theory requires the elimination of the passions from democratic politics would only go through if democratic politics for Habermas just is what goes on in practical discourse. But that would imply that Habermas thinks democratic politics is, to recall his characterisation of practical discourse, an 'exceptional' or 'fleeting' engagement, something that his two-track model of the public sphere explicitly denies. Democratic politics, for Habermas, is not reducible to what happens on the 'improbable' islands of discourse. Just as islands are situated in a surrounding sea, so democratic politics is set within a broader public sphere of struggle and contestation: 'Practical discourses cannot be relieved of the burden of social conflicts . . . Even if it is conducted by discursive means, a dispute about norms is still rooted in struggles for recognition' (IO, 106). It is to this informal sphere of public struggles for recognition, overlooked by Mouffe, that I shall now turn.

In not paying sufficient attention to Habermas's account of the informal public sphere, Mouffe appears to reduce Habermas's account of political life to entering practical discourse. But this fails to appreciate key aspects of Habermas's picture of democratic politics. When he straightforwardly asserts that '[d]eliberative politics . . . lives off the interplay between democratically institutionalized will formation and informal opinion formation' (BFN, 308), any account of Habermas's understanding of democratic politics that fails to include the informal public sphere will be missing half of the story.[39] Even a cursory glance at Habermas's two-track model undermines the elimination of the passions claim.[40] The distinction that Habermas draws between formal and informal public spheres is crucial, for it is within the informal public sphere that we see the passionate mobilisation of collective actors that Mouffe charges Habermas's 'rationalist and individualistic framework' with being blind to (A, 54).

A closer look at Habermas's account of democratic politics reveals that it includes moral, ethical and pragmatic components, and various forms of communication. 'Political communication', Habermas notes, 'assumes a different form in respective arenas' (E, 159). Bohman captures this well:

> [Deliberative politics] does not take place [solely] within a specialized form of discourse . . . Deliberative politics for Habermas is instead a complex 'discursive network' that includes argumentation of various sorts, bargaining and compromise, and, above all, unrestricted communication and free expression of opinions by all citizens in the informal public sphere. (PD, 175)

Habermas's account of the informal public sphere is set within a 'centre-periphery axis' picture of the political system (BFN, 354). This is (to simplify) a three-tiered system, with the informal public sphere constituting 'an intermediate system of mass communication, situated between the formally organized deliberations and negotiations at the centre and the arranged or informal conversations which take place in civil society at the periphery' (E, 159). The formally organised deliberations at the centre unfold within the administrative core of the political system, which is composed of highly regulated bodies set within formal state institutions, such as parliaments and courts. This is the formal sphere of democratic will-formation, whose 'institutionalized discourses' are orientated towards decision-making (E, 135; cf. BFN, 354). The 'episodic and informal' conversations at the periphery circulate through civil society (E, 135), which is comprised of 'more or less spontaneously emergent' non-governmental and non-economic organisations, such as voluntary associations and social movements (BFN, 367). These episodic conversations articulate personal experiences of suffering in the 'existential language' of the lifeworld (BFN, 359).

As an intermediate system, Habermas understands the informal public sphere as 'an open and inclusive network of overlapping, subcultural publics having fluid temporal, social, and substantive boundaries'. This overlapping network is the sphere of opinion-formation. It is here, in what Habermas characterises as a 'wild', 'anarchic' complex of '*unrestricted* communication' (BFN, 307–8), that the 'struggle over needs' takes place through public struggles for recognition (BFN, 314, 359). Habermas's emphasis on the 'unrestricted' nature of communication in the informal public sphere – he also describes it as 'unconstrained' – signals that communication here is 'not regulated by procedures', as it is in the formal sphere (BFN, 314). Thus the 'collective identities and need interpretations' that are articulated as part of public struggles for recognition can 'be conducted more . . . expressively' (BFN, 308).

The way that Habermas describes the unconstrained, expressive conduct of collective actors involved in these struggles suggests a sphere of passionate mobilisation.[41] In bringing 'conflict from the periphery into the centre of the political system' (BFN, 330), emergent actors need to '*dramatize* contributions' (BFN, 381) and engage in '*extraordinary* modes of posing . . . problems' (BFN, 358) so as to '*amplify the pressure* of problems' (BFN, 359) and, thereby, '*ignite the pressure* of public opinion' (BFN, 357). This dramatic, extraordinary, pressure-igniting amplification of problems is carried out through '*controversial* presentation . . . *sensational* actions, mass protests and incessant campaigning' (BFN, 381). This is no dispassionate, rationalistic realm for individuals to calmly and impartially identify new issues to talk about. Rather, this is a 'wild' arena for the passionate dramatisation of problems and needs, such that they '*force* their way' into the informal public sphere (BFN, 381) and, eventually, into the '*besieged* fortress' at the core of the political system (BFN, 487).

Habermas's picture of the informal public sphere, then, presents democratic politics as being conducted less in the manner of an academic seminar and more 'in the manner of a siege' (BFN, 486). And the way that Habermas characterises the various publics and forms of communication that circulate in this wild sphere suggests that for such a siege to be successful – in dramatising, amplifying, igniting, pressurising, forcing – emergent actors need to grip their audience. The term that Habermas repeatedly employs in this context is 'resonate' (BFN, 330, 358, 364, 366, 367). If emergent actors do not produce publics and forms of communication that resonate with their intended audience, then the 'signals that they send out' will remain 'too weak' to ignite public opinion and influence the political system (BFN, 373). As Habermas writes: 'the political influence that actors gain through communication must *ultimately* rest on the resonance and indeed the approval of a lay public' (BFN, 364).

Aiming for 'resonance' and 'approval' so as to 'ignite' the public hardly seems compatible with an account of politics that would require the elimination of the passions. The picture of the informal public sphere that emerges here is, accordingly, a little 'more theatrical and symbolic' than Mouffe's rationalistic charge suggests.[42] Habermas points to 'literary publics, religious and artistic publics, feminist and "alternative" publics', as well as '*episodic* publics found in taverns, coffee houses, or on the streets' and '*occasional* or "arranged" publics . . . such as theatre performances [and] rock concerts . . .' (BFN, 373–4). Far from requiring the elimination of the passions, such publics would seem to mobilise them. Given that Habermas holds that 'political communication assumes a different form in respective arenas' (E, 159), and given the multiplicity of publics that he points to, what might otherwise seem a surprising acknowledgement is not: 'non-discursive modes of expression such as story-telling and images, facial and bodily expressions in general, testimonies, appeals, and the like are ... normal parts of political communication' (E, 154). Indeed, the formation of such publics, and the more expressive modes of communication that circulate throughout these publics, play a crucial role in generating the 'ultimate' source of influence in the informal public sphere – resonance.

Hopefully, what emerges from this brief sketch of Habermas's account of the informal public sphere is the very thing that Mouffe charges Habermas with being blind to: the passions. When Habermas describes the informal public sphere as 'jumpy or in a constant state of vibration' (BFN, 488), rational convincing may well play a part. But, as we have seen, ultimately it is the affective dimension of resonance that vibrates throughout the multiple publics that make up this wild sphere. Mouffe's claim that, for Habermas, 'democratic politics requires the elimination of the passions from the public sphere' (A, 55) thus overlooks the crucial role that the informal public sphere plays in his account of democratic politics. Even if that account does not explicitly discuss the role of the passions in democratic politics, it does not require their elimination. Indeed, it would be hard to make sense of the picture of the informal public sphere that Habermas presents were the passions eliminated.

Furthermore, not only does this account recognise the passions in democratic politics, but it also acknowledges dimensions of power. When Mouffe claims that Habermas postulates 'the availability of a public sphere where power would have been eliminated' (DP, 98–9), she ignores Habermas's insistence on the weakness of the informal public sphere that results from its anarchic *structure*. The informal public sphere is more vulnerable to the repressive and exclusionary effects of unequally distributed social power, structural violence and systematically distorted communication than the more formal spheres (BFN, 306; E, 168–70).[43] This is not a mere empirical weakness; it is a structural one. Indeed, Habermas observes that the '*structures* of the public sphere' contain '*unavoidable* asymmetries' in terms of social actors' ability to generate, shape, present and validate information (BFN, 325, my emphasis). If the informal public sphere is the arena for struggles for recognition, informational asymmetries of this sort translate into asymmetries in social power.[44] Habermas holds to Enlightenment ideals, but not naïvely so. This is a postmetaphysical enlightenment, where one is caught in the vertigo of an anarchic, but also deeply fragile, communicative freedom (BFN, 185–6).

While Mouffe fails to demonstrate that Habermas's picture of democratic politics requires the elimination of the passions, she does point to a certain blindness in the lack of any detailed account of the role that the passions play in democratic politics. But, as I suggest in the next section, this is also a problem for Mouffe.

Which passions? What kind of fantasy?

As we have seen, in her critique of the deliberative approach Mouffe claims that politics is rooted in the passions of collective identifications and that the construction of a 'we' is only possible through the formation of a frontier that excludes an external 'they'. Hence the inescapable dimension of antagonism in social relations. If we were to remain at this point, then Mouffe would find herself in an uncomfortable position. Such an account would leave us with a picture of politics as revolving around the antagonistic frontier of the friend/enemy distinction. Insofar as collective identifications mobilise the affective dimension, and given that 'in the field of politics it is group and collective identities we encounter, not individuals', it would seem that there wouldn't be much else beside the affective bonds of friends and the antagonistic exclusion of enemies. This is one of the reasons why Mouffe maintains that the lessons Freud teaches us about collective passions have such 'devastating consequences for the liberal approach' (RP, 140; cf. A, 46–7; OP, 25–30). It is also the reason why she insists that the insights of Schmitt 'should shatter the illusions' of deliberative democrats.[45] Given the irreducible nature of antagonism, 'ignoring it doesn't make it disappear'; it simply leaves us 'bewildered and impotent in the face of its manifestations' (RP, 140). Hence Mouffe's insistence that we should abandon the deliberative model of consensus-formation for a partisan politics that mobilises the passions around conflicting poles of identification, thereby ensuring that politics has a real purchase on people's passions and fantasies.

These are important insights. While many of us are still rubbing our eyes in disbelief at the visceral politics that has recently exploded in the US and across Europe, Mouffe has consistently warned of such explosions, in which 'supposedly archaic passions' of a 'bygone age' re-emerge around dangerous forms of passionate collective identification (A, 4).[46] In 1993, for example, Mouffe argued that failure to acknowledge and mobilise the passions around progressive collective identifications would see 'the growth of other collective identities around religious, nationalist or ethnic forms of identification' (RP, 5). In 2000 she warned of the 'crystallization of collective passions' that would see an 'explosion of antagonism that can tear up the very basis of civility' (DP, 104). And in 2007 she described how these developments can lead to political discourse being 'played out in the moral register, using the vocabulary of good and evil to discriminate between 'we good democrats and "they the evil ones"'.[47] Six years later, Mouffe observes:

> This can be seen . . . in the reactions to the rise of right-wing populist parties, where moral condemnation has generally replaced a properly political type of struggle. Instead of trying to grasp the reasons for the success of right-wing parties, the 'good' democrat parties have often limited themselves to calling for a '*cordon sanitaire*' to be established in order to stop the return of what they see as the 'brown plague'. (A, 142)

While Mouffe's emphasis on the role of the passions and fantasy in political life yields important insights into the causes and consequences of non-progressive forms of collective identification, the picture she presents needs to be more fully worked out.

Troubling questions remain. For example, is fantasy a realm that remains free of the pathologies of social processes or is it enmeshed in them? How significant a role do the passions have? What is the relation between the affective and the cognitive? There are politically troubling effects of fantasy (of which Mouffe herself is clearly aware). Discussing the 'asymmetries of power between the sexes', for example, Anthony Elliot notes that 'phantasy processes have been deeply engrained historically in the vast exploitations, brutalities and violent tensions of sexual relations'.[48] And this could be extended to relations around race, ethnicity, nationality, religion and so forth. Given the anti-essentialist position of Mouffe, which sees her maintaining that 'the construction of social identity is an act of power' (RP, 141), she would presumably accept Elliot's claim that 'needs, affects, desires, and phantasies are internally connected with social relations of power'.[49] If so, then how does one distinguish between those passions and fantasies that can contribute to the kind of democratic politics Mouffe favours and those that threaten it? As a democrat, there are various passions one would not want to mobilise and all sorts of fantasies one would not want to see emerge. This is precisely what Mouffe's insights reveal. But isn't this also the reason why we ought to try to facilitate the kind of public deliberation deliberative democrats suggest? If one is interested in *democratic* politics, then shouldn't one, following Iris Young's deliberative democrat, attempt to 'limit domination and the naked imposition of partisan interests' through sites and processes of deliberation within any given context of dissensus?[50] If one abandons rational argumentation and the search for consensus and leaves politics to partisan interests grounded in the mobilisation of passions, then aren't we locked into 'Schmitt's deadly, existential antagonism of friend and enemy' or, at best, back to the logic of 'slogans and marching tunes' *à la* Schumpeter?[51]

If we take the Schmittian slope of this, the worry is that by insisting on the necessity of antagonistic exclusion, and in calling for a politics that abandons rational argumentation and the search for consensus in favour of a politics of partisan passions and fantasies, one is left in a potentially 'irrational, power-soaked . . . politics' with no way out.[52] Here we can hear echoes of Plato's warnings about the democrat 'becoming in his waking life what he was only occasionally in his dreams'[53] and glimpse the nightmarish flashes of 'bloody colours' and 'blind phenomena' that Adorno reminds us of when he writes: 'The German critics who found Kantian formalism too rationalistic have shown their bloody colours in the fascist practice of making blind phenomena, men's membership or nonmembership in a designated race, the criteria of who was to be killed.'[54]

While Mouffe rightly attempts to bring the affective dimension back into a politics blinded by rationalism, she risks adopting a perspective that is itself blinded by the passions. Her rationalism charge is too quick and too one-sided, for it fails to take into consideration the ambiguous nature of reason: while one must be aware of the dangers of reason and critical of its oppressive aspects, this should not blind one to the progressive dimension that remains within it, 'despite and because of its abstractness', as Adorno subtly puts it.[55]

IV. The Antagonistic Exclusion Thesis

This brings me to the antagonistic exclusion thesis. Here there are three issues I want to raise. Returning to the account of the informal public sphere discussed above, I shall show that, *pace* Mouffe, Habermas's account of democratic politics is not blind to collective identities. His picture of the informal public sphere is one populated by collective actors. However, this is not without its problems for Habermas's account. I then turn to Mouffe's account of collective identifications, and here I identify two problems. The first is the problem of modal slippage between a necessary and possible antagonism. The second problem concerns her argument for the constitutive outside thesis and the way she deploys this to support her antagonistic exclusion thesis. My aim will be to highlight an ambiguity in Mouffe's account that has significant consequences not only for her own position, but for her critique of Habermas and the deliberative approach more generally. In doing so, I also question Mouffe's appropriation of Derrida in her attack on the deliberative approach.

Collective identities and oppositional consciousness

As we saw above, Habermas describes public struggles for recognition as involving 'collective identities and need interpretations' (BFN, 308). This is no mere passing remark. Habermas makes it clear that the struggles that take place in the informal public sphere are waged by collective actors: 'in the political arena those who encounter one another are collective actors contending about collective goals' (IO, 203–4; cf. BFN, 355, 366, 370, 373). Among those collective actors, Habermas identifies 'indigenous actors' who emerge from the public, and 'mere users' who appear before the public. The former refers to loosely organised actors, such as social movements and citizen-initiatives, who aim to force unrecognised problems, experienced in the lifeworld, into the public domain. The latter refers to interest groups, such as established parties, labour unions and business associations, who are able to draw on pre-existing organised power, resources and sanctions with the aim of utilising the public sphere for specific organisations (BFN, 375–6).

While interest-group actors may not involve the forms of collective identification that Mouffe emphasises (insofar as such groups are already constituted actors who engage in a logic of negotiated concessions and benefits), indigenous actors seem to point to precisely this. These emergent actors cannot draw on pre-existing group identities with pre-existing interests that can be negotiated. Rather, they have to produce, and continuously consolidate, collective identities of solidarity (that do not operate according to the logic of negotiated compromises (BFN, 182)). As Habermas writes:

> [They] must first *produce* identifying features. This is especially evident with social movements that initially go through a phase of self-identification and self-legitimation. Even after that, they still pursue self-referential 'identity politics' parallel to their goal-directed politics – they must continually reassure themselves of their identity. (BFN, 376)

Drawing attention to invisible suffering requires that indigenous actors not only clarify specific needs and transform what was taken to be a private problem into a social problem, but also forge collective identities – through ongoing processes of collective self-understanding and identification – so that suffering and needs can be articulated, and solutions to address them can be identified. And to do this, actors produce both the publics in which they emerge and the collective solidarities that sustain them (BFN, 376). As Cohen (cf. BFN, 367–70) observes: 'collective actors often create public spaces and transform formerly private domains into social arenas for the creation of their collective identities and demands.'[56] Through the production of publics and collective identities, emerging actors are able to create social movements that transform 'unmobilized sentiment pools' into pressing public problems.[57] Given that these are particular forms of collective identification (that is, the construction of a specific 'we'), and given that these processes of collective identification take place amidst struggles for recognition, they are unlikely to emerge from the impartial, universal perspective of the moral point of view.[58]

Indeed, Habermas acknowledges that these 'cultural battles', in which disrespected minorities struggle against an insensitive majority culture, are 'inevitably permeated by ethics' (IO, 218; cf. 42, 225). Whereas moral discourse seeks to establish what is in the equal interest of all, ethical discourse seeks to establish what is good for us (BFN, 161). While the former 'requires a perspective freed of all egocentrism and ethnocentrism' in the search for a universally binding good for all (BFN, 97), the latter 'refer[s] to a shared ethos' (IO, 26) of a particular community 'orientated to the telos of . . . our good' (BFN, 97). The ongoing forms of collective identification that are forged in such battles construct a concrete 'we' that emerges from particular, shared experiences of suffering and establishes specific bonds of solidarity. While collective actors involved in such struggles may well issue demands in the abstract, impartial language of justice (for example, demands for equality and inclusion), such demands depend on ongoing processes of collective identification that forge particular identities around specific experiences of suffering. And, as Cohen points out (in terms not dissimilar to Mouffe's), the 'creation of identity [within social movements] involves social contestation' and the necessity of recognising 'the dimension of conflictual social relations between adversaries'.[59]

This contestation and conflict in the formation of collective identities in struggles for recognition is not restricted to the vertical opposition of a minority against a dominating majority. Struggles of collective actors within the informal public sphere are also oppositional in a horizontal sense. We can see this in the battered women's movement that emerged in the 1970s. A crucial part of the success of feminist actors in transforming the issue of 'wife beating . . . from a subject of private shame and misery' into 'an object of public concern' lay in creating and sustaining oppositional collective identities against a dominating majority.[60] The need for shelters for women seeking refuge from violent partners emerged from consciousness-raising groups, speak-outs and peer counselling, in which battered women shared their experiences of suffering and, through this, underwent transforming processes of self-understanding and need interpretation.[61] Gagné persuasively shows the centrality for this movement of 'developing a collective identity and how that is used to build social movement networks and change institutions' (13). While a collective identity needed to be constructed vertically against a dominating majority culture that failed to recognise the existence of domestic violence against women, horizontal oppositional collective identifications were also crucial in struggles over the framing of, and thus proposed solutions to, that problem.[62] Feminist groups within the battered women's movement, for example, distinguished themselves from, and actively contested, conflicting action frames – and thus conflicting collective identifications – that presented the problem of domestic violence as an 'individual pathology or dysfunction within the family system' that required a therapeutic response (48), rather than a societal problem of power and domination over women that demanded a political response. The former resulted in a collective identity that distinguished between battered and non-battered women, while the latter constructed a collective identity that made no such distinction, precisely because all women were perceived to be threatened with such violence (60–1). Feminist collective actors, then, set themselves 'apart from non-members' through adherence to a shared feminist collective action frame. Those who did not share such a frame were deemed 'suspect' and 'frozen out' or 'ostracized'. Thus the 'oppositional collective identity' (161–5) created by this feminist collective action frame was oppositional both vertically and horizontally. This account of oppositional feminist collective identities, forged within the battered women's movement, accords with Taylor's broader claim that 'by definition, social movements create a collective oppositional consciousness'.[63]

I have repeatedly referred to the particularity and specificity of the collective identities of emergent actors in the informal public sphere to underscore the oppositional nature of such collective identifications. These are specific identities constructed along adversarial we/they distinctions. There is nothing in Habermas's model of democratic politics in the informal public sphere that rules out these sociological accounts of collective we/they identifications in struggles for recognition. Indeed, not only does Habermas draw on Cohen's work and vice versa, but in acknowledging the irreducible ethical dimension of collective struggles, his own account points to the necessity of particular, collective identifications.

While Habermas's acknowledgement of an ethical dimension to practical discourse, and the account of collective identities that I have set out, provides a response to the charge that the deliberative approach fails to recognise collective actors (and thus collective identifications) in the public sphere, it comes at a cost for Habermas's account.[64] Recall that, for Habermas, in pluralistic societies rational consensus is crucial to securing the legitimacy of norms to which we are bound. And being orientated towards a rational consensus compels participants to adopt the impartial perspective of the moral point of view, where we reason not from the perspective of a 'particular community [but from] the perspective of *all* those possibly affected'.[65] Earlier I noted that Habermas introduces 'value orientations' into his principle of universalisation and acknowledges that practical discourse is 'necessarily permeated by ethics'. But this raises the question of how one can still hold to the abstract, impartial perspective of the moral point of view. Ethical questions pull in the opposite direction to moral questions, referring as they do to a specific good of a particular, concrete 'we'. This would seem to block the exercise of abstraction that participants in discourse are compelled to make in order 'to *transcend* the social and historical context of their particular form of life' and thereby orientate themselves to a rational consensus.[66] It would also block the move to fair bargaining and negotiated compromise that Habermas suggests as a response to persistent ethico-political disagreements. Values, unlike interests, are not easily traded in a process of negotiation. Values express who we are (or want to be), as well as what we take the good to be, rather than interests that we seek to maximise.

Discussing this problem, Thomas McCarthy persuasively argues, firstly, that 'value disagreements will often translate into disagreements about what is right or just' and, secondly, that in multicultural societies democratic deliberation will '*normally* be shot through with ethical disputes' grounded in fundamental value disagreements that may remain both intractable and reasonable (LD, 1089, 1095). As such, McCarthy concludes that 'democratic public life [will be] decidedly less centred on rational consensus' than Habermas suggests (LD, 1095). Though this poses a problem for Habermas's account, McCarthy thinks that it 'can be addressed without surrendering the discourse approach to democratic deliberation' (LD, 1083).

While a detailed discussion of this would require far more space than I have here,[67] McCarthy's argument that moral and ethical discourse are not two kinds of discourse (as Habermas maintains), but rather two aspects that are dialectically interdependent, seems a promising response. Seeking to resist conflating deliberation about politico-legal norms with deliberation about moral norms, McCarthy argues that when faced with questions of justice, we are not compelled to adopt the abstract, impartial perspective of the moral point of view, in which we consider what would be equally good for all (beyond our particular form of life). Rather, we are called upon to adopt the perspective of what would be *equally good for all of us affected*' (LD, 1097). By 'all of us affected', McCarthy means to emphasise my perspective as a member of a concrete community with its own intersubjective shared form of life. While seeking to arrive at decisions that are just will require 'a degree' of abstraction, deliberators 'have to take particulars of time, place . . . identities, values and so on into account' (LD, 1097).[68] And in modern, pluralistic societies this leaves open the possibility that, 'owing to basic differences in collective identities and fundamental values', discourse may fail to achieve rational consensus (LD, 1120). While this would not entail a rejection of Habermas's deliberative approach, McCarthy does think that it requires reworking that approach.

McCarthy makes a number of suggestions to this end. Rejecting a difference in kind between moral and ethical discourse, he proposes a 'dialectic model of legitimacy' (LD, 1111) grounded on:

> [A] model of practical discourse in which the thematization of any single aspect [moral, ethical, pragmatic] can take place only against the *background* of implicit assumptions about other aspects, which can themselves be contested and thematised at any time. Thus, *in practice* political deliberation is not so much an interweaving of separate discourses as a multifaceted communication process that allows for fluid transitions among questions and argument of different sorts. (LD, 1105)

This model calls for a shift towards a more procedural notion of legitimacy. Rather than understanding legitimacy as requiring that all participants succumb to the force of the better argument (and thus agree for the same substantive reasons), McCarthy argues that we should allow for rational agreement, and thus legitimacy, to be understood as accepting outcomes 'for the same procedural reasons but different substantive ones' (LD, 1117). This 'indirect' form of acceptance, or what Moore calls 'deliberative acceptance',[69] would weaken the cognitive thrust of Habermas's account of legitimacy by severing the connection between procedure and outcome that remains central to his account.[70]

Given that both rational consensus and strategic bargaining might not be possible in the face of persistent, reasonable disagreements grounded in differences in collective identities and fundamental values, McCarthy suggests 'mutual accommodation' as an option. This would be achieved through 'ethical-political dialogue' based on 'respect for, and desire to accommodate, ineliminable difference' (LD, 1125). On McCarthy's dialectical model of discourse, then, participants in democratic deliberation would still strive in discourse for consensus, but they would do so with a keen awareness of the possibilities of failure. As he puts it: 'Practical rationality in the face of diversity is as much a matter of recognizing, respecting, and accommodating differences as one of transcending them' (LD, 1124). This is something that deliberativists, as we shall see in the next chapter, will agree on.[71]

Modal slippage

I turn now to Mouffe's own account and, in particular, the problem of modal slippage. While the antagonistic exclusion thesis may well be an accurate description of a tendency to construct political identity through an oppositional logic, the question is why view this *possibility* of antagonism as a *necessary*, ineliminable feature of political identification and human relations more generally? It is odd that Mouffe draws on Derrida to support this Schmittian antagonistic exclusion thesis even though Derrida raises a similar question about modality in his reading of Schmitt in *Politics of Friendship*. There, one of the things Derrida circles around is the unthematised passage in Schmitt's discourse from the 'possibility' to the 'potentiality' and then 'actuality' of the friend/enemy relation (PF, 86, 124–33).[72] From the mere possibility-potentiality of this distinction, Schmitt moves to its 'inherent reality' without accounting for this passage.[73] As Derrida notes, from Schmitt's account it would seem that '[a]s soon as war is possible-eventual the enemy is present; he is there, his possibility is presently, effectively, supposed and structuring'. The issue of whether war is in fact decided upon 'is a mere empirical alternative in the face of an essential necessity' (PF, 86). Similarly, Mouffe moves from a claim about the possibility of the friend/enemy distinction emerging in various forms of collective identification, to the assertion that it is a necessary, inherent feature in human relations. Where Schmitt talks seamlessly of 'the *inherent* reality and real *possibility* of such a distinction', so Mouffe talks of 'the dimension of antagonism that is *inherent* in human relations' and of 'trying to defuse the *potential* antagonism that exists in human relations' (DP, 101).[74] This modal slippage is made throughout Mouffe's work and seems to be uncritically carried over from Schmitt.[75]

It is clear that Mouffe does not want to rest within the Schmittian problematic and will try to move beyond the essentialism of the friend/enemy distinction. In trying to do so, however, this slippage between 'necessity' and 'possibility' is no mere slip; it is a central move for her project. Mouffe needs strong talk of necessity to attack the deliberative emphasis on rational consensus. But she requires the lesser claim of possibility to create the space for twisting free of Schmitt and moving towards an agonistic politics, where friend and enemy become 'adversaries'. Mouffe explains this adversarial relation as one of 'friendly enemies, that is, persons who are friends because they share a common symbolic space but also enemies because they want to organize this common symbolic space in a different way' (DP, 13). Hence the ambiguous modal register and difficulties Mouffe's project faces.

Despite Derrida putting a similar question to Schmitt as we are to Mouffe, the latter still draws on Derrida, and, in particular, the notion of 'constitutive outside', to make the case for the antagonistic exclusion thesis. As she writes: in 'the work of Jacques Derrida . . . it is the notion of the "constitutive outside" which *helps me emphasize the antagonism inherent* in all objectivity and the centrality of the us/them distinction in the constitution of collective political identities' (DP, 12, my emphasis).[76] This move is not without its problems. The reason why Mouffe turns to Derrida is because she wants to avoid a Schmittian politics of existential conflict, and this requires de-essentialising the identity of the friend/enemy. Doing so, Mouffe thinks, will enable her 'to develop his [Schmitt's] insights into a different direction and to visualize other understandings [of the friend/enemy distinction] compatible with democratic pluralism'.[77] While antagonism cannot be eradicated, it can be redirected. Just as Habermas will detranscendentalise Kant for a postmetaphysical age, so Mouffe will de-essentialise Schmitt for a democratic pluralist one. While the Schmittian picture may offer Mouffe inroads against the Habermasian emphasis on impartiality, rationality and consensus, the 'unrelenting intensity of conflict between friend and enemy' that would seem to emerge from the antagonistic exclusion thesis would leave no room for the democratic pluralism Mouffe is keen to see flourish.[78]

The problem Mouffe faces, then, is that she wants an agonistic politics that acknowledges the ineradicability of antagonism, while affirming the possibility of democratic pluralism. While Mouffe views the deliberative approach as attempting the impossible in trying to eliminate the former through a rational consensus, the Schmittian position is seen as accepting the unacceptable in extinguishing the latter in the existential conflicts of implacable enemies. Refusing to adopt the consensual approach of deliberation, and insisting on the necessity of Schmitt as a starting point, Mouffe will attempt to think 'with Schmitt against Schmitt' (OP, 14). With Schmitt she will maintain that there can be no 'we' that does not at the same time exclude a 'they'. Against Schmitt she will insist that this does not leave us locked in the existential clash of concrete friend/enemy groupings. The notion of 'constitutive outside' is the poststructuralist twist that Mouffe thinks will allow her to hold on to the 'ineradicability of the conflictual dimension of social life' (OP, 4), whilst avoiding the Schmittian either/or: either the totalising homogeneity of friends or the disintegrating pluralism of enemies.

The constitutive outside

Mouffe introduces the notion of constitutive outside as an insight of Derrida's.[79] But there is a problem in drawing on Derrida here to support the antagonistic exclusion thesis, namely, that Derrida attempts to put into question the very demarcation of inside/outside that such a thesis would seem to suggest. Not only is this evident in Derrida's reading of Schmitt – a reading which brings out the porous, fragile and contestable borders of a series of organising inside/outside oppositions in Schmitt's discourse[80] – but it is arguably one of *the* guiding provocations behind Derrida's work, perhaps most clearly evident in his early work. In *Speech and Phenomena*, for example, he attempts to show that 'there can no longer be any absolute inside, for the "outside" has insinuated itself in the movement by which the inside . . . is constituted' (SP, 86). While this formulation may well lend itself to the notion of a 'constitutive outside', it can only do so if one appreciates that it puts into question the very possibility of clearly demarcating the inside and the outside, and, I would suggest, friend and enemy. The mutual contamination of both means that the 'outside' will always appear in scare quotes, just as the inside remains forever marked by an 'irreducible openness' (SP, 86).

Understood in this way, the notion of 'constitutive outside', far from helping, would actually call into question the 'double identification' necessary for the drawing of antagonistic frontiers that exclude the enemy from the friend (PF, 106, 149–63). As Derrida argues in his reading of Schmitt, 'the purity of *pólemos* or the enemy, whereby Schmitt would define the political, remains unattainable' (PF, 114). It is thus difficult to see how the work of Derrida could be used to show the necessity of an antagonistic exclusion in the formation of political identity. In this context, it seems that the most that one could get from a Derridean approach would be a thesis concerning the movement of difference at the heart of self-presence and the impossibility of a self closing in upon itself in a pure interiority of ownness. This may provide Mouffe with the means to de-essentialise the Schmittian starting point and thereby avoid succumbing to the existential conflicts of the friend/enemy relation. But, once this move is made, it is difficult to see how one can hold on to claims regarding the necessary nature of the antagonistic exclusion thesis. The only conclusion that Mouffe could draw from the notion of a 'constitutive outside', as informed by the work of Derrida, is that identity constitution takes place through differential relations.[81] While this may entail a relational logic of identification, there is nothing to say that this necessarily involves an antagonistic exclusion. Indeed, on the Derridean account, the kind of closure required for antagonistic exclusion would appear to be 'im-possible'.[82]

Mouffe, then, faces a problem. While the move to Derrida allows her to de-essentialise Schmitt, it would also seem to require dropping the strong claim of necessity in the antagonistic exclusion thesis. Indeed, Mouffe seems to end up suggesting a weaker formulation of the thesis. Outlining the democratic task as one of trying to 'envisage how it is possible to diffuse the *tendencies* [my emphasis] to exclusion that are present in every construction of collective identities', Mouffe goes on to explain the contribution made by the notion of 'constitutive outside' to such a democratic task:

> [I]ts aim is to highlight the fact that the creation of an identity implies the establishment of a difference, difference that is *often* constructed on the basis of a hierarchy . . . *Once* we have understood that every identity is relational and that the affirmation of a difference is a precondition for any identity, i.e., the perception of an 'other' that will constitute the 'exterior', then we can begin to understand why such a relation *may* always become the breeding ground for antagonism.[83]

Mouffe seems to accept the point that the constitutive outside thesis is limited to the claim that 'identity requires the establishment of a difference'. But it does not support the further assertion that the establishment of a difference entails antagonistic exclusion. Indeed, this suggests a weaker account. It is only 'once' we have grasped the role of the constitutive outside that we understand antagonistic relations to be a 'tendency' that 'may' emerge.

There seems to be a general ambiguity around this point. In *On the Political* Mouffe repeats the passage cited above and, immediately after, notes: 'This does not mean, of course, that such a [we/they] relation is necessarily one of friend/enemy, i.e. an antagonistic one' (OP, 15). Here, then, we have the possibility of oppositional collective identifications without antagonistic exclusion. Indeed, in a more recent book, *Agonistics*, Mouffe states that many such we/they relations 'are merely a question of recognizing differences' (A, 5). Yet, a few pages later, she suggests that identifying a 'they' is not simply a recognition of difference, but of antagonism:

> [D]efining an adversary, a 'they', will serve as a 'constitutive outside' for a 'we'. This is what can be called 'the moment of the political', the recognition of the constitutive character of social division *and the ineradicability of antagonism*. (A, 18, my emphasis)

While the identification of a 'they' in the construction of a 'we' may indicate a conflictual character of social division, it is not clear why it is to be understood in terms of antagonism (the latter emerges only when we/they distinctions take the form of friend/enemy). Insofar as we/they relations are defined in terms of adversaries, we are not at the level of antagonistic friend/enemy relations, but rather remain at the level of differences within a conflictual social field.

Problems with both a strong and weak version of the antagonistic exclusion thesis come into view if we approach this from a different angle. Take Mouffe's insistence on the 'impossibility of a world without antagonism' (RP, 4). While one might agree that we could not have a world without antagonism (although, as we will see below, it is not immediately obvious why this should be ruled out as impossible), that is not quite the same thing as claiming that it would be impossible for a particular community to function in terms of non-antagonistic relations. As we have seen, Mouffe is committed to the idea that it is possible to organise we/they relations in terms of adversaries rather than enemies. Insofar as a political community of adversaries is possible, in what sense is such a community not 'without antagonism'?

The Mouffean reply would probably consist in referring back to the argument for the necessity of exclusion: the very condition of possibility for a particular political community to exist is the exclusion of a 'they'. A particular political community may be structured *internally* along adversarial we/they distinctions, but its existence as such is constituted through antagonistic friend/enemy relations *externally*. As Mouffe writes: 'while politics aims at constructing a political community . . . a fully inclusive community can never be realized since there will permanently be . . . an exterior to the community that makes its existence possible.' The conclusion that Mouffe draws from this is that '[a]ntagonistic forces will never disappear' (RP, 69).

Mouffe's characterisation of this 'they' as 'permanently' exterior may provide the grounds for understanding this 'they' to be an enemy rather than an adversary, and therefore the relation one of antagonism. When Mouffe refers to 'those who do not accept the democratic "rules of the game", and who thereby exclude themselves from the political community', the case could be made for her claim that 'the category of the enemy remains pertinent' (RP, 4). Here, then, we would have grounds to support a strong version of the antagonistic exclusion thesis as it applies at the level of the very existence of a political community. If a political community can only exist through permanently excluding a 'they', then antagonism would appear to be an unavoidable feature of political life.

There are two points I wish to make in response. Firstly, where such a state of affairs holds – where, for example, there is an anti-democratic 'they' that is permanently excluded from a democratic community – it is not clear what kind of liberal illusions have been shattered. That a democratic community can only exist by excluding to the exterior any anti-democratic 'they' is something few democrats have any illusions about.[84] A brief glance at my Facebook news feed provides ample evidence of self-described democrats insisting on the necessity of punching, rather than deliberating with, fascists. Of course, Mouffe's critique is directed at the liberal democrat, who would probably not advocate that particular form of exclusion. But that is not to say that they would not advocate excluding – as a permanent exterior – such a 'they'. The liberal democrat, I imagine, is fully aware of the fact that democracy must define itself in opposition to an anti-democratic 'they' of this sort and that such opposition would entail exclusion. Indeed, this is part of what is involved in insisting on democratic rules of the game. That is to say, democracy is, in its very definition, antagonistic to a 'they' that would threaten the very possibility of a democratic form of life.

When Derrida intervened in the civil war in Algeria in 1994, which was sparked by the cancellation of elections in 1992 (when it looked like a nondemocratic party would take power), he insisted:

> We ... take sides ... against whoever does not respect electoral arbitration and whoever would tend, directly or indirectly, before, during, or after such elections, to put into question the very principle that will have presided over such a process; that is, democratic life, the state of law, the respect for freedom of speech, the rights of the minority, of political change ... We are resolutely opposed – and this side we clearly take with all of its consequences – to whoever would claim to profit from democratic procedures without respecting democracy. (N, 121)

I imagine that liberal democrats would be just as resolute in their opposition. Indeed, there are liberal democrats who are under no illusions about the kind of exclusions that may be required in opposition to an anti-democrat 'they'. Consider the controversy in the UK over the decision by the BBC to invite the then British National Party (BNP) leader, Nick Griffin, to appear on *Question Time* (aired on 22 November 2009). Responding to an argument put forward by Norman Baker MP – that the BNP had two democratically elected MEPs and a number of UK councillors and therefore should be represented on *Question Time* – the Home Secretary at the time, Alan Johnson MP, responded by noting that 'the National Front had people elected'. Johnson went on to criticise the BBC's decision to invite the BNP to appear on the grounds that it would make a far-right party 'seem a normal [democratic] party'.[85] While Johnson would probably not have endorsed punching Nick Griffin, he had no hesitation in identifying the BNP as an anti-democratic 'they' that needed to be excluded from the public sphere in the name of defending liberal democracy. As Johnson put it: 'I won't share a platform with a fascist ... I don't have to sit and debate with these people.'[86] While many liberal democrats may be under the illusion that there is no need for exclusion, they are not necessarily so.

One might reply by suggesting that this recognition of the need for exclusion just goes to show that Derrida and Johnson are not liberals. I doubt Mouffe would avail herself of this move. Not only would it beg the question against the liberal, but it would require Mouffe to reformulate her critique. Mouffe identifies Habermas as an exemplary figure of liberal rationalism. But Habermas is far from blind about the need for exclusion:

> There can be no inclusion without exclusion . . . A democratic order . . . must take preventive protection against the enemies . . . [W]e in Germany have become aware of the necessity of the self-assertion of a 'militant' democracy that is 'prepared to defend itself' . . . A constitutional state must perform a two-fold task here: it must repel the animosity of existential enemies while avoiding the betrayal of its own principles.[87]

While there may be problems with Habermas's account, failure to acknowledge the necessity of exclusion does not appear to be one of them.[88] If Habermas is a liberal rationalist, then liberal blindness is not constitutive.[89]

Here, then, we might preserve a strong version of the antagonistic exclusion thesis at the level of securing a democratic form of life. But, at this level, it's not clear who thinks otherwise.

Secondly, it is questionable whether one can secure the strong version of this thesis even at the level of the existence of a particular community. To secure such a thesis one would have to show that it is impossible for there to be a 'we' identification that does not involve the antagonistic exclusion of a 'they'. This may be unlikely empirically, but Mouffe's account does not demonstrate that it is impossible conceptually. And if such a state of affairs is not conceptually impossible, then the possibility of a fully inclusive 'we' remains. (This is not to claim that such a state of affairs would eliminate the possibility of antagonism.) Indeed, if Mouffe's argument for we/they relations is sufficiently formal, then there could be a fully inclusive human 'we' in opposition to a non-human 'they', whether it be the gods, non-human animals or the environment. Or one could form a fully inclusive 'we' in opposition to an ancestral 'they'. In either case, it seems that one could, in principle, have we/they identifications in which the 'we' would be pragmatically universal.[90] Abizadeh goes further. Not only does he argue that there is nothing conceptually incoherent about identification with a universal human 'we', he claims that it is perfectly coherent to have a 'we' identification that goes beyond humanity, where one identifies with 'all sentient beings' or, more radical still, 'the entire existing universe'.[91] If this is conceptually impossible, Mouffe has yet to provide an argument that demonstrates it to be so.

Even if one rejects the strong version of the antagonistic exclusion thesis, Mouffe may still hold on to a weaker version of that thesis. Here antagonistic exclusion would remain an ever-present possibility. But there are two problems here. First, it's not clear who would deny this possibility. The second problem is signalled by the quotation marks around 'exterior' in the extended quotation above. Once we make the de-essentialising move of the constitutive outside thesis, then there is no 'exterior' as such. An exterior implies an interior to which it stands in relation, but the notion of an interior is precisely what the constitutive outside thesis puts into question. As Mouffe herself says: 'it reveals the impossibility of drawing an absolute distinction between interior and exterior.'[92] And having recognised this impossibility, antagonism, based as it is on the essentialist distinction between friend and enemy, can seemingly no longer emerge. If the constitutive outside thesis does the de-essentialising work Mouffe thinks it does, then it would seem to require abandoning the antagonistic exclusion thesis. Put in a more Derridean formulation: the condition of possibility of the antagonistic exclusion would seem to be, simultaneously, a condition of impossibility.

To sum up the discussion so far, I have suggested that the two aspects of Mouffe's critique of the Habermasian model of deliberative democracy, namely, the elimination of the passions argument and the antagonistic exclusion thesis, do not clinch the critical claims that Mouffe suggests. I have argued that the elimination of the passions argument fails to hit its mark insofar as it is based on an overly narrow reading of what entering discourse entails and fails to take into account Habermas's two-track model of democratic politics. In addition, while Mouffe's alternative approach insists on the centrality of the affective dimension of political identification, she provides an insufficient theorisation of the role of the passions and fantasy in political life. Regarding the antagonistic exclusion thesis, I have argued that far from being blind to collective identities, Habermas's account of democratic politics is grounded in a public sphere populated by collective identities and acknowledges (or at least need not rule out) the oppositional nature of collective identifications. Turning to Mouffe's position, I have argued that it suffers from a form of modal slippage that is no mere slip. The problem of modal slippage reveals an unresolved dilemma at the heart of Mouffe's project: holding to the strong claim of a necessary antagonism in order to attack the deliberative approach leaves Mouffe in a Schmittian embrace; weakening antagonism to a possibility in order to envisage an agonistic pluralism of we/they relations leaves little between Mouffe's agonistic pluralism of 'friendly enemies' and the more liberal approaches she wants to attack. I have also tried to show that Mouffe's constitutive outside thesis fails to demonstrate the conceptual impossibility of a universal 'we'. Moreover, I have suggested that the Derridean approach on which she draws would seem to rule out the very possibility of drawing the distinctions required for antagonistic relations of friend/enemy. Thus, both the strong and weak versions of the antagonistic thesis are insufficiently defended.

Mouffe's account does, however, raise pressing questions for deliberative theory. Her critique highlights the lack of any detailed account of both the role of the passions in democratic life and the affective dimension of collective identifications. This presents a serious challenge to the Habermasian demand for impartiality. In addition, she provides valuable insights into some of the more troubling developments in contemporary politics. Her account includes important observations concerning the regressive forms of identification that we are seeing form around notions of nationalism, ethnicity and religion, as well as the way in which political discourse takes on an increasingly moral tone and the threat this poses to democratic politics.

In the final section, I return to the broader issue alluded to at the start of this chapter, namely, 'the time-honoured debate about conflict and consensus-orientated social and political thought'.[93] I want to touch briefly on ways of rethinking these issues that may point towards the possibility of 'a deliberative vision of democratic politics which can also do justice to the agonistic spirit of democracy'.[94]

V. A Dialogue of Friendly Enemies?

In a 1996 paper discussing the contributions of normative and agonistic models of democracy, Ricardo Blaug succinctly stated the challenge facing democratic theory: 'The strengths of each ... need to be combined.' Immediately after, however, Blaug dropped in the following pessimistic footnote: 'The present level of hostility between normative and postmodern approaches, wherein each accuses the other of inadvertently lending theoretical support to unfairness, would seem to preclude this.'[95] In a 2002 review of Mouffe's *The Democratic Paradox*, James Tully hoped that Mouffe's critique of consensual approaches to democracy would elicit 'a response' that would lead to 'a constructive discussion'.[96] John Brady's remarks in 2004, about the stubborn binary opposition of contestation/consensus in discussions between agonistic and deliberative democrats, suggested little progress had been made: 'With remarkable regularity', noted Brady, 'theorists on both sides insist on the fundamental opposition between a democratic political practice based on contestation and one based on consensus formation.'[97] In his 2013 book *Agonistic Democracy*, Wenman confirms Brady's observation when he insists that 'there is no middle ground between agonistic and deliberative theory'.[98]

However, there are encouraging signs. A number of theorists are attempting to meet the challenge Blaug and Tully set, engaging in constructive responses no longer marked by the kind of fault lines that so exasperated Brady.[99] If this dialogue is to continue to be productive, then there needs to be not only critical exchange, but a mutual transformation of both positions. The current generation of deliberative theorists are busy doing just that. While these theorists differ in terms of the model of deliberation they favour, what they do share is a concern over conceptions of public deliberation modelled on restrictive accounts of rational argumentation and overly demanding idealisations of consensus and impartiality. These concerns have prompted deliberativists to develop a more expansive conception of deliberation and a more minimal account of democratic legitimacy.

John Dryzek, James Bohman and Simone Chambers, for example, have called for a substantial weakening of the idealisations governing the Habermasian model of deliberation. Dryzek rejects 'unnecessarily constraining' (DDB, 1) approaches to deliberation based on strong normative conditions of rational argumentation and idealising presuppositions of consensus, and advocates a more 'tolerant' (DDB, iv) approach that would be 'more expansive in the kinds of communication it allows' (DDB, 73). This not only opens up deliberation to a variety of forms of communication, including rhetoric, humour, greeting and testimony, but also drops the presuppositions of consensus and impartiality for the more 'feasible and attractive' notion of 'workable agreements' that may be arrived at for very different reasons (DDB, 170). Similarly, Bohman argues for a plural understanding of public reason (PD, 75) and 'a much more minimal account of justification' (PD, ix). As if responding to Mouffe's criticisms of Habermas, Bohman rejects regulative ideals of convergence, unanimity and impartiality and argues that not only are these not necessary presuppositions of democratic deliberation, but by making them so 'Habermas unnecessarily narrows the range of convincing reasons in ways that are especially problematic for vibrant political deliberation in pluralistic societies' (PD, 45). Bohman sets out 'an elaboration of the ideal of public reason in political life that permits, rather than denies or avoids, moral conflict and difference in democratic politics' (PD, 84). A similar approach can be found in Simone Chambers' work. Chambers acknowledges that 'tragedy, no right answer, the problem of otherness, and disagreement are *permanent* features of our collective life' (my emphasis), recognises that 'reason has its limits', and insists that heterogeneity, non-conformity and the clash of opposing forces not only have their place in deliberation, but are a critical and productive force driving it.[100]

I shall discuss developments within deliberative theory in more detail in the next chapter, where I shall try to show how the current debate can avoid the seemingly intractable oppositions lamented by Brady. But just as deliberative theorists have substantially weakened the idealisations governing the deliberative approach of Habermas, there needs to be a corresponding weakening of the ontological claims underpinning the agonistic approach of Mouffe.[101]

In some sense this is already under way in Mouffe's work. The attempt to move away from the antagonistic friend/enemy relation of Schmitt to the agonistic 'friendly enemies' of democratic pluralism substantially weakens the strong ontological claims of a necessary antagonism. Although Mouffe seems to feel the pull of this move, she never quite follows through, hence the ambiguous modal register I discussed above. However, I think this is precisely the path that Mouffe needs to take. At present, the agonistic approach of Mouffe has raised important questions about ideals of consensus and impartiality, and the thin picture (which she sees deliberative approaches working with) of a rational subject bereft of the passions that are crucial in the constitution of political identity. But with no account of the agonistic subject who, on the one hand, constitutes her identity through acts of exclusions of a 'they', but who, on the other hand, resists an ineradicable antagonism and greets her adversary in a shared symbolic space with a 'friendly' agonistic acknowledgement, Mouffe's agonistic approach is left with the difficulty of explaining how we ever move from the Schmittian understanding of democracy to the shared symbolic space of a vibrant pluralism. When Mouffe observes that 'coming to accept the position of the adversary is to undergo a radical change in political identity', she characterises that change as having 'more of a quality of a conversion than of rational persuasion'.[102] This not only leaves the process of agonistic identity-formation in the dark, but it also leaves social actors vulnerable to the threat of a procedureless night of power.

The insight into the affective dimension of collective identification is an important one, but it must be weakened to take into account the cognitive mechanisms operating in deliberation and the legitimating procedures of collective decision-making that secure the possibility of a vibrant democratic pluralism. The Habermasian procedural account of democratic deliberation, and his two-track model of democratic politics, in which a wild anarchic public sphere is set within a constitutional framework so as to enable an 'unleashed cultural pluralism to fully develop', has the advantage of outlining how we can have not only 'solidarity among strangers', but the equally important 'right to *remain* strangers' (BFN, 308). On a Mouffean picture, this would always seem to be a strategic decision. It is not clear why the agonist, who sees the other as a legitimate adversary, wouldn't, given different circumstances, antagonistically transform her adversary into an other who has no right to remain.

While the passions of collective identification are something deliberative theorists tend to leave under-theorised, the agonistic approach of Mouffe has yet to develop a satisfactory account of the movement from antagonism to agonism and the institutional structures and procedures of collective decision-making that would preserve the shared symbolic space her approach relies upon. This is problematic insofar as the agonism that Mouffe advocates can only take place, as she herself acknowledges, 'under conditions regulated by a set of democratic procedures accepted by the adversaries' (OP, 21). How adversaries come to an agreement on the conditions that regulate what Mouffe calls the 'clash of *legitimate* democratic political positions' (OP, 30, my emphasis) is something her account leaves unanswered. A sympathetic reader such as David Howarth, for example, notes that although agonistic theorists such as Mouffe 'allude to the importance of democratic rules and procedures, there is still something of an "institutional deficit" in their respective theories'.[103] Mouffe's assurance that the struggles she wishes to see emerge '*will* not be one of "enemies" but among "adversaries", since all participants *will* recognize the position of others in the contest as legitimate ones' (DP, 74, my emphasis) is not particularly reassuring. Mouffe's 'will' has all the normative force of crossing one's fingers. Commenting on this passage, Kapoor asks: 'What will compel these groups to act democratically? What will guarantee or impel their legitimacy?' Without answers to these kinds of questions, Kapoor warns that 'Mouffe's agonistic pluralism risks condoning authoritarian behaviour and decisions or practices that are participatory only in name'. Indeed, it isn't immediately obvious what the Mouffean agonist would say in response to the following remark – cited by Kapoor – of an *adivasi* woman in Madhya Pradesh, India: 'Today you are sitting on the ground [participating with us], tomorrow [what is to stop you from] sitting on our heads?'[104]

If Mouffe's agonistic politics is to be a passionate, non-violent clash of democratically legitimate positions, then it will require the non-partisan, abstract agreements and institutionalised procedures of the sort set out by deliberative democrats. Indeed, it is precisely with these agreements and procedures in the background that post-traditional societies are able to support, and further pluralise, the forms of life that make up the vibrant, democratic public sphere Mouffe advocates. As Habermas puts it:

> The transitory unity that is generated in the porous and refracted intersubjectively mediated consensus not only supports but furthers and accelerates the pluralization of forms of life and the individualization of lifestyles. More discourse means more contradiction and difference. The more abstract the agreements become, the more diverse the disagreements with which we can *non-violently* live.[105]

It is this transitory unity that provides the space for the diversity of democracy's voices.

If we weaken Mouffe's claims of a necessary antagonism, then a more promising vision of democratic engagement becomes possible, one that would begin with the possibilities of antagonism, before going on to build on Mouffe's insights to explore the conditions that make it more likely to emerge and set out ways in which one can secure the shared symbolic space required for a vibrant democratic pluralism. I think this marks out the terrain for a productive dialogue between the weakened deliberative vision that is now emerging, and the weakened agonistic approach we catch a glimpse of in Mouffe's own attempt 'to visualize other understandings compatible with democratic pluralism' (OP, 15).

The agonism of William Connolly, Bonnie Honig and James Tully offer promising approaches in this direction (see n. 101). So far, Mouffe has rejected any move of this sort. In recent work, for example, she criticises Connolly and Honig on the grounds that they each offer an 'agonism without antagonism' (A, 10).[106] Despite differences in their respective approaches, Mouffe charges both Connolly and Honig with conceptualising agonistic politics as 'a mere valorisation of multiplicity' that fails to 'account for the necessary moment of closure'. Such failure is no mere oversight, but a 'necessary consequence' of their 'fight against closure'. As a result, both are, according to Mouffe, unable to recognise 'antagonism as . . . being ineradicable' (A, 14–15). Mouffe, I imagine, would extend this criticism to Tully. In an exchange with Honig, Tully acknowledges the 'complex and unnoticed ways that our most prized forms of reason are deeply woven into forms of violence', yet he argues that:

> Non-violent practices of cooperation, disputation and dispute resolution are more basic and prevalent than violent antagonism . . . If this were not true, if violent struggles for existence and wars of all against all were primary, the human species would have perished long ago. Cooperation, not violent antagonism, is the primary factor in evolution, as Kropotkin first responded to Darwin and as many have since tested and substantiated.[107]

Here is an agonism that weakens Mouffe's ontological starting point of a primary, ineradicable antagonism. In his search for 'a non-violent alternative to the deadly nexus of reason and violence called power politics', Tully acknowledges the 'difficulty . . . of realising this peaceful way of being in the world' but, crucially, 'not the impossibility' of such a way of being.[108]

But this is precisely the problem for agonists of various stripes – talk like this and one ends up slipping into a 'Habermasian voice' (and, in agonistic circles, that is no compliment).[109] While Mouffe seems reluctant to move in the direction of weakening the ontological starting point of her agonistic model, in the next chapter I shall explore the various ways in which deliberativists are weakening core assumptions of Habermas's deliberative model.

Notes

1. Khan, 'Critical Republicanism'; Glover, 'Games without Frontiers?'; Erman, 'What Is Wrong with Agonistic Pluralism?'; Gürsözlü, 'Agonism and Deliberation – Recognizing the Difference'; Rummens, 'Democracy as a Non-Hegemonic Struggle?'; Fossen, 'Agonistic Critiques of Liberalism'; Schaap, 'Political Theory and the Agony of

Politics'; Knops, 'Debate: Agonism as Deliberation'; Little, 'Between Disagreement and Consensus'; Schaap, 'Agonism in Divided Societies'; Dahlberg, 'The Habermasian Public Sphere'; Brady, 'No Contest?'; White, 'After Critique'; Dryzek, *Deliberative Democracy and Beyond*; Kapoor, 'Deliberative Democracy or Agonistic Pluralism?'.
2. I focus on Mouffe's articulation of agonism as she has developed her account through a long-standing critique of Habermas's deliberative theory. For an overview of various conceptions of agonistic politics see Wenman, *Agonistic Democracy*; Wingenbach, *Institutionalizing Agonistic Democracy*; Schaap, *Law and Agonistic Politics*.
3. Mouffe identifies these two aspects when she points to the 'two reasons why liberal theory could not really apprehend the nature of the political: first, because of its rationalism; and second, because of its individualism' (A, 136; cf. A, 3–4, 54; OP, 11, 14; RP, 2).
4. Joseph Bessette is credited with coining the term in 'Deliberative Democracy: The Majority Principle in Republican Government'.
5. Mill, 'Considerations on Representative Government', 432.
6. Cited in Held, *Models of Democracy*, 46–8.
7. Thucydides, *The War of the Peloponnesians and Athenians*, 113.
8. Elster, 'Introduction', in *Deliberative Democracy*, 1.
9. Lefort, *The Political Forms of Modern Society*, 305.
10. Bohman and Rehg, 'Introduction', in *Deliberative Democracy*, x.
11. Blaug, 'New Theories of Discursive Democracy', 50.
12. Schumpeter, *Capitalism, Socialism and Democracy*, 283.
13. Habermas, *The Future of Human Nature*, 10.
14. Thomassen, *Deconstructing Habermas*, 25.
15. McCarthy, 'Reason in a Postmetaphysical Age', 50.
16. Habermas, *The Philosophical Discourse of Modernity*, 322.
17. Habermas, 'A Reply to my Critics', 221.
18. Habermas, *Moral Consciousness and Communicative Action*, 120, 66.
19. Habermas sees deliberation and basic rights as mediating one another and maps these onto the pairs popular sovereignty and the constitutional state, democracy and human rights, solidarity and justice, public autonomy and private autonomy, and argues that these are 'conceptually intertwined' or 'co-originally constituted' in his theory. See BFN, 122, 170, 274, 298; IO, 136. This will be taken up in the final chapter.
20. Schmitt, *The Concept of the Political*.
21. Mouffe, 'Politics and Passions', 616.
22. Cited in Mouffe, 'Carl Schmitt and the Paradox of Liberal Democracy', 39.

23. Schmitt, *The Concept of the Political*, 28.
24. Ibid.
25. Ibid. 27.
26. Habermas, 'A Reply to Symposium Participants', 1493.
27. Mouffe, 'Decision, Deliberation, and Democratic Ethos', 26.
28. Habermas, 'A Reply to my Critics', 235.
29. Ibid. 254.
30. Ibid. 255.
31. The reformulated principle reads: 'A norm is valid when the foreseeable consequences and side effects of its general observance for the interests and value-orientations of *each individual* could be *jointly* accepted by *all* concerned without coercion' (IO, 42). This acknowledgement of 'ethical reasons' and 'value orientations' within practical discourse generates problems that I will take up in the discussion of collective identities below.
32. The success of the latter is, of course, another issue. This will be the focus of the next chapter.
33. Markell, 'Contesting Consensus', 390.
34. Barber, 'Foundationalism and Democracy', 354.
35. Mouffe, 'Deliberative Democracy or Agonistic Pluralism', 752.
36. Habermas, 'A Reply to my Critics', 235.
37. See Dahlberg, 'The Habermasian Public Sphere'; Knops, 'Debate: Agonism as Deliberation'.
38. Cited in Dahlberg, 'The Habermasian Public Sphere', 120.
39. Habermas's account 'places a good part of the normative expectation connected with deliberative politics on the peripheral networks of opinion formation' (BFN, 358).
40. Although often described as a two-track model, Habermas's account is more of a multi-tiered systems theory, in which there is a 'functional division of labour' across multiple arenas (E, 146).
41. All italicised terms in this paragraph are mine.
42. Hirschkop, 'Justice and Drama', 52.
43. Hence Habermas's insistence on legal and constitutional safeguards. The tension between this and democratic sovereignty will be taken up in the final chapter.
44. In addition to these '*systemic* constraints', Habermas recognises 'accidental inequalities in the distribution of individual abilities', which, taken together, 'make us aware of *unavoidable* moments of inertia – specifically, the scarcity of those functionally *necessary* resources on which processes of deliberative opinion- and will-formation significantly depend' (BFN, 325–6, my emphasis). While Habermas

sees glimmers of hope for emergent actors to influence the political system (BFN, 149–52, 379–80), his overall picture, based on empirical research on mass communication, is rather pessimistic (see BFN, 369–80; E, 152–79).
45. Mouffe, 'Introduction: Schmitt's Challenge', 2.
46. In the US, supposedly archaic political forces have re-emerged with emboldened neo-Nazis and white supremacists marching on the streets. In the UK, the EU referendum has unleashed a violent resentment directed at immigrants, a trend that has emerged across Europe. As I write this, for example, it is reported that one of 'the biggest gatherings of far-right activists in Europe' is taking place in Poland, with banners proclaiming 'White Poland, Pure Poland' and 'Pray for Islamic Holocaust'. See Taylor, ' "White Europe": 60,000 nationalists march on Poland's independence day', *The Guardian*, 12 November 2017.
47. Mouffe and Wagner, 'Interview with Chantal Mouffe', 271.
48. Elliot, *Social Theory and Psychoanalysis in Transition*, 95.
49. Ibid. 97.
50. Young, 'Activist Challenges to Deliberative Democracy', 672.
51. White, 'After Critique', 212. No doubt Mouffe's agonistic pluralism differs markedly from Schumpeter's competitive elitism, yet there are certain assumptions that are shared (no doubt for different reasons). For example, the rejection of the very possibility of a common good which 'all people could agree on or be made to agree on by the force of rational argument' (Schumpeter, *Capitalism*, 251) and the emphasis on the importance of the affective dimension in politics. For why Mouffe should not be misread as a fellow traveller of Schumpeter, see Smith, *Laclau and Mouffe*, 147–50.
52. Brady, 'No Contest?', 338.
53. Plato, *The Republic*, 575a.
54. Adorno, *Negative Dialectics*, 236.
55. Ibid.
56. Cohen, 'Strategy or Identity', 670. Despite differences, Mouffe's account of collective actors seems vulnerable to Cohen's critique of traditional collective-behaviour theory for harbouring 'an implicit bias towards regarding collective behavior as a nonrational . . . response' to broader societal problems, a bias that 'precludes any examination of . . . learning on the part of collective actors' (672).
57. Snow, Rochford, Worden and Benford, 'Frame Alignment Processes, Micromobilization, and Movement Participation', 467.
58. Neither will they be formed through an interest-group logic of

political exchange. Cohen brings out well the different logics of interest-group actors and the emergent actors of social movements: 'The process of identity formation [of social movements] involves *nonnegotiable* demands. The model of political exchange [typical of interest-group actors] is thus . . . inadequate to the logic of collective action of new movements, because political exchange, like collective bargaining, requires negotiations between opponents. Strategic calculations on the part of adversaries in a political exchange revolve around the concession of benefits . . . Yet it is precisely the logic of exchange and negotiation that is *absent* in the case of NSMs [New Social Movements] involved in the creation of solidarity and identity' ('Strategy or Identity', 692).
59. Ibid. 694.
60. Tierney, 'The Battered Women Movement', 210.
61. Gagné, 'The Battered Women's Movement in the "Post-Feminist Era"', 15, 17, 70–1, 87. All subsequent page numbers in this paragraph refer to this text, unless otherwise indicated.
62. In the US in the early 1970s '"domestic violence" meant riots and terrorism' (Tierney, 'The Battered Women Movement', 213).
63. Taylor, 'Social Movement Continuity', 771.
64. I can only enter into a brief discussion of this (see n. 67 below). Part of my strategy here – and in Chapter 2 – is to focus on internal developments within deliberative theory and, in particular, attempts to rework Habermas's account in light of the kind of concerns that motivate Mouffe's critique. Mouffe's failure to engage with these internal debates means that even if her criticisms of Habermas prove to be right, her call to abandon the deliberative approach as such is premature.
65. Habermas, *Justification and Application*, 24.
66. Ibid.
67. See also Pierce, 'Justice without Solidarity?'; Carrabregu, 'Habermas on Solidarity'; Markell, 'Making Affect Safe for Democracy?'; Cooke, 'Habermas and Consensus'; McCarthy, *Ideals and Illusions*, 181–99.
68. On this issue of what degree of abstraction, see Cooke's distinction between taking a hypothetical stance on one's values and denying one's values ('Habermas and Consensus', 258–9).
69. Moore, 'Deliberative Elitism?'.
70. Cf. Cooke, 'Habermas and Consensus', 261–4.
71. For Habermas's response, see his 'Reply to Symposium Participants', 1487–503.

72. I am indebted to Matthias Fritsch's 'Antagonism and Democratic Citizenship (Schmitt, Mouffe, Derrida)'.
73. Schmitt, *The Concept of the Political*, 28.
74. Ibid.
75. See, *inter alia*, A, 4–5, 6, 9, 18, 19, 23, 26; DP, 13; OP, 15, 16, 19–21; RP, 2–5, 127–6.
76. The reference to deconstruction as the source for the notion of 'constitutive outside' appears across Mouffe's work: DP, 48, 135; OP, 15, 18; RP, 2, 69, 85, 114, 141, 152. However, see n. 79 below.
77. Mouffe, 'Introduction: Schmitt's Challenge', 5.
78. White, 'After Critique', 212.
79. The term is introduced in Staten, *Wittgenstein and Derrida*, 20.
80. For example, public *hostis*/private *inimicus* (87–8, 124, 136 n. 19, 144), *pólemos/stasis* (88–106, 119), external enemy/internal enemy (119–21).
81. I explore this in Chapter 4.
82. I discuss Derrida's notion of 'im-possibility' in Chapter 4. On the broader point made here, see Abizadeh, 'Does Collective Identity Presuppose an Other?'.
83. Mouffe, 'Decision, Deliberation, and Democratic Ethos', 26 (emphases mine).
84. All sorts of problems are generated by the manner in which one identifies such a 'they'. I take this up in the discussion of Derrida's notion of democratic auto-immunity in Chapters 5 and 6.
85. 'Johnson: I won't debate with BNP', *BBC Question Time*, 16 October 2009, <http://news.bbc.co.uk/1/hi/programmes/question_time/8309964.stm> (last accessed 31 January 2020).
86. *The Daily Telegraph*, 9 November 2009, <https://www.telegraph.co.uk/news/politics/labour/6527672/Alan-Johnson-Labour-has-helped-BNP-by-shying-away-from-immigration-debate.html> (last accessed 31 January 2020).
87. Habermas, 'Religious Tolerance', 6–8.
88. For a critical discussion of Habermas on toleration, see Thomassen, *Deconstructing Habermas*, chapter 3.
89. Note that, for Mouffe, acknowledging the necessity of exclusion is itself a recognition of antagonism (recall the passage from A, 18).
90. I am grateful to David McNeill for this point.
91. Abizadeh, 'Does Collective Identity Presuppose an Other?', 47.
92. Mouffe, 'Decision, Deliberation, and Democratic Ethos', 27.
93. Karagiannis and Wagner, 'Varieties of Agonism', 323.

94. Benhabib, 'Introduction: The Democratic Moment and the Problem of Difference', 9.
95. Blaug, 'New Theories of Discursive Democracy', 56, 74.
96. Tully, 'The Democratic Paradox by Chantal Mouffe', 864.
97. Brady, 'No Contest?', 333.
98. Wenman, *Agonistic Democracy*, 163.
99. See Chapter 2.
100. Chambers, *Reasonable Democracy*, 158–62.
101. For alternative agonistic approaches see, *inter alia*, Connolly, *Identity/Difference*; Connolly, *The Ethos of Pluralization*; Honig, *Political Theory and the Displacement of Politics*; Honig, 'The Politics of Agonism'; Honig, 'Difference, Dilemmas, and the Politics of Home'; Honig, 'Between Decision and Deliberation'; Tully, *Strange Multiplicity*; Tully, 'Dialogue'; White, *Sustaining Affirmation*.
102. Mouffe, 'Deliberative Democracy or Agonistic Pluralism?', 755.
103. Howarth, 'Ethos, Agonism and Populism', 189.
104. Kapoor, 'Deliberative Democracy or Agonistic Pluralism?', 473. Wingenbach seeks to remedy this on behalf of agonistic theory, but only because he recognises the danger: 'It seems far more likely that political contestation of the type described by agonistic democrats will, in the absence of strong institutional protections, lead to polarization and a hardening of divisions between groups . . . Agonism . . . in the absence of institutional securities, will in all probability generate undemocratic outcomes' (*Institutionalizing Agonistic Democracy*, 115).
105. Habermas, *Postmetaphysical Thinking*, 140.
106. See Dreyer Hansen and Sonnichsen, 'Radical Democracy, Agonism and the Limits of Pluralism'.
107. Tully, 'Dialogue', 158.
108. Ibid. Tully would appear to be closer to Derrida's thought here than Mouffe. Consider Derrida's response to Ernesto Laclau: 'there is, in the opening of a context of argumentation and discussion, a reference . . . to disarmament. I agree that such disarmament is never simply present . . . and therefore that a certain force and violence is irreducible, but nonetheless, this violence can only be practiced and can only appear as such on the basis of a non-violence . . . I do not believe in non-violence as a descriptive and determinable experience, but rather as an irreducible promise of the relation to the other as essentially non-instrumental. This is not the dream of a beatifically pacific relation, but of a certain experience of friendship . . . what I sometimes call an *aimance*, that excludes violence; a non-

appropriative relation to the other that occurs without violence and on the basis of which all violence detaches itself and is determined' (RDP, 83).
109. Honig, ' "[Un]Dazzled by the Ideal?" ', 139.

2
A More Expansive Conception of Deliberation

In the previous chapter I argued that while Mouffe raises some pressing questions for Habermas's deliberative theory, her critique fails to hit its mark in some important respects. Even if this were not the case, Mouffe overlooks debates between deliberative democrats and this leaves her call to abandon the deliberative approach premature. Mouffe's critique remains at the level of first-generation deliberative theory, ignoring the direct responses of second-generation deliberativists to the kind of concerns she and others have raised, and the more radical developments of fourth-generation deliberativists.[1] While contemporary deliberativists differ in terms of the model of deliberation they favour, what they do share is a concern over restrictive conceptions of public reason and the overly demanding idealisations of impartiality and rational consensus. This has led efforts to develop a more expansive conception of public deliberation and a more minimal account of democratic legitimacy. Critically assessing these developments within deliberative theory will show that the deliberative approach is far more sensitive to dissensus and difference than critics contend, and offers a more complex conception of deliberation.

In this chapter I focus on attempts by deliberativists to offer a more expansive conception of deliberation. Much of the motivation behind this effort is aimed at avoiding what I shall call the unjust exclusion charge (hereafter UEC). As I touched on at the end of the previous chapter, friends and critics alike worry that Habermas's account models deliberation on a restrictive account of rational argumentation that unjustly excludes certain voices from public deliberation. In the previous chapter I pointed to aspects of Habermas's account that suggest his overall account of democratic politics may not be as rationalistic or individualistic as Mouffe claims. I will not repeat those points here. My strategy in this chapter is to show that even if the rationalistic charge holds against Habermas, it does not hold against the deliberative approach as such. While I return to the rationalistic charge, I shall do so not to rehearse Habermasian responses to that charge, but to critically assess the more expansive conception of deliberation that deliberativists have sought to develop in response to the UEC.

After providing a brief sketch of the UEC, I consider two approaches that deliberativists have developed in response. The first, which I call the supplementing approach, seeks to address concerns about an overly rationalistic conception of deliberation by supplementing rational argumentation with 'other' forms of communication so as to accommodate difference. The second, which I call the systemic approach, replaces the categorical criteria of the supplementing approach with systemic criteria. This approach allows for a more expansive conception of deliberation, for it assesses political communication according to its effect on the deliberative system as whole. But this, I suggest, comes at the cost of sacrificing core deliberative ideals in specific instances, the likely result of which is the exclusion of those struggling to gain deliberative standing. Thus, while the systemic approach opens up deliberation more radically than the supplementing approach, it does not escape the UEC. Rather than resulting from overly restrictive ideals of rational argumentation, unjust exclusions result from allowing forms of speech that are judged to offer systemic benefits even where these are likely to exclude actors struggling in particular parts of the deliberative system. I suggest that a return to Aristotle's account of rhetoric and deliberation holds to the gains of each, whilst avoiding the problems of both.

I. The Unjust Exclusion Charge

The UEC emerges from a perceived problem with Habermas's initial account. To recall, while acknowledging cultural pluralism, and the fact that differently situated social actors may compromise and agree for different reasons, Habermas insists that 'the consensus brought about through argument must rest on *identical reasons* that are able to convince the parties in the same way' (BFN, 339). Orientated towards such a rational consensus, participants must 'look beyond what is good *for them* and examine what lies equally in the interest of all' (BFN, 102). This demand for an 'impartial evaluation of action conflicts' (BFN, 97) is seen as providing a procedural answer to the fact of pluralism. The strategy is to anchor the validity of any particular norm in the processes of a rational deliberation that would be open to all affected, where participants adopt an impartial perspective and put forward claims equally in the interest of all with the aim of reaching a rational consensus. In such a deliberative process 'only . . . the compelling force of the better argument' would move participants (BFN, 10). The reasons offered in such a process would thus be empowered with a consensus-producing force, enabling differently situated actors to arrive at collective decisions that would be seen by all as legitimate.

Critics, however, have argued that this approach models deliberation on a restrictive account of rational argumentation that leaves certain voices unjustly excluded from public deliberation. Although Habermas's deliberative theory sets out formal procedures that guarantee all those affected by a norm a place at the deliberative table, critics claim that privileging certain modes of speech denies certain participants an effective voice in deliberation. Included formally, they are excluded actually.[2] According to this critical position, deliberative approaches such as Habermas's fail to appreciate what James Tully calls '[d]ifferent practices of reasoning-with-others'. As they are grounded in culturally distinctive repertoires of practical skills, know-how and ways of relating to one another, Tully argues that 'culturally diverse practices of deliberation' are not something from which we can unproblematically abstract away. 'The exchange of public reason', writes Tully, 'cannot be separated from the cultural, linguistic, ethnic and gendered identities of those participating.'[3] Iris Young makes a related point when she argues that 'the norms of deliberation are culturally specific' and that by failing to acknowledge this deliberative theorists are in fact defending views that serve to unjustly silence alternative forms of speech.[4]

To find oneself excluded by the dominant model of deliberation is therefore to confront a choice. One can either refuse to play the game, in which case one is left excluded on the margins. Or one can conform to the dominant model, which would require that one 'gradually develops the form of identity and comportment characteristic of participants in this kind of practice'.[5] In the former case we have straightforward exclusion. In the latter case we have formal inclusion but actual exclusion, for actors are included but denied the voice to challenge the dominant model. If, as Habermas suggests, doing justice to the other requires processes of deliberation that ensure a '*nonleveling* and *nonappropriating* inclusion of the other in his otherness*' (IO, 40), then the UEC strikes at the very heart of that project. Because they perceive the UEC to be a genuine problem, deliberativists have attempted to develop a more expansive conception of deliberation. Without this more expansive account, the worry is that deliberative theory will be left vulnerable to the charge of leading to unjust exclusions, in the form of what Tully calls the 'unfreedom of assimilation' or what Young refers to as 'internal exclusion'.[6]

II. The Supplementing Approach

Recent attempts to 'rehabilitate rhetoric as a legitimate component of deliberation' have been made largely in response to the UEC.[7] By seeking a place for rhetoric within deliberation, deliberativists aim to provide an account of public deliberation that ensures, to recall Habermas, a non-levelling and non-appropriating inclusion of the other in her otherness. In concert with critics of traditional deliberative theories, Bohman rejects Habermas's 'overly rationalistic' approach to deliberation, which he claims 'unnecessarily narrows the range of convincing reasons in ways that are especially problematic for vibrant political deliberation in pluralistic societies' (PD, 44–5). Instead, Bohman sets out an account of public deliberation that includes 'the use of argument and rhetoric' and 'jarring speech acts', such as irony and jokes (PD, 7, 205). Bohman points to the important role such forms of communication can play in helping social actors break through 'community-wide biases' that prevent marginalised groups from introducing new themes for public deliberation and drawing attention to unrecognised needs

(PD, 205). Similarly, Gutmann and Thompson suggest that rhetoric can enable members of marginalised groups, whose interests are often systematically ignored, to place issues onto the deliberative agenda. Discussing Carol Moseley-Braun's impassioned performance on the floor of the US senate over the decision to renew the patent of the Confederate flag insignia, they describe how her 'oratory of impassioned tears and shouts' helped reach an otherwise deaf audience.[8] Likewise, Dryzek argues that 'rhetoric plays an important role in deliberating across difference' (DDB, 167), whether this be differences between differently situated social actors or between the public sphere and the state (DDB, 54).

The aim to rehabilitate rhetoric in deliberative theory is to be welcomed. The problem is that rhetoric is here conceived merely as a supplement to deliberation.[9] That is to say, rhetoric is what social actors resort to in particularly difficult situations; it is not a legitimate component of deliberation itself. As I will try to show, this supplementing approach operates with a restrictive conception of rhetoric and provides an inadequate answer to the UEC.

Dryzek: Supplementing rational argumentation

John Dryzek's supplementing approach emerges from his dissatisfaction with 'unnecessarily constraining' approaches to deliberation based on strong normative conditions of rational argumentation and idealising presuppositions of consensus (DDB, 1). Dryzek seeks to offer a more 'tolerant' approach to deliberation that would be 'more expansive in the kinds of communication it allows' (DDB, iv, 73). This would require opening up deliberation to a variety of forms of communication, including rhetoric, humour, greeting and testimony (DDB, 1). Dryzek is, however, quick to assure Habermasians that he is not opening the doors of deliberation and offering an unconditional 'let them in!' (DDB, 68). Dryzek's assurance that deliberation will still be 'answerable to reason' (DDB, 54) is meant to address 'Habermasian antipathy to deception, self-deception, manipulation, strategizing, and coercion' (DDB, 67). Dryzek's deliberative hospitality is thus conditional. Dryzek sets out 'the extent to which deliberation can and should admit alternative forms of communication', and how best to 'accommodate' them while still maintaining a critical vigilance regarding the dangers they pose (DDB, 67). On the one hand, Dryzek is keen to open up deliberation to styles of communication that are more inclusive. On the other hand, he wants to ensure that we do not welcome these 'additional' modes of communication uncritically, as he takes some critics of the deliberative approach to be doing.[10]

In opening up deliberation, Dryzek looks to rhetoric, testimony and greeting. While acknowledging the ways in which these forms of communication may function coercively, he stresses that they can have important roles to play in deliberation (DDB, 68–70).[11] Recognising both the limitations and the possibilities of various forms of political speech, the condition of entry for participants in deliberation is no longer conformity to an overly rationalistic conception of argumentation, but the weaker, and more inclusive, notion of engaging in non-coercive communication (DDB, 167).

Dryzek's attempt to move away from a conception of public deliberation restricted to 'arguments in particular kinds of terms' (DDB, 1), and to extend the notion of deliberation to include modes of communication such as rhetoric and testimony, is to be welcomed. However, conceiving of these as 'additional modes of communication' or 'supplements' presents a problem (DDB, 5). When Dryzek describes these 'other' modes of communication as 'supplements', what is being supplemented is rational argument, which 'always has to be central' to public deliberation (DDB, 71). The status of these supplements is, however, 'a bit different'. These 'other' forms of communication are conceived of as optional extras which 'can be present', but need not be (DDB, 71). This presents a picture of rational argumentation as being something separate from, and crucially untouched by, these 'other' modes of communication. The former remains the central core of deliberation, the latter mere peripheral appendages. This picture enables Dryzek to admit the 'additional' modes of communication emphasised by critics of deliberation, without having to give up any of those Habermasian antipathies. The danger that Dryzek wants to avoid is the one he thinks critics tend to succumb to, namely, taking these modes of communication as being alternatives to rational argument. While these 'other' forms of communication can be accommodated, they leave rational argumentation untouched.

Dryzek singles out Iris Young as one critic who does not make this mistake, and briefly looking at Dryzek's reading here will reveal the importance of this supplementing approach for his response to the UEC. Rather than banishing rational argument, Dryzek reads Young as wanting 'simply to supplement rational argument with other kinds of communication that better represent difference'. It is precisely this supplementing approach that keeps her account of democracy within a deliberative trajectory. As Dryzek continues: 'Thus she can present her own model of communicative democracy as a development of the deliberative model rather than a negation of it' (DDB, 78, n. 6). It is this supplementary approach, then, that enables one to admit 'other' modes of communication, and through this include difference, while preserving an uncontaminated sphere of rational argument, thereby maintaining the possibility of critically informed deliberation. Without this supplementing approach deliberative theory would be unjustly exclusive (in denying difference) or excessively open (in dropping criteria).

Dryzek misses an important aspect of Young's account and exploring this will bring out the difficulties the supplementing approach faces. While Young does not wish to abandon talk of rational argument, nor does she want 'simply to supplement rational argument', as Dryzek suggests. Young's approach cuts a little deeper than this. When Young tells us that she offers practices of greeting, rhetoric and narrative 'as enriching both a descriptive and normative account of public discussion and deliberation', 'enriching' is to be understood as a transforming addition, not an accommodating supplement.[12] As Young makes clear, she is not concerned with merely describing different styles of speech that occur in deliberation. There is a normative dimension here too. In our earlier discussion we noted that Young emphasises the cultural specificity of norms of deliberation and argues that if deliberation is to be inclusive, effectively and not merely procedurally, then it must be open to multiple forms of political communication. Greater inclusion means greater diversity in the voices heard in deliberation and this, for Young, ultimately means transforming deliberation itself. This transformation is seen not simply as a happy side effect of inclusion; it is a key reason for calling for greater inclusion in the first place. As she explains: 'one of the purposes of advocating inclusion is to allow transformation of the style *and terms* of public debate' (my emphasis). And the reason why this kind of transformation is important is because it 'opens the possibility for significant changes in outcomes'.[13]

By conceiving of this as wanting to 'simply supplement' rational argumentation, Dryzek's accommodating approach domesticates Young's project to that of transforming the style of deliberation. But as I have emphasised, it is not simply the style of deliberation that Young seeks to transform, but the very terms of deliberation. The latter, I suggest, implies transforming the processes of deliberative reasoning through which arguments are formed, rather than simply providing additional ways in which such arguments can be delivered. While Dryzek accommodates diverse forms of communication so that deliberative democracy can 'cope with issues of difference' (DDB, 71), for Young the point is not merely to 'cope' with difference, but to encourage difference, to open up public debate to different voices in order to bring about a transformation of deliberative practices. Difference is here approached not as a danger, but as a resource.[14]

Once we appreciate that transforming the style and terms of deliberation drives Young's project, we begin to see the problems this presents for an approach that attempts to 'cope with' difference by 'simply supplementing' rational argumentation with 'other' modes of communication. Dryzek's supplementing move seeks to preserve a realm of rational argumentation that is untouched by these 'alternative' modes of communication, hence the different status he assigns to each. Although not wishing to nail Dryzek to the choice of one word, I think the notion of 'coping' with difference is indicative of his broader defensive strategy: the need to include difference is acknowledged, but the approach is about managing its dangers, by 'accommodating' it in peripheral supplements (that we may opt for but need not), thereby ensuring that the dangers posed do not seep into the core structure of rational argumentation and bring the whole deliberative house down.[15] This leaves one with an approach that calls for the inclusion of 'additional' extras, but no transformation of the 'essential' features. From Young's perspective, this kind of move remains inadequate. The whole point of inclusion is to bring about a transformation of deliberation, rather than adding on various supplements.[16]

Thus, different pictures emerge. Dryzek's supplementing approach leaves one with a picture of deliberation in which rational argumentation remains separate from the supplements one may opt for. Young, however, offers a picture in which rhetoric 'constitutes the flesh and blood of *any* political communication'.[17] When Young maintains that one 'ought to attend' to rhetoric, this is not an *ad hoc* move to better represent difference through a change in style, but a requirement for any adequate account of deliberation as such.[18] While Dryzek accepts a positive role for rhetoric as an 'aid' to argument (as we shall see), his supplementing approach seems to hold to the idea that one can have a rhetoric-free zone of pure rational argument. Rhetoric is a supplement that may be present, but need not be. Insofar as this is the case, Dryzek's approach would seem vulnerable to Young's criticism of those 'theories of deliberative democracy [that] tend to bracket rhetoric, even when they do not explicitly denigrate rhetorical modes of discourse'.[19] The lesson that Young wants us to take away, however, is this: 'Because rhetoric is an aspect of all discourse, the temptation should be resisted to base a theory of deliberative democracy on a notion of non-rhetorical speech that is coolly and purely argumentative.'[20] I shall return to this claim.

That Dryzek avoids this temptation seems evident in both his criticism of deliberative theorists such as Habermas for (as he sees it) wanting to jettison rhetoric, and his insistence that 'rhetoric plays an important role in deliberating across difference' (DDB, 167).[21] Dryzek points to the role of rhetoric in deliberating across differences in two ways. Firstly, rhetoric can help with deliberation across the differences between social actors within the public sphere. Dryzek suggests that the success of Martin Luther King Jr's appeals – in reaching into the hearts of white Americans – 'was aided' by the 'accompanying rhetoric'. Secondly, rhetoric can aid deliberation across differences between the public sphere and the state. Dryzek argues that 'rhetoric plays an especially important function as a transmission mechanism' in trying to reach state actors who 'almost by definition' hold 'frames of reference initially very different from, and potentially unsympathetic to, discourse generated within the public sphere' (DDB, 52–4). These are important observations and constitute an advance on deliberative theories that see in rhetoric only a threat to deliberation. However, even here, at the moment when he points to its importance for deliberation, rhetoric for Dryzek is still conceived of as an 'aid' or 'transmission mechanism' that deliberators resort to in particularly difficult situations. Where frames of reference are very different, *then* we resort to rhetoric.

Another way of approaching this problem is to consider the scope of Dryzek's observations regarding those moments where rhetoric plays an 'especially important function' or is needed 'almost by definition'. While Dryzek's observations about deliberating across difference seem right, the scope he assigns to such situations does not. Rather than describing problematic situations that may occasionally occur within deliberation, these observations describe the deliberative situation as such (a point Bohman will emphasise). In the differentiated and pluralised lifeworlds of modern democratic societies, deliberating across different frames becomes increasingly common in public deliberation (a point that we saw McCarthy make in the last chapter). This is not simply a problematic situation *within* deliberation, but the problematic situation *of* deliberation. The need to deliberate emerges in response to a situation in which our frames diverge such that we cannot continue any longer. Understood in this way, the deliberative situation itself is 'problematic' in the way in which Dryzek describes particular situations that may or may not emerge within deliberation. If this is so, then the rhetoric that Dryzek sees as essential in these situations is extended to deliberation as such. In the words of Young, rhetoric 'constitutes the flesh and blood of any political communication'.

Although Dryzek's supplementing approach constitutes a significant advance in deliberative theory, the attempt to cope with issues of difference by conceiving of rational argumentation as a necessary, central core that remains untouched by optional, peripheral supplements does not adequately address the need to transform the very terms of public deliberation. An approach like Young's, however, does not make sense without this transformation, a transformation that presents a picture of deliberation where the kind of distinctions that hold Dryzek's picture together – argument/rhetoric, core/supplement, necessary/optional – cannot be drawn in the way that Dryzek's supplementing position requires.

Bohman: Pluralising public reason

James Bohman offers a more expansive conception of deliberation by arguing for a plural understanding of public reason. Bohman thinks his account of a pluralised public reason would require 'a much more minimal account of justification' than the Habermasian approach (PD, 75). Bohman rejects Habermasian regulative ideals of unanimity and impartiality, and argues that not only are these not necessary presuppositions of public deliberation, but by making them so 'Habermas unnecessarily narrows the range of convincing reasons in ways that are especially problematic for vibrant political deliberation in pluralistic societies' (PD, 45). In contrast, Bohman offers 'an elaboration of the ideal of public reason in political life that permits, rather than denies or avoids, moral conflict and difference in democratic politics' (PD, 84).

Noting that various forms of argumentation have emerged and gradually specialised into institutions to deal with recurring problems, Bohman maintains that these 'are not the proper model for deliberation' precisely because when it comes to 'ordinary deliberation' standardised norms of argumentation and routine practices are put into question (PD, 42). Here we see the problematic situation *of* deliberation that Dryzek seemed to miss. Public deliberation, for Bohman, emerges when there is a need 'to resolve atypical and non-standard problematic situations' and the difficulty this presents for deliberative theories that base their accounts on a particular conception of rational argumentation is that 'usually there is no well-established means for resolving these problems, or these means themselves are called into question' (PD, 42). While formal institutions require specialised discourses that demand specific types of reasons, the various problems that give rise to a deliberative situation mean that the use of public reason will require a variety of public reasons, 'including pragmatic goals, considerations of justice, and cultural understandings' (PD, 44). In short, public deliberation 'has no single domain' and therefore it 'must take many forms' (PD, 53). That is to say, deliberation must be opened up.

For Bohman, this process of opening up and transforming deliberation is unnecessarily constrained by the ideals of impartiality and rational consensus that Habermas holds to be necessary to

A MORE EXPANSIVE CONCEPTION OF DELIBERATION 73

deal with the problem of plurality. Recall that, for Habermas, 'the consensus brought about through argument must rest on *identical reasons* that are able to convince the parties in the same way' (BFN, 339). Abstracting away to an impartial perspective is seen as the way to achieve this. For Bohman, this picture of producing publicly convincing reasons would require making 'the assumption of singularity' (PD, 89). Democratic deliberation would involve the assumption of convergence towards a single point where all agree for the same reasons, and this would call for abstracting away to an impartial perspective. This is one of the problems that emerged from Mouffe's critique of Habermas. But it does not apply to the deliberative approach as such. Bohman rejects the impartiality requirement. While abstracting away to an impartial perspective may lead to convergence and agreement, Bohman maintains that this is not required for reason to be publicly convincing. 'Expressive communication can be publicly convincing', argues Bohman, 'without being impartial in the strict sense; my needs remain mine even if they are publicly convincing' (PD, 45). Publicity does not require impartiality.

What we are looking for in the deliberative situation, according to Bohman, is not unanimity, impartiality and rational consensus, but to convince those involved to continue to cooperate in trying to solve the problem. This, Bohman argues, does not require unanimous agreement on standards of rational justification. In the movement of dialogue, the kind of reasons that one finds convincing may change, and in cases of deep conflict 'standards of rationality are themselves subject to deeply conflicting interpretations' (PD, 73). In other words, public reason is essentially contestable (PD, 75). Continued cooperation in trying to resolve a problem requires that deliberators offer and take up reasons in conditions where all are exercising their deliberative capacities freely and where all are accountable to all for their contributions. Deliberative success would be seen in terms of the continued cooperation of those involved in the process of deliberation. Here we see a move to drop the idea of a single norm of public reason and, with it, the requirements of impartiality and orientation towards rational consensus. Instead, Bohman conceives of deliberation as a dialogue where no single norm of reasonableness is presupposed and this opens the way for agreements to be reached for different publicly accessible reasons (PD, 83). Engagement in democratic deliberation need not assume an ideal we-perspective, but instead requires recognising the deliberative freedom of others and opening one's own beliefs to the possibility of revision. Here public reason would not be 'beyond political contestation'. Indeed, public reason would remain open to transformation 'at its most basic levels of evidence, relevance, and inference' (PD, 86–7). Such transformation goes beyond matters of style and delivery.

Such contestation is crucial if one is to avoid the UEC. For Bohman, exclusion from deliberation can lead to a situation where sections of society become powerless to contest conditions they perceive to be unjust. Insofar as this is the case, we have failed to do justice to the other. This unjust exclusion consigns actors to what Bohman terms 'political poverty', which he introduces as follows:

> Just as economic agents must have the capacity to avoid acute hunger and malnourishment, so too public actors must have the ability to avoid being excluded from public life and to avoid having their concerns consistently ignored. (PD, 109–10)

Political poverty is indicated by any one of the following: (1) being unable to enter the public sphere; (2) being unable to make effective use of resources and capacities so that one cannot initiate public dialogue about a theme; (3) failing to have one's arguments receive deliberative uptake. Political poverty can be understood as the inability of social actors to reach this basic threshold. In concert with critics such as Young and Tully, Bohman is aware that relying on formal procedures to solve this issue fails to address the problem, for even with formal equality factors that can persistently disadvantage some from having an effective voice may still be in play. As Bohman observes:

> The opportunity to speak does not lend any convincing force or effectiveness to what one says. More often, ineffective and disadvantaged participants lack a public voice rather than procedural opportunities; that is, they lack a vocabulary in which to express their needs and perspectives publicly. (PD, 121)

Formal inclusion at the procedural level does not solve the problem of sedimented practices of deliberation or prevailing conceptions of rationality denying participants the vocabulary in which to articulate their needs and perspectives. Bohman's account highlights how, even in procedurally structured public exchanges, subtle forms of communicatively embedded inequalities can operate in all sorts of ways, whether through the imposition of particular forms of communication that favour a dominant section of society; forms of intimidation which may operate unintentionally (in claims to expertise based on accumulated cultural resources, for example, which only work on those predisposed to feel it); unnoticed norms of interruption; or the framing of problems in ways that ensure the success of powerful groups (PD, 114–20). Now, these forms of deliberative inequality need not be of the explicit Fox News variety, which are textbook examples of non-public forms of communication. In many cases, deliberative inequalities will be the effect of implicit inequalities embedded in social relationships that go unnoticed by those engaged in public deliberation. To modify Sanders: 'Prejudice and privilege do not [always] emerge as bad reasons, and they are not [always] countered by good arguments.' They will often be 'sneaky', but they may equally be invisible to those engaged in a deliberative process.[22] So, while politically impoverished actors may be included formally, they may remain excluded actually. Effectively denied the voice and resources to convert those formal opportunities into the ability to introduce new problems and to contest decisions, they remain vulnerable to the consequences of decisions they are unable to influence. The politically impoverished remain addressees to laws they have no influence over, further perpetuating the cycle of political poverty. Here there is a loss of democratic legitimacy.

For Bohman, then, a crucial task in doing justice to the other is to create processes of deliberation in which those without effective voice can gain such voice and, through this, cross the threshold of political poverty. Without an effective voice in deliberation, the other may be included, but not in their otherness. Here we confront the difficulty facing those who are excluded: the very thing that could help them cross the threshold of political poverty and push for inclusion is the very thing they lack, namely, deliberative uptake. Without this there is little chance of excluded groups entering the public sphere to contest current arrangements and thus little reason for such groups to recognise those arrangements as legitimate. Often what is needed is the capacity to change the current situation into a problematic situation – precisely what social facts of inequality and sedimented structures of deliberation often disable (PD, 200).

In exploring what is required to change the situation, Bohman looks to the speech of social critics and new social movements and how their 'use of argument and rhetoric' and 'jarring speech acts', such as irony and jokes (PD, 7, 205), can help 'unblock the capacity for perspective taking' (PD, 205). This capacity is a crucial element of deliberation as alternative perspectives and interpretations play a vital role in resolving the problematic situation that has stopped us in our tracks. But this is not restricted to one's style of delivery. 'A dynamic public sphere', writes Bohman, 'must be able to alter the framework of deliberation' (PD, 198). Here, then, we have a deliberative approach that appears more promising in meeting the UEC, as articulated by Young and others. Bohman's aim is not simply to supplement rational argumentation, but, like Young, to transform the very framework of deliberation.

While Bohman's account avoids some of the problems identified in Dryzek's account, he nevertheless appears to restrict these alternative forms of communication to particular moments of deliberative breakdown (PD, 200, 205). That is to say, they seem to be conceived by Bohman as tools in the deliberative box that help jumpstart stalled processes of public deliberation. While Bohman does not seek to circumscribe a pure realm of rational argumentation that would be untouched by optional supplements, he appears to repeat Dryzek's gesture of allowing alternative forms of communication to enter deliberation, but limiting their field of operation. That is to say, despite Bohman's promising insights, a supplementing move seems to be repeated. Describing the conditions that call for indirect or strategic forms of communication, Bohman writes:

> If the conditions of public discourse about a topic make it difficult for all speakers to achieve similar uptake (as when deliberative dialogue is disturbed by social inequalities and power

asymmetries), it is often the case that speakers must *resort to* indirect or strategic forms of communication to get any sort of uptake. (PD, 205, my emphasis)

As a description of what is often required in real-world processes of deliberation, this seems right. The question is whether such forms of communication are to be restricted to such situations. It would appear so. Bohman repeatedly describes these forms of communication as something speakers 'resort to' when 'deliberation fails' or is 'blocked' (PD, 199, 201, 203, 206). It is during these moments, where actors are 'deceived by their own ideologies and other self-deceptions' or where there are 'community-wide biases', that one has 'recourse to *other* means of achieving understanding' (PD, 205, 229). And similarly, when he refers to the deliberative possibilities of rhetoric, Bohman describes rhetoric as 'necessary' in 'extraordinary periods' of democratic renewal, where there is a need 'to overcome the impasses of public deliberation at critical junctures when the public finds community-wide biases and restriction in communication keeping its input out of normal institutional channels' (PD, 231). If recourse to these 'other' forms of communication is prompted by breakdowns or impasses in deliberation, the aim of such communication appears to be that of '*restoring* the conditions of direct communication' and '*restarting* stalled processes of ... deliberation' (PD, 205, 206, my emphasis).

Like Dryzek, then, Bohman's account appears to present these forms of communication as 'other' means of achieving understanding that we deploy in particularly difficult situations. That is to say, they function as supplements that speakers 'resort to' to help us get back on the deliberative track. The implication seems to be that, where successful, such forms of communication would not (or need not) feature in 'normal [democratic] politics' (PD, 230).[23]

Aristotle on rhetoric

As a response to the UEC, the supplementing approach fails. And it fails because the rehabilitation of rhetoric that is key to this approach results in a 'restricted rhetoric', understood merely as a matter of style.[24] That is to say, rhetoric is conceived as the outer garments of captivating speech that speakers resort to when trying to reach an audience insensible to rational argumentation. The restrictive aspect of this conception of rhetoric can be shown by contrast with a more expansive conception. In Aristotle's view, notably, a central element of rhetoric is *logos*, understood as seeing what is persuasive in each case and showing (*deixis*), through arguments (*enthumema*), the persuasive grounds for opinion (R, 1354a14–29, 1354b2–22, 1355a3–18).[25] To conceive of rhetoric merely as a supplement to rational argumentation is to make the very same mistake that Aristotle charged his own predecessors of having made, namely, of focusing on 'accessories' (*prosthekai*) to rhetorical persuasion rather than the 'body' of such persuasion (R, 1354a15–16). For his part, Cicero rejects such an approach in still more colourful terms: as an 'unprofitable and reprehensible severance between the tongue and brain'.[26]

If deliberativists wish to rehabilitate rhetoric to avoid the UEC, then rhetoric needs to be reconceived. In place of the supplementing approach to rhetoric, I shall argue for a constitutive understanding of rhetoric. By 'constitutive' I mean, firstly, that *ethos*, *pathos* and *logos* are constitutive elements of rhetoric and, secondly, that rhetoric, so understood, constitutes political judgement. To make the case for this constitutive account, I will turn briefly to Aristotle.

In designating rhetoric as a 'counterpart [*antistrophe*] of dialectic', Aristotle sets out an account of rhetoric that directly challenges the restricted conception of the supplementing approach (R, 1354a).[27] Dialectic is the capacity to examine arguments and, through strict and rigorous reasoning, to show the way from opinions towards the starting points of knowledge. As a counterpart, rhetoric is the capacity to see what is persuasive in each case and, through enthymemes and examples, to show the persuasive grounds for opinion. Rather than being mere accessories that orators drape around the body of reason, rhetoric is persuasive speech whose body consists of 'providing arguments' (R, 1356a34). But there is a difference with dialectic, hence the term '*antistrophe*'. Unlike dialectic, which reasons about that which admits of certain knowledge, rhetoric is located within a deliberative situation, where 'things admit of going different ways' (R, 1356a8–9, 1357a5–6). To use a Socratic image: while the movement of dialectic is an ascent out of the cave of opinion into the sunlight of knowledge, rhetoric is a descent into the cave of a particular community, where citizens struggle, in the flickering 'firelight of opinion', with questions about the just, the advantageous and the beautiful for their political community.[28] Although rhetoric is a theoretical activity of seeing and showing the persuasive grounds for opinion in the matter at hand, it is neither detached nor separable from our emotional orientation to the world of our concern. And knowing how the emotions, commitments and evaluations of her fellow citizens can affect judgement is something a speaker cannot ignore if she is to see and show her listeners persuasive grounds for opinion in each case.[29] It is for this reason that Aristotle describes rhetoric as an 'outgrowth' (*paraphues*) of dialectic into politics (R, 1356a27–9, 1359b11).

Understood as such an outgrowth, the way the art of rhetoric engages the emotions is no mere last resort because of an irrational audience. Rather, the emotions play a constitutive role in judgement because of the complexity and indeterminacy of the deliberative situation, in which arguments are presented by a particular speaker to a particular audience on some matter of concern which admits of going different ways. That is to say, the deliberative situation is one in which we are called upon to exercise judgement on issues that matter to us, in light of arguments that appear convincing to us. 'Rhetoric', Aristotle observes, 'is for the sake of judgement' (R, 1377b21). And given that the 'emotions are those things through which, by undergoing change, people come to differ in their judgements', they are a constitutive element of the deliberative situation, rather than a mere accessory.[30] The judgement we eventually arrive at in a particular situation will depend on how we perceive that situation and experiencing the appropriate emotions is crucial if it is to be properly perceived as a situation that matters to us.[31]

The complexity and indeterminacy of the deliberative situation is also the reason why *ethos* is a constitutive element of public deliberation:

> But since rhetoric is for the sake of judgement . . . it is *necessary* not only to look to the argument . . . but also to present oneself as a certain sort of person . . . for it makes a big difference as far

as persuasion is concerned, in deliberations especially, . . . what sort of person the speaker appears to be . . . (R, 1377b21–9, my emphasis)

Just as the emotions of the audience affect how things appear to them, and thus the judgements they make concerning the arguments presented to them, so too will the character of the speaker, *qua* speaker, affect the way a speaker's arguments appear to them. In Aristotle's account, the speaker being trustworthy is crucial. In pointing to judgement and virtue as two elements 'on account of which we feel trust' (the third is goodwill), Aristotle's account of *ethos* has, accordingly, an epistemic and an ethical dimension. Two of the ways in which trust can be lost make this clear: 'they [speakers] either have incorrect opinions on account of lack of judgment, or while they have correct opinions they do not say what seems true to them on account of vice' (R, 1356a5–9, 1378a6–17).[32] If the audience judges the speaker to have failed in either dimension, the speaker's arguments will fail to have probative force.

It is salutary to note, however, that the centrality of *ethos* to public deliberation does not leave us lost in the cult of personality. Recall that *logos* is the body of persuasion and that persuasion through *ethos* (as well as *pathos*) is legitimate only where it is made through argument. Aristotle insists that persuasion through character 'ought to come about through the argument, not because the speaker has a prior reputation for being a certain sort of person' (R, 1356a9–11).[33] Persuasion through *ethos* is to be achieved not by listing one's past triumphs, but by exhibiting one's character through argument.

While Habermasians are right to emphasise the force of the better argument, I submit that the real significance of the rhetorical turn in deliberative theory is that '[t]he force of an argumentation is always relative [to the specific audience]'.[34] And given this, the rhetorician cannot afford to ignore *pathos* or *ethos* if her arguments, as presented in a deliberative situation, are to be persuasive to her audience. As Abizadeh puts it: 'the art of rhetoric requires that *ethos*, *pathos*, and *logos* operate every time.'[35] That is to say, rhetoric is no optional supplement.

By presenting rhetoric merely as a supplement to rational argument, and by setting up the latter as a normative standard that remains untouched by the former, deliberativists assume the very framework that generates the problems associated with the UEC in the first place. If we accept Young's point that rhetoric is an aspect of all discourse, we are still left with a problem that the supplementing approach rightly identifies and aims to address – the problem of manipulation. This is why Dryzek seeks to reassure the Habermasians that deliberation would still be 'answerable to reason' (DDB, 54, 67). But herein lies the tension that the supplementing approach fails adequately to resolve: how to develop a deliberative theory that recognises rhetoric as a legitimate aspect of deliberation, but without giving up those Habermasian antipathies. By accommodating rhetoric as a mere supplement to deliberation, however, deliberativists fail to admit rhetoric as a legitimate component of deliberation. This failure leaves the supplementing approach with a restrictive conception of rhetoric and an inadequate answer to the UEC.

III. The Systemic Approach

One of the attractions of the systemic approach is that it significantly weakens the normative criteria for the kinds of political speech that can be included in public deliberation. Rather than evaluating political speech according to categorical criteria based on a rationalistic conception of deliberation, the systemic approach evaluates political speech according to its overall effect on the deliberative system. As the authors of the key text of this approach put it:

> A systemic approach . . . allows us to conclude that a single part, which in itself may have low or even negative deliberative quality on one of the several deliberative ideals, may nevertheless make an important contribution to the overall deliberative system.[36]

This 'functional division of labour' within the system expands significantly the kinds of communication that could count as legitimate components of public deliberation.[37] Forms of communication we would reject as violating deliberative ideals in specific instances would count as legitimate where they benefit the system as a whole. Thus, even 'highly partisan rhetoric' that violates principles of mutual respect and accountability is deemed legitimate where it has net systemic benefits.[38] Accordingly, the task is to assess the function of political speech at the level of the system. If the UEC calls for a more expansive notion of deliberation that remains normatively guided, the systemic approach appears to provide the answer.[39]

I shall focus on the approach Dryzek develops in his later work, since he specifically addresses the role of rhetoric from a systemic perspective. In contrast to his earlier advocacy of the supplementing approach, Dryzek now drops the Habermasian insistence that 'rhetoric stops at reason's door' and argues instead that rhetoric should answer to the deliberative system as a whole.[40] When judging the proper place of rhetoric in deliberation, we should apply 'systemic tests' that track the consequences any particular use of rhetoric has for the deliberative system. As Dryzek puts it: 'The key test is, does the rhetoric in question help constitute an effective deliberative system?'[41] From this, Dryzek draws radical conclusions. While Rawls and Habermas 'are reluctant to allow that its [rhetoric's] non-*logos* aspects can ever substitute for reason', Dryzek argues that 'the systemic view developed here shows that such a substitution can sometimes be fruitful'.[42] Dryzek previously rejected the latter as effectively abandoning the deliberative approach. But once we shift to systemic tests, Dryzek suggests that *ethos* or *pathos* may legitimately replace *logos*.[43]

This systemic approach is certainly a move beyond the supplementing approach. However, it evidently comes with significant costs. 'Categorically ugly rhetoric', Dryzek argues, is welcomed if it 'produces good systemic results'.[44] Discussing the extreme rhetoric of Australian politician Pauline Hanson, Dryzek writes:

> She had little in the way of commitment to any categorical deliberative norms, and was not averse to racial stereotyping. Yet the net result of her activities was a more deliberate polity, at least in the sense that a number of discourses that were either taken for granted or had yet to crystallize or had been marginalized took shape in a way that *could* have allowed for their engagement in the public sphere.[45]

This is a puzzling place for a *deliberative* democrat to be in.[46] Recall that the UEC is directed at deliberative theory's model of rational argumentation, which, critics argue, leads to the unjust exclusion of certain voices from deliberation and, in so doing, violates deliberative ideals of equality, mutual respect and democratic legitimacy. While the supplementing approach failed to open the door wide enough, the systemic approach seems to remove the door from its hinges. By focusing on net benefits, the systemic approach accepts speech that may cause, or entrench, pockets of political poverty. Where this is the case, such approach fails to do justice to the other. While Hanson's rhetoric is admitted for its (perceived) net contribution to the deliberative system, one wonders what those targeted by Hanson's rhetoric would make of this.

Consider the concerns one may have regarding the rhetoric deployed by Nigel Farage, the former leader of the UK Independence Party.[47] Even if this rhetoric – about British people feeling uneasy hearing foreign accents on public transport or having Romanians move next door – gives voice to a 'previously marginalised discourse' and stimulates a 'counter-mobilisation',[48] it is very plausible that the price of any purported systemic benefits will appear too high to those on its receiving end. It is not clear why news that the deliberative system as a whole benefits from such rhetoric ought to persuade those directly suffering the effects of that rhetoric not to return their democratic ticket. One of the likely local effects of such rhetoric is to perpetuate political poverty.

Imogen Tyler convincingly shows how extreme rhetoric directed at Travellers and Gypsies by elements of the British media and politicians created conditions that led not only to specific instances of political poverty, but to psychological suffering, physical intimidation and violence. Tyler notes how the culminating event of this extreme rhetoric – the mass eviction of Travellers and Gypsies from Dale Farm in Essex in 2011 – produced counter-mobilisations that have created solidarity between Traveller and Gypsy groups and activists across the political system and, with that, the promise of resistance to exclusions in the future.[49] Even if one accepts that resulting counter-mobilisations guarantee a future net reduction in political poverty across the system as a whole, it is not obvious why those now suffering in particular pockets of the system ought to accept their suffering as a justifiable cost. As Owen and Smith succinctly put it: there is 'a real danger of treating certain subjects as means to "deliberative" ends'.[50] The singularity of the other seems to get lost in the system's functional division of labour.

The systemic approach, then, admits discourses that, in specific parts of the system, contribute to instances of political poverty. At the very least, this result is in *prima facie* tension with the ideals that, as deliberativists of various stripes agree, are constitutive of deliberative democracy.[51] One might try to ease this tension by appealing to categorical criteria when judging certain forms of rhetoric. But such tests would most likely exclude the kind of communication that can help actors escape political poverty. Indeed, avoiding categorical exclusions is a key motivation of the systemic approach in the first place. Consider the case of Frederick Douglass's speeches aimed at promoting the abolitionist cause. Douglass rejected demands to 'argue more and denounce less' and instead insisted on 'scorching irony' and a 'fiery stream of biting ridicule', for 'it is not light that is needed, but fire'.[52] While the fire of Douglass's rhetoric would be welcomed from a systemic perspective, it would be condemned on categorical grounds. The systemic approach is right to reject categorical tests if deliberative theory is to avoid the UEC. By opening up deliberation to all kinds of political speech, the systemic approach avoids the kind of unjust exclusions generated by the supplementing approach. But it does so by throwing the deliberative baby out with the categorical bathwater. And in doing so, it remains vulnerable to a variant of the UEC: voices are excluded by accepting forms of speech that are likely to produce or entrench pockets of political poverty within the system.

Let me summarise the discussion so far. The supplementing approach fails as a response to the UEC insofar as it casts 'alternative' modes of communication as mere supplements, suitable only for situations of deliberative breakdown. The systemic approach, in contrast, attempts to eliminate unjust exclusions by replacing categorical with systemic criteria. But this move sacrifices core deliberative ideals, not least the ideal of equality of deliberative standing. The systemic approach, as it stands, does not escape unjust exclusions. Rather than resulting from overly restrictive ideals of rational argumentation, unjust exclusions now result from forms of speech that are judged to offer systemic benefits, even where these are likely to exclude actors struggling in particular parts of the system. Unjust exclusion in the form of political poverty is a cost that deliberativists ought to be unwilling to accept.

IV. The Manipulation Problem

Above, I touched on Aristotle's account of rhetoric in response to the restricted conception of rhetoric deployed by defenders of the supplementing approach. A key claim there was that *ethos*, *pathos* and *logos* are constitutive elements of rhetoric, and, so conceived, rhetoric is constitutive of deliberative argumentation and judgement, rather than a mere supplement. This offers a more promising response to the UEC. Firstly, the Aristotelian account admits rhetoric into public deliberation in a way that provides the more expansive conception of deliberation that deliberativists seek. Secondly, it avoids presupposing the very framework that gives rise to the UEC charge in the first place. But there's a problem. If rhetoric is constitutive of public deliberation, then how are we to avoid the dangerous kind of rhetoric that merely manipulates the audience? Once *ethos* and *pathos* are admitted as intrinsic elements of public deliberation, rather than optional supplements, then do we not leave ourselves open to precisely what the supplementing approach sought to prevent – the threat of manipulation? When Dryzek moves from a supplementing approach to a systemic approach, for example, he allows for non-*logos* aspects of rhetoric to 'substitute for reason'. While I have argued that *logos* cannot be jettisoned on the constitutive approach, one might still be worried about how such an account responds when a Gorgias knocks the door. In other words, wouldn't the Aristotelian approach leave us facing similar problems to the systemic approach?

While Gorgias's image of rhetoric as a 'force of incantation', which 'by entering into the opinion of the soul' is 'wont to beguile . . . and alter it by witchcraft', may not strike us with quite the force that it once did,[53] Kant's description of rhetoric as 'an insidious art' that moves men 'like machines to a judgment' and thus 'robs their verdict of its freedom' is still very much with us.[54] The question, then, is whether the constitutive approach provides a principled distinction between manipulative and non-manipulative practices.[55] If it does, then this would answer the kind of worries that motivate the supplementing approach. It would also justify the more expansive approach advocated by defenders of the systemic approach, whilst avoiding some of the unwelcome consequences that result.

A key argument of Aristotle's is that rhetoric is an art (*techne*). While this is a seemingly dry, academic point, what is at issue here is the 'politics of demagoguery'.[56] If rhetoric is not an art, then it does not have technical standards internal to that practice to guide it. In the absence of such standards, the speaker is free to deploy whatever strategy to help her achieve her goal of winning her audience over. Imagine someone who wins a game of pool by randomly hitting the balls and distracting her opponent when the latter is taking a shot. While this player achieved the goal of winning the game, we would hardly describe her as having engaged in the art of pool. However, we may describe her opponent in these terms, despite her having lost. And we would do so by judging how well the opponent played the game in reference to standards internal to the art of pool (for example, she showed skill in reading the table, displayed good judgement in shot selection, demonstrated sound positional awareness). If rhetoric is a *techne*, then the rhetorician, like any practitioner of an art, will be guided by standards internal to the art, rather than external standards. This does not mean that the goal of persuading the audience drops out of the picture for the rhetorician, any more than the goal of winning the game drops out for the pool player. As Garver notes, 'Unless achieving the external end were desirable, no one would even develop an art.'[57] Rather, the point is that the rhetorician will be guided by, and judged in reference to, standards internal to that art.

Garver helpfully distinguishes between a 'guiding end' (which is 'constitutive' of an art) and a 'given end' (which is 'external' to an art):

> Every art . . . has two ends. Activities for which there is no corresponding art have only one end, achieving the external, given good . . . Some activities, those with only an external end, are . . . complete only when they are over and successful.

Other activities, those with guiding ends, aim at a good outside themselves but also answer to internal standards of completion and perfection.[58]

When Aristotle counter-intuitively insists that rhetoric's 'work [*ergon*] is not to persuade but to see the means of persuasion that are available on each matter' (R, 1355b10–11), he is shifting the normative standards of the practice from the external, non-technical goal of winning, to the internal, technical standard of seeing the available means of persuasion. With this shift, rhetorical success is no longer evaluated by reference to the external, given end of winning, but by the internal, guiding end of discovering the best available means of persuasion in the particular situation. It is this normative distinction that provides the ground for Aristotle's attack on his predecessors.

It is because they looked solely to the external, given end of winning that Aristotle charges his predecessors with focusing on practices that are 'not even . . . part of the art' (R, 1354a13). When his predecessors outline ways to causally move an audience through appeals to the passions, Aristotle argues that they

> busy themselves with things that are extraneous to the matter at hand; for prejudice and the passions of the soul such as pity and anger are not concerned with the matter at hand . . . one ought not to lead the juror astray by provoking . . . anger or envy or pity, since that would be as if someone made the very thing crooked that he was about to use as a ruler. (R, 1354a14–27)

Two points are needed here. Firstly, this may seem to contradict the claim that the emotions are essential to rhetoric. But it does not.[59] Aristotle's predecessors go wrong not by appealing to emotions, but by focusing on the atechnical practice of simply manipulating emotions to causally bring about their desired decision. Recall that to engage in the *art* of rhetoric, a speaker will be directed by the guiding end of seeing the available means of persuasion in the matter at hand. And, as we have seen, on the constitutive approach, those means are the 'technical proofs' of *ethos*, *pathos* and *logos* (R, 1355b35), which conjointly operate every time. In addition, these proofs must be demonstrated 'through the argument' (R, 1356a9–11). Aiming straight for the external end of getting one's desired decision, and attempting to achieve this through such manipulative strategies, circumvents both requirements and therefore fails as an exercise in rhetorical expertise.

Secondly, as well as being guided by the internal end of *seeing* the available means of persuasion, the rhetorician needs to *show* her audience those means. The reason for this is, as noted above, that 'rhetoric is for the sake of judgement' (R, 1377b2). The rhetorician must show her audience the available means of persuasion to help them arrive at a judgement. This is not just any judgement, but a well-grounded judgement.[60] Above, I described the 'means of persuasion' as 'proofs'. The term Aristotle uses here, *pisteis*, is often translated in both ways. But while the singular, *pistis*, is related to *peitho* (to persuade), it is a distinct concept (it can mean 'trust', 'credence', 'credit').[61] When Aristotle charges his predecessors with failing to say anything about the art of rhetoric, he explains: 'for the means of persuasion [*pisteis*] alone are intrinsic to the art' (R, 1354a14). If rhetoric is for the sake of judgement, and if the rhetorician's role is to see and show her audience *pisteis* relevant to the particular matter, then the task of the rhetorician is nothing more, but nothing less, than providing her audience with 'proofs' that serve as credible grounds for judgement. As Aristotle insists, 'there is nothing appropriate . . . to do outside of showing' (R, 1354a27–8).

In taking these *pisteis* as credible grounds for judgement, the audience must understand themselves to be doing just that. As Garver notes, 'proof depends on the hearer recognizing what a speaker is doing. I cannot prove something to you unless you realize that that is what I am doing.' And to be a process of persuasion it

> has to be intentional and require this mutual awareness, because belief . . . is similarly intentional. *Pistis* is best rendered here as trust: You can arouse my indignation without my knowing that this is what you are doing, but I cannot trust you without being aware that I am trusting you. Making the audience do the speaker's bidding because he has made them indignant is in this sense *not* persuasion.[62]

Persuasion, then, presupposes what Garsten calls the 'active independence' of the audience. Despite the passive voice, Garsten observes that when 'someone . . . decides, "All right, you have persuaded me," he is not merely describing something that has happened to him . . . he is describing something he has done'.[63] If mutual awareness and active independence are essential aspects of showing an audience the relevant proofs to ground judgement, then causally moving an audience by manipulating their emotions would not be an exercise of rhetorical expertise. Such a practice not only fails to show any credible grounds, but it depends on concealing one's intentions and, through this, destroying mutual awareness and undermining the active independence of the audience, both of which are crucial for seeing and showing an audience credible grounds for the sake of good judgement. Adopting the predecessors' approach would be to warp and coerce the audience for the sake of winning.

On the constitutive approach, then, the kinds of manipulative tactics that worry advocates of the supplementing approach remain outside the art of rhetoric. In addition, such an approach would prohibit dangerous forms of rhetoric that would be admitted by defenders of the systemic approach. One might object that the constitutive approach does not provide a principle that would clearly demarcate manipulation from non-manipulation. Moreover, Aristotle's *Rhetoric* seems an unlikely place to find such a principle. While providing resources for the constitutive approach, the *Rhetoric* seems also to provide resources for less reputable practices. I will briefly address each, taking the latter point first.

Numerous attempts have been made to address the manipulation problem in the *Rhetoric*. Some commentators deploy a version of the ideal/normal rhetoric distinction and argue that Aristotle, in the name of political efficacy, adopts a pragmatic attitude when it comes to less-than-ideal conditions. Others identify epistemic and/or moral principles that serve as constraints.[64] None of these responses are entirely satisfactory. Indeed, when Aristotle considers the manipulation problem, he seems to concede the point:

> As for the claim that someone using such a power with speeches might do great harm, this applies in common to all good things,

except virtue, and most of all to the most useful things, like strength, health, riches, and skill at leading armies; for one might confer the greatest benefits by using these justly and do the greatest harm using them unjustly. (R, 1355b3–8)

Although rhetoric, as a *techne*, has guiding ends with their own internal standards of evaluation, these standards do not provide a principle to solve the manipulation problem. And the reason for this is because 'sophistry is present not in the power but in the intention' (R, 1355b17–18). And if there is no neutral principle that we can apply to track intentions, then the search for a principle to solve the manipulation problem is doomed:

> If the difference is not one of art but motive, then there are no aspects of the art that cannot be used sophistically for external purposes. There is no distinction between rhetoric and sophistic, only between the rhetorician and the sophist. Everything the rhetorician does artfully, the sophist can also use for ulterior motives.[65]

This does not mean giving up on the manipulation problem; it means giving up on the search for principles. The constitutive approach provides an account of non-manipulative rhetoric and the normative standards internal to the art. But, empirically distinguishing a rhetorician from a sophist will be a matter of judgement. While there will be paradigm cases of manipulation, we will mostly face difficult cases. Such cases will not be decided by the disengaged theorising of the deliberative theorist; they will be first-order questions for deliberators.

While the internal standards of the art of rhetoric could help identify some forms of manipulation, difficult cases will require *ethos*-based judgements. As Garver suggests above, the judgement we need to make is not between rhetoric and sophistic, but 'between the rhetorician and the sophist'. Recall, *ethos*-based judgements concern *ethos qua* speaker, rather than direct appeals to character. When the former White House Communications Director Anthony Scaramucci was asked about 'credibility' and whether he would 'give accurate information and truth', his response – 'I feel like I don't even need to answer that question . . . that's the kind of person I am' – was a direct appeal to *ethos*, rather than a display of *ethos qua* speaker.[66] But how would one arrive at an *ethos*-based judgement, *qua* speaker? Garver provides a helpful suggestion:

> The principal thing I would have to point to would be . . . the *logos* of the speech. It is the primary evidence for the speech's *ēthos*. Turning attention to *ēthos* would . . . change the focus slightly. The speaker's *ēthos* would . . . answer such questions as: Why choose this decision and argument and not another? Why this example? Why these probabilities and signs and why weight them as you did?[67]

The manipulation problem, then, requires *ethos*-based judgements that look to a speaker's character as revealed through their 'pattern of deliberation and choice'.[68] While such judgements do not provide a principle to solve the manipulation problem, they do offer a way of approaching that problem.

One might object that this still leaves the door open to manipulative speakers. That is true. But principles will not bar that door. Whether or not the sophist is able to trick her way in will depend largely on the audience's capacity for judgement and, specifically, 'understanding' (*sunesis*).[69] The deliberative situation requires not only artful speakers, but an educated audience. Reeve provides helpful suggestions about the latter. In *On the Parts of Animals*, Aristotle states that 'it is the mark of an educated man to be able to judge successfully what is properly expounded and what is not'. In the *Eudemian Ethics*, Aristotle suggests that 'a lack of education' will reveal itself in an 'inability to judge which reasonings are appropriate to the subject and which foreign to it'.[70] The capacity to judge when something is properly expounded and when reasoning is or is not appropriate to the subject is precisely the kind of skill an audience needs to exercise in a deliberative situation. Addressing the manipulation problem, then, requires looking to both speakers *and* audience. The advice Aristotle offers to speakers is useful for us, the audience, too: we need to know how one might be persuasive about opposite things 'so that the way things are might not go unnoticed, and in order that, if someone else uses arguments unjustly, we ourselves will have the means to refute them' (R, 1354a32–5). We need not assume Aristotle's so-called 'epistemological optimism' for this;[71] we need only assume that we can develop and exercise such capacities. While the so-called dark arts that Aristotle describes in the *Rhetoric* generate the contradiction problem, these sections of the text may help us, a modern-day audience, mitigate the manipulation problem.

Deliberative standing

While the constitutive account of rhetoric avoids unjust exclusions that result from invoking categorical criteria, and while it avoids sacrificing core deliberative ideals for systemic gains, it is not clear how this approach deals with the suffering of those who are targets of certain forms of extreme political speech. One can imagine speakers meeting the internal standards of the art of rhetoric and still deploying political speech that impoverishes certain groups. Such speech is likely to produce the kind of suffering that I criticised the systemic approach for accepting. We therefore need to develop a response that also addresses the suffering of those who are struggling against political poverty. Again, Aristotle can help us here.

A crucial aspect of the art of rhetoric is knowledge of the soul of one's political community. But as Aristotle suggests, that, in turn, requires knowledge of one's political regime and, specifically, the end sought by that regime, as this will shape the character of one's fellow citizens (R, 1366a14–16). Now, Aristotle notes that 'the end sought by democracy is freedom' and its guiding principle is equality (R, 1366a4). What characterises the citizen in a democracy is 'participation in judgement and authority', whether deliberative or juridical, for without such participation democratic freedom and equality cannot be realised.[72] Excluded from participation, one would be like 'some interloper of no standing [*timē*]'.[73] To be excluded from such participation, then, is to be denied the kind of standing required to be seen, and to see oneself, as a fellow citizen. If participation in judgement and authority is essential to what it is to be a democratic citizen, then exercising that function well means that 'a good [democratic] citizen must have the knowledge and capacity both to rule and be ruled'.[74] But that can only be gained through active participation in deliberative processes. As Owen and Smith note, deliberation is 'a practice which must itself be practiced'.[75]

Being excluded from such active participation, then, not only denies one the status crucial to one's standing as a democratic citizen, but it also denies one the opportunity to develop the knowledge and capacities through which one can gain such standing. As Rostbøll suggests (when setting out his own account of deliberative freedom):

> [I]s it not rather the case that democracy *gives* citizens such capability and such a standing? Discursive capability . . . and status are attributes that can only develop in the presence of others . . . It is by living in a democracy — in particular, a democracy that promotes public deliberation — that we become citizens whose opinions matter . . . It is as participants in deliberative politics that we have discursive status . . .[76]

What Aristotle identifies, then, is what deliberativists call equal deliberative standing. Furthermore, Aristotle emphasises, along with deliberativists, the importance of certain insights and capacities, developed through participation in deliberation, for gaining such standing.[77] If the end sought by democracy is freedom, and if its guiding principle is equality, then fundamental to freedom in a deliberative democracy is participating in public discourse such that I gain equal deliberative standing and, thus, deliberative uptake. And this is a virtuous democratic circle: the more I participate in public deliberation, the more I develop the insights and capacities necessary to contribute to the forms of collective judgement and self-legislation constitutive of a deliberative democracy. And the more I develop those capacities and insights, the more likely it is that I will receive deliberative uptake and thus enhance my standing as a democratic citizen.[78] In participating in public deliberation, I enjoy 'deliberative freedom' (to recall Rostbøll). Where I am excluded from public deliberation, I fall into 'political poverty' (PD, 131).

To promote equal deliberative standing is to seek to protect citizens' deliberative freedom by ensuring that no citizen falls into political poverty. If a political speech either undermines the deliberative standing of citizens vulnerable to the threat of political poverty or further entrenches citizens in such poverty, then deliberativists ought to disavow such speech, as it denies citizens their deliberative freedom. In the absence of such deliberative freedom, it is hard to see how one could still talk of mutual respect, equality and inclusion – key deliberative ideals. In Aristotelian terms, we can say that the end sought by any deliberative democracy should be to cultivate, maintain and enhance the deliberative standing of its citizens. And that means exposing any particular instance of unjust political impoverishment and attacking the conditions that create or sustain it. To accept an instance of unjust political poverty, therefore, would be to accept instances in which deliberative freedom is denied.[79] Such a denial can neither be dissolved by distributing the value of deliberative standing across a system, nor compensated for by overall gains in other parts of the system.

Securing deliberative standing, then, is a way of protecting those struggling against political poverty. Following Bohman, I take 'political poverty' as a minimal 'threshold requirement': to avoid political poverty participants must enjoy 'equal capacities to participate effectively' in public deliberation (PD, 131).[80] The reason for adopting this minimal approach is to avoid closing off 'critical oppositional activity' that may need to violate core deliberative ideals, such as mutual respect, in the very struggle against political poverty in non-ideal circumstances.[81] Mutual respect is a weighted ideal: where particular forms of speech undermine the deliberative standing of those struggling against political poverty, the ideal should be taken as an immovable weight. However, this should not tie those struggling against political poverty to ideal deliberative processes that are skewed by background conditions of inequality and power. This would turn the protective immovable weight of mutual respect into a dead weight that would anchor those struggling for deliberative uptake more firmly in political poverty.

V. Redrawing the Philosophical Map of Reason

I have argued that the charge that deliberative approaches to public deliberation are overly rationalistic and exclude difference needs to be rethought. We have seen how deliberative theorists have substantially weakened the norms governing democratic deliberation and offer a more expansive conception of public deliberation. However, one of the concerns running throughout this chapter has been how deliberativists fail to provide a satisfactory response to the UEC. In the next chapter I shall approach this issue in the context of arguments over the work of Jacques Derrida. Indeed, it will be an argument over argumentation itself. What I hope to show is that Derrida has been engaged in a long-term project of opening up argumentation in ways that will prove useful in trying to think through the problems we have been concerned with here. In particular, Derrida's deconstructive approach is guided by the demand to do justice to the other in their otherness. In the light of such a demand, both the supplementing and systemic approaches remain inadequate. The former presupposes the very picture that gives rise to the UEC in the first place. The latter risks sacrificing singular others in the name of systemic gains. Before we exit, however, I want to suggest that Bohman is already inviting us through the door to this next chapter.

While setting out his account for pluralising public reason, there is a moment where Bohman directs us to one of his earlier articles (PD, 279, n. 9).[82] Although Bohman makes a similar bracketing move in this article, and although his talk of 'the argumentative and rhetorical' (202) suggests the kind of distinction we saw in (early) Dryzek, there are aspects to the argument developed in this article that point the way to the kind of concerns that occupy Derrida.[83] In this article it is clear that Bohman is unsympathetic to any attempt to purge public deliberation of rhetorical elements and thereby preserve a pure realm of rational argumentation. Attempting to loosen Habermas's distinction between illocutions and perlocutions, Bohman criticises Habermas's 'philosophical strategy of holding back rhetoric by isolating a purified area of language use orientated to understanding and validity'. In contrast, Bohman suggests that there is 'a proper place for strategy, rhetoric, and perlocutions' in communicative language (193). This place is the 'emancipatory speech' that social critics employ – 'perlocutionary acts in the service of communicative aims' (199). What is interesting about this move is not only the rejection of a purified realm of argumentation and the loosening up of these distinctions, but the way Bohman characterises his own project. Bohman sees himself as engaged in a project of 'redrawing the traditional philosophical map of reason' (189), where distinctions governing argumentation and rhetoric 'must give way to a continuum' (202). The 'toll booths of the map of reason', insists Bohman, must be rethought if social critics are to be 'both effective and rational' (202). In seeking to redraw the tradition philosophical map of reason and argumentation, Bohman's work seems to cross over in interesting ways with the kind of concerns that have engaged Derrida. As we will see in the next chapter, Derridean deconstruction attempts to elaborate the subtle differences between various forms of speech in order to resist the idea that one could simply oppose argument to rhetoric. In doing so, Derrida has consistently attempted to redraw the philosophical map of reason in ways that would enable the new and different to emerge. Similar to Bohman, Derrida insists that 'reason must let itself be reasoned with' (RS, 159), that the philosophical map of reasoned argumentation must be redrawn if we are to do justice to the other in their otherness. This is why, in both theory and practice, Derrida has always insisted on the importance of precisely those forms of communication that deliberativists have increasingly turned to in order to respond to the UEC. With this in mind, let's open the deliberative door to deconstruction.

Notes

1. See Elstub, Ercan and Fabrino, 'Editorial Introduction: The Fourth Generation of Deliberative Democracy'.
2. Sanders, 'Against Deliberation'; Young, 'Activist Challenges to Deliberative Democracy'.
3. Tully, 'The Unfreedom of the Moderns', 223.
4. Young, 'Communication and the Other', 123.
5. Tully, 'The Unfreedom of the Moderns', 223.
6. Ibid. See Young, *Inclusion and Democracy*, 55.
7. Chambers, 'Rhetoric and the Public Sphere', 325.
8. Gutmann and Thompson, *Democracy and Disagreement*, 135; Gutmann and Thompson, *Why Deliberative Democracy?*, 50–1.
9. In later work, Dryzek and Bohman develop a systemic approach. Setting out these two approaches as independent alternative responses,

A MORE EXPANSIVE CONCEPTION OF DELIBERATION   97

however, will not only help us see what is at stake in the debate over the UEC, but will also allow me to bring out the strengths and weaknesses of each approach.
10. As we shall see, Derrida's account of doing justice to the other (Chapters 4, 5) and his account of hospitality (Chapter 6) struggle with precisely this problem.
11. He also looks at 'argument'. What is interesting here is that these are put under separate headings, and while this is no doubt motivated by a desire for clarity, it also reflects Dryzek's general approach here of wanting to treat argument as something separate from these modes of communication. That is to say, it seems to be presented not merely as an analytic distinction, but as a real distinction.
12. Young, *Inclusion and Democracy*, 57.
13. Ibid. 12.
14. Ibid. 115–20.
15. cope, $v.^1$ 2. *Arch.* to cover with a coping [i.e. an angled roof to throw off the rain] (*OED*).
16. Cf. Derrida's insistence that a general theory of speech acts must include those speech acts said to be non-serious, extrinsic, accidental, where ' "include" here does not simply mean "to incorporate" it (in the psychoanalytical sense, i.e., retaining the object within itself but as something excluded, as a foreign body . . .)' (LI, 77).
17. Young, *Inclusion and Democracy*, 65.
18. Ibid. 64.
19. Ibid.
20. Ibid.
21. Dryzek goes as far as to say that 'rhetoric is necessary in deliberative democracy' (DDB, 165, 177) and this would seem to be in tension with his earlier claim that other modes of communication, such as rhetoric, 'can be present' but 'do not *have* to be present' (DDB, 71).
22. Sanders, 'Against Deliberation', 353.
23. Similar to both Dryzek and Bohman, Gutmann and Thompson offer a supplementing response to the problem of unjust exclusion. In their discussion of the impassioned oratory of Senator Moseley-Braun, they claim that her 'oratory of impassioned tears and shouts' helped reach an otherwise deaf audience. The senator had to 'resort' to the 'high drama' of passionate oratory as a 'nondeliberative' step to deliberation. Such non-deliberative rhetoric successfully 'provoked deliberation' and 'stimulated debate' (*Democracy and Disagreement*, 135; *Why Deliberative Democracy?*, 50–1). In his discussion of theorists who allow

these moments of rhetoric into deliberation, Parkinson accurately describes the general move as follows: 'This is not to say that rhetoric should replace reasoned debate, but only that it has a legitimate role in prising open the doors of deliberative moments' (*Deliberating in the Real World*, 26). While rhetorical speech may occasionally be utilised to open the doors of deliberation, for the supplementing approach, at the doors is where it ought to remain.
24. Ricoeur, *The Rule of Metaphor*, 9.
25. Showing through enthymemes involves 'the presentation of evidence for an opinion' and this is 'the central and characteristic activity of rhetorical speaking'; 'Aristotle's great innovation in the *Rhetoric* is the discovery that argument is the *centre* of the art of persuasion.' See Sachs, *Plato* Gorgias and *Aristotle* Rhetoric, 289.
26. Fontana, 'Rhetoric and the Roots of Democratic Politics', 51.
27. 'Antistrophe' is 'a stanza in a choral ode in the same metric meter as the preceding stanza, and dances in the same steps, but in the opposite ... direction across the stage' (Sachs, *Plato* Gorgias and *Aristotle* Rhetoric, 113, n. 1).
28. Sachs, 'Introduction', in *Plato* Gorgias and *Aristotle* Rhetoric, 19.
29. As Aristotle observes, 'we do not render our judgements the same way when grieved as when delighted' (R, 1356a13–15; cf. 1377b32–5, 1378a19–22).
30. Aristotle does not take the emotions to be mere brute causes of judgements: 'And when people believe they themselves are in the wrong and suffering justly no anger arises ... since they no longer regard themselves as being treated inappropriately, and that is what anger was taken to be' (R, 1380b15–18). Similarly, we feel pity when an evil 'strikes someone who does not deserve it' (R, 1385b12–14).
31. Nussbaum calls this the 'inclusive view of perception' (*Love's Knowledge*, 80).
32. Goodwill is discussed under the *pathe* (R, 1378a6–17).
33. See Cooper, 'Ethical-Political Theory in Aristotle's *Rhetoric*'.
34. Manin, 'On Legitimacy and Political Deliberation', 353.
35. Abizadeh, 'The Passions of the Wise', 274.
36. Mansbridge et al., 'A Systemic Approach to Deliberative Democracy', 3.
37. Ibid. 4.
38. Ibid. 3, 9. Cf. Bohman, 'Representation in the Deliberative System': 'a systems approach suggests that the reduction of bias *overall* is the proper goal for the system as a whole' (84). As such, 'we do not need to idealize deliberation in each dimension ... but rather test the

deliberative system as a whole and how well it functions according to a basic list of democratic functions' (85).
39. For an excellent critical survey of the systemic approach see Owen and Smith, 'Survey Article: Deliberation, Democracy, and the Systemic Turn'.
40. Dryzek, 'Rhetoric in Democracy', 323.
41. Ibid. 320.
42. Ibid. 322.
43. This separation of the three proofs of rhetorical persuasion misses Aristotle's insistences that *logos* is the 'body' of persuasion. Aristotle (R, 1356a1–20) insists that all three forms of persuasion are made through argument. Were this not so, such persuasion would remain an atechnical practice of merely moving the audience through an appeal to the passions (R, 1354b16–23, 1355b36).
44. Dryzek, 'Rhetoric in Democracy', 322.
45. Ibid. 334.
46. See Owen and Smith, 'Survey Article', for an incisive critique of the systems approach for allowing actual deliberation between citizens to be replaced by functionally equivalent non-deliberative speech. As they note, one could end up judging a system to be deliberative 'with little, or even nothing, in the way of actual deliberation between citizens taking place' (218).
47. Dryzek, 'Rhetoric in Democracy', 322. Farage offered a systemic-sounding defence of campaign posters in 2014, which many regarded as reproducing the racist rhetoric of the British National Party: 'The posters are . . . going to get people talking. I'll have a little bet with you . . . there'll be pubs and clubs and restaurants up and down this country tonight where a big conversation will be going on.' See Wintour and Collier, 'Nigel Farage launches UKIP campaign amid criticism of "racist" rhetoric', *The Guardian*, 22 April 2014.
48. Dryzek is not discussing UKIP but net benefits more generally.
49. Tyler, *Revolting Subjects*.
50. Owen and Smith, 'Survey Article', 223.
51. See Mansbridge et al., 'A Systemic Approach': a primary function of the deliberative system is to 'produce mutual respect among citizens' because this 'is *intrinsically* part of deliberation' linked, as it is, to the moral status of citizens as co-authors and to non-domination (11–13).
52. Frank, 'Staging the Dissensus', 98.
53. Gorgias, 'Encomium of Helen', §10.
54. Kant, *The Critique of Judgement*, §53. Kant's horror seems to have been fully realised: 'On its website, Cambridge Analytica makes the

astonishing boast that it has psychological profiles based on 5,000 separate pieces of data on 220 million American voters – its USP is to use this data to understand people's deepest emotions and then target them accordingly. The system, according to Albright [a professor of communications at Elon University], amounted to a "propaganda machine".' See Cadwalladr, 'Robert Mercer: The big data billionaire waging war on mainstream media', *The Guardian*, 26 February 2017.
55. Below I suggest that seeking principles is misguided.
56. Garsten, *Saving Persuasion*, 129.
57. Garver, *Aristotle's Rhetoric*, 28.
58. Ibid.
59. The contradiction problem has generated a vast amount of literature. Some argue that the contradiction dissolves once we realise that the account of rhetoric offered in 1.1 is different from the account offered in the rest of the text. For a summary of this see Gormley, 'Deliberation, Unjust Exclusion, and the Rhetorical Turn'. Dow provides a detailed discussion in *Passions and Persuasion in Aristotle's Rhetoric*, chapter 7.
60. See Dow, *Passions and Persuasion*, 31; Garsten, *Saving Persuasion*, 190.
61. I am grateful to David McNeill for drawing my attention to this.
62. Garver, *Aristotle's Rhetoric*, 38, 153.
63. Garsten, *Saving Persuasion*, 7.
64. See Dow, *Passions and Persuasion*, chapters 5 and 7.
65. Garver, *Aristotle's Rhetoric*, 222.
66. Fox 10, 'New White House Communications Director Anthony Scaramucci speaks after Sean Spicer resigns', 21 July 2017, <https://www.youtube.com/watch?v=fz-VaIjXorQ> (last accessed 31 January 2020).
67. Garver, *Aristotle's Rhetoric*, 195. The ridiculing of the British Prime Minister Theresa May as 'Maybot' – on account of her repetition of the phrase 'strong and stable leadership' – expressed a negative *ethos*-based judgement of her *qua* speaker.
68. Garver, *Aristotle's Rhetoric*, 195.
69. See Aristotle, *The Nicomachean Ethics*, 1142b31–1143a16.
70. Cited in Reeve, 'Philosophy, Politics, and Rhetoric in Aristotle', 192–3.
71. Wardy, 'Mighty Is the Truth and It Shall Prevail'.
72. Aristotle, *The Politics*, III.1, IV.4. Cf. 'For where all do *not* participate, this is in general a mark of oligarchy' (IV.6).
73. Ibid. III.5.
74. Ibid.

75. Owen and Smith, 'Survey Article', 229.
76. Rostbøll, *Deliberative Freedom*, 66.
77. See Bohman, 'Deliberative Democracy and Effective Social Freedom'; Knight and Johnson, 'What Sort of Equality Does Deliberative Democracy Require?'; Rostbøll, *Deliberative Freedom*. This is not to claim Aristotle as a deliberative democrat. The point is that Aristotle's thinking about what being a democratic citizen involves is helpful for contemporary deliberative theory.
78. In *The Politics*, Aristotle emphasises the importance of 'educating citizens for the way of living that belongs to the constitution in each case' and that citizens should be 'trained and have their habits formed by that *politeia*, that is to live democratically if the laws . . . are democratic, oligarchically, if they are oligarchic' (IV.9; cf. III.5). If one wishes to secure a deliberative democracy, then the process outlined here would be a crucial part of the education, training and habituation of deliberative citizens. Not only would this be a necessary requirement for achieving deliberative standing, but it would also contribute to the general education of deliberative citizens and, thus, to addressing the manipulation problem.
79. Qualification is needed here. There may be cases where we might want to politically impoverish certain discourses (e.g. white supremacist discourse). To be afforded the protections of deliberative standing, one would need to respect the deliberative standing of other democratic actors. Deliberative standing, then, would be a democratic principle that operates according to what Blaug calls the 'principle of preservation' (see Chapter 6).
80. Owen and Smith speak of a 'deliberative minimum' of treating others with mutual respect that would disavow the kind of extreme rhetoric system-theorists are seemingly willing to include. This deliberative minimum would involve taking a 'deliberative stance' to others, that is 'a relation to others as equals engaged in the mutual exchange of reasons' ('Survey Article', 227–8).
81. Young, 'Activist Challenges to Deliberative Democracy', 671; Fung, 'Deliberation before the Revolution'.
82. Bohman, 'Emancipation and Rhetoric'. Subsequent page numbers refer to this article unless otherwise indicated.
83. Bohman talks of critics' use of rhetoric as enabling communication with the 'systematically deceived' (198, 200, 201) or the 'self-deceived and deluded' (202).

3
Arguments and Hearing Something New

For those who fervently repeated the line that deconstruction is a brand of apolitical irresponsibility or nihilism, intent on dismantling Western laws and culture and leaving us lost in some apocalyptic landscape of swirling negations and withering absence, in what Roger Scruton characterised as a world 'without hope or faith or love . . . in short, the world of the Devil', the advice would be clear: close the door as quickly as possible and nail a few boards up for good measure.[1] For such critics, the bluntness of Derrida's remark in *Politics of Friendship* – 'no democracy without deconstruction, no deconstruction without democracy' (PF, 105) – should have reached out from the deceptively comforting parentheses in which it appeared and struck with a sobering force. While it is difficult to make sense of such characterisations of Derrida's work, one only has to recall the 'de Man affair',[2] the 'Cambridge affair'[3] and the kind of reactions after Derrida's death to recall the intensity of responses deconstruction provoked.[4] But as Derrida once remarked, 'When the door is slammed too quickly, at least one knows there is a door' (PS, 74).

But there have been more measured responses. While unsympathetic to deconstruction's 'ersatz textual politics', Terry Eagleton matter-of-factly notes that 'there is no doubt that Derridean deconstruction was a political project from the outset'.[5] And Habermas's choice of the word 'enlightening' in the title of a piece written shortly after Derrida's death in 2004, 'A Final Farewell: Derrida's Enlightening Impact', signals the kind of shifts that have taken place in response to Derrida's work. 'Enlightening' and 'no doubt . . . a political project' is something few would have applied to Derrida's work a few decades ago. But is it the case that, assured of the political concerns of deconstruction, we can now simply slide back into those parentheses? The formulation of that parenthetical claim may still appear somewhat hyperbolic. Does Derridean deconstruction contain an injunction that *necessarily* points towards democracy?

This is a question that both friends and critics raise. For example, while sympathetic to Derridean deconstruction, Ernesto Laclau rejects any notion of deconstruction providing ethico-political injunctions. From the undecidability of constitutive openness revealed by deconstruction, Laclau argues that 'no course of action necessarily follows' (TJ, 78). While Laclau acknowledges that deconstructive undecidability may give rise to 'ethico-political moves', he insists that these may be 'different from or even opposite to democracy'. Laclau thus maintains that 'the case for totalitarianism can be presented starting from deconstructionist premises . . . either direction is equally possible' (TJ, 77). We may summarise Laclau's position with an alternative claim: no deconstruction without undecidability; no undecidability with normativity.

Richard Rorty goes further in denying any political significance whatsoever to deconstruction. For Rorty, the 'over-philosophication'[6] of deconstruction transforms the contingent and ironic Derrida, who 'weave[s] bits of books together with bits of other books', into 'a man with a great big theory' (TP, 314). It is precisely the urge to make 'big swooshy transcendental claims' – an urge that Derrida occasionally succumbs to – that Rorty thinks we should give up (TP, 331). The sooner we realise that Derrida's work is that of an ironist's private struggle for autonomy with little relevance to social justice, the sooner we can leave all this 'problematizing for weekends' and return to the 'banal' discussions of everyday politics.[7] Rorty's alternative formulation would be something like this: no deconstruction without irony; no irony with big swooshy transcendental claims.

The issue of the normativity of deconstruction is something that will re-emerge in criticisms levelled by friends and critics alike. I will explore this in more detail later. In this chapter, I want to take a step back to consider a recurring claim made about Derrida's work, namely, that it does not engage in argumentation. Showing why this claim is incorrect is important for at least two reasons. Firstly, it will allow me to highlight the way in which Derrida's work has been engaged in a long-standing effort to multiply the possibilities of reasoned argument. In doing so, I aim to show that Derrida's work contributes to the democratic task, explored in the previous chapter, of developing a more expansive conception of reasoned argument so as to avoid unjust exclusions. Secondly, building on this account, I shall argue that this project is not limited to contesting the delimitations of certain kinds of academic discourse, but points to a much broader political dimension of Derrida's work, what I call a politics of the stage. This, I hope, will open up a space for a more productive dialogue between deliberative theory and deconstruction. While I will consider various formulations of the 'no argument' charge, I will focus on Richard Rorty's version, responding in particular to his central claim that Derrida has no arguments and is therefore publicly useless.[8] I start with Rorty's version because rather than deploying this to justify a certain non-engagement, he arrives at this position through a longstanding engagement with Derrida's work. As such, I think Rorty's argument requires an answer and provides for a more productive discussion.

Now, one might think that Rorty's reading has been left behind with Derrida's later work, and therefore there is little point in returning to Rorty here. I disagree. Beneath all the talk of jokes and irony, Rorty makes a claim that brings out some of the difficulties surrounding argumentation that we have been considering in the previous two chapters. Here is the claim: 'philosophers like Heidegger and Derrida . . . do not *have* arguments or theses' (CP, 93). This claim has proven influential in the reception of Derrida's work. Most responses to Rorty, however, have concentrated on showing that Rorty's distinction between early and late Derrida does not hold up. While important, the significance of Rorty's reading goes beyond the issue of how one should understand deconstruction and touches on issues regarding argumentation, humour, rhetoric and irony. The 'no arguments' charge seems to bring out precisely the kind of concerns about exclusionary approaches to reason and argumentation that occupied us in the previous chapters. In addition, it also brings to the surface the political dimension to these arguments about arguments. Rorty, to his credit, makes it very clear that one of the things underlying this issue is a disagreement about politics.

I. Rorty, Transcendental Jacques and 'Bad Brother' Derrida

In a book review of 2004, Pascal Engel begins with the following observation: 'There is something of the Dr Jekyll and Mr Hyde about Richard Rorty.'[9] While Engel sees this as a split between the analytic Dr Richard and the postmodern Mr Rorty, when it comes to the work of Derrida, the postmodern Mr Rorty seems just as split. Most of the time Rorty allows himself to be carried away by the ingenious performances of Derrida, whom he ranks among the 'most powerful and fascinating writers' of his time, a writer who not only displays an 'incredible, almost Nabokovian polylingual linguistic facility', but one who is also 'a great *comic* writer', perhaps 'the funniest . . . since Kierkegaard' (EHO, 112–13). In the family drama of Western philosophy 'bad brother Derrida' (CP, 92) has some of the best lines and Rorty loves him for it. And yet there are moments when Jacques gets pulled into conversations with overbearing Father Heidegger and honest Uncle Kant, and instead of cracking jokes and deconstructing them, he gets a little too serious, speaking in what Rorty characterises as a 'metalinguistic jargon, full of words like *trace* and *différance*' (EHO, 93). In these moments, Jacques comes perilously close to going all transcendental at the knees and this has the unfortunate consequence of encouraging interpreters to start talking about Derrida's rigorous or 'quasi-transcendental' arguments. This sees an exasperated Rorty pushing past the likes of Norris and Gasché and heading for the door exclaiming: 'I have reached the end of my tether. I do not know how to use the notion of "quasi-transcendentality"' (TP, 337). But Rorty cannot quite close the door; he cannot quite give up on Derrida. 'I find myself returning to his work over and over again,' writes Rorty, 'always unable to get a clear synoptic view of his intent, but always fascinated' (TP, 13). While transcendental Jacques may be a rather dull boy, bad brother Derrida remains irresistible.

Hence Rorty's engagement with Derrida and his interpreters, an engagement that has been a long-standing struggle to rescue the poetic, inventive flesh-and-blood writer from those 'professional' deconstructionists he finds so 'hilarious' for all their talk about rigour (CP, 246, n. 21). As early as his 1978 paper 'Philosophy as a Kind of Writing', Rorty makes a claim that will turn out to be the red thread running throughout his later essays on Derrida: 'philosophers like Heidegger and Derrida . . . do not *have* arguments or theses' (CP, 93). To claim otherwise would be to place Derrida in the Kantian tradition, which sees itself as giving clearer and clearer views of the persistent problems of philosophy and helping to complete the 'unfinished walls and roofs of the great Kantian edifice' through a series of shared arguments based on common methods (CP, 92–3). This is precisely the position commentators such as Norris put forward. For Norris, whether it's issues of language and reference, the idealism/materialism, transcendental/empiricist debates of modern epistemology, or an interrogation of the principle of reason itself, Derrida's work engages in problems that 'belong within the Kantian tradition of enlightened critique'.[10] While Norris notes that it would be a mistake to interpret Derridean deconstruction as simply carrying on that tradition, he insists that it would be to completely misunderstand what Derrida is up to if we did not 'take stock of the problems created by Kant and his successors'.[11] Derrida may well problematise the Kantian tradition, but his work would be 'inconceivable' outside of it.[12]

The problem for Rorty is that Derrida is not engaged in the Kantian project of attempting to resolve the persistent problems of philosophy and finally get the correct presentation of the way things really are. As the latest and largest flower to bloom in the non-Kantian dialectical tradition, whose roots stretch back to Hegel's *Phenomenology of Spirit*, Rorty sees Derrida as continuing the series of horizontal interpretations characteristic of Hegel's philosophy, while dropping 'its sense of direction' and 'seriousness' and, with that, the quest for that final, all-encompassing reinterpretation (CP, 95). In denying that truth can be discovered transcendentally in a realm beyond time, or that it unfolds teleologically through history without chance, Derrida, on this view, is, as Mark Dooley puts it, 'as good a nominalist/historicist as one is likely to get'.[13] Or as Rorty might put it, he is an ironist embracing the freedom of contingency, not a metaphysician seduced by the dream of a final vocabulary. Aware of the contingency of any vocabulary and the possibility of self-creation this opens up, what bad brother Derrida is really all about is making philosophy funnier and more allusive, nimbler and more impure (CIS, 93).

To claim that 'Derrida *argues* and moreover argues "rigorously"' is, for Rorty, to see Derrida as a metaphysician at heart, still believing that there are well-grounded theoretical arguments to resolve philosophical problems.[14] Rorty takes this up in a 1984 essay:

> Arguments work only if a vocabulary in which to state premises is shared by the speaker and audience. Philosophers as original and important as Nietzsche, Heidegger and Derrida are forging new ways of speaking, not making surprising philosophical discoveries about old ones. (EHO, 94)

If Derrida does have arguments, then, by Rorty's own lights, this brings Derrida into the public realm of a shared vocabulary. And if that is so, then one can no longer treat his books as purely private projects in which Derrida 'works out his private relationships to figures who have meant most to him' and engages in 'vivid and forceful forms of private self-creation'.[15]

This is precisely what Rorty fears when he hears talk of 'arguments' or 'rigor'. Philosophers like Derrida are important precisely because of their originality, precisely because they refuse to accept the banal language of a shared vocabulary. Aware of the contingency of any final vocabulary, they simply drop theory and argumentation in a never-ending attempt to create themselves by creating their own language. The great fear here is being reinterpreted as just one more footnote to Plato. The moment one starts talking about rigour and argumentation, the notion of a consensus of inquirers or community of practitioners is not far away and, with that, the subordination of the extraordinarily imaginative ways of talking that ironists like Derrida come up with. As Rorty puts it:

> Rigor, it seems to me, is something you can have only after entering into agreement with some other people to subordinate

your imagination to their consensus . . . It is hard to be rigorous *all by yourself* . . . When somebody does something *for the first time*, she may do it brilliantly, but she cannot do it rigorously. (TP, 339, my emphasis)

On this view, Derrida is not the rigorous philosopher of the professional deconstructionists offering arguments; he is more like Lyotard's postmodern artist, writing texts without the solace of good forms or a shared vocabulary, texts that create brilliant new vocabularies and endlessly imaginative reinterpretations that escape the judgement of a shared consensus or collective practice.[16] Derrida gives up the public realm of shared argumentation for the private realm of creative autonomy, writing texts that are truly original, the novel creations of an ironist producing something for the first time, not the discovery of the metaphysician offering something for the last time. Such texts have neither arguments nor rigour; what they do have is the character of an event.

This separation between a community of inquirers arguing in a shared vocabulary and judging according to a general consensus, and the imaginative individual striving 'all by herself' to create 'something for the first time' in a quest for private autonomy and self-creation, is not simply a desperate attempt to rescue bad brother Derrida from those professional deconstructionists so Rorty can continue having his postmodern fix. Underpinning this quarrel is a political disagreement. For what is at stake here is the question of whether Derrida is a private writer getting his ironist kicks by transfiguring the likes of Plato, Hegel and Heidegger and spinning them off into fascinating new contexts with little relevance for social justice, or whether he is a public writer who contributes to transforming existing institutions and bringing about emancipatory social change (IDT, 138–9). Rorty's desire to keep Derrida for the private realm of self-creating ironists is part of his wider political vision that sees public demands of social justice and private projects of self-creation as 'forever incommensurable' (CIS, xv). Philosophy has always been captivated by this distinction, tossing and turning between the public and private, at times dazzled by the glittering dream of their unity, but all too often waking to the blinding nightmare of darkness at noon. If we are to avoid future nightmares, then, for Rorty, we must give up this dream and accept that no theoretical discipline will ever allow us to bring these two realms together in a single, comprehensive vision. There is simply no way to bring justice and self-creation together and make them speak the same language (CIS, xiv–xv). Those who argue that Derrida offers arguments that get at the underlying structures of things and, in so doing, provide the tools of political critique are still seduced by the old metaphysical dream of reconciling private projects of creating oneself with the public mission of transforming the world. Fortunately, Derrida – the much 'misunderstood nominalist' – was aware of this dilemma. After the 'false start' of his earlier work (IDT, 145–6), in which he seemed to have a taste for the transcendental, Derrida 'had the courage to give up the attempt to unite the private and the public'. Derrida, according to Rorty, 'privatizes the sublime, having learned from his predecessors that the public can never be more than beautiful' (CIS, 125).[17]

Who needs Derrida? Are texts like 'Force of Law' or *Spectres of Marx* useful for public purposes?[18] For Rorty, the banal transactions of politics, the proposed reforms and compromises it deals in, do not need the esoteric allusions and ingenious re-readings offered by Derrida. Only polylingual sophisticates like Rorty need that. The concrete demands of everyday politics need the kind of detailed descriptions of the lives of those considered marginal that are offered by ethnographers, journalists and novelists. While Derrida is invaluable as an exemplar of private self-fashioning, his work is 'pretty much useless when it comes to politics' (CIS, 83).[19] What democracy needs is a Dickens, not a Derrida.

Argumentative macho metaphysicians or noninferential sidesteppers?

There are two issues that I would like to address regarding Rorty's reading of Derrida, namely, the 'Derrida has no arguments' argument and the 'Derrida is publicly useless' argument. Rorty gives at least two reasons for claiming that Derrida has no arguments. First, only 'macho metaphysicians' argue and Derrida is no macho metaphysician (EHO, 98). Call this the macho metaphysician claim. Second, arguments require a shared vocabulary between speaker and audience, but Derrida is one of those original philosophers who abandon such consensus to create a new language and thus a new self. Call this the original philosopher claim. From these two claims it is not a great leap to the conclusion that, concerned with creating himself through creating a new language, Derrida's work, while privately illuminating, is publicly useless.

While I find Rorty's readings of Derrida some of the more engaging and, as Derrida himself put it, 'at once tolerant and generous' (RDP, 78), his 'no arguments' argument is unconvincing. Take the macho metaphysician claim. Rorty argues that Derrida faces a dilemma. On the one hand, he wants to write about the philosophical tradition, to, as Rorty quotes Derrida, 'think – in the most faithful, interior way – the structured genealogy of philosophical concepts'. On the other hand, he wants to do so, again Rorty quoting Derrida, 'from a certain exterior that is unqualifiable or unnameable by philosophy' (EHO, 92). In Rorty's words, Derrida wants to 'write about philosophy unphilosophically', 'to get at it from the outside', in order to show where philosophy's dream of providing that final, closed vocabulary always comes undone. According to Rorty, Derrida thinks that to write in this way provides him with the possibility of talking about philosophy while 'step[ping] off the path' of the ontotheological tradition, with all its dreams of a final vocabulary (EHO, 95, 96). We might say that the aim here is to avoid being one more deceived metaphysician who fails to sidestep the Hegelian embrace that Foucault feared might be waiting for us all.

The problem that Derrida faces, as Rorty lays it out, is that in writing from a position unnameable by philosophy, Derrida risks losing all touch with philosophy and being left with nothing to say about it or simply being ignored by it. But if he is to talk about that tradition, then his words must stand in some kind of inferential relation to that tradition and this brings with it the danger of doing what macho metaphysicians always do – giving arguments about different vocabularies and propounding some new contender for that final, show-stopping vocabulary. But this would land Derrida right back in the ontotheological tradition from which he wants to escape. Thus the moment Derrida attempts to give arguments, he 'betrays his own project' because, as Rorty puts it, he 'can't *argue* without turning himself into a metaphysician' (EHO, 93, 101). Derrida, then, cannot have arguments.

But is it the case that we can have only argumentative macho metaphysicians or noninferential sidesteppers? Can sidesteppers have arguments, or do arguments immediately signal one out as macho metaphysician? Is it not precisely this kind of distinction that Derrida is trying to complicate when he insists, again quoted by Rorty, that 'one must interweave and interlace these two motifs . . . one must speak several languages and produce several texts at once'? A little further on, not quoted by Rorty, Derrida also talks about the need for a change in style, a style that he emphasises 'must be *plural*' (M, 135). In a later interview, a similar point is made: 'Deconstruction always consists in making more than one movement at a time, and writing with two hands, writing more than one sentence' (PM, 143). For Derrida, one does not simply choose between one language or another, one style or another; the languages are several just as the styles are plural, and they must be interweaved 'at once', beyond any either/or.

But Rorty immediately reinstates an either/or by suggesting that Derrida is here invoking a 'distinction between *inferential connections* between sentences . . . and *noninferential associations* between words' (EHO, 101). While Rorty is fully aware that this is a 'blurry distinction', he thinks that Derrida needs to 'make something of these distinctions' (EHO, 98) in order to appear original (everyone else simply rearranged the inferential connections, but I'm going to shake things up by bringing in noninferential associations!). But it is Rorty who needs to make something of this distinction because it is precisely the former that circumscribes the realm of argumentation, and thus marks out the domain reserved for the macho metaphysician, while the latter is irrelevant to argumentation and thus marks out the realm of the associative sidestepper. But if this distinction is a blurry one, then it blurs not only the distinction between arguments and associations, but also the distinction between macho metaphysicians and associative sidesteppers. Perhaps sidestepping their way through these blurry distinctions is something like a 'vulnerable' or, dare I say it, 'quasimetaphysician', speaking several languages and producing several texts at once.

'There is never something totally original or new' (N, 238)

And this brings me to the original philosopher claim. Is Derrida as original as Rorty thinks he is? Recall Rorty's claim:

> Arguments work only if a vocabulary in which to state premises is shared by the speaker and audience. Philosophers as original and important as . . . Derrida are forging new ways of speaking, not making surprising philosophical discoveries about old ones. (EHO, 94)

Making surprising philosophical discoveries about old philosophical problems is the 'unoriginal' realm of arguments and, as Rorty quips, 'I value Derrida's originality too much to praise him in those terms' (IDT, 139). The implication seems to be that originality comes at the expense of a shared vocabulary. Sacrificing argumentation is the price Derrida has to pay for creating new ways of speaking. Underlying this is another either/or: one has either a shared vocabulary or originality, arguments or new ways of speaking. Rorty talks here as if one must choose between these two options, as if they were incommensurable language games. But this would sit uncomfortably with Rorty's rejection of the very idea of incommensurable language games.[20]

In a 1995 interview Rorty makes the less radical claim that what he has in mind with such distinctions is the idea that 'the language of citizenship, of public responsibility . . . is not going to be an original, self-created language'.[21] But why is it the case that the language of public responsibility cannot be original? Much will depend on how strong a reading we should give to 'original'. On a weak reading, where 'original' means something like 'novel', it would seem plausible to say that public responsibility and originality can go together. If we take 'original' in a strong sense, which I take Rorty to be doing, then the question becomes, is that coherent? Let's look at each possibility in turn.

If we opt for the weaker reading, so that by 'original' we mean something like 'novel', then it is not clear why the language of public responsibility cannot be original. As Bohman points out, one of the things that social critics do all the time is come up with novel ways of talking that can change the situation or interpretative frame through which we see and relate to the social world. This is needed, according to Bohman, because institutions, social inequalities and power asymmetries supply inertia to social change, and this leaves public deliberation congealed into what William Connolly describes as 'the inertia of settled vocabularies' and fixed forms of identity.[22] Bohman refers to this as 'linguistic rigidity' (PD, 220) and argues that such rigidity makes it difficult for those struggling in political poverty to challenge dominant interpretations and entrenched taken-for-granted meanings: 'our values, modes of questioning, and ways of seeing things can become rigid and fixed, so that new aspects, new experiences, novel variations, and minority viewpoints are not even considered to be possibly relevant to deliberation' (PD, 219). For Bohman, this is a problem we encounter when cultural codes and entrenched ways of seeing oneself and the social world close off the capacity for perspective taking and, with that, possibilities of alternative self-interpretations.

Social critics play a crucial role in 'making such codes fluid' through 'disclosure', which Bohman is at pains to distance from Rorty's strong talk of inventing new languages. Bohman understands disclosure not as a 'mysterious event' of creation or an 'extraordinary event' of poetic invention, but as 'a certain effect of expressive speech ... on a specific audience' (PD, 220–2).[23] Here the social critic offers 'new possibilities of interpretation' (PD, 219) in order to get the hearer 'to see things in a new way, [to] take up a different perspective' (PD, 225). Critics enable this aspect change in all sorts of ways, including rhetoric, irony, jokes, metaphors, narrative and other 'jarring' speech acts. Whether it is getting the hearer to see that the existing field of meaning has become rigid and closes off other possibilities or recontextualising the background beliefs and assumptions of the audience, social critics aim to disclose other possibilities and aspects so that we 'are released from rigid interpretative frameworks'[24] and 'reoriented to the social world' (PD, 225). Bohman aptly expresses this through an analogy:

> Critics are thus disclosive in the sense described by Kafka's narrators: they don't talk like the rest of us, but they show us things

that we cannot fully describe in quite ordinary ways. Kafka's parables show indirectly how a shift in communicative context permits us to see things in a new and a different way – to see the relevance of what is not yet important to us. (PD, 218)

While the language of public responsibility is unlikely to be original in Rorty's sense, the conclusion to draw here is not that public responsibility and originality belong in separate realms, but that originality is to be understood differently. Social critics may not talk *like* the rest of us, but they do talk *to* us.

Even if one goes along with the stronger reading, it is difficult to see how it can clinch the kind of separation of public and private that Rorty wants to maintain with regard to 'original' philosophers like Derrida. The question here is whether Derrida has succeeded in creating a new, original language. We can address this by asking two slightly different questions: what would such a *new* language look like? And what would it mean to have a new, *self-created* language? Regarding the first, presumably the mere fact that one could recognise what Derrida is doing as new presupposes that it can be understood as such. And if it can be understood, then it is capable of being appropriated within a horizon of intelligibility. But if this is so, then it cannot be *entirely* new.[25] The condition of possibility of something being entirely new is that it breaks with any horizon of intelligibility, that it arrives as an absolute interruption. But this is what is impossible, for the arriving of the new can only take place – as an arriving of that which I recognise as new – within some horizon of intelligibility (otherwise it would be unrecognisable). Therefore, the condition of possibility of the entirely new is at the same time the condition of impossibility of the entirely new. When Rorty says that '*différance*' was not only new but 'unrecognisable' when Derrida first used it, he is overstating the case (EHO, 102–3). '*Différance*' was no doubt a new, unfamiliar word; however, it was recognised as a new, unfamiliar word and, as such, it was commensurable within a horizon of understanding. Without that horizon '*différance*' would have been a mere noise.[26]

Regarding the second question, a similar move can be made. If Derrida has come up with a new language, then presumably the very condition of it being a language is that it can be shared. By this I do not mean that Derrida's private creations become publicly mediated and thus no longer remain that 'original' self-creation we first encountered. Rather, I mean that there is no encountering of a purely idiomatic mark. As Derrida states: 'I do not believe in pure idioms.' As he goes on to explain: 'as soon as there is a mark, ... language, generality has entered the scene' (PS, 200). This generality is not something that a private creation falls into, but that which enables the mark to emerge at all. As Derrida argues, for any mark to function as a mark, 'to be legible ... it must be iterable ... it must be able to detach itself from the present and singular intention of its production' (M, 328). This possibility of being detached and re-marked does not befall a purely idiomatic mark as it emerges into the public realm; this possibility of being detached 'intervenes from the moment there is a mark, at once ... And it is not negative, but rather the positive condition of the emergence of the mark' (LI, 53). Whether we think of the lapidary inscriptions of buried civilisations or the secret diary jotting a young Rorty may have made about wild orchids, any mark is constituted *as* a mark by this structure of iterability. The latter denies the very thing that Rorty would need for his argument, namely, 'the self-identity of an isolated element' – precisely the thing that the structure of iterability 'divides at once' (LI, 63). Without this division or re-marking no mark would emerge; because of this division, there is no pure, idiomatic mark.[27]

It is hard to see, then, why Derrida cannot be original and argumentative, why he cannot submit himself 'to the most demanding norms of classical philosophical discussion' whilst 'multiplying statements, discursive gestures, forms of writing' (LI, 114). This 'dual writing' is evident in Derrida's response to Searle. Despite the performative nature of a text like *Limited Inc*, Derrida tries 'to respond point by point ... to Searle's arguments' (LI, 114). And Searle's arguments are themselves a response to arguments put forward by Derrida. Searle has no problem pointing to 'what is wrong with [Derrida's] arguments' or revealing the 'internal weaknesses of his arguments' (cited in LI, 4). It would be hard to make sense of all this if, as Rorty maintains, Derrida has no arguments.

Indeed, Rorty himself credits Derrida with arguments when he refers to the 'antiessentialist arguments Derrida shares with many of his contemporaries' and how Derrida 'is giving arguments against [the] quest for ultimate, self-validating truths' (EHO, 11, 113). Not to mention his agreement with Searle 'that a lot of Derrida's arguments . . . are just awful' (EHO, 93, n. 12). However awful Derrida's arguments may be, if they are, indeed, arguments, then presumably they are part of a shared vocabulary that Searle and Rorty among others at least recognise. And once we grant this, then the kind of either/or structuring Rorty's 'Derrida has no arguments' argument can no longer do the job that Rorty would like it to do. Instead of seeing Derrida as either an ironic sidestepper, free-associating in a world of contingency, or a macho metaphysician arguing in the realm of the transcendental, perhaps we could think of Derrida as an argumentative sidestepper, posing what he himself describes as 'transcendental questions' that are continually renewed in light of the 'possibility of accidentality and contingency' (RDP, 81).[28] If we can see things this way – and Rorty seems to acknowledge such a possibility when he admits that 'Derrida makes noises of both sorts' (CIS, 128) – then one cannot simply seal Derrida off in the private realm of ironic self-creation. Derrida is free to sidestep his way into the public realm, perhaps lacking the swagger of the macho metaphysician, but nevertheless not as useless as one may have thought. To put this in a Rortian idiom: Derrida would be 'dreaming out loud' (WA, 214).

II. 'Midway between California and Europe . . . Oxford and Paris' (LI, 38)

Variations of this 'no arguments' charge recur, as I shall indicate in a moment. I shall not give detailed responses to these charges. Rather, I shall use these charges to bring out what I think is at stake in this dispute. I have already suggested that Derrida is complicating the kind of distinctions that Rorty deploys in order to circumscribe the domain of argumentation. Like the efforts made by the deliberativists in the previous chapter, Derrida is attempting to develop a more expansive conception of argumentation. Derridean deconstruction is not rejecting logic for rhetoric, nor philosophy for literature; what it is doing is 'raising the stakes of argumentation' (RDP, 78). I shall come to this shortly, but first I want to touch on some of the more prominent 'no arguments' charges made against deconstruction.

In a 1984 paper, Nancy Fraser claims that in 'refusing the very genre of political debate' Jean-Luc Nancy and Philippe Lacoue-Labarthe 'maintain the ethos of deconstruction'. Fraser elaborates:

> For there is one sort of difference that deconstruction cannot tolerate: namely, difference as dispute, as good old-fashioned, political fight. And so, Nancy and Lacoue-Labarthe are utterly – one might say terribly – faithful to deconstruction in refusing to engage in political debate.[29]

While both Rorty and Fraser appear frustrated, it is for different reasons. Rorty is frustrated by those who seem determined to get Derrida caught up in argumentation, while Fraser is frustrated by the fact that deconstruction always seems to sidestep the fight. With the play on 'terribly' we catch a glimpse of a certain impatience for the fight, as if Fraser 'cannot tolerate' these overcautious deconstructionists any longer. While this ironic play on 'terribly' may be an attempt to provoke such thinkers out of their 'transcendental safe house',[30] might it not be the case that some are engaging in disputes, just not in a way recognised by the norms and procedures of the 'good old-fashioned' type?

A year later we glimpse a similar frustrated desire for a good old-fashioned dispute in Habermas's well-known remark: 'Since Derrida does not belong to those philosophers who like to argue, it is expedient to take a closer look at his disciples in literary criticism within the Anglo-Saxon climate of argument.'[31] Habermas and Fraser seem to have been successful in provoking the deconstructionists (much to Rorty's dismay). By 1994, we are presented with a very different picture. Not only does deconstruction now appear to have left the transcendental safe house, but, according to Amy Gutmann, the 'will to power of deconstructionists' starts being flexed across multiple fields.[32] No longer hovering timidly on the sidelines of the fight, deconstruction, Gutmann tells us, is now concerned solely with getting on the 'path to political power'. The problem, as Gutmann sees it, is that deconstruction comes out fighting, not arguing. Everything – shared norms, intellectual standards, the 'most careful, compelling philosophical arguments' – is reduced to 'the antagonistic interests and will to power of political groups'. Those timid deconstructionists that Fraser tried to provoke into arguments are, on this picture, 'dangerous': 'the threat of deconstruction', Gutmann warns us, is that it turns everything into 'a political battlefield'. Not concerned with engaging those with whom they disagree in 'intellectual dialogue' and the 'pursuit of reasoned argument', deconstructionists, according to Gutmann, see others as mere opponents, 'unworthy of intellectual respect'. This picture leads Gutmann to the rather surprising conclusion that deconstruction is characterised by an 'unwillingness to learn anything from the other or recognize any value in the other'. Far from doing justice to the other, deconstruction, on this reading, seeks only to overpower and silence the other.

I do not intend to give a detailed response to the specifics of these claims, or address the differing paths that Rorty et al. head down from their shared 'no arguments' starting point. I take up Fraser's position in the next chapter. While Habermas's position shifts later (recall the 'Enlightening' remark referred to earlier), I do think this explicit dismissing of Derrida from the stage, and with it the possibility of any discussion or exchange, is of interest beyond the specifics of the Habermas-Derrida debate, and so I will return to this. Regarding Gutmann's charge, I confess I can make no sense of this attack. But one thing is clear: such charges present their own difficulties for those insisting on the importance of reasoned argument. What kind of understanding of 'reasoned argument' is in play here? How reasonable is Habermas's dismissal of Derrida? Does Gutmann offer us an argument? To whom are Habermas and Gutmann talking? Does the phrase 'the Anglo-Saxon climate of argument' not already suggest alternative climates of argumentation (otherwise why not simply '*the* climate of argument')? And, if so, does this not raise the stakes of what one takes to be reasoned argument and the kind of exclusions that are justified by that determination?

'Raising the stakes of argumentation' (RDP, 78)

Derrida responds to the 'no arguments' charge in the following way:

[T]he question that is often raised on the subject of deconstruction is that of argumentation. I am reproached – deconstructionists are reproached – with not arguing or not liking argumentation etc., etc. This is obviously a defamation. But this defamation derives from the fact that there is argumentation and argumentation, and this is often because in contexts of discussion like the present one where the propositional form, a certain type of propositional form, governs . . . where the attention to language is necessarily reduced, argument is clearly essential. And what interests me, obviously, are other protocols, other argumentative situations where one does not renounce argumentation simply because one refuses to discuss under certain conditions. As a consequence, I think the question of argumentation is central, discussion here is central, and I think the accusations that are often made against deconstruction derive from the fact that its raising the stakes of argumentation is not taken into account. (RDP, 78)

In referring to contexts of discussion and argumentative situations (both plural), a question is already being raised against the idea that reasoned argument is an unvarying form of speech that remains indifferent to the multiple climates of discussion. Instead, the suggestion is that there is a multiplicity of argumentative climates, where other protocols give rise to different forms of arguing. This is not to deny situations that may call for 'good old-fashioned' dispute, but one must be sensitive to different forms of arguing that emerge in the many contexts of discussion. Without exploring the latter, one remains deaf to those trying to raise claims and arguments that may not fit established forms of reasoned argument. Hence the importance of there being an 'And' and not a 'But' in the middle of this passage. Derrida is not renouncing the kind of argumentation that Habermas likes, Fraser is eager for, and Rorty wants him to leave behind. Rather, he is interested in complicating it, opening it up to, or, more precisely, being opened up to, the various modes and registers of reasoned argument (recall Tully's 'different practices of reasoning with others'). 'There is argumentation and argumentation.' In this respect, Derrida is engaged in the same kind of problems that we saw Young, Tully, Dryzek, Bohman and others grappling with in the previous chapter.

We can begin to see this if we look at a possible Derridean response to Habermas. Habermas's 'no argument' charge is part of a more general critique of Derrida for what he sees as Derrida's levelling of the distinction between logic and rhetoric, philosophy and literature. To recall, Habermas argues that the totalising critique of reason that he understands deconstruction to be engaged in leaves it caught in a performative contradiction. Derrida denounces reason as authoritarian, but he can only do so by employing the tools of reason.[33] Derrida, according to Habermas, attempts to get out of this 'aporia of self-referentiality' by 'standing the primacy of logic over rhetoric, canonized since Aristotle, on its head'. By inverting the philosophical tradition in this way, the grounds that would make 'contradiction' an issue simply dissolve. Once the 'sovereignty of rhetoric over the realm of the logical' has been established, philosophy can be treated as a form of literature and one is no longer constrained by demands of logical consistency. Derrida, according to Habermas, is now free to wander in the 'indirect communications' of texts, and the only criterion for his interpretations is 'rhetorical success'.[34]

Not that Habermas is dismissing any role for rhetoric. Indeed, he states that not only is everyday language 'ineradicably rhetorical', but so too is the language of law, morality, science and philosophy.[35] But, and here is the crucial thing for Habermas, the rhetorical elements are to be 'tamed'.[36] Not only tamed, but placed in check: 'the tools of rhetoric are subordinated to the discipline of a *distinct* form of argumentation.'[37] On this view, if one does not maintain this hierarchical distinction between argumentation and rhetoric, then not only do we undermine the emancipatory ideals of democracy, but we leave the door open to 'the worst' (see Chapter 5). In dropping argumentation and philosophy and taking up the tools of rhetoric and literature, Derrida is charged with letting the sword of critique slip from his grasp.[38]

But how can Habermas wield this sword with such confidence? How can Habermas be so certain about what is and is not reasoned argument, what is and is not philosophy? Habermas appears to be held captive by a particular picture of philosophy and argumentation. As we saw in the exchange with Searle, Derrida insists that he does argue according to the classical norms and standards of philosophical discussion. But this does not exhaust reasoned argument. This is the reason why he tells us that he is interested in forms of argumentation that take a certain propositional form *and* other protocols of argumentation that emerge in different contexts of discussion. In exploring the multiple possibilities of reasoned argument, Derrida maintains that he is not levelling the difference between logic and rhetoric, philosophy and literature. Whether he inserts Mallarmé into Plato or brings Genet into play with Hegel, the motivation is not to 'create confusions', but rather to 'articulate different registers' so that 'it causes one to think' both (PS, 374). In trying to show 'that the limits between the two are more complex' and 'less given than people think or say' (PS, 217), Derrida maintains that he is not effacing the distinctions, but trying to 'elaborate finer, more complex differences' (LI, 156; cf. PM, 142).

Like Bohman's social critic, Derrida's work attempts to make our philosophical codes more fluid so that our modes of questioning, forms of arguing, and ways of seeing things do not become rigid and fixed. This is not against philosophy, but a way of doing philosophy:

> Some [Derrida is here referring to his texts] are, I hope, recognizable as being philosophical in a very classical way; others try to change the norms of philosophical discussion from inside philosophy; still others bear philosophical traits without being limited to that . . . In any case, whether I practice philosophy or ask questions bearing on philosophy . . . I always place myself in relation to philosophy. I will always find it hard to understand how it can be said of a question *about philosophy* that it is simply *non-philosophical*. (PS, 412)

This is not a rejection of philosophy or reasoned argument, but an attempt to analyse philosophy, its 'multiple' and 'mobile' 'regimes of demonstrativity' (PS, 217). For Derrida, asking questions about these multiple regimes, about the language, logic and rhetoric of philosophy, is carried out not against philosophy, but in the name of philosophy. These questions are 'indistinguishable from philosophy itself' (PS, 217). This debate is what keeps philosophy alive: 'The question of knowing what can be called "philosophy" has always been the *very question* of philosophy, its heart, its origin, its life-principle' (PS, 411). From this perspective, then, the dismissal of Derrida from the stage of philosophical argumentation is a gesture based on a rigidity that not only remains blind to alternative perspectives and novel variations, but one which closes down any discussion about philosophy and reasoned argument. That is to say, it is a move that denies 'the historical nature of philosophy' (PS, 411) and excludes from the philosophical stage those who seek to re-examine, modify, contest or transform current norms of argumentation.[39] Upping the ante a little, perhaps this would be excluding philosophy itself from the stage.[40]

This is where Derrida raises the stakes. If it is the case that the history of philosophy is marked by multiple regimes of demonstrativity, and if we understand the debate over philosophy and argumentation to be itself part of the practice of doing philosophy (its life principle), then so long as one is doing philosophy, one will be without clear criteria that would enable one to definitively determine, in non-trivial cases, what is and is not reasoned argument.[41] This does not mean that one simply gives up all debate over argumentation and philosophy. Indeed, this debate is the life principle of philosophy. Neither does it mean that there may not be a consensus about the norms of 'good old-fashioned' politico-philosophical discussion (to recall Fraser). The point is that these norms are non-natural, historical forms that have emerged in particular 'climates' (to recall Habermas's apt choice of phrase). As such, these forms can always be re-examined, modified, contested and transformed. While one can carry on getting stuck in to good old-fashioned arguments, this should not blind one to new, alternative, forms of arguing and questioning. From this perspective, then, the absence of definitive criteria about what constitutes 'philosophy' means that the debate of what is and is not 'philosophy', and what is and is not 'reasoned argument', remains interminable.[42]

Raising the stakes a little higher, Derrida argues that those who exclude his work on the grounds that it rejects reasoned argument often violate the very norms of reasoned argument to which they appeal. Broadening out the issue beyond Habermas, Derrida points to the political dimension in this disagreement:

If I insist here on the example of Habermas, after that of Searle, it . . . is to underscore a situation that is unfortunately typical and politically very serious . . . [T]hose who ceaselessly claim to reinstate the classical ethics of proof, discussion, and exchange, are most often those who excuse themselves from attentively reading and listening to the other, who demonstrate precipitation and dogmatism . . . as though they had not the slightest taste for communication or rather as though they were afraid of it at bottom . . . Why? That is the real question. What is going on at this moment, above all around 'deconstruction', to explain this fear and this dogmatism? Exposed to the slightest difficulty, the slightest complication, the slightest transformation of the rules, the self-declared advocates of communication denounce the absence of rules and confusion. And they allow themselves to confuse everything in the most authoritarian manner. (LI, 157–8)

While claiming to be engaging in rational discussion, those who denounce deconstruction in the terms we have touched on do so in a manner that effectively closes down any discussion about what is or is not reasoned argumentation. For Derrida, this not only violates any ethics of dialogue, but imposes a particular conception of philosophy and reasoned argument that is not up for discussion. From this perspective, what pushes the likes of Habermas, Gutmann, or the signatories of the letter denouncing Derrida's work as a 'question of honour' into this violation of their own norms of reasoned argument is the struggle to protect a particular form of philosophy:[43]

> Those who protest against all these questions mean to protect a certain institutional authority of philosophy, in the form in which it was frozen at a given moment. By protecting themselves against these questions and the transformations that these questions call for or suppose, they are also protecting the institution against philosophy. (PS, 218)[44]

For Derrida, then, many of these moves against the kind of questions that deconstruction raises are due to the privileging of a particular picture of philosophy and argumentation. The appeal to reasoned argument is made in such a way as to dismiss alternative ways of doing philosophy and to exclude certain questions from contesting dominant discursive modes and demonstrative procedures. Not only does this violate an ethics of discussion, but it also leads to an uncritical, rigid attitude that shields a particular form of philosophy from the ever-new and ever-disturbing (philosophico-political) question: What is philosophy? What is reasoned argument?

To hear something new

Now, there may well be something less than innocent going on here.[45] However, I would suggest that at the bottom of these dismissals of Derrida's work is something like what David Owen has termed 'aspectival captivity'.[46] Drawing on Wittgenstein's remark about pictures holding us captive (in both senses of captivated/captive), Owen describes aspectival captivity as the inability to reorientate one's view in relation to the issue in question (in this case, what is and is not reasoned argument). In pointing to regimes of demonstration, and in multiplying the protocols of argumentation, Derrida's aim is to loosen the grip of aspectival captivity by showing other possibilities. It is an attempt to get us to see, or, perhaps, hear, something new. Nietzsche reminds us of how difficult this can be:

> It is more comfortable for our eye to react to a particular object by producing again an image it has often produced before than by retaining what is new and different in an impression . . . To hear something new is hard and painful to the ear; we hear the music of foreigners badly. When we hear a foreign language we involuntarily attempt to form the sounds we hear into words which have a more familiar and homely ring.[47]

In Fraser's desire for 'good old-fashioned dispute' and Habermas's reference to the 'Anglo-Saxon climate of argument' we see the force exerted by the familiar and homely. And in Gutmann's attack we see how painful to the ear the new and different can be. It seems that it has been more comfortable to reproduce the image of deconstruction as not engaging in reasoned argument, than to engage deconstruction. That is to say, Derrida has been heard badly.[48]

A more nuanced approach is needed if we are to see and hear what Derrida is trying to do. Rather than rejecting argumentation or levelling the distinction between logic and rhetoric, Derrida's work seeks to elaborate finer, more complex differences, in order to open up the possibility for the new and different to be heard. By tirelessly re-examining, modifying, multiplying and transforming existing practices of reasoned argument, Derrida's work attempts to strike the tympanum of the philosophical ear with a 'heterogeneous percussion' (M, xii). And the motivation for this is to open up our practices of argumentation so that the new and different can resonate. In the vocabulary of the previous chapter, Derrida is seeking to develop a more expansive notion of argumentation, such that the other is not simply included formally, but effectively. By seeking to pluralise public reason in this way, Derridean deconstruction seeks forms of inclusion in which the other has an effective voice, such that they can raise new issues and challenge current understandings. That is to say, Derridean deconstruction seeks to do justice to the other in their otherness.[49]

Above, I suggested that Derrida can be thought of as playing a similar role to Bohman's social critic. While not dismissing the existing codes governing philosophical practice and reasoned argument, Derrida does see them as overly rigid. In order to counter perceived tendencies 'to protect a certain institutionalised authority of philosophy, in the form in which it was frozen at a given moment' (PS, 218), Derrida multiplies modes of communication and tries to expose the reader/hearer to different possibilities of reasoned argumentation. The motivation behind this is to make existing codes fluid and to thereby enable us to see multiple aspects of reasoned argumentation, such that a multiplicity of voices can be heard. This, in turn, would open up alternative ways of relating to oneself and the social world.

Derridean deconstruction, then, is concerned with bringing about the conditions that would enable the loosening up of what Bohman calls 'linguistic rigidity'. Bohman, however, reproduces the same kind of image of Derrida that we have encountered in this chapter.[50] This is unfortunate because had Bohman been able to hear Derrida differently, he would have understood Derrida to be engaged in a similar task of loosening up the pictures that hold us captive, and multiplying the possibilities of reasoned argumentation. That is to say, he would have recognised that Derrida's work is engaged in a similar project – to pluralise public reason. And the motivation for both is the same: to enable those excluded from the stage of discussion to gain an effective voice and receive uptake.

Bohman's attempt to redraw the map of reason so as to enable a more nuanced account of rhetoric and argumentation to emerge (see the end of the last chapter) is a task that Derrida has been engaged in from the very beginning. Derrida's attempt to elaborate more complex differences between various forms of speech resists the idea that one could simply oppose, for example, argument to rhetoric. In doing so, Derrida has consistently attempted to redraw the philosophical map of reason in way that would enable the new and different to emerge. This is not to reject reason, but to insist that 'reason must let itself be reasoned with' (RS, 159). Reasoning with reason so that it sees reason is a way of being 'faithful to reason's call', a faithfulness that requires keener ears and a sharper sight:

> Who is more faithful to reason's call, who hears it with a keener ear, who better sees the difference, the one who offers questions in return and tries to think through the possibility of that summons, or the one who does not want to hear any question about the reason of reason?[51]

This is why Derrida has always insisted on the importance of precisely those forms of communication that deliberativists have recently started to include in their respective accounts of public deliberation. Like Bohman, Derrida realises that reason must be reasoned with, that the philosophical maps of reason and argumentation must be continually redrawn if we are to hear the new and the different. While this may be painful to the ear at times, it is the chance for the other to make their way onto the stage.

Derrida, however, does not restrict these forms of communication to moments of blockage or trying to communicate with the systematically deceived. Neither does he conceive of them as instrumental supplements. Given this, Derrida opens up the doors of reasoned argument in ways that go beyond the supplementing approach. The more recent, and more expansive, conception of reasoned argument defended by advocates of the systemic approach is something that Derridean deconstruction has been developing for decades. Crucial for Derrida, however, is the demand to do justice to the other as other. This clearly rules out treating certain others, to recall Owen and Smith, 'as a means to deliberative ends' – a threat that remains with the systemic approach.[52]

Derrida, then, has been engaged in a long-standing task of making our forms of communication more fluid. And this is motivated by the desire to loosen the grip of rigid interpretative frameworks that prevent the other from being included in their otherness. This is not a mere private project of self-creation, but an ongoing attempt to open up different forms of communication so as to transform the way we see and relate to the social world. What William Connolly says of Foucault could equally be applied to Derrida: his work attempts 'to incite the experience of discord or discrepancy' between prevailing conceptions of 'self, truth, and rationality and that which does not fit neatly within their folds'.[53] This task, and the concerns driving it, point to a political dimension of Derrida's work, one that attempts to politicise 'the places that the code of politics leaves out of the picture'. This, according to Derrida, is a 'certain political deconstruction', one that he insists is 'indispensable' (PS, 28). The politics of this may not be immediately recognisable, but it is, to recall Eagleton, 'no doubt' there.

Politics of the stage and the work of resistance

One can see this politics at work in a 1977 interview, where Derrida refers to 'apparatus effects'. According to Derrida, via a whole complex of institutions and apparatus, certain 'laws of production and receivability' operate according to 'framing or coded forms' that can stifle what appears to be even the most revolutionary contents.[54] This, he insists, imposes 'an imperative' to 'transform the structure of apparatus'. As he writes:

> What seems necessary to me, in principle . . . is to try and avoid separation, to partition as little as possible, and never to engage

in an action, a discourse, or so-called revolutionary 'force' within framing or coded forms that either cancel them out or absorb their shock right away. There are laws of production and receivability; they are very complex and overdetermined, but one can sometimes easily verify the constraints they impose. What appear the most revolutionary or subversive 'contents' (whether acts of discourses) are perfectly well received, neutralized, assimilated by the systems which they claim to oppose as long as certain rules of formal decency are respected. (PS, 57)[55]

This imperative 'calls for a multiplicity of apparently heterogeneous gestures' that aim to raise the question of the politics of the codes and forms that determine the range of 'acceptable' (that is, 'receivable') contents. Alluding no doubt to his own work (but not only his work), Derrida points to 'ruptures and disruptions of the code in one's manner of writing, teaching, practicing, or trafficking in language or the instruments of logic and rhetoric' (PS, 57). This neither fetishises avant-gardism nor excludes forms of intervention that operate according to conventional codes. Rather, such disruptions aim to develop a multiplicity of forms of intervening in the apparatus. It is the failure to recognise the need for such intervention that often leaves one, despite a 'revolutionary eloquence' (PS, 63), 'sleepily installed' in the apparatus (PS, 67), conforming to 'the dominant force [that] forbids one to tamper with [the governing codes]' (PS, 57).[56] This would limit transformation in advance. In more concrete terms, it would lead to the exclusion of those voices, discourses or actions that do not conform to the dominant codes or forms.[57]

Just as certain discourses may appear to contain subversive content but in fact have very little effect on the governing apparatus (insofar as they do not touch the dominant codes that structure the system), so certain discourses that appear to have no subversive content may introduce a disruptive force into the apparatus by pluralising the codes that govern the system. 'Without having revolution on one's lips nor wearing it on one's sleeve', writes Derrida, 'one has only to graze "formally" the surface of whatever the guardian forms are guarding for the censorship machine to be engaged' (PS, 57). This 'censorship machine' need not 'proceed by acts, decrees, or deliberate rejections'; it can result instead from 'apparatus effects'.[58]

This, it seems to me, parallels the kind of issues discussed in the previous chapter concerning overly restricted conceptions of rational argumentation and the problem of inclusion being merely formal, not effective. The forms and codes of certain conceptions of reasoned argument can 'cancel' or 'neutralise' potentially subversive voices. Just as Tully calls for an acknowledgement of different practices of reasoning with others, just as Bohman calls for a pluralised public reason and a transformation of the framework of deliberation, and just as Young calls for a transformation not only of the style but of the very terms of public deliberation, so Derrida, here, in 1977, insists on pluralising codes and forms: 'one must . . . work in several directions, in several rhythms. The monorhythmic and the monocode always spell immediate reappropriation. One must, then, tamper with the code' (PS, 58). If one is to develop processes of deliberation that enable a 'nonappropriating inclusion of the other' (to recall Habermas), then such tampering will be indispensable, for this plays a key role in resisting reappropriating codes and forms. Recalling Young, such tampering would be essential in avoiding 'internal exclusion'. As Derrida puts it: 'I must try and write in such a way that the language of the other does not suffer in mine, [that it] receives the hospitality of mine without getting lost and integrated there' (PS, 363).

In a 1982 interview, Derrida takes up this theme again and discusses it explicitly in terms of exclusion. Asked about his manner of writing, Derrida explains: 'By distributing the norms and etiquette of academic writing, one can hope to exhibit . . . what they are protecting or excluding . . . This is why it is important to tamper with . . . the "form" and the code, to write otherwise' (PS, 85).[59] Such tampering, then, is not the ingenuous work of an ironist getting his private kicks, as Rorty would have us believe. Nor is it the work of the nihilistic destroyer of culture that Scruton and others would have us fear. While this 'tampering' requires rethinking the codes that determine a whole series of inclusions-exclusions, Derrida's call for 'highly differentiated practical and critical interventions' does not counsel the cynical dismantling of reason nor any nihilistic destruction of Western culture: '[A]nalysis can lead one, in a specific, concrete situation, to advance "classical" discourses or actions', to advance a 'simple, clear, univocal form'. The point is not to destroy classical codes, but 'to do several things at once and in several ways at once' (PS, 58).

Give this analysis of the codes of the apparatus, it is unsurprising that the political aspect of these deconstructive interventions is often missed. Noting that 'the research, the questions, or the undertakings that interest me (along with a few others) may appear politically silent', Derrida suggests that '[p]erhaps it is a matter there of a political thinking, of a culture ... that are almost inaudible in the codes that I have just mentioned' (PS, 88). Returning to the discussion of Rorty, we can see this in his reference to the uselessness of Derrida's work for the 'banal' transactions of everyday politics. But the particular political dimension of deconstruction that I am attempting to identify here operates not at the level of the content of policy statements, but at the level of the codes and frames that determine the forms that structure such transactions.[60] There is a politics that appears *on* the stage, and there is a politics *of* the stage. The latter is a politics of the forms and codes that determine who or what appears.

One can see this politics at work in Derrida's 'unspoken' contribution to a 1983 colloquium, 'Creation and Development', held in the Sorbonne and organised by the French Ministry of Culture. Derrida remained silent throughout the colloquium, but published a paper afterwards explaining that silence.[61] Derrida begins by affirming that his attendance signalled solidarity with the colloquium in principle, before outlining a series of questions that, if left unconsidered, would leave the community assembled for the colloquium unable to 'even begin to understand itself, to think about its responsibility'. Derrida then raises the following question about the forms and codes structuring the colloquium: 'Was it possible to do them [the series of questions he had in mind] justice in these conditions, given the protocols, the speaking arrangements, the rules of an implicit deontology, the constraints of the rhetoric and time?' (N, 59). Derrida remained off-stage, silently listening in the wings of the colloquium, where he 'ended up thinking that this public demonstration had been *silent*'. That silence was discerned by listening '*with a certain ear*' for 'what could interrogate or disturb the depths of the consensus' that the colloquium seemed to be structured around and constrained by (N, 57). Derrida then begins to articulate what he was thinking and what he would have said:

> [I]f there is a responsibility for those who are called, in such a confused manner, 'intellectuals,' 'artists,' 'men and women of culture,' then today it can only be exercised on one condition, at least. The condition: never participate in a demonstration, whether it be organized by the state or by private organizations, without asking oneself . . . and especially without asking *publicly* . . . the following questions:
> a) Who is really behind things, at every moment of the process?
> b) Who is mediating it, by what means, in view of what?
> c) Who is excluded from it? This last question is the most indispensable. It provides the most reliable guiding thread for the analysis of any socio-institutional or socio-cultural phenomenon. (N, 57)

Here, then, is a demand for a certain political practice. Before analysing that which appears on stage, political responsibility demands that we begin by raising the question of exclusion, of who or what does not appear on the stage. Note that Derrida generalises this political demand: it is a key question not just for the specific conference, but for the analysis of 'any' socio-institutional or cultural phenomenon. I will come back to this. While Derrida acknowledges that exclusions are not an automatic target for criticism, he insists that it is 'always better to bring the modalities, the mechanisms, and, each time, the singularities of this exclusion to light' (N, 57). Not only must one begin by asking about who or what has been excluded, but one must then analyse the discourses and evaluations that explain those exclusions and the norms and authority that legitimise them.

Despite the fact that the community formed at the colloquium remained 'tolerant' and 'pluralistic', the question of 'what discourses *could not* be put forth, what gestures *could not* be made' was never raised (N, 59). And it is here that Derrida discerns a certain silence. Similar to his remarks above about 'apparatus effects', the silence surrounding this 'could not' is not taken as arising 'merely from a powerful contract', but rather, in keeping with this politics of the stage, 'from constrains that are linked simultaneously to the scenographic plan, the technical conditions governing interventions, and especially the imperatives for immediate translatability' (N, 59). Here, then, certain 'laws of receivability' constrained, silently and in advance, the contents that could appear on stage.

I am not suggesting that this political aspect of Derrida's work — what I am calling a politics of the stage — can or ought to replace the kind of 'banal' transactions of everyday politics that seem to determine the scope of the political for Rorty and others. I am suggesting that this is a political practice, and one that is not entirely separate from such transactions. I can only indicate briefly some of the ways here.

Such a politics could be understood as operating, initially, in an indirect way. Asked in the early 1980s whether the 'theoretical radicality' of his work can be 'translated into a radical political practice', Derrida responded: 'I must confess that I have never succeeded in directly relating deconstruction to existing political codes and programs.' But it would be a mistake, Derrida insisted, to take this as implying that 'deconstruction is opposed to politics, or is at best apolitical'. Such a view 'only prevails' where politics is reduced to our existing 'political codes and terminologies'.[62] Opening up, multiplying or transforming such codes with a view to critically intervening in the 'apparatus effects' can have practical consequences for what happens further downstream. But a crucial preliminary step is needed. That step would be a stepping back, a pausing to open up the space to raise the 'indispensable' question of exclusion. Such stepping back would direct us (as a 'guiding thread') into a detailed analysis of the concrete context in each case — its codes, frames, rhythms, structuring and so forth. It is a prescription to resist immediately taking to the stage to deliver one's contents, a demand to take the time to analyse the very staging of such contents and the structuring codes and forms that determine who and what counts. As Derrida puts it in an interview:

> If I rush to say that . . . politics is always allied with whatever regulates the time to look for one's words, or the words of others, I will have allowed myself to be hurried along by a determined

urgency . . . (determined does not mean unjustified, but belonging to a set of determinations that some would like to have the time to interrogate, analyze, define, name before answering) . . . Political analysis must be . . . adjusted, refined in each situation, taking into account its greatest complexity, the forces of the current that one is plugging into, or attempting to plug into, immediately or through some media. (PS, 32)

There are three things to note here. Firstly, there is a call to resist the urgency to respond, to resist what Adorno called the 'compulsive pressure to deliver oneself'.[63] This is not counselling disengagement; it is a way of contributing to the development of a 'critical culture' through the 'work of resistance' (N, 86). Resisting the urge to plug immediately into contemporary currents is crucial if we are to avoid unconsciously succumbing to the 'compulsive, feverish, hyperactive management' of those who determine the codes of the apparatus (PS, 28), and blindly reproducing the current state of things, with all the silent exclusions they involve.

Secondly, this work of resistance will not issue in any political programme. Although motivated by the general question of exclusion and directed towards intervening in the codes and forms that structure contemporary apparatus, this can only be taken up in singular contexts, to which one will have to adjust one's analyses in each case. This is evident in Derrida's own practice. We have already seen how, as a philosopher, his manner of writing attempts to highlight and transform the codes and forms that delimit certain academic discourses and forms of argumentation. In the context of the conference organised by the French Ministry of Culture, a certain non-participation was judged to be the best response (which, as we saw, enabled the concrete analysis that followed). We see a different form of resistance in the context of the French education system, and, specifically, in response to 'the reassertion of control by the most conservative, even retrograde forces' in the aftermath of the events of May 1968 (PS, 348).[64] For an author publishing books and articles, the work of resistance takes the form of a certain kind of prescription: 'How can one accept to "publish" without putting on the "published stage" the forces, the conditions . . . of the editorial machine? Without at least trying . . . to transform it?' (PS, 29).

And in the context of the public sphere more broadly, this extends even further: 'to attack solely the scholarly or publishing apparatus, to believe . . . that an internal action suffices – this is a comfortable alibi' (PS, 64).

Picking up on the last point, such a politics of the stage, and the work of resistance it calls for, would also require addressing what Derrida describes (in an interview with an organ of the mass media, *Le Monde*) as 'one of the most serious problems today', namely, 'this responsibility before the current forms of the mass media and especially before their monopolization, their framing, their axiomatics'.[65] The terms in which Derrida describes this problem suggests that this is part of a much broader politics of the stage: those frames and axiomatics all too often reduce 'to silence everything that does not conform to very determinate and very powerful frames or codes, or still yet to phantasms of what is "receivable"' (PS, 87). One strategy that Derrida deploys in order to take up this 'responsibility' is to put on stage, as an interview unfolds, the particular frames and codes silently structuring that interview.

In one of his earliest interviews, for example, the interviewer opens by asking what has determined, 'here and now', Derrida extending the multiplicity of forms of writing into multiple forms of activity. Derrida alludes to the implicit constraints of the interview (what he ought to say, what he ought to avoid, the demand not to delay), before putting them in full view:

> Here and now an 'interview' is taking place . . . and it implies all kinds of codes, demands, contracts, investments and surplus values. What is expected from an interview? Who requests interviews from whom? Who gets what out of them? Who avoids what? Who avoids whom? There are all sorts of questions and programmes that we should not run away from. Here and now . . . I wonder if it is not necessary to begin with these kinds of questions? They are, finally, the ones that have always interested me the most and the most consistently (even though I don't speak of them directly) since I began taking part for better or worse in this theatre . . . Okay, you are now going to think I am piling up the protocols in order to run away from an impossible question. So running away is a bad thing? And why is that? Does one have

to be noble and brave? What if all the questions put to me about what I write came down to fleeing what I write? Okay. I give in and return to your highly differentiated question . . . (PS, 9–11)

Putting on stage the implicit codes of the interview does not mean dismissing those codes, as the 'return' in the last sentence of the passage indicates. Rather, the strategy is the following. On the one hand, in agreeing to do an interview, Derrida agrees 'to pay the price' of that contract. He responds to the questions asked, knowing (and registering in the interview) that this will involve simplification, distortion, the displacement of arguments, and so on (PS, 10). On the other hand, he responds in such a way as to highlight, and expand as far as possible, those codes. The particular form this work of resistance takes, then, proceeds by negotiating that contract, with all the codes and demands that are contained in the small print, a small print that is often passed over, but which all too often determines who or what gets passed over.

Thirdly, given that this negotiation is adjusted to a context that is each time singular, there is no method, rule or theory that could determine the form such analyses should take or ensure that such negotiations will be successful. Derrida insists not only that 'there is no ready-made programme' and that such attempts 'can always go wrong', but that, 'to a certain degree, even, it goes wrong every time' (PS, 27).[66]

To broaden this last point out, and to anticipate some of the key issues that will concern us throughout, part of the reason for this 'going wrong' is that these negotiations are always negotiations that attempt to do justice to the other in their otherness, that attempt to resist the silencing of those heterogeneous voices that currently have no place in the codes and forms that structure the political stage. This resistance requires one to negotiate a series of contradictory injunctions. In an interview with *Le Magazine Littéraire*, Derrida gives the following example:

> [H]ow is one to, *on the one hand*, reaffirm the singularity of the idiom . . . the right of minorities, linguistic and cultural difference, and so forth? How is one to resist uniformization, homogenization, cultural or linguistico-media leveling, its order

of representation and spectacular profitability? But, *on the other hand*, how is one to struggle for all this without sacrificing the most univocal communication possible, translation, information, democratic discussion, and the law of majority? Each time one must *invent* so as to betray as little as possible both one and the other – *without any prior assurance* of success. (PS, 360)

For Derrida, to think that one can escape these kind of negotiations and contradictions, such that one could be assured of doing justice to the other in their otherness, 'is an optimistic gesticulation, an act of good conscience and irresponsibility', a form of 'indecision and profound inactivity beneath the appearance of activism or resolution' (PS, 360). This is a key issue that we shall return to in the remaining chapters.

The question of how to 'translate' the theoretical aspects of deconstruction into a political practice thus misses the point. Derrida's attempt to pluralise the codes that structure the dominant forms of academic discourse, reasoned argument and media representations is crucial to any democratic politics that aspires to a 'non-appropriating inclusion of the other in their otherness'. For an indispensable aspect of that task is to bring to light the various exclusions that take place off-stage and to analyse the procedures, norms and codes that determine and legitimise such exclusions. Such a democratic demand requires a politics that situates itself 'between what arrives on stage and what does not' (N, 82). It is here that a 'certain political deconstruction' is to be found (PS, 28).

Notes

1. Scruton, 'Upon Nothing'. See also Smith and Sims, 'Revisiting the Derrida Affair', where Smith claims that '[m]any minds have been corroded by Derridean acid' (159) and describes the wider, cultural impact of Derrida's work as 'something like a spiritual death, as when a psychopath throws acid at a Rembrandt painting' (155).
2. The 'de Man affair' was sparked in the 1980s by the uncovering of some of Paul de Man's journalism in the pro-Nazi magazine *Le Soir* in the early 1940s in occupied Belgium. This led some not only to question Paul de Man's past but to put deconstruction in the dock. An example here would be Jeffrey Mehlman's comment that 'there

are grounds for viewing the whole of deconstruction as a vast amnesty project for the politics of collaboration in France during World War II' (cited by Wolin, 'Deconstruction at Auschwitz', 2). For more on this see Hamacher and Keenan, *Responses: On Paul de Man's Wartime Journalism*.
3. This involved a number of academics signing a letter that was sent to *The Times* (9 May 1992) protesting the nomination of Derrida for an honorary degree (see N, 399–421; LI, 111–60).
4. See Kandell, 'Jacques Derrida, abstruse theorist, dies at 74', *New York Times*, 10 October 2004. See also Leiter, 'The Derrida Industry'.
5. Eagleton, 'Marxism without Marxism', 83–4.
6. Rorty, 'Response to Ernesto Laclau', 69.
7. Rorty, 'Response to Simon Critchley', 44.
8. I discuss Laclau's rejection of any normativity in deconstruction in the next chapter.
9. Engel, 'Richard Rorty', *Notre Dame Philosophical Reviews*.
10. Norris, *Derrida*, 169. See also Gasché, *The Tain of the Mirror*, 2: 'what Derrida has to say is mediated by the canon of the traditional problems and methods of philosophical problem solving, as well as by the history of these problems and methods, even if his work cannot be fully situated within the confines of that canon and history.'
11. Ibid. 150.
12. Ibid. 162; cf. PS, 411.
13. Dooley, 'The Civic Religion of Social Hope', 39.
14. Norris, *Contest of Faculties*, 219. See also Norris, 'Analytic Philosophy in Another Key'.
15. Rorty, 'Remarks on Deconstruction and Pragmatism', 17.
16. Lyotard, *The Postmodern Condition*, 81.
17. This split between the public and private is something Derrida explicitly rejects: 'between politics – that is public life – and private life the communication is never broken. I do not believe in the conceptual value of a rigorous distinction between private and public . . . In what I write one should be able to perceive that the boundary between the autobiographical and the political is subject to a certain strain' (N, 18).
18. See Rorty, *Philosophy and Social Hope*, 218.
19. Rorty makes a much stronger claim elsewhere, arguing that attempts to derive a politics from deconstruction are 'at best useless and at worst dangerous' (CIS, 69); or again: 'attempts to get a political message out of Heidegger, Derrida, or Nietzsche are ill fated . . . they don't succeed very well. Hitler tried to get a message out of Nietzsche . . . And people who try to get a political message out of Derrida produce

something perfectly banal. I suspect it isn't worth bothering with.' See Rorty, 'Towards a Postmetaphysical Culture', 51. This potential danger of taking deconstruction as one's starting point for politics is something that Habermas, McCarthy, Fraser, Wolin and Laclau all raise (see Chapters 4 and 5).
20. Rorty, 'Universality and Truth', 12.
21. Rorty, 'Towards a Postmetaphysical Culture', 50.
22. Connolly, *The Ethos of Pluralization*, 100.
23. See also Bohman, 'Two Versions of the Linguistic Turn'.
24. Ibid. 209.
25. I am indebted to conversations with David McNeill for the formulation of this point. See Derrida, N, 238.
26. I suspect that those with no knowledge of Derrida's work would still see in *différance* a family resemblance to 'differ', 'difference' and so on.
27. One would also need to re-read Derrida's remarks regarding invention, where he argues that the appearance of something for 'the first time' would itself require a system of conventions, a tradition, a social consensus to arrive: 'Invention *begins* by being susceptible to repetition . . . re-inscription' (PSY, 6; cf. 25, 34).
28. I will return to this in the next chapter.
29. Fraser, 'The French Derrideans', 65. Part of Fraser's critique of deconstruction is that it withdraws from the ontic realm and remains at the transcendental level where it sets to work uncovering metaphysical necessities. I take up this 'withdrawal' reading of deconstruction in the next chapter.
30. Fraser, 'The French Derrideans', 76.
31. Habermas, *The Philosophical Discourse of Modernity*, 193.
32. Gutmann, 'Introduction', in *Multiculturalism*, 18. Subsequent references in this paragraph refer to this text, 19–21.
33. I address this claim in the discussion of McCarthy in Chapter 4.
34. Habermas, *The Philosophical Discourse of Modernity*, 187–90.
35. Clearly criticisms that Habermas is somehow blind to rhetoric miss the point. Not only does Habermas see rhetoric as ineradicable, but he also acknowledges its 'illuminating power' in certain contexts (*The Philosophical Discourse of Modernity*, 209). The issue is rather the scope he assigns rhetoric and how one decides whether the taming and keeping in check is benign. See Morris, 'Deliberation and Deconstruction'.
36. Habermas, *The Philosophical Discourse of Modernity*, 209.
37. Ibid. 210.
38. Ibid.
39. Much of Derrida's work involves looking back over the history of

philosophy and how different thinkers have approached a particular concept. While this is often attacked as a sign of Derrida's disengagement with 'real world' issues, I would argue that one effect of this approach is to elicit different ways of seeing issues and concepts. It can, in the words of Quentin Skinner, 'prevent us from becoming too readily bewitched [by our heritage]' by contributing to an 'awareness [that] can help to liberate us from the grip of any one hegemonal account of those values and how they should be interpreted'. Skinner goes on to suggest that this enables us to 'stand back' from our present way of life and present ways of thinking and 'ask ourselves in a new spirit of inquiry what we should think of them'. This, I would argue, is one of the things that Derrida is engaged in, trying to provoke a reorientation in our way of thinking about a particular heritage. Skinner is cited in Owen, 'Genealogy as Perspicuous Representation', 87.

40. Derrida argues that those who accuse deconstruction of not arguing are trying to protect a certain institutional authority of philosophy but in doing so they 'protect the institution from philosophy' (PS, 218). Elsewhere he identifies the philosopher as someone who is always questioning philosophy, modifying and transforming it: 'A philosopher is always someone for whom philosophy is not given, someone who in essence must question the self about the essence and destination of philosophy. And who reinvents it.' See Derrida, 'The Right to Philosophy from the Cosmopolitical Point of View', in *Ethics, Institutions, and the Right to Philosophy*, 4.

41. See Bernstein, *The New Constellation*, 220–2.

42. Lasse Thomassen has an interesting take on this in his *Deconstructing Habermas*, 126–7. Thomassen points to the difficulties involved in philosophy asking the question 'What is philosophy?'. Doing philosophy, Thomassen observes, requires answering a question ('What is philosophy?') that must remain open if we are to do philosophy. For philosophy to continue, the identity and limits of philosophy cannot be definitively given. Philosophy, like democracy (see Chapters 5 and 6), is 'to come'.

43. The title of the letter protesting Derrida's nomination for an honorary degree from Cambridge was 'Derrida Degree: A Question of Honour' (*The Times*, 9 May 1992). By putting these dismissals in the same sentence I do not wish to suggest that they are of the same order. I take the concerns of Habermas to be very different from those who signed the letter. Unfortunately, Habermas does seem to endorse Gutmann's critique of what Habermas calls the 'deconstructionist method'. See Habermas, 'Struggles for Recognition', 120, n. 13.

44. Habermas's dismissal is the most surprising given that he is concerned with the same problem that drives Derrida, namely, how to include 'the other in his or her otherness' (IO, xxxv). Indeed, we can see the same concerns over restricted forms of argumentation when Habermas insists on an 'argumentative practice that is as inclusive and continuous as possible' and which is 'subsumed by the ideal of continually going beyond the limitations of current forms of communication'. See Habermas, 'From Kant's "Ideas" of Pure Reason to the "Idealizing" Presuppositions of Communicative Action', 29.
45. As Bernstein remarks: 'We should not be innocent about the ways in which "tough minded" appeals to argumentation become ideological weapons for dismissing or excluding philosophical alternatives.' See Bernstein, *The New Constellation*, 220.
46. Owen, 'Genealogy as Perspicuous Representation'.
47. Nietzsche, *Beyond Good and Evil*, aphorism 192.
48. Having said this, Habermas and Derrida did seem to hear one another better towards the end of Derrida's life.
49. Continuing with the imagery of the ear, Derrida describes a dilemma that all those seeking to contest the dominant codes and forms confront: 'In order effectively, practically to transform what one decries . . . must one still be heard and understood within it, henceforth subjecting oneself to the law of the inner hammer?' A little later, he suggests a possible, indirect strategy: 'to luxate the philosophical ear, to set the *loxos* in the *logos* to work, is to avoid frontal and symmetrical protest' (M, xiii, xv). Parallels with Bohman's account (from the last chapter) are clear: those who are excluded from the public sphere and consigned to political poverty often face the following difficulty: the very thing that is needed in order to escape political poverty is the very thing that they lack – an effective voice. But to gain such an effective voice, one would have to accept the very thing that has consigned one to political poverty, namely, the current norms of argumentation. Thus, in trying to contest and transform those norms, the politically poor remain inaudible; but so do they if they subject themselves to those norms. It is in response to this that Bohman points to the indirect (or oblique) forms of communication of social critics, which, he argues, provide the means to transform the current situation into a 'problematic situation'.
50. Bohman takes Derrida to be claiming that 'all discourse is mere rhetoric' (see his 'Two Versions', 206). See also Bohman's account of Derrida's work as a one-sided critique of reason and an anti-political scepticism, in 'The Politics of Modern Reason'.

51. Derrida, 'The Principle of Reason', 9.
52. Owen and Smith, 'Survey Article: Deliberation, Democracy, and the Systemic Turn', 223.
53. Connolly, 'Taylor, Foucault, and Otherness', 368.
54. For Derrida, this reference to apparatus involves 'not only technical or political powers, procedures of editorial and media appropriation, the structure of public space (and thus the supposed addressees one is addressing or whom one should be addressing); it also involves a logic, a rhetoric, an experience of language, and all the sedimentations this presupposes' (PS, 113). Thus beyond the explicit context of the mass media, publishing houses, journals, and the determinations of what is proper to philosophy, one should extend this discussion of the apparatus to other areas that Derrida has explicitly engaged in, including the structure of the university system and the teaching of philosophy in France, the codes of philosophical and political discourse and, thus, the norms of democratic discussion that structure a whole range of institutions and forums within the deliberative system.
55. In the background here is Walter Benjamin's 'The Author as Producer'. In this essay, Benjamin argues that intellectuals 'should not supply the production apparatus without, at the same time . . . changing the apparatus'. This, Benjamin insists, is a political demand insofar as, even where the 'material supplied appears to be of a revolutionary nature', it will do very little, in political terms, if such works do not seek to transform the very apparatus through which they are produced (93–4). Without reflection on, and transformation of, the processes of production within which they work, Benjamin (citing Brecht) argues that such authors would be left '[b]elieving themselves to be in possession of an apparatus which in reality possesses them [and] over which they no longer have control' (98).
56. Cf. 'There are discourses and gestures whose code and rhetoric are apparently highly political, but whose foreseeable submission to exhausted programmes seems to be seriously apolitical or depoliticizing' (PS, 363).
57. An example here might be the dominant codes that silenced the political nature of the riots in England in 2011. These codes operated not only in the mass media, but also in certain academic discourses.
58. This would parallel Bohman's concerns about 'communicative inequalities' embedded in prevailing forms of argumentation which may not be the result of strategic intentions (PD, 114–20).
59. 'Must one not be interested in the conventions, the institutions, the

interpretations that produce or maintain this apparatus of limitations, with all the norms and thus all the exclusions they imply?' (PS, 217).
60. Of course, this is not to say that Derrida's work does not provide direct 'contents' of this sort (for example, his work on the teaching of philosophy in France, his call for different laws of immigration, proposals for cities of refuge, to name but a few).
61. 'I was not able to take the floor or thought I had better not, neither within the group "Creation and Changing Society" nor in the plenary session, even when I was explicitly invited to do so' (N, 55). I include this to draw attention to two things. Firstly, the theme of the group and the colloquium as a whole was explicitly political, concerned as it was with how creation and development can contribute to changing society. Secondly, Derrida expresses his non-engagement in terms of a practical necessity.
62. Derrida and Kearney, 'Deconstruction and the Other', 119.
63. 'A Conversation with Theodor W. Adorno', *Der Spiegel*, 1969. Asked about the events of May 1968, Derrida notes that although he organised one of the first meetings at the École Normale (where he was teaching) and participated in demonstrations, he was 'worried in the face of a certain cult of spontaneity, a fusionist, anti-unionist euphoria. I never believed in it . . . I have always had trouble vibrating in unison' (PS, 348).
64. 'I began to give a more visibly, let us say "militant" form to my work as a teacher' (PS, 348). This led to, among other things, his work with GREPH (Groupe de Recherches sur l'Enseignement Philosophique) and his role as one of the founders of the Collège International de Philosophie. See Derrida, *Who's Afraid of Philosophy? Right to Philosophy 1* and *Eyes of the University: Right to Philosophy 2*.
65. Derrida was initially reluctant to engage with the mass media. In an interview broadcast on French radio in 1986, the interviewer opened by noting that there are 'very few public photographs of you, very few interviews in the press' (PS, 196). Derrida explains his 'misgivings as regards the way in which the modalities of appearing are generally programmed by what is called the cultural field'. In terms that suggest a political demand not to join in (to recall Adorno), he continues: 'During the fifteen or twenty years in which I tried . . . to forbid photographs . . . it was because the code that dominates at once the production of these images, the framing they are made to undergo, the social implications (showing the writer's head framed in front of his bookshelves, the whole scenario) seemed to me . . . contrary to what I am trying to write and work on. So it seemed to me consistent

not to give in to all of this . . . You also mentioned interviews, live broadcasts . . . there too I have the same worry. I have never found a kind of rule or coherent protocol in this regard' (PS, 197). Despite these misgivings, Derrida, presumably under the imperative indicated above, increasingly engaged with the mass media.

66. This emerges from his account of undecidability (Chapter 4) and the resulting claim that we can never have a good conscience (Chapter 5).

4

The Possibility of Political Thought and the Experience of Undecidability

In the previous chapter I argued that the 'no arguments' charges directed at Derridean deconstruction are based on a misunderstanding. Derrida's work can neither be characterised as that of a side-stepping ironist free-associating in the private world of self-creation, as Rorty suggests, nor that of a frivolous sophist wandering in the indirect communications of texts, as Habermas suggests. Instead, I tried to show that Derrida's work attempts to open up a more expansive notion of reasoned argument and, more broadly, seeks to transform the forms and codes of public discourse. This, I suggested, reveals a political dimension of deconstruction: a politics of the stage that is motivated by the question of exclusion. If the account offered so far is correct, then deconstruction has, perhaps, got its foot in the door. But a number of objections still potentially block the entrance. In the first half of this chapter I shall address two key criticisms raised by critical theorists, what I call the withdrawal charge and the totalised critique charge. The former claims that deconstruction rejects the empirical realm and withdraws into a politically disabling transcendental reflection. The latter takes Derridean deconstruction to be engaged in a totalised critique of reason and wholesale sceptical subversion of systems of thought. As such, deconstruction is judged to undercut any appeal to reason and justice, leaving it unable to say anything that could contribute to politics. After showing that both criticisms are based on a misreading of Derrida, I turn to Ernesto Laclau's critical reading of deconstruction. While Laclau insists on the political usefulness of deconstruction, he nevertheless arrives at a similar conclusion to the critical theorists, arguing that, as a matter of principle, no ethico-political injunctions guide the quasi-transcendental reflections of deconstruction. In responding to Laclau's reading, I develop a detailed account of a central aspect of Derrida's work, namely, the 'experience of undecidability'. I argue that this is key to trying to respond justly to the other as other. I leave it to the following chapter to unpack the ethico-political demands that flow from this, and the type of politics it points towards.

I. Speeding up on the Political Highway

In a 2005 interview Derrida responded to a question about whether the discussion of more explicit political issues in his later work was in response to outside demands by insisting that his 'speeding up on the political highway' was not the result of outside pressure (PM, 153). That Derrida began speeding up on the political highway may raise a few eyebrows. Was not Derrida off-roading somewhere in the slippery terrain of signifiers and supplements? Some would argue that, never on the highway to begin with, Derrida came crashing through the barrier – sometime around 1989 – and careered across the lanes without ever managing to firmly grip the road (despite some dazzling driving). His fixation on marginal aspects of selected texts related to broader cultural criticism in the way 'the obsessive polishing of a car bonnet related to a repair of the engine'.[1] For a number of critics, Derrida did not need to point to the 'scene of the car accident . . . imprinted . . . in quite a few of my texts' (PM, 153) – many of them were already at the roadside dialling the emergency services. Scruton was one of the more alarmed voices at the scene. Not only an eyewitness to Derrida's 'delirious' (482, 483, 484, 496) 'sideways slipping' (496) all over the road (due, perhaps, to the 'cryptic syllables' stuck to the windscreen and the lack of tread on his '*jeux-de-mots*' (498)), Scruton was also an investigator finding incriminating associations with the world of Orwell's *Nineteen Eighty-Four* (504–5), and evidence of connections with 'radical feminists', '"gay" activists', '"multiculturalists"' (492), 'left-ists' and 'malcontents' strewn all across the highway (502). Despite the caricature that emerges in Scruton's response, he was not entirely off the mark. One of the things that seems to worry

Scruton is the political implications of deconstruction, hence his decision to set his response within 'its [i.e. deconstruction's] cultural and political context' (482).

While deconstruction is too political for some, for others it is not political enough.[2] For a number of thinkers, both critics and those more sympathetic to deconstruction, it is the apparent lack of political dimension that has been the problem. A sympathetic reader such as Simon Critchley, for example, suggests that there is an 'implicit refusal of the ontic, the factical, the empirical' in Derrida's work and this leads to a political impasse.[3] A similar claim is made, more polemically, by Habermas, when he accuses Derrida of 'degrad[ing] politics and contemporary history to the status of the ontic . . . so as to romp all the more freely, and with greater wealth of associations, in the sphere of the ontological'.[4] In both cases, deconstruction is seen as lacking a political dimension; it removes itself from the concrete context of politics to carry out transcendental analyses that leave it, in the words of Thomas McCarthy, with 'nothing substantial to say' (PI, 11). The two criticisms I mentioned above, namely, the withdrawal charge and the totalised critique charge, are key to addressing the more general question of what kind of politics, if any, deconstruction points to.

The withdrawal charge

The withdrawal charge is subtly laid out by Peter Dews. Returning to Derrida's engagement with Husserl, Dews argues that although Derrida's critique of Husserl's phenomenology appears to open up and expose transcendental consciousness to an outside (an alterity and difference that fractures immanence), Derrida takes this outside to be a transcendental structure and in doing so he erases the contingency of historical processes.[5] While the fracturing of immanence could have prompted a move downstream into concrete experiences of consciousness unfolding in history, Derrida moves upstream in search of the transcendental condition of appearing and thereby withdraws his discourse from the contingency of socio-historical forces. Derrida thus refuses the road taken by much post-Hegelian philosophy, which sees historical content bursting forth to deny philosophical claims to mastery over socio-historical reality, and attempts to '*preserve* the security and priority of philosophical discourse'.[6] According to Dews, this presents at least two problems for any politics of deconstruction. Firstly, by taking the transcendental route, Derridean deconstruction is concerned only with laying bare structures rather than transforming them. Secondly, the determination 'to prevent any contamination of the transcendental with the empirical' means that deconstruction refuses to expose its discourse to other forms of inquiry.[7] As Dews puts it:

> Deconstruction cannot learn from its objects, but occupies a position of superior insight . . . in this way the successor of philosophy continues to evade the exposure of thought to the contingency of interpretation, and the revisability of empirical knowledge.[8]

For Dews, a more promising path would have been to think the end of the metaphysics of presence 'precisely in terms of this exposure'.[9] For critics, as we shall see, it is Derrida's failure to take such a path that disables deconstruction from offering any contribution to politics.

Drawing directly on Dews, Thomas McCarthy argues that this move upstream effectively constitutes 'a withdrawal from the specificity of politics and of empirical research' (PI, 115). This, McCarthy suggests, is evidenced in Derrida's approach to political questions. Rather than entering into historical, social and cultural inquiry, Derrida abstracts away from such inquiries in an effort to think the essence of the political itself. With empirical inquiry 'devalue[d]', Derrida carries this out through the reading of selected texts, an approach that results in 'an airy abstraction' at best (PI, 116). While Derrida denies the charge of textualism (which resulted from the famous 'there is no outside-text' claim; see LI, 136), his methodological approach to politics – limited, according to McCarthy, to the reading of texts and not the exploration of socio-historical contexts – only confirms it (PI, 117). McCarthy maintains that this is not to reject an approach to political theory that engages with texts, but one that thinks this suffices (PI, 130, n. 75).[10] In short, Derrida's commitment to a transcendental thinking of the political leaves deconstruction 'seriously disabling where morals and politics are concerned' (PI, 98). More worryingly, it leaves a vacuum that could be filled in all sorts of ways (PI, 118).[11]

A similar critique is developed by Nancy Fraser. In her 'The Force of Law: Metaphysical or Political?', which is a response to Derrida's 'Force of Law', Fraser identifies two possible approaches to analysing the relation between force and law in Derrida's account. The first is an empirical approach that seeks to expose the way in which the force of law operates violently in the service of contingent social, economic and political forces external to the law. The second is a transcendental approach that seeks to reveal the inescapable relation between violence and law that lies beneath specific institutional and social arrangements. The former, according to Fraser, leads to a political critique of contingent empirical forces that could be altered, the latter to a transcendental reflection on an unalterable metaphysical necessity. Derrida, Fraser argues, bypasses the political approach as 'merely empirical' or 'merely ontic' and instead takes the transcendental route, believing this to get at the heart of the relation between force and law.[12] To privilege transcendental reflection so as to get beneath the merely ontic realm in the way that Derrida does, however, 'incurs a disability when it comes to thinking politically'. In concentrating all its efforts on getting behind every merely ontic state of affairs, Derrida's work leaves those affairs untouched.[13] That is to say, while busy laying bare the structure of a necessary and irreducible relation between violence and law, deconstruction leaves untouched the specific empirical forms of unnecessary violence rooted in unjust, but alterable, social arrangements. So long as it privileges the transcendental over the empirical in this way, not only will deconstruction 'never get to politics', but it will 'disable or impede the possibility of political thought'.[14]

It is not immediately obvious how this general withdrawal charge can be sustained in light of the politics of the stage and work of resistance outlined in the previous chapter. Take McCarthy's formulation of this criticism. Whatever one thinks of the political dimension outlined in the previous chapter, it is neither limited to the reading of texts nor guilty of abstracting away from cultural criticism. On the contrary, it engages with institutions and calls, precisely, for cultural criticism. Instead of returning to those points here, I will respond to the central claim underpinning the various formulations of this withdrawal charge, namely, that Derridean deconstruction cuts itself off from the empirical to remain at the level of the transcendental, a move that, as Dews puts it, seeks to prevent any contamination of the transcendental with the empirical.

Deferring for the moment a more detailed discussion of Derrida's reading of Husserl, there is reason to think that Derrida's engagement with Husserl is intended to do the opposite. It seems that the whole labour of Derrida's reading of Husserl is aimed at revealing how Husserl never quite manages to achieve the closure that would secure an inner realm of pure interiority uncontaminated by the contingency of 'the outside, the world, the body' (SP, 82). As I shall argue, we can see this in Derrida's attempt to demonstrate that expression is irreducibly contaminated by indication and therefore Husserl's attempt to expel the latter is impossible.[15] Insofar as indication covers 'factuality, worldly existence, essential non-necessity and physicality', the attempt to show this irreducible contamination would seem to put into question the whole set of conceptual distinctions, such as contingency/necessity and worldliness/transcendentality, through which the reduction is articulated (SP, 30).[16]

Rather than trying to maintain the purity of such oppositions, Derrida's work seems to be engaged in an attempt to complicate the opposition between the transcendental and the empirical. Whether we think of this in terms of contamination or aporia, the move is always aimed at showing an irreducible interweaving of the transcendental and empirical that would require a rethinking of both. As Richard Beardsworth has persuasively argued, the whole thrust of Derrida's approach is concerned with locating a 'middle ground' that, on the one hand, insists on the 'inescapability of inscription' (and this would mean contingency, worldliness, materiality), while, on the other hand, not losing the 'inescapable gesture of the transcendental'.[17] This double move seems to be precisely what Derrida describes when he insists on

> the necessity of posing transcendental questions in order not to be held within the fragility of an incompetent empiricism . . . But such questioning must be renewed in taking into account the possibility of . . . accidentality and contingency . . . (RDP, 81)[18]

While one cannot settle for roaming in the labyrinthine field of the empirical, it is equally the case that one cannot simply soar off into the ether of the transcendental. The transcendental gesture is not abandoned, but it is rethought by Derrida in terms of a quasi-transcendentality. The possibility of accidentality and contingency is not erased from this 'new form of transcendental questioning' but remains in the 'quasi' that continually disturbs any transcendental exposition (RDP, 82). Derrida's transcendental questioning is always put out of place, exposed, in its very ex-position, to an outside that denies the purity of closure and thereby interrupts the (classical) transcendental gesture. While this is the very movement of philosophy, it is also what 'makes philosophy trip and fall'.[19] This is the reason why Derrida so often describes the condition of possibility as also being a condition of impossibility.

Secondly, it would seem that, far from attempting to preserve the security of philosophy, Derrida's work seeks to expose philosophy to an outside, an otherness that philosophy cannot master. For Derrida, philosophical discourse has 'always insisted upon assuring itself mastery over the limit'. That is to say, it has always believed that it is able to control the borders that mark it off from its other. It is through this marking off that philosophy 'derives its essence' and thinks its other (M, x). Now if, as Derrida maintains, philosophy always thinks the other as *its* other, such that it reappropriates and thereby misses the other; and if, in doing so, philosophy neutralises any possible surprises and protects itself from blows to its knowledge from outside, then in seeking to mark philosophy in a way that it could not reappropriate and interiorise as its own, in trying to strike the tympanum of philosophy with a 'heterogeneous percussion', such that philosophy could not muffle and thereby 'forbid the blows from the outside', would not Derridean deconstruction be the search for a 'non-philosophical site from which to question philosophy' (M, xi–xvi)? Rather than preserving the security of philosophy, deconstruction would be the attempt to 'interrogate philosophy anew' from a site it could not master.[20] This is not to say that Derrida thinks one can occupy a site totally free of the marks of philosophical language. However, it would be a site that remains irreducible to philosophy (M, xxv).

As with the empirico-transcendental relation, Derrida seeks to occupy an in-between position, this time '[g]nawing away at the border' between philosophy and the other to philosophy, moving along the margins, working the cracks and fissures between the two (M, xxiii). As he goes on to explain, the move would be to

> interrogate philosophy beyond its meaning, treating it not only as a discourse but as a determined text inscribed in a general text . . . to recall that beyond the philosophical text there is . . . another text, a weave of differences of force without any present centre (everything – 'history', 'politics', 'economy' . . . said not to be in books . . .); and also to recall that the *written* text of philosophy (this time in books) overflows and cracks its meaning. (M, xxiii)

Here, then, there is a double movement of overflowing. On the one hand, the borders that enclose and secure philosophical discourse would be overflowed by philosophy's inscription within the forces of a more general text (the empirical realm of history, politics, economy and so forth). On the other hand, there would be an overflowing of those securing borders from the fissures and cracks within the philosophical text itself. While this would not disqualify the distinction between philosophy and non-philosophy, it would seek to rework and complicate it (see Chapter 3). At the very least, it would involve the attempt to 'put philosophy back . . . on a stage it does not govern'.[21]

Could we not say that Derrida is thinking in terms of exposure?[22] Indeed, one could go even further and argue that not only does Derridean deconstruction not reject other fields of inquiry, but its search for a site that works the margins and cracks would seem to call for such inquiries. In a 1989 interview Derrida responded to a question about the weight of theoretical discourse in political life as follows:

> I have never thought or hoped . . . that a deconstructive practice . . . would invade the entire field and occupy a dominant position . . . It is absolutely indispensable that other types of practices . . . be pursued . . . [T]he idea that a deconstructive discourse might come to command and replace other practices . . . is a

kind of madness or comedy that doesn't interest me in the least. Deconstruction's motif, impulse or stimulus is doubtless necessary and at work in places one least expects (today in numerous non-literary and nonphilosophical fields), but without it replacing or substituting for anything else. (N, 196)[23]

Not only does Derrida not reject other practices and discourses, he explicitly insists on their importance. It is not by chance that, while insisting on the necessity of a deconstructive approach, Derrida refers to this as an impulse or stimulus that would be put to work in all sorts of fields of inquiry.[24] As a stimulus, deconstruction relinquishes any claims to mastery or dominance and calls for the kind of complementary practices that the thinkers we have been discussing rightly stress.

The totalising critique charge

Given the account outlined above, we should be sceptical of attempts to characterise the relation between deconstruction and empirical inquiry as one where the former 'rejects' (PI, 114) or 'rules out' the latter.[25] Not only do McCarthy and other critics claim this is so, but they make the stronger claim that this is 'no accident' (PI, 98), that deconstruction remains 'as a matter of principle, *empirically uninformed*'.[26] For simplicity, I will follow McCarthy's more influential version of this argument.

McCarthy thinks that Derrida's rejection of other modes of inquiry is 'no accident' because he (1) understands deconstruction to be engaged in a 'totalized critique of reason' and a 'wholesale attack' on the logocentric discourse of philosophy and (2) identifies this discourse as present in every social science (PI, 101, 107, 108, 111). This leads (3) to the rejection of the latter as part of Derrida's 'general deconstruction of philosophy' (PI, 113). While I think McCarthy's critique of Derrida raises some important points, his reading of deconstruction here misfires. Taking up move (1) of the argument, McCarthy tells us that 'Derrida's deconstructionism is generally taken to be a sceptical enterprise' (PI, 107), a 'totalized critique of reason' (PI, 101), a 'wholesale attack on "logocentrism"' (PI, 107, 108), a 'wholesale subversion' (PI, 111). Two brief points by way of response. Firstly, McCarthy seems rather too easily taken by this 'generally taken'. McCarthy supports this 'totalizing' or 'wholesale' critique reading by noting that Derrida tells us that to deconstruct is to 'desediment', 'destabilize', 'uproot' and 'overturn' inherited concepts and schemas, 'to turn them against their own presuppositions', to 'loosen', 'undo', 'decompose' and 'dismantle them' (PI, 107). To conclude from this that deconstruction is fundamentally a sceptical enterprise is too quick. Not all attempts at destabilising inherited concepts and schemas are necessarily in the service of a totalising critique. If, for example, one aims to deconstruct the logic of a racist discourse, and if one carries that out by attempting to 'loosen', 'undo', 'decompose' and 'dismantle' its governing concepts, would one thereby be engaged in a sceptical enterprise? If one attempts to 'destabilize' or 'desediment' what one perceives to be a system of 'ethical-ontological hierarchies in which there is subordination and violence', as Richard Bernstein understands Derrida's critique of metaphysics, would one describe this as sceptical? Are acts of desedimenting, destabilising or overturning perceived tendencies toward subordination and violence sceptical *per se*? Could we not see this as a critique that is 'primarily ethical-political', as Bernstein suggests?[27]

Secondly, McCarthy's insistence on the 'wholesale' or 'totalized' nature of Derrida's critique of reason appears inconsistent with other aspects of his account. McCarthy acknowledges that Derrida does not renounce the principle of reason, nor does he junk the concepts of Western metaphysics. As McCarthy points out, Derridean deconstruction seeks to transform or reinscribe those concepts so as to release new concepts (PI, 99–102). This does not sound like a 'wholesale' critique. When McCarthy argues that Derrida's claims, in 'The Principle of Reason', that the reduction of knowledge to 'informatization' and the intermingling of the metaphysical and the technical 'makes the principle of reason a principle of integral calculability' (PI, 104), this needs to be balanced by the final point Derrida makes (and McCarthy overlooks) at the end of the paragraph that McCarthy refers to:

All of this has to be pondered as the effect of the principle of reason, or, put more rigorously, has to be analyzed as the effect of the *dominant interpretation* of that principle, or a *certain emphasis* in the way we heed its summons.[28]

These crucial qualifications caution against any straightforward assertion about a totalised attack on reason or claims that Derrida shares Heidegger's pessimistic diagnosis of modernity, where 'Western reason is in the end *nothing more* than the subjectification and objectification in the service of domination' (PI, 110, my emphasis). Derrida's qualification suggests the possibility of an alternative interpretation or emphasis that could release a different understanding of the principle, one that would not be reducible to a principle of integral calculability.[29] Neither straightforward acceptance nor outright rejection, Derrida's approach is something other than a totalised critique or wholesale subversion.

The second half of McCarthy's argument – moves (2) and (3) – is also problematic. Recall that McCarthy charges Derridean deconstruction with sealing off 'the foundational domain reserved for philosophy' from the penetration of the human sciences, of 'withdraw[ing] philosophical thought' from any exposure to an outside (PI, 114), thereby preserving the security of philosophy from contingency and revisability. Yet Derridean deconstruction is also seen as carrying out 'a general deconstruction of philosophy' in its wholesale, totalised attack on reason, and it is precisely as part of this that the human sciences, permeated with such a philosophical discourse, are to be rejected according to McCarthy's reading (PI, 104, 113). Is Derrida preserving or attacking philosophical discourse? If it is the former, then it is not clear why the mere presence of such a discourse in the human sciences is a reason to reject them nor why Derrida is charged with a 'totalized' critique (PI, 113). If it is the latter, then it is not clear in what way Derrida is preserving the security of philosophical discourse. I would argue that, as we have seen above, Derrida is seeking an in-between ground where there is no simple 'either accept or reject', but instead a reworking. Just as he is reworking the relation between the transcendental and empirical, just as he is reworking the borders between philosophy and non-philosophy, so he is trying to rework the principle of reason in a way that will release alternative understandings. If this account is correct (see Chapter 3), then

Derridean deconstruction should not be understood as trying to preserve the security of philosophy against non-philosophy, of attempting a totalised critique or wholesale subversion, nor as rejecting other forms of inquiry.

The scepticism expressed by these critical voices regarding the relation between politics and deconstruction is understandable given the hesitancy Derrida himself expresses regarding the political possibilities of his work. For example, in the early 1980s Derrida responded to a question about whether the theoretical moves of deconstruction could be translated into a political praxis by saying: 'I must confess that I have never succeeded in directly relating deconstruction to existing political codes and programmes.' One of the reasons Derrida offers for this is because 'our political codes and terminologies still remain fundamentally metaphysical'.[30] Derrida says he has not succeeded (and specifically, not succeeded in 'directly' doing so), but there is nothing to say that a reworking of existing political codes is not possible. If Derrida's work, as I have argued in the previous chapter, aims at reworking those codes in an attempt to release new concepts and thus the possibility of new perspectives, then the claim that because Derrida takes political concepts to be metaphysical deconstruction is rendered politically speechless would be too quick. Returning to the comments above, Derrida says that the reason for the lack of success is because such codes 'remain' 'fundamentally' metaphysical. The possibility of reworking these codes in a way that releases new concepts that no longer remain so fundamentally marked by metaphysics is not ruled out, however hesitant Derrida may be about its success.

I take the increasing prominence of directly political issues in Derrida's later work (on apartheid, justice, forgiveness, hospitality, immigration) as an attempt to rework existing political codes. This reworking was already under way, as I have suggested in the previous chapter, much earlier, but in a form that was, perhaps, less recognisable as political. When asked in 2005 about the political dimension to his work, Derrida responded by saying that he would like to think that his various forms of political engagement 'and the discourses that supported them were themselves in agreement . . . with the ongoing work of deconstruction'. In the same interview he goes on to explain:

> I tried to adjust a discourse or a political practice to the demands of deconstruction, with more or less success, but never enough. I don't feel a divorce between my writings and my engagements, only differences of rhythm, mode of discourse, context, and so on. I am more aware of the continuity than of what has been called abroad the 'political turn' or the 'ethical turn' of deconstruction. (PM, 152)[31]

Although I have tried to counter the withdrawal charge, there are difficulties, brought out by these critical readings, which still remain. When McCarthy stresses that deconstruction needs to be complemented by some kind of constructive practice (PI, 107), and that 'Derrida rarely mentions this side of the ledger' (PI, 110), he raises an important point.[32] Where I differ with McCarthy on this issue is whether deconstruction *could* say something about this side of the ledger. McCarthy seems to think not. Because he sees Derrida as engaged in a totalised critique of reason and wholesale sceptical subversion, McCarthy thinks that Derrida is unable to say anything on this score (PI, 96, 106, 110, 112, 113, 118). This is a common charge from critical theorists, as we have seen. Although I have argued that the analysis that leads to this conclusion should be resisted, this does not mean that the conclusion itself is unwarranted. Indeed, thinkers more sympathetic to deconstruction, including Richard Rorty, Ernesto Laclau and Martin Hägglund, arrive at a similar conclusion. When McCarthy concludes that Derrida's work 'points us in no *particular* direction' (PI, 117) he is joined by Ernesto Laclau. 'Theoretical and political arguments that take deconstruction as their starting point', argues Laclau, 'can go in *many* directions, democracy being just one of them.'[33]

Although Laclau disagrees with Rorty and the thinkers discussed above (he thinks that deconstruction is useful for political purposes), he agrees with them that deconstruction does not provide any ethico-political injunction. I shall respond to Laclau's account by arguing that his overly structuralist reading of deconstruction crucially overlooks Derrida's rearticulation of the concept of experience and his emphasis on the 'ordeal' of undecidability. By reconstructing the former and unpacking the latter, I hope to show that the 'experience of undecidability' should not be understood as a mere openness, as Laclau and others suggest. Rather, I argue that the experience of undecidability is better understood as a crucial aspect of our basic ethical experience of trying to respond justly to the other as other. The kind of demands that flow from this, and the kind of political direction it points towards, will be taken up in the following chapter.

II. Laclau: A Directionless Deconstruction?

Not only has Laclau had a long-standing engagement with deconstruction, but, as Geoffrey Bennington notes, his work (along with Mouffe's) 'is arguably the only political theory as such to have engaged seriously with Derrida's work'.[34] Although Laclau's engagement goes right back to *Hegemony and Socialist Strategy*, here I concentrate on two essays in which Laclau specifically addresses the question of the ethico-political significance of deconstruction (as opposed to incorporating some of its insights into his own theory of hegemony).

Laclau attempts to offer an 'optimistic reading' of Derrida that seeks to bring out the possibility of 'rethinking . . . politics in a deconstructive fashion' (TJ, 81–2), while still raising a number of critical questions regarding the ethico-political injunctions that many see flowing from undecidability (TJ, 79), injunctions that remain 'hovering in Derrida's text' (TJ, 82). Laclau's reading brings into view two dimensions of deconstruction: the promise as a structural feature of all experience, whose openness to the coming of the other leaves it without content (TJ, 73), and the ethico-political injunction of a 'democracy to come', which Derrida links to the classical notion of emancipation (TJ, 75). While Laclau endorses the former, which does away with any teleological eschatology and reveals the terrain of structural undecidability, he is less convinced by the latter insofar as the classical notion of emancipation, which 'Derrida is not at all prepared to put . . . into question' (TJ, 75), requires the synthesis of a series of contents and is thus 'intimately connected to the teleological eschatology that Derrida is deconstructing' (TJ, 76). The problem that arises for Laclau is this: how is one to conceive the transition between the contentless openness as a general structure of experience, and the ethico-political contents of emancipation understood in terms of a democracy to come? While Laclau is not dismissing the latter, he thinks that it remains incompatible with the former. Derrida seems to want both the radical openness of a promise without content and the fulfilled ethico-political contents of the classical emancipatory project linked to democracy.

For Laclau, this problem only arises if one makes the 'illegitimate transition' from the 'ontological' position of constitutive openness and structural undecidability, to an ethico-political injunction that necessarily commits one to a democratic society (TJ, 77). 'Undecidability', argues Laclau, 'should be literally taken as that condition from which no course of action necessarily follows. This means that we should not make it the source of *any* concrete decision in the ethical or political sphere' (TJ, 78). Undecidability may give rise to 'ethico-political moves', but these may well be 'different from or even opposite to democracy to come'. Thus Laclau maintains that 'the case for totalitarianism can be presented starting from deconstructionist premises . . . either direction [democracy or totalitarianism] is equally possible' (TJ, 77). While this rules out any necessary connection to an emancipatory project or democratic ethos, it is not a denial of the 'important consequences [deconstruction has] for both ethics and politics' (TJ, 78).

But given this reading, one might wonder what kind of political consequences could there possibly be here? If deconstruction is unable to offer any proposals for particular courses of action, then all this talk of political consequences would seem confined to what Rorty called 'a never-never land of theory'.[35] While Laclau rejects any normative reading of deconstruction, unlike Fraser, McCarthy, Rorty and others, one of his key concerns is 'to present the main consequences of deconstruction . . . for politics'.[36] Deconstruction, for Laclau, 'makes possible a crucial turn in Political Theory'.[37] According to Laclau, deconstruction politicises the social by showing that the political is the instituting moment of society, a contingent act not predetermined by some underlying logic. And the flipside of this politico-discursive production of the social is that society remains structurally incomplete because ultimately no contingent act of institution is fully achievable. It remains undecidable. By widening the field of structural undecidability, deconstruction reactivates the contingent moment of decision that underlies any sedimented set of social relations, thus clearing the way for further political decisions. As Laclau puts it: 'Deconstruction is primarily a political logic in the sense that, by showing the structural undecidability of increasingly larger areas of the social, it also expands the area of operation of the various moments of political institution.'

However, Laclau is quick to add a sobering note to those wishing to get a political message out of deconstruction. The above quotation continues:

> This does not imply that . . . one can derive, from deconstructionist premises, a decision about concrete political arrangements in a particular situation . . . Theoretical and political arguments that take deconstruction as their starting point can go in *many* directions, democracy being just one of them.[38]

By widening the terrain of structural undecidability, deconstruction is unable to furnish one with any particular ethico-political injunction. But, for Laclau, it does provide us with 'one of the most powerful tools at hand for thinking strategically' (TJ, 81–2). We can summarise Laclau's position in the following way:

1. Derrida's talk of an openness to the other that is inscribed within the very structure of experience leaves it without determinable content.
2. This is good news because (a) it does away with all teleology and eschatology and (b) it reactivates the contingency of sedimented practices, thereby extending the terrain of structural undecidability to larger areas of social relations.
3. Because undecidability is inherent in constitutive openness, the kind of political moves that take place on this undecidable terrain cannot be determined by any ethico-political injunction.
4. Therefore, from deconstruction one cannot derive an ethico-political imperative to be committed to democracy. Deconstruction leaves the field wide open; one could go in a totalitarian just as much as a democratic direction.

I think point 3 misconceives the notion of undecidability. Once we realise this, we will see that the argument that deconstruction is a neutral practice, which merely reveals a structural undecidability that points in no particular direction, does not follow. When Laclau talks of 'structural undecidability' as being 'inherent in constitutive openness' (TJ, 77), or when he describes the necessity of having to make decisions within incomplete systems, and that 'incompletion here means undecidability' (TJ, 79), he seems to see undecidability in the following two ways: (a) as a structural feature *out there* in social systems and relations and (b) as a mere openness or incompleteness. In both cases Laclau misses the emphasis Derrida places on the 'experience' of undecidability. Sensitivity to the latter casts doubt on both aspects of Laclau's understanding of undecidability, and, consequently, his mere openness thesis. Rather than being seen in these terms, deconstruction is better understood as an *experience* of undecidability, an experience that is crucial to the possibility of responding justly to the other as other.[39]

III. Reactivating the Concept of Experience

Before we begin, however, a doubt may be raised about the very appeal to the concept of experience. Surely for Derrida, the concept of 'experience' is a thoroughly metaphysical concept and one he would be reluctant to appeal to, determined as it is by the theme of presence? In *Of Grammatology*, for example, Derrida writes:

> As for the concept of experience, it is most unwieldy here . . . it belongs to the history of metaphysics and we can only use it under erasure [*sous rature*]. 'Experience' has always designated the relationship with a presence. (OG, 60)

And similarly, in 'Violence and Metaphysics', he asks: 'Has not the concept of experience always been determined by the metaphysics of presence? Is not experience always an encountering of irreducible presence?' (VM, 190). This seems particularly bad news for any account of Derrida's work that seeks to emphasise the concept of experience. In his later work, however, Derrida continually emphasises 'experience', whether it's 'the *experience* of the *perhaps*'

(PF, 67), 'the *experience* of what happens unforeseeably' (PSY, 349), 'the *experience* . . . *of the impossible*' (TOH, 45), or even 'the necessity of *experience* itself' (AP, 19).[40] What is Derrida up to here? Why does he lift the *sous rature* from the 'unwieldy' concept of experience? Why does he allow 'experience' not only to go out without being escorted by quotation marks, but to stride around in italics? What happened to the metaphysics of presence and the discipline of quotation marks that was demanded in response? In short, how does Derrida get from the 'torturous prudence' of his earlier work[41] to the claim that, '[a]s for some philosophy of "mine" . . . I prefer to speak of *experience*' (PS, 362)?[42]

Despite appearances, this emphasis on experience in the latter work is not an abrupt about-face. When Derrida opts for the word 'experience' to describe his own work, he crucially adds: 'The word experience, once dusted off and reactivated a little . . . is perhaps the one I would choose' (PS, 207). This dusting off and reactivating is already under way in the earlier work. That is to say, experience under erasure was never the whole story.

We can get a better understanding of this story of suspicion and reactivation if we take a brief detour into Derrida's engagement with Husserl. It is in response to the phenomenological attempt to uncover the universal form of experience, or the transcendentality of what Husserl terms the 'living present', that Derrida will suspect the concept of experience of failing to take into account the movement of *différance* and participating in the reduction of the trace. But, as we will see, at the very moment when Derrida raises this suspicion against the concept of experience, a 'to the extent that' introduces an opening in which the possibility of an alternative concept of experience can already be heard: 'To the extent that the concept of experience in general – and of transcendental experience, in Husserl in particular – remains governed by the theme of presence it participates in the movement of the reduction of the trace' (OG, 61–2). Despite this suspicion, the possibility of another concept of experience, opened up by this 'to the extent that', begins to emerge, a rearticulated concept of experience that Derrida will call 'experience as arche-writing'. Exploring Derrida's engagement with Husserl no doubt raises a host of issues, but my concern here is to focus on the way in which it enables one to see the transformation of the concept of experience that Derrida is attempting to bring about.[43]

Experience as arche-writing

So, firstly, why the suspicion? In *Speech and Phenomena*, Derrida argues that Husserl determines being as ideality (SP, 53). Ideality is the possibility of the indefinite repetition of what is given as an object to intuition. Such ideality is not dependent on empirical instances, but is instead constituted by the possibility of acts of repetition that secure the permanence of the object, in the sameness of its identity, to consciousness. The ideal object *is* insofar as it can be repeated as the same to a self-present consciousness. And it is precisely the non-existence or non-reality of the ideal object (it remains independent of the empirical world) which gives 'the assurance that presence to consciousness can be indefinitely repeated' (SP, 9). In this sense, ideality, requiring both the presence of the object to intuition and the self-presence of the acts which intend it, 'is the preservation or mastery of presence in repetition' (SP, 9–10). While ideality secures the repeatability of the object as the same to consciousness, Derrida argues that what makes ideality itself possible for Husserl is the living present: 'The ultimate form of ideality . . . is the *living present*' (SP, 6). The living present is the inner certitude of the self relating to itself in absolute proximity, and this absolute self-relation, requiring no detour into the contingent empirical realm, is what ensures the purity of ideality. Hence, for Derrida, 'the presence of the living present' is the conceptual foundation of Husserlian phenomenology (SP, 99). It is only in the experience of the immediate self-relation of the living present, the self-presence of transcendental life, that the 'absolute beginning' of the phenomenological unfolding of what presents itself in intuition finds its source of 'authority'.[44] That is to say, Husserl's 'principle of principles', the foundation for a phenomenological understanding of experience, is itself founded upon the self-presence of the living present. Thus, Derrida writes: 'The universal form of all experience (*Erlebnis*) and therefore of all life has always been and will always be the present' (SP, 53).

There are two things to note here. Firstly, although Derrida is suspicious of the concept of experience, he is equally suspicious of what he calls the '"naïve" critiques of experience' (OG, 60). There is no suggestion of simply dropping this concept, but rather of rearticulating it. And if one is going to do so, then, as he will say later, the 'word experience itself would have to refer to another concept' (PF, 67). However, this is already under way in Derrida's earlier work. Some eleven lines after telling us in *Of Grammatology* that 'the concept of experience ... belongs to the metaphysics of presence and we can only use it under erasure', Derrida refers, without quotation marks and under no erasure, to 'experience as arche-writing' (OG, 60–1). Arche-writing is a 'new concept' that Derrida introduces five pages earlier, linking it to a 'formidable difference' that 'breache[s] living speech *from within and from the very beginning*' (OG, 56–7, my emphasis). Before I outline what is at stake in Derrida's notion of arche-writing, we can already see that 'experience as arche-writing' is referring 'experience' to another concept, a concept that seeks to reveal within the metaphysics of presence a difference that would breach the immediacy of any self-relation or pure presence, not as some belated empirical accident from without, but 'from within and from the very beginning'.

We shall see why Derrida thinks this is so. However, we can anticipate this a little if we focus for a moment on 'arche-writing'. By referring experience to 'arche-writing', Derrida is seeking to generalise the difference, mediation and non-presence associated with writing (in the everyday sense) to the possibility of any appearing or presenting as such. That is to say, by rearticulating experience as arche-writing, Derrida is going to argue that all experience is conditioned by these features that are seen as characterising writing. The 'writing' in arche-writing refers us to difference and non-presence, while the 'arche' seeks to emphasise that these are not derivative of some pure presence, but are in fact 'originary'. This is clear from the 1968 essay 'Différance', where Derrida introduces arche-writing through a discussion of signification:

> [T]he movement of signification is possible only if each so-called 'present' element ... appearing on the scene of presence, is related to something other than itself, thereby keeping within itself the mark of the past element, and already letting itself be

vitiated by the mark of its relation to the future element, this trace being related no less to what is called the future than to what is called the past, and constituting what is called the present by means of this very relation to what it is not ... An interval must separate the present from what it is not in order to be itself, but this interval that constitutes it as present must, by the same token, divide the present in and of itself, thereby also dividing, along with the present, everything that is thought on the basis of the present ... And it is this constitution of the present, as an 'originary' and irreducibly nonsimple (and therefore, *stricto sensu* nonoriginary) synthesis of marks ... that I propose to call arche-writing. (M, 13; cf. OG, 56)

These themes will be explored shortly when we take up the discussion of Husserl in *Speech and Phenomena*. What I want to highlight here is the move Derrida is making with the introduction of arche-writing: it is an attempt to show that the difference and non-presence associated with writing conditions every experience 'from the beginning'. In making this 'experience as arche-writing' move, Derrida is claiming that difference and non-presence are not to be understood as a modification of a simple presence, but as that through which presence itself appears.

Secondly, just as Derrida is not simply dropping the concept of experience but rearticulating it, likewise he is not trying to do away with any notion of presence; rather, he is trying to rethink it. One need only recall the discussion of the egoity of experience in 'Violence and Metaphysics' to realise this:

For egological life has as its irreducible and absolutely universal form the living present. There is no experience which can be lived other than in the present. The *absolute impossibility* of living other than in the present, this eternal impossibility, defines the unthinkable as the limit of reason. (VM, 165, my emphasis; cf. N, 16)

Thus there is no simple rejection of 'presence'. Indeed, there would be no experience without this form. An experience beyond the presence of the 'living present' would be unthinkable given that the

'I am' is, as Husserl says, 'the primordial intentional foundation of my world' (cited in VM, 164). While my experience lived outside the form of presence would be impossible, this does not mean that experience can only be thought on the basis of a pure, simple self-presence. Derrida's reference to 'experience as arche-writing' is the first indication of a possible rearticulation of experience that simultaneously seeks to transform the notion of presence from 'within'.

As we have seen with the empirical/transcendental, non-philosophy/philosophy distinctions, Derrida's deconstructive move is not simply to reject concepts, but rather to put them to work otherwise with the aim of intervening in the discourse of which they are part. Deconstruction is a transformation from within. As he writes in *Of Grammatology*:

> Of course, it is not a question of 'rejecting' these notions; they are necessary and, at least at present, nothing is conceivable for us without them. It is a question at first of demonstrating the systematic and historical solidarity of the concepts and gestures of thought that one often believes can be innocently separated. (OG, 13)

When Derrida takes up concepts like 'democracy' and 'writing' and reworks them as 'democracy to come' and 'arche-writing', for example, an attempt is being made to unsettle the heritage to which they belong, not in order to destroy that heritage (otherwise why hold on to the old terms at all?), but in order that one may 'designate the crevice through which the yet unnameable glimmer beyond the closure [of that particular heritage or discourse] can be glimpsed' (OG, 13, 24).[45] In other words, deconstruction operates within a heritage or discourse and uses the resources within it to make appear those crevices through which a new way of thinking that tradition can come about.

Returning to the concept of experience, we can see this transformation from within in *Speech and Phenomena*, where the rearticulation of experience as arche-writing will attempt to 'make appear' an 'irreducible nonpresence . . . or nonself-belonging of the living present' (SP, 7). Here it will not be a question of rejecting experience or dismissing presence. Indeed, as Leonard Lawlor perceptively notes, it would seem that the whole labour here would be aiming 'precisely to bring something to presence, to an experience, for us'. The aim is to carry out a mutual rearticulation and transformation of both that will help us 'recognise' the 'irreducible void' of non-presence 'on the basis of which the security of presence is decided and raised up'.[46] What Derrida is concerned with here is to make appear the 'nonpresence and difference at the heart of self-presence' (SP, 15).

We can see this in Derrida's discussion of Husserl's claim that in the silent soliloquy of inner life we do not communicate or indicate anything to ourselves for our meaning-acts and expressions 'are themselves experienced by us at that very moment [*im selben Augenblick*]' (cited SP, 49). Here Husserl is attempting to exclude from the inner monologue of solitary mental life mediation, alterity, difference, non-presence – in short, all that is implied by the term 'indication' – in order to hold on to the unmediated self-presence of lived experience, thereby securing the purity of ideality and the inner certitude of transcendental experience. By arguing that the sign is always already caught up in a structure of repetition and re-presentation, which is not a reduplication that befalls a simple presence but is itself primordial (SP, 7, n. 6), and that the 'very moment' of the 'now' of the living present is composed 'essentially and indispensably' with the 'not-now' of retention and protention (SP, 64), Derrida is attempting to show that the self-presence of the living present, the identity of experience instantaneously present to itself, does not happen to be contingently affected by re-presentation and non-presence, but is constituted through them.

This seems to be suggested by Husserl's own account of inner time consciousness (SP, 65). John Caputo summarises this:

> For the now is not altogether now . . . is not self-identity, pure and simple. Instead, in virtue of his own doctrine of retention, Husserl insists that now must be continuously compounded with [not-]now . . . presence with non-presence, in order to make up . . . the present . . . which is a protential-retentional synthesis. This means that the present depends on the function of representation, of retentional making present again . . . Here representation makes presence possible . . .[47]

Just as presentation is already worked by a trace structure of re-presentation, so the retentional-protential traces of the 'not-now' require the re-presentational synthesis that makes up the 'now'. If this is so, then 're-presentation belongs by essence to every experience' and non-presence and alterity insinuate themselves ineradicably at the core of living consciousness (SP, 68). This irreducible interweaving of the now and not-now, this 'dialectic' of presence and non-presence, 'open[s] up living to difference, and constitute[s], in the pure immanence of experience, the *divergence* involved in indicative communication and even signification in general' (SP, 69).[48] What begins to 'appear', then, is a concept of experience which cannot be thought on the basis of a simple self-presence or self-identity, but as emerging through the trace structure of re-presentation and the movement of *différance* it introduces – what Derrida calls '[t]his arche-writing' (SP, 85).

This reference to arche-writing, echoing the 'experience as arche-writing' remark in *Of Grammatology*, does not mean that Derrida is concerned only with the system of linguistic differences and traces. If this were the case, one would still be faced with the question that Derrida himself raises: 'But can one not conceive of a presence, and of a presence to itself of the subject before speech and signs, a presence to itself of the subject in a silent and intuitive consciousness?' (M, 16). Derrida's answer is 'no': 'this arche-writing is at work at the origin of sense' (SP, 85). Derrida's point here is not simply that the speaking subject, whether it be in dialogue with another or the inner discourse with oneself, could not be present to itself without inscribing itself within a system of linguistic differences or indicative detours, but the deeper point that the presence to itself of the subject, the self-identity of living consciousness itself, emerges through the movement of *différance* and not the reverse. 'This movement of différance', writes Derrida, 'is not something that happens to a transcendental subject; it produces a subject' (SP, 82). While experience would be impossible outside the form of presence, presence itself is constituted through the trace structure and movement of *différance*. The experience of presence and self-identity would thus be an experience of the trace and alterity. This 'irreducible void', as Derrida referred to it above, is nothing other than arche-writing:

> [I]t is this constitution of the present, as an 'originary' and irreducibly nonsimple (and therefore, *stricto sensu* nonoriginary) synthesis or marks, or traces of retentions and protentions . . . that I propose to call arche-writing . . . or *différance*. (M, 13)

In rearticulating experience as arche-writing, Derrida is attempting to make appear 'an irreducible non-presence or nonself-belonging of the living present' (SP, 6), the divergence of the movement of *différance* that opens up the pure immanence of experience to reveal the alterity 'at the heart of self-presence' (SP, 15).

Experience as interruption

This rearticulation of the concept of experience opens up the way for Derrida to redeploy this concept in later work. No longer understood simply in terms of a metaphysics of presence, 'experience' now comes to be understood as that which opens up self-sameness and self-identity to difference and alterity. No longer requiring the constraints of quotation marks, experience now comes to be understood as a passage to those 'undecidable' moments variously described as 'the aporia', 'the impossible', 'the perhaps', 'the event' and so forth. What I want to focus on here is what I shall call experience as interruption.

We can begin to approach this by turning to a remark from one of Derrida's later essays, where he rather bluntly writes: 'The event ought to *happen* to someone . . . who is thus affected by it . . . No event without *experience* (and this is basically what 'experience' means)' (WA, 72). Experience is here linked to the event which happens to a subject and affects that subject. The passive language is not by chance. What is being emphasised here is the unforeseeable arriving of the event that interrupts the order of what is presently possible, familiar, and under the mastery of a subject. This is an interruption that happens to a subject, beyond its control and mastery. Before we begin to approach this 'experience as interruption' I want to avoid a possible confusion. Talk of interruption, of 'happening to', would seem to presuppose an already existing subject simply present to itself and this was something that the rearticulation of experience as arche-writing sought to question. Hence, we need to get clear about the order of priority.

To recall, what 'experience as arche-writing' seeks to show is that just as there is no linguistic meaning without the indicative detour through the mediation of the sign, likewise there is no subjectivity, no self-relation, without the movement of *différance*. As Derrida puts it:

> The movement of *différance* is not something that happens to a transcendental subject; it produces a subject. Auto-affection is not a modality of experience that characterizes a being that would already be itself (*autos*). It produces sameness as self-relation within self-difference; it produces sameness as the nonidentical. (SP, 82)

That is to say, difference and non-presence do not come to befall some pre-existing subject relating to itself in a pure auto-affection. Rather, subjectivity issues forth through the differing and deferring (*différance*) that opens up the experience of auto-affection. Experience as interruption needs to be understood as part of this story. Derrida's reactivation of the concept of experience in terms of 'experience as arche-writing' attempts to make appear the constitutive difference and nonself-belonging at the heart of self-identity. But this attempt to 'make appear' also involves the attempt to show that the alterity within self-presence does not appear. As Derrida emphasises: 'All the concepts of metaphysics . . . *cover up* the strange "movement" of this difference' (SP, 85; cf. OG, 43, 166). Through the concept of pure auto-affection, for example, the immediate presence to itself of the subject is taken as a primordial starting point and what this covers over is that subjectivity is itself an effect of the movement of *différance*: 'The concept of *subjectivity* belongs . . . to the order of the *constituted*', as Derrida puts it (SP, 84, n. 9; cf. M, 16–17). Experience as interruption is to be understood as an interruption of *the assurance* of a subject that takes itself to be immediately given to itself in a pure interiority of ownness. It is an interruption in the sense that it makes appear the more 'originary' 'experience as arche-writing', revealing the subject's dependency on difference, mediation, the outside world; in short, my irreducible exposure to who or what is other. It is precisely this vulnerability to the who or what is other that will prompt Derrida to describe this experience

– as an event that interrupts – as 'traumatic' (FL, 27; FWT, 52–3; GD, 5; PS, 362; SM, 127; WA, 241).

We can begin to understand this traumatic interruption through David Wood's 'The Experience of the Ethical'. In an insightful argument that goes via Heidegger's thinking of ethics as a dwelling that preserves (and this notion of preserving will become very important) the disruptive experience of the unfamiliar (Gods) in the familiar (hearth), Wood understands Derrida to be reworking this account through an understanding of experience as that which interrupts the domesticated at-homeness and mastery of the subject. This interruption is experienced through the unforeseeable visitation of the *arrivant* (the arriving of who or what is other). Although Wood does not refer to it in these terms, the way he describes this interruption captures what I have been emphasising: 'an experience in which the forces of difference constitutive of any . . . identity or presence are activated and acknowledged'.[49] Having followed the rearticulation of the concept of experience (as arche-writing) through his engagement with Husserl, we can now see what this reactivation involves. What is reactivated through this experience as interruption is the constitutive difference and nonself-belonging at the heart of self-identity, the 'experience as arche-writing' that is concealed beneath the security of self-presence. Through this experience as interruption, the unfamiliar erupts into the domain of the familiar, disrupting the domesticated security and at-homeness of the subject. It is for this reason that Derrida writes: 'An event [and here we can now read experience] is always traumatic' (WA, 136).

Although we do not get any phenomenological account of experience as interruption, in the way, for example, that we do get a phenomenological description of 'experience as arche-writing' in Derrida's discussion of hearing oneself speak (SP, chapter 6), this reference to 'traumatic' may point the way a little. Pausing for a moment to see what this might entail will prove useful in bringing out what many readings of Derrida, and Laclau's in particular, seem to miss.

At first sight this reference to trauma may seem a little odd. It is repeated a little later when, discussing Paul de Man's association of the unforeseeability of the event with the suffering of the subject, Derrida goes on to radicalise de Man's point:

By reason of the unforeseeability, this irreducible and inappropriable exteriority for the subject of experience, every event as such is *traumatic*. Even an event experienced as a 'happy' one ... An event is traumatic or it does not happen. (WA, 159; cf. ARSS, 96)

No doubt this is a rather idiosyncratic use of the word 'trauma'. One can hardly imagine a 'happy' trauma. One way of understanding Derrida's generalising of 'trauma' here is to see it as an attempt to bring out the sense in which, for an event to arrive, one must be exposed to an outside, vulnerable to an unforeseeable arriving that is beyond one's control or mastery, such that the subject of this experience is disturbed (WA, 159; AP, 12; PF, 68; RS, 152). In 'disturb' one can hear not only interruption but also dispossession,[50] and in both a relation to an outside, to the coming of a who or what, is implied. Saying that an event is traumatic in that it disturbs is to suggest an experience of interruption and dispossession; an arriving that throws into disorder my subjectivity.

Understood in terms of the disturbing arrival of the other, one can make sense of a 'happy' trauma. 'When love arrives', writes Derrida, 'one is exposed' (FWT, 60). Part of the experience of love is an experience of being disarmed, exposed and disturbed by the other. Here one can turn to a brief passage in David Velleman's 'Love as Moral Emotions'. Velleman points to this being-exposed of love when he describes love as that which 'arrests our tendencies toward emotional self-protection from another person, tendencies to draw ourselves in and close ourselves off from being affected by him. Love disarms our emotional defenses; it makes us vulnerable to the other.'[51] When Velleman talks of being 'arrested' or 'disarmed' by this experience, he seems to be pointing to a certain loss of mastery that I have been highlighting in the deconstructive account. We can see this by the way in which Velleman's phenomenological description of love changes the perspective through which one understands this experience: from a perspective which would see love as an impulse or inclination issuing from a subject out towards the loved object, to one where the subject is affected by something, taken by surprise, and thrown into a state similar to 'amazement or awe'.[52] Although not expressed in precisely these terms, what Velleman seems to be describing here is an arriving that not only interrupts a subject (and any attempt to close oneself off from the other), but is experienced, if we are to take amazement literally, as a loss of self-possession. This switch of perspective (from the active going forth of the subject to the passivity of the arriving of the other) seems to be further underlined when Velleman maintains that what we ordinarily take to be our motives are in fact the 'independent responses that love merely unleashes' (recall that for Derrida the other is the who or what that arrives). Hence, love 'lays us open' not only to feelings of attraction and sympathy, but to hurt and resentment. This laying open and unleashing suggests an experience of arriving and vulnerability, a disturbing of the self that is beyond the mastery of the subject. As Iris Murdoch put it, with the arrival of love 'the centre of significance is suddenly ripped out of the self' and one 'is shocked into an awareness of an entirely separate reality'.[53] In other words, love is a 'traumatic' experience.

Understood in this way, 'trauma' is not referring to the particular contents of an event or a particular effect of a particular cause. Rather, trauma would name the very being-exposed of the subject. When Derrida describes the experience of love as one where 'the other . . . disturbs or effects [sic] my own property, my own relation to myself' (ROD, 25), it is not particular unhappy experiences of love that make this disturbance traumatic; rather, it is the fact that one is exposed, vulnerable, 'without protection' (AP, 12) to disturbance as such (FWT, 58). Here one could be 'happily vulnerable' (FWT, 53). The 'trauma' of experience as interruption, then, can be understood in terms of this being-exposed to a disturbance beyond one's control or mastery, what Derrida describes as 'a vulnerable exposure to what arrives' (N, 363).

Having fleshed out experience as interruption, we see that although it may initially suggest a pre-existing subject in an undisturbed realm of interiority that subsequently comes to be affected by an external difference, it is better understood as that which interrupts the security of self-presence and 'makes appear' the constitutive difference at the heart of self-identity. That is to say, experience as interruption reveals a subject that is always already interrupted and forever exposed to a 'traumatic' arriving.

If I have interpreted this rearticulated concept of experience (as arche-writing and interruption) correctly, one may still wonder what follows from this reactivation. Above I touched on Wood's suggestion that the significance of this lay in the activation and acknowledgement of the constitutive difference at the heart of self-identity, and it is here that we can begin to see the stakes involved. I take Derrida's earlier work to involve the attempt to activate this constitutive difference through 'experience as arche-writing', while I take his later work, on what I have called experience as interruption, as an attempt to bring about an acknowledgement of this difference that is in some way transformative. Acknowledgement would involve what Wood describes as the formation of 'certain complex dispositions, ways of remembering, bearing witness to . . . the significance of such experience'.[54] This is a crucial observation and something that is overlooked in the kind of reading Laclau offers. In his focus on structural undecidability, Laclau misses the importance of Derrida's rearticulation of experience. Once we understand this rearticulation of experience, we can no longer think of the 'experience of undecidability' as merely a structural moment that makes way for the decision that follows. Rather, it is meant to be transformative. Before taking this up in the next chapter, I want to clarify what Derrida means by 'undecidability', because there is an aspect to this, crucial to the account I am offering, that is overlooked in most readings of Derrida.

IV. Understanding Undecidability

In the previous section I unpacked Derrida's rearticulation of 'experience' in terms of, firstly, reactivating the difference at the heart of self-presence through the rearticulation of experience as arche-writing, and, secondly, attempting to make this difference appear through the disturbing arriving of the other, understood in terms of experience as interruption. This is the first step in clarifying what Derrida means by the 'experience' of undecidability. In this section, I shall turn to the concept of 'undecidability' and attempt to bring out three things. First, there is a specific understanding of undecidability as an ordeal that is crucially overlooked by most readings of Derrida. Second, this notion of an ordeal relates undecidability to the rearticulation of the concept of experience. Third, the ordeal of undecidability is the necessary experience for the possibility of responding justly to the other as other. This may not seem immediately obvious if we understand undecidability to be limited to the claim that no rule or norm can specify its application in a particular case. No doubt this is an aspect of undecidability. But this does not capture Derrida's insistence that undecidability is an 'ordeal' that one must go through (FL, 24; GD, 5; SM, 75; WA, 241). Accordingly, I shall unpack the concept of undecidability, firstly, in terms of a formal account of having to decide without the assurance of a pre-existing rule and, secondly, in terms of an ordeal we must undergo. I shall then argue that without the ordeal of undecidability there would be no ethical decision. Finally, I show that this ordeal presupposes 'experience as interruption'.

Undecidability as a formal moment of any decision

Although often taken to imply indecisiveness or paralysing uncertainty, undecidability figures in Derrida's work as part of an analysis of the concept of decision.[55] Rather than being something that is opposed to the taking of a decision, undecidability emerges as the condition of any decision. I am not going to explore the radical version of this account in any great detail, but shall instead focus on how Derrida brings it to bear on ethico-political decisions.

In 'Force of Law' one of the things that Derrida seeks to show is that the relation between law and justice is undecidable because 'the decision between just and unjust is never insured by a rule' (FL, 16). If a decision were insured by a pre-existing rule that one merely applies in a given situation, then, for Derrida, we might say that such a decision is legal, that it conforms to law, but not that it is just. For a decision to be a just decision, there must be a moment where there is an 'épokhè of the rule' (FL, 22), a moment where the law is suspended and a 'fresh judgement' that 're-invents' the law emerges (FL, 17, 23).[56] This claim emerges from Derrida's more general account of decision, which can be summarised as follows. Insofar as being just or exercising justice presupposes freedom and responsibility, a just decision must exceed the order of the calculable. Why? Because a decision that would be calculable, that would be determined simply by the application of a pre-existing rule offering guarantees and assurances, such that I would know what is to be done in a given situation, 'would not be, in the rigorous sense of the term, an act of responsibility or freedom' (N, 200). Instead, Derrida claims, it would be the 'unfolding of a programme' (ROD, 20) or the 'effecting of a calculation' (FL, 23).[57] And given that a decision presupposes freedom and responsibility, and given that the latter would be incompatible with the mere application of a rule or norm, for there to be a decision there must be a moment that is discontinuous with the order of the calculable. As Derrida puts it:

> If I know what is to be done, if my theoretical analysis of the situation shows me what is to be done . . . then there is no moment of decision, simply the application of a body of knowledge, of, at the very least, a rule or norm. For there to be a decision, the decision must be heterogeneous to knowledge as such . . . [o]therwise, there is no responsibility. (N, 231)

A similar point is made in his later work:

> Whenever I have at my disposal a determinate rule, I know what must be done, and as soon as knowledge dictates the law, action follows knowledge as a calculable consequence: one *knows* what path to take . . . The decision then no longer decides anything but is made in advance and is thus annulled in advance . . . There is no longer any place for justice or responsibility. (RS, 85)

If there is to be a decision, then there must be a moment where one is no longer following the consequence of some determinate knowledge or rule, a 'leap' that 'takes off' and 'frees itself' from any calculable process, since it is here that one's freedom and responsibility is engaged (PF, 69, 219; cf. ARSS, 133; FWT, 53; N, 200). Such a leap is the 'structurally necessary moment' of undecidability within the very concept of decision (FL, 20; cf. LI, 116).

But this formal account of undecidability seems to return us to the kind of reading that Laclau offers. While Derrida is engaged in giving such an account – at various moments he reminds us of this: 'All that I am saying here is nothing but the modest analysis of the concept of decision', an analysis which points to something in 'the very structure of any decision' (N, 232) – his insistence on the 'ordeal' of undecidability goes beyond this. 'Ordeal' suggests a trying, protracted experience that one undergoes, and this is what Laclau's structural reading leaves out. Undecidability without the ordeal gives us only half of the story. If we were to see undecidability simply in terms of the structural reading, then one would be left wondering why this should be understood as an 'ordeal' at all. Derrida leaves us with work to do here for we never get any fully worked out account of what kind of experience 'ordeal' is referring us to. However, a brief look at the way in which Derrida characterises the moment of decision does suggest that, unlike 'trauma', 'ordeal' is pointing to a difficult experience. There is no happy ordeal. I also hope to show that a particular understanding of undecidability, which is not captured in the structural account, is also suggested.[58]

The ordeal of undecidability: 'I am not here to reassure anyone'[59]

Derrida tells us that the moment of decision, of making the leap, is an 'anxiety ridden moment' (FL, 20), a 'madness' in which we find ourselves confronted with a 'terrible choice' (ROD, 11; N, 195) and the necessity of having to act in a 'night of non-knowledge and non-rule' (FL, 26). Here, at the 'crossroads of chance and necessity' (PF, 30), we are 'given over in darkness to the exception of singularity without rule' (PF, 219), to a 'test' or 'endurance' (AP, 19; DE, 63; GD, 5), where we are 'never at peace' but continually 'haunted' by the possibility that we have gone wrong (ROD, 20, 11; PF, 219). Alone in this darkness, faced with decisions 'that I alone will have to answer for' (GD, 91), there are no principles, no system or dialectical story, that can conjure away the 'ghost of the undecidable' and relieve me of this ordeal (FL, 24). Here 'remorse' – understood not in terms of self-accusation but in the sense of 'never being happy with the decision' – is 'irreducible'. As Derrida rather darkly puts it: 'A decision has to be paid for' (ROD, 23).[60]

This is a disquieting picture. Is Derrida offering nothing more than the modest analysis of the concept of decision? Is this the only story that one could tell of the moment of decision? From the account of undecidability as the structurally necessary moment of making a leap that breaks with existing laws and rules, must we necessarily undergo such an ordeal? Could we not experience this leap as a moment of freedom, where a space opens up for creative acts that break free of determined laws and structures? Indeed, would not this moment of deciding without any determining ground be, as Laclau puts it, 'like impersonating God'?[61] And, if so, might we not experience this as an exhilarating moment of freedom, a moment 'we mortal gods' relish?[62] To say that a decision requires freedom and responsibility, and that one must exceed the order of the calculable to exercise the latter, only licenses the claim that a decision requires the undecidable moment of an incalculable leap. Something more is needed for the further claim that such a leap is experienced as an ordeal. If we are to make sense of undecidability as an ordeal, we cannot remain with the structural account.

In trying to clarify how the notion of 'ordeal' functions in Derrida's account of undecidability, two readings are possible. The first, more radical reading would be to say that the ordeal of the undecidable, understood in terms of the kind of disquieting experience characterised above, is what any decision must go through. The second, more restricted reading would be to say that such an ordeal is the condition of not just *any* decision, but rather of any *just* decision. That is to say, it is only once we are confronted with an ethical or political decision that the undecidability that attends any decision is experienced as an ordeal. Although Derrida at times seems to suggest the former, as far as I can tell he never really provides an argument as to why every decision would be an ordeal.[63] Furthermore, if we were to go for radical reading it would be hard to avoid the charge of 'dramatising our difficulties'.[64] Adapting a remark from Sartre, we would not want to say that whenever I choose between a millefeuille and a chocolate éclair I go through an ordeal.[65]

So it seems there are good reasons to go with the restricted reading and understand 'ordeal' not as a structurally necessary moment of any decision, but as the necessary experience one undergoes when trying to respond justly to the other. If we take the attempt to respond justly to the other as our basic ethical experience, then the ordeal of undecidability would be the condition of such experience. This would suggest that, in order to regard ourselves as ethical agents, we must see ourselves through this ordeal of undecidability. More than a mere polemic response to ethico-political surety, Derrida's description of the ordeal of undecidability seeks to 'make appear' an experience that is not some local imperfection or mistake that we could put right or free ourselves from, but a basic state for an ethical subject. Prior to responding to the demand to do justice to the other, one must experience oneself as one who is vulnerable to the aporias revealed by the ordeal, for it is this that opens up a space for ethics, what we might call a pre-ethical space of ethics. As Derrida insists: 'we must not hide it [the aporia] from ourselves. I will even venture to say that ethics, politics, and responsibility . . . will only ever have begun with the experience . . . of the aporia' (TOH, 41).

The reason for thinking that the 'ordeal' of undecidability is the necessary experience of any just decision is that justice, according to Derrida, concerns the 'singularity' of irreplaceable lives in a unique situation, a situation that is always different and always in need of a 'fresh judgement'. Such a judgement or decision is one 'which no existing, coded rule can or ought to guarantee absolutely' (FL, 23). If a judge merely follows a rule that guarantees her decision, then such a judge would, according to Derrida, be a sort of 'calculating machine' (FL, 23), subsuming cases to the generality of a given law and missing the 'singularity of the decision that has to be made' (PS, 359). Here we would be in the order of the calculable, not the 'irreplaceably singular' situation of justice (LI, 148). A just decision is, in this sense, incalculable.

Now this might still leave us with the exhilarating freedom of the incalculable leap referred to above. Indeed, talk of a leap, and especially talk of a leap that 'would liberate one' (N, 181), does lend itself to the 'exhilarating freedom' interpretation. If this is what Derrida means, then he would seem to have made the same mistake as Kierkegaard's dancer who confuses being able to leap very high with the ability to fly.[66] While the latter suggests a 'being emancipated from telluric conditions', the former is 'the accomplishment of a being essentially earthly, one who respects the earth's gravitational forces'. Derrida, however, is not assuming the privilege of 'winged creatures'. Although he insists that a just decision demands a leap that exceeds the order of the calculable, he is not suggesting that one simply abandon all rules whatsoever. While (on this account) we would not describe someone who merely applies pre-existing rules or laws to cases as making a just or responsible decision, neither would we do so, Derrida maintains, if one makes no reference to any law or rule. The claim is not that one must decide without rules, but that one must decide by exceeding rules without assurance or certainty (PS, 360). Exceeding does not equal destroying. A just decision, then, is not one that destroys all rules – it 'is not the absence of rules' – for in the moment of suspending law or rules what would allow us to call a decision just? (AD, 117; FL, 26).

Indeed, the moment of suspension leaves itself open to the threat of 'the most perverse calculation' and so although a just decision requires a leap that exceeds law and calculation, it simultaneously requires calculation (FL, 28). Here we encounter the aporia. For a decision to be just it must be both 'regulated and without regulation' (FL, 23). It must be without regulation so that the decision that responds to the singular other is not neutralised in advance by the mechanical application of a rule, but it must also be regulated insofar as a just decision must take account of existing laws and rules so as not to be left to arbitrary improvisations that can always be close 'to the worst'. And so 'incalculable justice *requires* us to calculate' (FL, 28). It is here, in this obligation to calculate the incalculable, that the 'ordeal' of the undecidable emerges. As Derrida puts it:

> The undecidable is not merely the oscillation . . . between two decisions; it is the experience of that which, though heterogeneous, foreign to the order of the calculable and the rule, is still obligated – *it is of obligation that we must speak* – to give itself up to the impossible decision, while taking account of law and rules. A decision that did not go through the ordeal of the undecidable . . . might be legal; it would not be just. (FL, 24, my emphasis)

From this we can see that undecidability is not simply the structural necessity of making a leap that breaks with existing rules or norms, as Laclau's reading suggests. It should also be understood as the ordeal of having to respond to 'antinomic injunctions' or a 'contradictory obligation' that we unavoidably experience the moment it is a question of doing justice to the other (PS, 359, 360). Rather than a leap that liberates my possibilities from constraining laws, this understanding of undecidability demands a decision which, in needing to be both regulated and unregulated, calculable and incalculable, is one we experience as an 'im-possible' decision.[67] Paine's 'ghosts of departed wisdom' jostle with Derrida's ghosts of the undecidable.[68]

Justice as the experience of interruption

So far I have argued that although the formal account of undecidability captures an aspect of undecidability, it fails to make sense of Derrida's repeated insistence on the 'ordeal' of undecidability. I then tried to show that the latter is to be understood as the unavoidable experience of the 'antinomic injunctions' any attempt to do justice to the other places on us. Not only does this avoid the more decisionistic interpretations of the leap, but it also follows from the characterisation of justice as concerning the singularity of the other. And it is here that 'experience as interruption' is crucial.

To say that justice 'concerns the other', however, does not capture the disturbing arriving of an interruption that opens up the demands of justice. Justice concerns the other, but not simply a determinable other that could be foreseen and assigned a place in the calculable framework of a generalised system of norms or rules. Justice concerns the singularity of the other, and this singularity marks an interruption, an experience of interruption. Commenting on the word 'justice', Derrida writes: 'It is the experience of the other as other' (N, 105). To experience the other *as other* suggests an experience of interruption, for the 'as other' gestures towards a singularity which exceeds, and so interrupts, the conceptualisations, calculations and strategies of my present possibilities. Here the other, as other, is experienced as that which resists being appropriated within my current framework. In the experience of the other as other 'something incalculable comes on the scene' (VR, 17). This incalculable something, this coming of the *arrivant*, is 'experience as interruption'. Not only does Derrida maintain that '[a]s soon as justice implies a relation to the other, it supposes an interruption' (N, 230; SM, 27), he more robustly claims that there would be 'no justice without interruption' (FWT, 81). Without the interruption of an incalculable other we would remain in the ordeal-free order of applying calculable norms and conditions to an other who never appears *as other*. Here, then, the ordeal of undecidability we undergo in experiencing the antinomic injunctions of doing justice to the other is itself opened up through an experience of interruption: no justice without the ordeal of undecidability; no ordeal without experience as interruption.

In the first section of this chapter I argued that Derrida seeks to rework the empirical/transcendental relation and expose philosophy to that which it could not appropriate and master. I did so in order to counter the claim that deconstruction rejects the empirical realm of politics and withdraws into a politically disabling transcendental reflection. I then tried to correct the idea that the 'experience of undecidability' refers simply to a structural openness by showing that (1) from the early work through to the later work Derrida has been engaged in an attempt to rearticulate the concept of experience in a way that brings out the difference at the heart of self-presence and our 'traumatic' relation to the arrival of an incalculable other; that (2) there is a particular understanding of undecidability as an ordeal that (a) is a response to the experience of a conflictual obligation and so already situates us in the zone of a particular kind of ethico-political decision and (b) is the condition of our basic ethical experience of trying to respond justly to the other as other; and that (3) experience as interruption is what opens up the ordeal of undecidability and that this ordeal is necessary for the possibility of any just decision. That is to say, the possibility of doing justice to the other requires undergoing this experience. If this account is correct, then Derrida's rearticulation of the concept of experience, and his understanding of the ordeal of undecidability, are crucial to the possibility of doing justice to the other as other (something the 'withdrawal' and the 'mere openness' readings overlook). This is a crucial step in understanding Derrida's work. But it is only a step. I have yet to answer positively the question concerning the kind of demands or injunctions this account leads to, and the political direction it points us towards. Both questions will be taken up in the next chapter.

Notes

1. Scruton, 'Upon Nothing', 493. Page references in this paragraph refer to this text. I have taken the liberty of overworking Scruton's initial car analogy, which is limited to this quoted sentence.
2. Derrida, 'Mochlos; or, The Conflict of the Faculties', 22–3.
3. Critchley, *The Ethics of Deconstruction*, 189, 220.
4. Habermas, *The Philosophical Discourse of Modernity*, 181.
5. Dews, *Logics of Disintegration*, 19, 43.
6. Ibid. 37.
7. Ibid. 19.
8. Ibid. 37–8.
9. Ibid.
10. McCarthy would need to say more here. It cannot be the fact that Derrida is reading texts (or that he thinks this suffices) that is the problem. Reading texts can be a politically significant activity. One assumes that it must be the way Derrida reads texts that is the problem.
11. Thus the withdrawal charge leads to the 'mere openness' charge (which I take up in the next chapter).
12. Fraser, 'The Force of Law', 1326.
13. Ibid.
14. Ibid. 1326–7.
15. I am not saying anything here of which Dews is not aware. Dews notes that Derrida's work appears to be 'connected to a fracturing of the immanence of transcendental consciousness, its exposure to its repressed "outside"'. The difficulty that Dews identifies is that given this, why does Derrida seek to prevent any contamination between the transcendental and empirical? (Dews, *Logics of Disintegration*, 17–18). This difficulty, I suggest, may be avoided if we attend to what I perceive to be a complication of the relation between the two.
16. We can also see this move as governing the critique of phonocentrism in Derrida's early work. Derrida argues that when hearing oneself speak, the need for inscription seemingly falls away because 'the phonic substance . . . *presents itself* as the non-exterior, non-mundane therefore non-empirical or non-contingent signifier' (OG, 7). Derrida's move is to show that this apparent immateriality is inescapably marked by these very qualities and this means that the non-worldly will always be contaminated with the worldly – what we might call 'the necessity of reinscription' (Derrida, *Positions*, 77). This does not mean that Derrida does not hold on to the importance of the transcendental. However, it does mean that the nature of the transcendental itself

would be rethought and the relation between the transcendental and the empirical reorganised (see Beardsworth, *Derrida and the Political*, chapter 1). This necessity of inscription seems to be precisely what Derrida is getting at when he says: 'the only possibility for philosophy ... to speak itself ... is to pass through idioms ... to translate itself ... in the body of idioms which are not closures' but 'passages to the other' ('Onto-Theology of National Humanism', 4). Signs of this may be glimpsed even earlier in IOG where Derrida is already trying to bring out the 'paradox' of the necessary fall back into language and history which simultaneously sets free and alienates the pure ideality of sense (77). No doubt this calls for a detailed reading of IOG that cannot be carried out here. But this would involve returning to (1) Derrida's insistence on the necessity of truth being 'engraved in the world' and therefore 'exposed'; this necessity puts truth in 'danger' and here Derrida identifies a moment of empiricism that unavoidably appears (92–3), and (2) Derrida's denial of a pure univocity that would remove truth out of history's reach and his insistence on an irreducible equivocity (105). These are tentative suggestions, but, at the very least, this would suggest the need to rethink the relation between the transcendental and empirical in Derrida's earlier work in a way that already seems to be pointing to the irreducible contamination that becomes more explicit later (for example, LI, 119). As Derrida puts it: 'The historical incarnation sets free the transcendental, instead of binding it. This last notion, the transcendental, must be rethought' (IOG, 77).
17. Beardsworth, *Derrida and the Political*, 5.
18. It is necessary not 'to give up the transcendental motif' while still affirming 'the coming of the event or other' that would 'resist all reappropriation' (N, 367).
19. Derrida, 'Onto-Theology of National Humanism', 3.
20. Derrida and Kearney, 'Deconstruction and the Other', 108.
21. Derrida, *Positions*, 45; cf. 'What I call *text* is also what practically inscribes and overflows the limits of such a [philosophical] discourse. *There is* such a general text everywhere that (that is everywhere) this discourse and its order (essence, sense, truth ... ideality) are *overflowed*, that is, everywhere that their authority is put back into the position of a *mark* in a chain that this authority intrinsically and illusorily believes ... it does in fact govern' (52). Derrida explicitly sees his work as questioning the subordination of regional sciences to philosophical jurisdiction. Discussing two types of appropriating mastery of philosophy, Derrida writes: 'On the one hand, a *hierarchy*: the

particular sciences and regional ontologies are subordinated to general ontology, and then to fundamental ontology. [Derrida here inserts a footnote: 'The putting into question of this ontological subordination was begun in *Of Grammatology*.'] From this point of view, all the questions that solicit Being and the proper upset the order that submits the determined fields of science, its formal objects or materials (logic and mathematics, or semantics, linguistics, rhetoric, science of literature, political economy, psychoanalysis, etc.), to philosophical jurisdiction' (M, xix–xx). These claims form a recurring theme in Derrida's more practical interventions around the teaching of philosophy in France, particularly with the Groupe de Recherches sur l'Enseignement Philosophique (Research Group on the Teaching of Philosophy) and his work as one of the founders of the Collège International de Philosophie. Particularly relevant here would be the report 'Titles (for the Collège International de Philosophie)' where Derrida argues for a 'transversal intersection of fields of knowledge' that would involve a reciprocal transformation of disciplines. As he explains: 'the recourse to philosophy no longer takes its classical and hierarchizing form: the arbitrating of an ontological or transcendental authority . . . What is being sought now is . . . a different relation of philosophical language to other discourses (a more horizontal relation, without hierarchy . . .)' (see *Eyes of the University*, 195–215). In an interview discussing the College, Derrida insists on this: 'more philosophy is still necessary, in less hierarchically organized spaces and more exposed to the most irruptive provocations of the "sciences," of "technologies," of the "arts"' (PS, 110).

22. Indeed, one could argue that this early account of an arriving that philosophy could not reappropriate, an arriving that would unleash blows to its knowledge from an outside that could not be comprehended and interiorized by a philosophical discourse, meets up with Derrida's later rearticulation of the concept of experience as interruption (see below). In this sense, Derridean deconstruction has always been thinking in terms of exposure.

23. Similarly: 'I have tried to show how in apparently regional scientific practices, in ontologies that philosophy say are regional, one can find general deconstructive movements, where the ground falls away or shifts, disorganising or calling into question the order of dependence between a fundamental ontology and regional ontologies.' See Derrida, 'Onto-Theology of National Humanism', 8.

24. This is why Derrida resists describing deconstruction as a method that exists outside the fields and contexts in which it operates. Rather than

being a method that one simply applies to contexts, deconstruction is put to work differently by the contexts in which it operates.
25. Wolin, *The Seduction of Unreason*, 214.
26. Ibid. Fraser's reading of deconstruction appears to leave open the possibility of a deconstructive approach that may have something to say about politics.
27. Bernstein, *The New Constellation*, 176.
28. Derrida, 'The Principle of Reason', 14 (my emphasis).
29. This differentiated approach to reason seems straightforwardly asserted in the 'Principle of Reason' article that McCarthy focuses on: 'the principle of reason is not simply reason' (7). This differentiated approach to reason remains consistent throughout Derrida's work, right up until his later work (see part II of *Rogues*, for example).
30. Derrida and Kearney, 'Deconstruction and the Other', 119.
31. Cf. 'I had first of all to prepare the premises of a political discourse in harmony with the demands of deconstruction, and avoid prevailing codes and criteria that it's thought necessary to rely on for deciding whether or not a language is political. These shared codes often have a depoliticizing effect, which I try to avoid' (PM, 115).
32. Although one should be cautious about assuming that the absence of constructive proposals is, in itself, fatal to political thinking. See Adorno, 'Critique', in *Critical Models*, 281–9.
33. Laclau, 'Deconstruction, Pragmatism, Hegemony', 58.
34. Bennington, *Interrupting Derrida*, 198, n. 4.
35. Rorty, 'Universality and Truth', 24.
36. Laclau, 'Deconstruction, Pragmatism, Hegemony', 54.
37. Ibid. 48.
38. Ibid. 58.
39. In Chapter 5 I argue that not only does this point to a series of ethical injunctions, but it also points in a democratic direction. See Norval, 'Hegemony after Deconstruction'.
40. The concept of experience in Derrida's work has been overlooked by most commentators. Notable exceptions would include Norval, 'Hegemony after Deconstruction'; Wood, 'The Experience of the Ethical'; Lawlor, *Derrida and Husserl*.
41. Derrida, *Of Spirit*, 32.
42. In an interview Derrida is asked: 'If one were to try and measure your . . . route, path, adventure, experience, trajectory . . . Which one do you prefer from among all these words? Perhaps it is in fact a different one?' His reply: 'I don't know. I rather like the word experience' (PS, 207; cf. AP, 15; N, 192; SM, 35).

43. For a critical discussion of Derrida's reading of Husserl see, *inter alia*, Caputo, 'The Economy of Signs in Husserl and Derrida'; Mulligan, 'How Not to Read'; McKenna and Evans, *Derrida and Phenomenology*; Lawlor, *Derrida and Husserl*; Mooney, 'How to Read Once Again'; *Journal of the British Society for Phenomenology*, 'Husserl and Derrida Special Issue', 36:2 (2005); Schwab, 'The Fate of Phenomenology in Deconstruction'.
44. See Husserl, *Ideas: General Introduction to Pure Phenomenology*, I §24.
45. Keeping the old name serves as a 'lever of intervention' (Derrida, *Positions*, 77; cf. 39, 60).
46. Cited in Lawlor, *Derrida and Husserl*, 173.
47. Caputo, 'The Economy of Signs in Husserl and Derrida', 101.
48. While Derrida here is still using the word 'dialectic' in inverted commas, he goes on to caution that he is using this 'in every sense of the word and before any speculative subsumption of this concept' (SP, 69).
49. Wood, 'The Experience of the Ethical', 115. This immediately raises the question of what the relation is between activation and acknowledgement. The former is concerned with how the subject is constituted, the latter with how the subject takes itself to be. This is an important point and something to which I shall return.
50. *disturb, v.* 4b. *Law.* To deprive the peaceful enjoyment or possession of. (*OED*)
51. Velleman, 'Love as Moral Emotions', 361.
52. Ibid.
53. Murdoch, *Fire and the Sun*, 36.
54. Wood, 'The Experience of the Ethical', 116.
55. See Fraser, 'The French Derrideans', 65; Negri, 'The Spectre's Smile'; Žižek, *Did Somebody Say Totalitarianism?*, 152.
56. According to Derrida, this would be the case even where the decision conforms to existing law. If the decision to follow the law is to be just, then in following the law one would still need 'to assume it, approve it, confirm its value, by a reinstituting act of interpretation, as if ultimately nothing previously existed of the law, as if the judge himself invented the law himself in every case' (FL, 23).
57. See, *inter alia*, AD, 117; AP, 16, 19; ARSS, 118; FWT, 53; GD, 5, 24–6; LI, 116; N, 31, 200, 231; PS, 359–60; ROD, 34; TOH, 41, 44.
58. Derrida distinguishes at least three meanings of undecidability: (1) that which resists binarity; (2) that which limits calculability; (3) that which calls for a decision in the order of ethico-political responsibility. Most approaches to undecidability seem to remain within the second mean-

ing (what I refer to as the structural account). Limited to this second meaning, however, Derrida's insistence on the 'ordeal' of undecidability would remain inexplicably dramatic (LI, 116).
59. Derrida, 'Interview with Alan Montefiore', 13 February 1992.
60. Derrida suggests that in fact we have always, to a greater or lesser extent, gone wrong with our decision: 'A decision has to be paid for, there is always some bad consequence for even the best decision' (ROD, 23). Given Derrida's account of decision, one can see how the argument would run for the claim that a decision is always haunted by the *possibility* of going wrong, but it's not clear what support there is, from the formal account of decision, for the claim that there is always, necessarily, some bad consequence for even the best decision. I think the argument for this claim is to be found in Derrida's reading of Kierkegaard, in particular the unavoidable 'sacrifice' of my duty to 'all the others' that I, as a finite creature, necessarily carry out when responding to the singular other. In this sense, no matter how well I respond to the singular other – which would be the condition of a just decision – there is always some sacrifice, some failure regarding those other others that I have not responded to in turning to this singular other (see GD, 66–71; cf. PS, 363). For a critical response see Wood, 'Responsibility Reinscribed (and How)'.
61. Laclau, 'Deconstruction, Pragmatism, Hegemony', 54–5.
62. Ibid. 56.
63. There are moments where Derrida seems to slip between 'any decision' and any 'just decision'. For example, Derrida insists, in what appears to be a straightforward claim for the radical thesis, that a 'decision that did not go through the ordeal of the undecidable would not be a free decision, it would be . . . the unfolding of a calculable process'. However, this is immediately followed by what appears to be a limited claim, namely, 'it might be legal; it would not be just' (FL, 24).
64. Rorty, 'Response to Simon Critchley', 42.
65. See Sartre, 'Discussion', 57.
66. Kierkegaard, *Concluding Unscientific Postscript*, 112–13. The subsequent three quotations refer to this passage.
67. Derrida insists that 'im-possibility' is not to be understood negatively: 'For me, the experience of the impossible is not simply the experience of something not given in actuality, not accessible, but something through which a possibility is given' (DE, 64). I think one way of understanding this is to think of 'impossibility' not as a metaphysically robust claim that X cannot be, but rather a claim about the way in

which the possibility of X reveals itself as beyond the order of the possible, calculable; the possibility of X appears as im-possible or non-possible (see N, 358–63). As Derrida puts it in *Rogues*, the im-possible is what 'must remain (in a nonnegative fashion) foreign to the order of my possibilities . . . [but it is] not privative' (RS, 84). Insofar as a just decision becomes possible only by exceeding such an order, its possibility emerges as im-possible, as beyond the order of my possibilities. We might say that doing justice to the other is only possible if it is experienced as im-possible. If my experience of the demand to do justice to the other was along the lines of 'ok, it's possible for me to do justice in this situation by doing X', then, for Derrida I would be in the calculable order of the possible where no just decision can emerge (TOH, 45). As Derrida claims: when we deem something as possible 'it means we have already mastered, anticipated, pre-understood' it (N, 194) and this means we miss the singularity of justice. I shall return to this in the discussion of hospitality in Chapter 6. See also Gormley, 'The Impossible Demand of Forgiveness'.
68. Paine, *The Rights of Man*, 197. I shall return to this in Chapter 6.

5

The Demands of Deconstruction

In Chapter 3 I pointed to a deconstructive politics of the stage by examining the various forms of intervention in Derrida's work. Often commentators acknowledge the political positions that Derrida, the individual, has taken up, but maintain that these interventions are incompatible with the theoretical commitments of deconstruction. In Chapter 4 I attempted to respond to two key arguments that underpin this claim, what I called the 'withdrawal' and 'wholesale critique' charges. I tried to show that both are mistaken to claim that Derridean deconstruction is, as a matter of principle, disabled from engaging in politics. I also responded to what I called the 'mere openness' charge. This, I argued, misread deconstruction by suggesting that even though deconstruction may be politically useful strategically, it is not, as a matter of principle, orientated by any ethico-political injunction. Setting out Derrida's rearticulation of the concept of experience, and unpacking his account of the ordeal of undecidability, I argued that both are crucial aspects of trying to do justice to the other as other. That is to say, deconstruction is normatively orientated. A key aim of that chapter was to avoid the door being closed on deconstruction in relation to ethics and politics. The task in this chapter is to develop the account now that deconstruction has its foot in the door.

Building on the account of the experience of undecidability in the previous chapter, the first section of this chapter outlines a number of injunctions that flow from that account. In developing this, I respond in more detail to the argument that, in advocating an ethics of openness to the other, deconstruction fails to offer any normative orientation. Emphasising openness to the other, but pointing in no particular direction, deconstruction is seen as leaving us open to *any* other. In response, I argue that the injunctions of deconstruction are best thought of not in terms of openness to the other, but in terms of maintaining an ethos of interruption. It is in response to this demand that we can understand Derrida's insistence on the necessity of laws, calculation, deliberation, and the need to recognise and close off from that which would put an end to such an ethos. I suggest that the normativity of deconstruction is best understood as a form of negativism (which is not to be mistaken as negative or pessimistic). With deconstruction reconceived in terms of an ethos of interruption, the second section explores the political challenges this presents. While I show that the demand to maintain an ethos of interruption points to a democratic form of politics, I suggest that Derrida's account of democracy remains overly abstract.

I. A Quiet Conscience Sleeps through Thunder[1]

Iris Murdoch once remarked that it is 'always a significant question to ask any philosopher: what is he afraid of?'.[2] In the case of Derrida, the answer would probably be 'the worst' (I will come back to this). If Murdoch's question aims to capture something about the idiosyncratic gesture of thought that marks a particular thinker, however, I think that before we get to 'the worst', a key place to start when it comes to Derrida might be wanting or having a good conscience. It is also the place where we can begin to unpack the demands of deconstruction.

Throughout his work Derrida continually returns to good conscience and issues straightforward injunctions against it.[3] The clearest example of this is to be found in *Aporias*, where he tells us: 'one must avoid good conscience' (AP, 19). To begin to understand this we need to take a closer look at what having a good conscience implies. The *OED* defines 'good conscience' as 'a consciousness that one's acts, or one's moral state, are right'. Having a good conscience is a knowing: 'my action was right', 'I fulfilled my obligations', 'I did the just thing'. Having a good conscience, then, implies that we can be certain about our ethical decisions or state, that responding justly to the other is of the order of knowledge. This, for Derrida, is anything but responsible. Put polemically, this assurance of a good conscience reassures us that we have assumed and fulfilled our ethical responsibilities, allowing us the peace of a 'sweet sound sleep' while the thunder continues to shake the world outside.[4] I say polemically because it's clear that Derrida is engaged in a polemic. When he criticises the 'moralizing moralists and good consciences who preach to us with assurance' about ethical and political responsibility, when he reminds the 'knights of good conscience' that one cannot avoid or dissolve the conflictual obligation of doing justice to the other as other, that when it comes to our ethical experience we are all inhabitants of the 'land of Moriah' every second of every day (GD, 67–9), the rhetoric deployed is clearly engaged in a polemic against ethical certainty. Similarly, the way in which he characterises the disquieting experience of the ordeal of undecidability (see Chapter 4) seems aimed not merely at giving an analysis of a structural feature of the concept of 'decision', but at reaching out and ethically shaking the reader. When it comes to our basic ethical experience, Derrida seems to say, we cannot wrap ourselves up in the certainty of knowledge and rules and enjoy that sweet sound sleep of a good conscience. Just as he seeks to remind the knights of good conscience that they are in the land of Moriah, so Derrida's characterisation of the ordeal of undecidability seeks to make us see that in such a thunderous night there is no knowledge to assure us of having responded justly. The only certainty here seems to be the insomnia of a bad conscience.[5]

While the polemical element is clearly there in Derrida's account, it is not mere polemics. If having a good conscience is to be understood in terms of knowledge that assures one that one has fulfilled one's ethical responsibilities, then from the account of the ordeal of undecidability as a necessary condition for responding justly to the other (see Chapter 4), we can see why Derrida thinks having a good conscience is something that must be avoided. Returning to the context of the injunction against a good conscience cited above, Derrida explains:

> Good conscience as subjective certainty is incompatible with the absolute risk that . . . every responsible decision . . . must run.

> To protect the decision or the responsibility by knowledge, by some theoretical assurance, or by the certainty of being right . . . is to transform this experience into the deployment of a program, into the technical application of a rule or a norm, or into the subsumption of a determined case. (AP, 19)

Knowing or having certainty about responding justly to the other dissolves the very ordeal of undecidability through which the possibility of doing justice to the other is given. Without this ordeal, without this experience of the antinomic injunctions of justice opened up by the interruption of an incalculable other, 'one might as well give up on . . . justice' (SM, 65). Behind Derrida's polemics against good conscience is the demand not to dissolve the ordeal of undecidability, not to close off this experience of having to respond, without assurance, to the interruption of an incalculable other.

Before fleshing out this demand a little more, I want to consider an immediate response. One might think that although a just decision must 'go through' the ordeal of undecidability, once through the ordeal one can have the kind of certainty of having *done* the just thing that Derrida denies. The very language of 'going through' would seem to suggest an understanding of the ordeal as momentary. Knowledge or certainty could be had about our ethical decisions, they could be calculated with assurance, it is just that we lack the resources for this (such as time and knowledge). Hence the ordeal. Indeed, Derrida tells us that 'justice doesn't wait', that 'a just decision is always required *immediately*' (FL, 26). Perhaps the ordeal of undecidability emerges because of the empirical limitations we unavoidably encounter in responding to the urgency of justice with a decision that 'cannot furnish itself with infinite information and unlimited knowledge of conditions, rules or hypothetical imperatives' (FL, 26). That is to say, the ordeal of undecidability would be the name for the empirical limitations that we unavoidably experience in having to decide with finite resources. There would be nothing to rule out achieving certainty after the decision. And so the good conscience of *having responded* justly to the other remains compatible with the ordeal of undecidability we experience when trying to decide what *would be* the just response.

But this would reduce the ordeal of undecidability to the indecisiveness of an empirical moment and this, as we have seen, is what Derrida insists it is not. Recall that, for Derrida, a just decision cannot fall from a pre-existing rule or norm or be the consequence of some determinate knowledge. And the reason for this is because it is a response to the singularity of the other, a singularity that interrupts any calculating framework. So even if we had all resources at our disposal, '[c]enturies of preparatory reflection and theoretical deliberation' (PF, 79), the decision itself, if it is to be a just decision, cannot be the consequence of such knowledge. Where it is such a consequence, one applies or unfolds a programme (FL, 24–6). And this, as we have seen, is incompatible with responding justly to the other as other. As we saw in the previous chapter, for Derrida a just decision presupposes a leap that is discontinuous with the order of knowledge, hence the characterisation of the ordeal as 'acting in the night of non-knowledge and non-rule'. Unlimited resources may help us penetrate this night, but they will not dispel it.

This is also the reason why Derrida characterises this experience as one where we are 'never at peace' but continually 'haunted' by our decisions (see Chapter 4). And here we see a second response to the momentary understanding of undecidability. We can think about it in the following way. I find myself in a situation of trying to respond justly to the other. After making what I take to be a just decision, I reflect on what happened. I faced the ordeal of having to respond to the antinomic injunctions placed on me by the interruption of the other and made the discontinuous leap that any just decision requires. But now I have landed back on the ground (as it were) and, on reflection, I say to myself, 'it's all clear now, I *know* I made a just decision'. But what is enabling me to see the justice of my decision with such certainty? It cannot be the laws and rules of yesterday, otherwise there would have been, in principle, no need of a leap. Perhaps it is the reaffirmed or reinvented laws and rules which I find myself with after the leap? But then the question comes back: if the moment of the leap, where I reaffirm or reinvent the law, is both necessary and yet discontinuous with knowledge, then what assurance do I have here? Moreover, if I could guarantee that these laws and rules of today provide me with the knowledge that I did do the just thing, then this implies that the decision I faced was of the order of knowledge – I just needed to calculate it correctly. But if this is the case, then the decision slips back into the order of the calculable that justice demands it break with. What I faced was an incalculability that remained of the order of the calculable, but which 'escape[d] it for contingent reasons, such as finitude, a limited power' (FWT, 49). The upshot of this account seems to be that at no point can I be certain of the justness of my decision. Hence the haunting and lack of peace:

> That is why the ordeal of the undecidable that . . . must be gone through . . . is never past or passed, it is not a surmounted or sublated (*aufgehoben*) moment in the decision. The undecidable remains caught, lodged, at least as a ghost – but an essential ghost – in every decision. Its ghostliness deconstructs from within . . . any certitude . . . that would assure us of the justice of a decision. (FL, 24)

The ordeal of undecidability, as Derrida understands it, cannot be understood as a momentary indecisiveness that we leave behind. Rather, it is an experience that remains to disturb any good conscience and keep us ethically off balance, something we experience as an 'interminable . . . remainder' (AP, 19). Our sleep will always be interrupted.

'Not a moment to be . . . forgotten or suppressed' (PF, 219)

Behind the polemics against the 'irresponsibility' of having a good conscience,[6] and the insistence that '[n]o-one could or should . . . be quietly reassured about their decisions' (ROD, 20), is the demand not to suppress or forget the ordeal of undecidability. As I argued in the previous chapter, the ordeal of undecidability is an experience of a conflictual obligation that emerges from the interruption of an incalculable other and the 'im-possible' demand placed on me to do justice to the other as other. This, as we have seen, is an interminable experience and not a passing moment. So what would it mean to suppress or forget this ordeal?

The former suggests neutralising the ordeal in advance by applying norms or rules in the certainty that the road ahead is clear. Here I would know what to do and so would not experience the ordeal. The latter suggests dissolving the ordeal with the knowledge of having taken the right road. Here the ordeal would become a mere contingent moment in a calculable process. In both cases there is no interrupting arrival of the other as other. Suppressing the ordeal closes off the interruption of the other by transforming the conflictual obligation to respond justly to the other into a technical problem to be solved by the application of a rule or norm for within a given framework. This, in turn, would imply missing the 'always unheard of singularity of the decision that needs to be made' (PS, 360). The other would never arrive as other. Forgetting the ordeal would involve transforming the ordeal from an interminable experience that remains to disturb and affect me, to a momentary indecisiveness that merely makes way for the decision that follows, a decision that I know to be just. Here I would not be affected by the ordeal and so would remain untouched by the other. And this is another way of saying that the other, as other, does not arrive.

I suggested that the problem with having a good conscience is that it dissolves the ordeal of undecidability. We can now see that the problem with the latter is that it closes off or denies the arriving of the other as other. Thus the demand not to dissolve the ordeal of undecidability, which I identified as motivating the injunctions against a good conscience, is itself motivated by the demand to remain open to the interruption of the other, that is to say, to experience as interruption. Insofar as closing oneself off from such interruption destroys the possibility of responding justly to the other, the demand to remain open to the arrival of the other would be an ethical demand.

'Openness to the other', however, is not the most helpful way of formulating this demand. Although most of the literature speaks of it in this way, it leads to at least two problems. The first is that 'openness to the other' suggests a passive stance of openness and this invites the charge of being open to *any* other. Laclau, for example, argues that being open to the other regardless of the content of that otherness would appear to be more like ethical nihilism than an ethical injunction (TJ, 70). Kearney thinks that Derrida's account leaves us unable to decide between 'benign and malign strangers'.[7] Wolin, pointing to those ' "others" – neo-Nazis, white supremacists, and other racists – who have forfeited their right to my openness', suggests that a deconstructive ethics of openness would leave us vulnerable to such others. 'Openness to the other', then, would remain normatively impotent and politically suspect.[8] The second problem, recently articulated by Martin Hägglund, argues that as a constitutive structure of experience, openness to the other is unavoidable and therefore it simply makes no sense to make any normative demand here. As Hägglund puts it: 'openness to the other cannot be an ethical principle since it is not a matter of choice.'[9]

A more promising way of understanding the demands of deconstruction might be to think in terms of maintaining the experience of undecidability (as interruption and ordeal). This avoids the charge of a normative deficit – such maintaining would require closure – and the suspicion that Derrida is trying to derive an 'ought' from an 'is'. I will address both of these points, starting with Hägglund's point first.

Hägglund is right to say that openness to the other is not a matter of choice. However, speaking of an ethical demand here is not incoherent. Things become a little clearer if we recall the two layers to the structure of experience outlined in the previous chapter. The first layer, 'experience as arche-writing', points to a constitutive openness to the other in terms of the difference and alterity at the heart of self-identity. Here openness to the other is unavoidable, for there would be no identity, no self-relation, without it. Hägglund is right insofar as this cannot be a matter of choice and therefore it makes no sense to talk of an ethical demand here. On the second level, however, there is the disturbing arrival of the other, what I called 'experience as interruption'. Now, this can be thought of as unavoidable insofar as it reveals or reactivates one's 'traumatic' relation to an incalculable other (see Chapter 4). However, as we have seen, one can suppress or forget this experience. That is to say, one can choose to deny it. Derrida emphasises this when he refers to 'the undeniable, and I underscore *undeniable*, experience of the alterity of the other' and goes on to explain: 'I underscore *undeniable* to suggest *only deniable*' (RS, 38). Similarly, when Derrida insists that 'we must not hide it [the aporia] from ourselves' (TOH, 41), this suggests that we could indeed hide the aporia from ourselves (through suppressing or forgetting the ordeal). Given that the aporia is the ordeal we experience in having to respond to the conflictual obligations placed on us by the interruption of the other as other, hiding the aporia would be a way of denying the interruption of the other as other. In this respect, it is probably more appropriate to describe this second layer as undeniable rather than unavoidable. So, when Derrida insists that one cannot and should not close off the relation to the other, we have to bear in mind both the unavoidable and undeniable layers. Once this is recognised, one can make ethical demands here.

One could avoid the ambiguity that leads to the kind of response from Hägglund if we think of the demand not so much in terms of 'openness to the other', but rather as the demand to maintain the experience of undecidability (as interruption and ordeal) through which a space is held open for the arriving of the other. This would be a demand not to forget or suppress this experience (RS, 38). In *The Other Heading* Derrida links these two layers of experience – the constitutive difference at the heart of identity and the relation to the other as other – with the demand to respond to and remember this experience. Discussing what, in this context, he calls the 'experience of the other heading' (TOH, 17), Derrida emphasises that one needs 'to recall that there is another heading', what he describes as 'the *heading of the other*, before which we must respond, and which we must *remember, of which* we must *remind ourselves*' (TOH, 15). This demand not to deny this experience, but to respond to and remember it, would involve, to recall Wood, 'the formation of complex dispositions' that would 'bear witness to' such an experience. This would not be bearing witness to the memory of a past moment that disappears with the decision that follows, but to an experience that remains and leaves one exposed to, and transformed by, the interruption of the other.

To summarise this, we could think of this demand as being called upon to maintain an ethos of interruption.[10] Such an ethos would involve 'cultivating the difference-to-oneself . . . that constitutes identity' and developing a disposition of openness to the coming of the other, what Derrida describes as a 'culture of oneself *as* the culture *of* the other' (TOH, 10–11). The politics of the stage and work of resistance discussed in Chapter 3 would be one way of taking this up (see also the discussion of hospitality in Chapter 6).

Maintaining interruption might seem like a paradoxical demand; the newness and heterogeneity of 'interruption' seemingly puts an end to the preserving and holding of 'maintaining'. However, it is in the tension between these two that deconstruction operates. As Derrida says, this 'is what deconstruction is made of . . . the tension between memory . . . the preservation of something . . . and, at the same time, heterogeneity . . . and a break' (VR, 6). From this we can perhaps glimpse a fourth injunction emerging that would orientate the maintaining of such an ethos, namely, a commitment to preserving a space for the possibility of the new, the heterogeneous; what we might call a 'fidelity . . . to the to come' (RS, 4).

'Preventing certain things from coming to pass' (N, 194)

Let me summarise the account so far. I initially identified three injunctions in Derrida's work and suggested that the first, 'avoid a good conscience', is motivated by a second, 'do not deny the ordeal of undecidability', which was in turn motivated by a third, 'remain open to the arriving of the other'. I then argued that instead of thinking of the latter in terms of openness to the other, it is better to think of this as demanding that we hold open a space for the arriving of the incalculable other, what I referred to as maintaining an ethos of interruption. At the end of the last section, I suggested that maintaining this ethos of interruption would itself be orientated by a fourth injunction, namely, a fidelity to the 'to come'.

I take 'to come' to denote the promise of the arriving of an incalculable other (and, as always with Derrida, the other refers to who or what comes). This is captured by Derrida's discussion of the event in *Rogues*. There he describes the event as an 'incalculable irruption, the singular and exceptional alterity of *what* . . . or indeed of *who* . . . comes' (RS, 128; cf. N, 182). But this irruption is not to be understood as the not-yet-present of a future arrival or something we can have certainty about. The 'to come' is not a modality of the present, and neither is it of the order of knowledge; it belongs 'to the time of the promise' (PF, 306). Whether it is a reason to come (RS, 148), a democracy to come (RS, 90–1; TOH, 78) or a friendship to come (RS, 4), each is structured like a promise, never present but always remaining to be thought and rethought. A fidelity to the 'to come', then, would place on us the duty to remain faithful to the promise of the arriving of the other as other, to create the conditions that would open up and maintain spaces for the incalculable arrival of who or what comes (see Chapter 6). With this in place, we can now address the problem of openness.

From these brief remarks, we begin to see that the injunction to maintain the ordeal of undecidability, understood not in terms of 'openness to the other' but in terms of maintaining an ethos of interruption, does not imply a passive stance of mere openness, as both friends and critics suggest. In creating and maintaining the conditions for the arrival of the other, such an ethos demands that we prevent the arriving of that which would close off the space for the arriving of the other, that would put an end to the very possibility of any interruption, any culture *of* the other. Such a demand means that we cannot remain neutral, that we must do everything within our power to prevent certain events or others from arriving. Derrida is unambiguous on this point:

> The coming of the event is what cannot and should not be prevented; it is another name for the future itself. This does not mean that it is good – good in itself – for everything and anything to arrive; it is not that one should give up trying to prevent certain things from coming to pass . . . But one should only ever oppose events that one thinks will block the future or that bring death with them: events that would put an end to the possibility of the event. (N, 194)

Being faithful to the 'to come' involves creating the conditions for maintaining the space for the arriving of the other. One is not left open to anything. One's fidelity to maintaining such a space itself calls for forms of action, practice and intervention. As Derrida insists: 'a promise must promise to be kept, that is not to remain "spiritual" or "abstract," but to produce events, new effective forms of action, practice, [and] organization' (SM, 89). The affirmation of such an ethos requires taking a position. Without the latter, the former remains spiritual, abstract.[11] Out of a fidelity to the 'to come', then, one must close off the arriving of that which would destroy the very space for the interruption of the other. The demand to maintain a space for the arriving of the other, then, cannot be reduced to the 'moralizing and unpalatable stereotype' of mere openness that Derrida feared (N, 194). Nor can it be characterised as a paralysing inaction that is, as a matter of principle, unable to decide which others to welcome, as many have suggested. Instead, fidelity to the 'to come' demands that we calculate in order to prevent the emergence of discourses that close the 'to come'.[12]

This demand to prevent certain discourses from emerging is taken up in a 1994 roundtable where, in response to a question about the political dangers of too much diversity and what deconstruction has to say in favour of the unity of the community, Derrida responds by noting that while deconstruction is not out to destroy all totality, it does insist on

> the heterogeneity, the difference, the dissociation, which is absolutely necessary for the relation to the other. What disrupts totality is the condition for the relation to the other. The privilege granted to unity, to totality . . . to community as a homogenized whole – this is a danger for responsibility, for decision, for ethics, for politics. *That is why I insisted* on what prevents unity from closing upon itself, from being closed up. (VR, 13, my emphasis)

What Derrida describes here as a disruption – the heterogeneity, difference, dissociation which makes possible the relation to the other – is part of an ethos of interruption. The reason why the attempt to totalise or gather a community into a homogenised whole would present such a danger is precisely because it would leave no room for the conditions necessary for the interruption of the other and, hence, the very 'possibility of responsibility, of a decision, of ethical commitments' (VR, 13). That is to say, it would deny the experience of undecidability (as interruption and ordeal) and close off the space an ethos of interruption seeks to hold open. And it is for this reason that Derrida does not simply *describe* this relation to the other which prevents such closure, but, as he notes in the response above, *insists* upon it. This insistence points beyond a neutral description of a structural openness to a demand, 'an ethical and political duty', that is made in response to such danger, and which is presumably motivated by seeking to prevent that danger from emerging (VR, 14).

Indeed, Derrida will go on in this response to link his insistence on that which prevents closing off with an orientation that, as he puts it, 'prevents totalitarianism, nationalism, ethnocentrism'. Discussing these issues under the more concrete experience of struggles for cultural identity, Derrida links both of the layers of experience that I have pointed to – the inner difference at the heart of self-identity and the difference that appears with the interruption of the other – with that which prevents the turn to totalitarianism and nationalism:

> People who fight for their identity must pay attention to the fact that identity is not the self-identity of a thing . . . but implies a difference within identity . . . a culture is different from itself . . . the person is different from itself. Once you take into account this inner and other difference, then you pay attention to the other and you understand that fighting for your own identity is not exclusive of another identity, is open to another identity. And this prevents totalitarianism, nationalism, egocentrism and so on. (VR, 13–14)

Here we see Derrida pointing to the importance of the two layers of experience I identified in the previous chapter (arche-writing and interruption) in terms of this 'inner and other difference'. Of particular interest in this passage is the reference to 'take into account' and 'pay attention to' because it is this that contributes to blocking the emergence of certain discourses. That is to say, it seems to go against the mere openness reading. The claim seems to be that 'taking into account' these two layers of experience leads to a 'paying attention', and this brings about an 'understanding' that can help prevent the turn to totalitarianism, nationalism and so forth. My claim here is that 'taking into account' is part of what I have been referring to as maintaining an ethos of interruption. It would answer to the demand not to 'leave out' or ignore, not to forget or suppress the experience of undecidability (as interruption and ordeal), but 'to consider', 'to notice', to remember and recall it in every decision or judgement (see above). This would involve the formation of complex dispositions referred to by Wood, or what Derrida describes as 'cultivating the difference-to-oneself . . . that constitutes identity' (TOH, 10–11). And it is through the formation or cultivation of such dispositions that this 'taking into account' would reorient one's attending to the other and transform one's understanding of the 'inner and other difference'. That is to say, one is transformed through the ongoing practice of maintaining an ethos of interruption.

II. Negotiating the Ethical–Political Challenge

The deconstructive injunctions I have so far identified emerge from the account of the experience of undecidability. As a way of capturing what these injunctions call for, I have referred to this as the demand to maintain an ethos of interruption. In the remainder of this chapter, I shall identify some of the political challenges this presents. Although I have focused on undecidability and the incalculable, here I turn to Derrida's insistence on the need for calculation, an aspect of Derrida's work that is often overlooked. While this shows that deconstruction does not wash its hands of politics, it does raise questions about the kind of politics to which deconstruction points. This will be a democratic form of politics. Derrida's account of the latter, however, remains under-theorised.

'One must calculate' (N, 13)

The need for calculation, laws and rules is something that Derrida continually insists on.[13] This is often overlooked in accounts of Derrida's work. While Derrida is at his most lyrical, controversial and hyperbolic when emphasising the incalculable, non-knowledge or the impossible, this is no excuse for not attending to this dimension of his work. If we recall Derrida's account of the ordeal of undecidability (see Chapter 4), we are presented with a disquieting picture of our ethico-political life, one in which we are confronted with a terrible choice in a night of non-knowledge, anxiety and remorse. The only action seemingly open to us is to make a 'mad' leap the justice of which remains uncertain. While Derrida presents us with a disconcerting picture of our basic ethical experience, it hardly licenses claims that Derrida is a 'philosopher of the undecidable' who 'glorifies the moment of particularity' and 'relish[es]' the madness of decision. And even less so can one claim that Derrida is '*for* "singularity," "madness," and the "mystical," [and] *against* formal procedures, rules, and rationality'.[14] As I argued in the previous chapter, Derrida's whole account of the ordeal of undecidability would not make sense without the obligation to calculate, to refer to laws and rules, what he describes as a 'feeling of duty – a respect for the law' (N, 13). It is precisely in the tension between the calculable and the incalculable, the regulated and the unregulated, that the ordeal of undecidability emerges. In the absence of either pole there would be no ordeal and, as we have seen, for Derrida this would mean no possibility of doing justice to the other. While Derrida describes the instant of a decision as a madness, this is a madness that feels the gravitational burden of doing justice, not a sovereign madness that frees itself entirely.

So while it may be understandable for some to detect a 'distress' in Derrida's work,[15] it is harder to make sense of claims that his account leaves us with a 'political existentialism' where we 'simply *decide*'.[16] Yes, we do have to decide, but if there's one thing that Derridean deconstruction denies us, it is this 'simply'. When Derrida describes the instant of decision as a madness there are two things to bear in mind. Firstly, by the 'madness' of decision Derrida does not mean randomness or ignorance, but rather that which exceeds calculation or, as he often puts it, is discontinuous with knowledge. Secondly, Derrida is talking about the 'instant' or, as he emphasises elsewhere, 'the *moment* of decision' (N, 231). Derrida's claim, then, is that the instant or moment of decision is one which is discontinuous with knowledge. But this does not mean that one simply decides. Derrida is 'not advocating that a decision ends up deciding *anything* at *any* moment' (N, 231). His account does not rule out (is not 'against') accumulating knowledge and preparing for the decision in the most cautious and considered way possible (ROD, 11). Indeed, it calls for it. Derrida insists that 'it is necessary to know as much and as well as possible before deciding' (FWT, 53; N, 298), that 'one must deliberate, reflect' (N, 231) before the decision, that 'we need to have . . . the best and most comprehensive [knowledge] available, in order to . . . take a responsibility'

(RS, 145; N, 299). The ordeal of undecidability, and thus the very possibility of responding justly to the other, emerges from, and would dissolve without, the necessity of this 'must' or 'need'. While Derrida argues that there would be no possibility of a just decision if one merely applied existing norms or rules, it would equally be the case if one 'simply' decided without taking knowledge, norms and rules into account. The instant of a just decision may be a madness, but we must draw on knowledge, calculate and deliberate so that we venture into that 'night of non-knowledge' with a decision which, while discontinuous with knowledge, is 'as lucid as possible' (N, 232).

Given this, Simon Critchley is not entirely fair in his discussion of Derrida's work when he suggests:

> I take a risk one way or the other – I am for x or against x – but ultimately I do not know why I made the decision . . . But is the madness of decision an adequate account of political life? Is it even a valid description of how one arrives at one's political preferences and engages in political action?[17]

Derrida's reference to the madness of decision is not offering an account of how people arrive at their political preferences. I may arrive at my political preferences in all sorts of ways. I may come under the influence of a family member, teacher or friend; my preferences could be informed by a particular experience in my past, a historical event, a documentary I saw on television, a book I read, and so on. Neither is the madness of decision attempting to give an account of political life; it is attempting to point to something about the concept of a just, responsible decision, which is, no doubt, an important aspect of political life. Furthermore, describing the instant of decision as a madness does not mean that we cannot give reasons for why we made a particular decision. The knowledge, deliberation, reflection and calculation that leads up to a decision that would be 'as lucid as possible' would furnish one with reasons that inform the way in which one calculated the risks in the way that one did. What the madness of decision tries to bring out is not the absence of reasons in arriving at a decision, but the absence of any knowledge that assures us about the justness of our decision.

That is to say, it points to an irreducible risk that no calculation, knowledge or set of reasons will be able to dissolve.

Derrida is acutely aware that without this deliberation, calculation and knowledge, without the light of the most lucid decision possible, insistence on the incalculable 'can become politically quite dangerous' and 'allow for the worst abuses' or 'most perverse calculations' (N, 194; FL, 28). It would leave us vulnerable to those discourses that close off the space for the arrival of the other, discourses that, as Derrida put it above, 'block the future or bring death with them'. Put differently, without the light of the most lucid decision possible, we would leave the other vulnerable to the violence of an impenetrable night. While we can never eliminate this risk, we must do all we can to combat it: 'we have to circumscribe or surround a decision with the maximum of guarantees, knowledge, precautions, and so on, *even if* we know that the decision belongs to an order which is heterogeneous to knowledge' (ROD, 34; cf. PS, 198).

This is a tricky path to negotiate. On the one hand, Derrida wants to go as far as possible in leaving a space for the interruption of an incalculable other. On the other hand, he recognises that we must continually negotiate and calculate the risks involved in order to block the arriving of that which would close off such a space. We must run this risk in the surest possible way. The question that Derrida puts to Lévinas is not simply a question for Lévinas:

> [T]o save the interruption without, by keeping it safe, losing and ruining it all the more, without the fatality of . . . interrupt[ing] the interruption . . . EL takes calculated risks in this regard, risks as calculated as possible. But how does he calculate . . . so as to leave room for the incalculable? (PSY, 166)

But however difficult this may be (and we will come back to this), the insistence is clear: while one cannot have guarantees that would eliminate this vulnerability to the worst, we should do all we can – accumulate knowledge, deliberate, calculate, prepare, anticipate – to combat it.

This call to combat the worst is not a thought that arrives only in the later work. Above we saw how the attempt to hold open a space for the incalculable arriving of the other requires that one calculate and anticipate. Without the latter, the space we leave for the other would be left open to the possibility of the most perverse calculations and worst violence. And so the light of the most lucid decision is required in order to prevent the other being abandoned to an impenetrable night. We might say that here we would have to combat calculations with calculations so as to leave a space for the incalculable. A similar move appears in the 1964 text on Lévinas, 'Violence and Metaphysics'. One of the things that Derrida's reading focuses on is Lévinas's attempt to locate an ethical relation in the encounter with singularity of an interrupting other, an encounter that would not be subject to the violence of light. The latter refers to the violence of onto-phenomenological discourse which, in seeking to bring to light and grasp, appropriates and reduces the alterity of the other to the identity of the same. Free of the phenomenal violence of light, the ethical encounter would take place in the silent signification of the face – the appeal of a gaze that tears me out of the light of familiarity. This is not the place to rehearse debates about Derrida's reading of Lévinas. What is important here is that we see Derrida responding in a similar way to what we have already encountered. Just as the incalculable left to itself could succumb to the most perverse calculations and worst abuses, so this encounter before light would itself be vulnerable to the worst kind of violence, a violence that does not even come to light to be named but is lost to an 'unimaginable night' (VM, 185, 172). Thus, one must accept the violence of light. Just as 'one must combat light with a certain light' (VM, 145) in order to protect the (certain) silence of peace, so one must combat calculation with certain calculations in order to keep open a space for the incalculable. As Derrida puts it in a later text on Lévinas: 'everything has to be calculated so that calculation does not win out over everything' (PSY, 161).

Returning to the injunctions outlined above, we see that while one cannot have a good conscience about one's decisions, and while the ordeal of undecidability must not be dissolved, the demand to hold open a space for the arriving of the other 'must not be an "anything whatsoever"' (SM, 168).[18] This 'anything whatsoever' harbours behind it 'those too familiar ghosts, the very ones we must practice recognizing' (SM, 168). These are ghosts that bring with them discourses 'of the blood, nationalisms of the native soil' and systems that 'close themselves off from the coming of the other' (N, 182). In short, discourses that *'open onto no future'* (ARSS, 113; cf. SM, 168). Here, at the very moment when he rejects the 'anything whatsoever' reading of deconstruction, when he demands vigilance with regard to those others who presumably we must not remain open to, Derrida talks of a practice of recognising. Recognising these others is something we must practise doing. A similar demand is made in *The Other Heading*, where Derrida insists that we must anticipate and not simply give ourselves over to the rhetoric of the absolutely new, for under this banner of the 'unanticipatable' or absolutely new 'we can fear seeing return the phantoms of the worst'. Thus, one 'must' be suspicious of the 'exposure to what would no longer be identifiable at all' and 'learn to identify' these ghosts in all their guises (TOH, 18, 77).

Understood in these terms, deconstruction does not call for an 'anything whatsoever' openness, but for the development of complex dispositions and practices that seek to hold open a space for a relation to the other. And in doing so, deconstruction demands that we oppose and attempt to prevent the arrival of those others that would close off such a space. '[W]e must not be open to whatever comes' (ROD, 11). That is to say, deconstruction does not remain paralysed. It calculates.

Normativity without a good conscience

Before exploring the kind of politics that this account points to, I want to set out a little more explicitly the kind of normativity at work in deconstruction. When asked of his work, 'Is there anything normative?' Derrida responded: 'Of course there is. There is nothing but that.' Unsurprisingly, a cautioning 'but' quickly followed: 'But if you are asking me implicitly whether . . . there is [anything] normative in the ordinary sense of that term, I would have more trouble answering you' (PS, 361). What, ultimately, causes this trouble for Derrida is the requirement of a conception – or knowledge – of the good that normativity ordinarily presupposes. Such knowledge is often taken as necessary for grounding one's critique of existing conditions and for providing a standard, rule or norm that justifies our judgements, guides our actions, and offers positive alternatives.[19] But Derrida's whole account, as we have seen, aims to reveal that doing justice to the other cannot be thought of in terms of knowledge. As he says in the same interview, one must respond to the interruption of the other 'without anything that would finally be the object of knowledge' (PS, 362). If one's response was not discontinuous with the calculable order of knowledge, then it would deny the incalculable singularity signalled by 'as other'. Not only would we miss the very singularity of the other that justice demands we respond to, but we would do so in good conscience.[20]

But given this, how are we to understand Derrida's emphatic response to the question of normativity? Derrida's work, I suggest, should be understood as a form of negativism and, in particular, a form of epistemic and meta-ethical negativism.[21] The former is the view that we cannot know the good, the latter that we can ground normative judgements in the identification of a wrong. That Derrida's work is a form of epistemic negativism is, I hope, evident from the account outlined in this and the previous chapter. Derrida has consistently argued that our attempts to respond to the antinomic injunctions placed on us by the demand to do justice to the other will always be 'heterogeneous to knowledge' (N, 231; cf. ARSS, 118; ROD, 20; RS, 145). That Derrida's work is a form of meta-ethical negativism is evident in his identification of a whole series of wrongs and his insistence that we ought to do all we can to prevent or minimise those wrongs.[22] The thought here is that those normative judgements are not grounded in any positive conception or knowledge of the good, but rather in comparative judgements about the wrongs one is confronted with. Judgements such as 'the world will be a worse place if we do not prevent this' or 'reducing this suffering would be better' would be of this form.

To return to the opening of this chapter, and to what is no doubt *the* wrong, consider Derrida's numerous references to 'the worst'. When, for example, Derrida insists that we must 'remember the worst' – to officially commemorate the round-up of the Jews at the Vélodrome d'Hiver, or to recognise the responsibility of the French state for what took place under the occupation (N, 107) – this is not only to preserve the memory of the victims and the historical truth;

it is also for the sake of current struggles against the 'return of phantoms of the worst' (TOH, 18; N, 106), signs of which Derrida sees emerging all across Europe (TOH, 6). One must prevent the return of these 'ghosts' of 'nationalism, racism, xenophobia, antisemitism' (N, 107) and oppose the discourses they bring with them (N, 182, 194). Here we have a negative demand – prevent 'the return of the worst' (N, 106). This demand is not preceded by a theory of the good and no such theory is needed to reveal the wrongness of that which we are called upon to prevent. Nor is such a theory required to motivate us to do all we can to prevent its re-emergence. To insist that one must provide a standard that justifies such a demand or a conception of the good that grounds it would be more a sign of ethical failure than of moral rigour.

Or consider another wrong that Derrida continually returns to, that of the treatment of immigrants by the French state. Here is the opening of a public speech Derrida gave during a particularly fraught situation:

> I remember a bad day last year: It just about took my breath away, it sickened me when I heard the expression the first time, barely understanding it, the expression *crime of hospitality* . . . In fact, I am not sure that I heard it, because I wonder how anyone could ever have pronounced it, taken it on his palate, this venomous expression; no, I did not hear it, and I can barely repeat it; I read it voicelessly in an official text . . . (I still wonder who dared put these words together) . . . What becomes of a country, one must wonder, what becomes of a culture, what becomes of a language when one admits of a 'crime of hospitality'. (N, 133; cf. FWT, 59)[23]

The wrongness that Derrida describes here is one that is felt. The sickness is immediate; it is there the moment he encounters this expression (even though he can barely understand it). He cannot breathe. With the reference to 'palate' the expression takes on a revolting materiality – one can almost feel its poison oozing down the throat. The expression assails his senses: he thought he heard it but didn't; he couldn't actually say the words. Much later, in the moment of the speech itself, he still struggles to say the words; he is still reeling at the thought that the expression actually exists and describes feeling 'suffocate[ed] and . . . ashamed to live like this' (N, 135). Later in the speech, he does go on to set out a series of arguments against the law, and, citing the history of unjust laws targeting refugees in France, he raises the stakes considerably, recalling the subsequent murder of refugees sent to the camps and warning of echoes, today, 'of a sort of pre-Vichyite night' (N, 137).[24] As he approaches the end of his speech he calls for civil disobedience and campaigns to change the law, before immersing his audience back into the immediate wrongness of the situation: 'This will have to be done so we can finally live, speak, breathe' (N, 144).

To see the wrongness of the law, and to recognise the force behind the demand to oppose and eliminate it, does not require the legal, political, economic, historical and moral arguments that Derrida develops in the middle of his speech (though they no doubt strengthen his appeal). The wrongness is there, in the situation itself, and in the physical and intellectual disorientation and sickness that it immediately induces. The normative judgement – that one must engage in civil disobedience and commit to eliminating this law – is not grounded on a theory of the good; it is grounded in the thought that we cannot live in a world where such suffering exists, in the feeling that we are not able to breathe in such wrongness, and in the judgement that the world would be less bad were such a law eliminated.[25]

The normativity at work in deconstruction is to be found in comparative judgements of this sort. We see this across Derrida's work. In his early text on Lévinas, briefly touched on above, Derrida argues that one is always in an 'economy of violence' and, as such, one's ethico-political decisions will be guided by what one judges, in the particular situation one finds oneself in, to be 'the lesser violence' (VM, 400, n. 21). In relation to the concrete issue of an ethics of hospitality, Derrida insists that 'it is necessary to deduce a politics and law from ethics. This deduction is necessary in order to determine the "better" or the "less bad"' law (AD, 115). In a much later interview he writes:

> [T]he only response is *economic*: up to a certain point, there is always a measure, a better measure to take . . . I certainly cannot eradicate or extirpate the roots of violence against animals . . . racism, anti-Semitism, etc., but, under the pretext that I

cannot eradicate them, I do not want to allow them to develop unchecked. Therefore, according to the historical situation, it is necessary to invent the least bad solution. (FWT, 76; cf. 73–5)

And similarly:

> For example, how is one to, *on the one hand*, reaffirm singularity of the idiom . . . the rights of minorities, linguistic and cultural differences . . . How is one to resist uniformization, homogenization . . .? But, *on the other hand*, how is one to struggle for all that without sacrificing the most univocal communication . . . democratic discussion, and the law of the majority? Each time one must *invent* so as to *betray as little as possible* [my emphasis] both one and the other – *without any prior assurance* of success. (PS, 360)

Although we always find ourselves within an economy of violence, not all forms are equivalent. While we must practise 'violence against violence', we must do so in order to 'avoid the worst violence' in the singular situation in which we find ourselves (VM, 145–6). This will always be a context-specific judgement, but one that calls on us to 'distinguish between different modalities of violence' (ROD, 15) so as to arrive at 'violence chosen as the least violent' (VM, 146). In the realm of politics, this will often mean contesting what one perceives to be an unjust law and, as above, trying to eliminate, transform or, at the very least, arrive at 'the least bad law' (DE, 87). While I understand those sympathetic readers of deconstruction who resist the idea that there is any normativity to deconstruction (a resistance that is, perhaps, partly motivated by trying to avoid the kind of complacency that one might summarise as 'duty accomplished'[26]), I hope that the account I have set out so far removes that particular worry.

'A perpetually indispensable negotiation . . . This is perhaps what politics is!' (N, 195)

For Derrida, then, one is always caught in an inescapable economy of calculation, where we 'try to outsmart the worst' through perilous negotiations that are never assured (PS, 118). And this strategy of outsmarting plays itself out on all levels of politics. Not only must we calculate and anticipate in order to outsmart the worst of an unimaginable night, but we must also outsmart the danger of erasing singularity and heterogeneity through the potentially blinding light of calculation, for this would only abandon the other to a different sort of night. As Derrida says:

> [T]o be responsible in ethics and politics implies that we try to programme, to anticipate, to define laws and rules . . . to do our best to predict, prepare . . . to organise ethics and politics . . . to soften or cancel the surprise: we have to do this, master the surprise, without . . . erasing the heterogeneity, the alterity of what is coming, and that is the political and ethical challenge. (ROD, 7)

If we do not try to predict and prepare, then we leave the other abandoned and exposed to the surprises of injustice. Hence the need for knowledge, laws and calculation. The ethico-political challenge is to do this without erasing the singularity of the other. This is the ethico-political challenge that the demand to maintain an ethos of interruption calls on us to negotiate continually.

Derrida's insistence that such negotiations require the most comprehensive knowledge available would involve drawing on all sorts of fields of inquiry. This provides another reason to question the reading of Derridean deconstruction that sees it as rejecting the concrete realm of empirical inquiry (see Chapter 4). Far from 'withdrawing' from (McCarthy) or 'degrading' (Habermas) the ontic realm of politics, Derrida's account points to the opposite: a perpetual negotiation in an inescapable economy of calculation. 'I prefer the word "negotiation" to more noble words,' notes Derrida, because 'there is always something about negotiation . . . that gets one's hands dirty . . . it does not disguise the anxiety . . . one thinks of force . . . compromise . . . impure things' (N, 13). Rather than disabling the possibility of political thought (as we have seen McCarthy, Fraser and others suggest), or avoiding the dirtying of one's hands (as Critchley, Fraser and others suggest),[27] in calling for this interminable negotiation, deconstruction signals the impossibility of clean hands.

From the ordeal of undecidability and the conflictual demand to make a decision that is both regulated and unregulated, to maintaining an ethos of interruption by calculating the incalculable, the picture of ethico-political life we see emerging from Derrida could perhaps be summed up with the following slogan: 'doing the impossible'. For critics such as McCarthy, Derrida needs, but fails, to specify what, concretely, this might entail (PI, 130).[28] On this view, Derrida insists on the need to negotiate between justice and laws, the incalculable and the calculable, but he fails to set out the possible ways of politically organising this ordeal, the 'forms of action, practice, [and] organization' it would call for (SM, 89). How does one maintain the 'im-possible' stance of calculating the incalculable? What would it mean, and what would it require, to acknowledge what Derrida refers to above as 'the inner and outer difference'? What would it mean, in terms of our practical engagements, to insist that 'one must cross . . . situations of undecidability, always maintaining the "possibly" open . . . all the while engaging in a consistent decision' (N, 31)?

Returning to Murdoch's question, one gets the feeling that Derrida's fear of a calculated ethical world, in which there would be 'the worst along with a good conscience' (N, 179), sees him grabbing his lantern and heading for the ethico-political marketplace to seize those there and shake them out of their complacent calculations. No doubt a necessary task. But if Nietzsche's madman arrived too soon for his astonished listeners, Derrida, according to both friends and critics, leaves too quickly. Derrida points us towards an im-possible ethico-political world that maintains a space for the arriving of the other, but he does not adumbrate its terrain.[29] While Derrida is rightly worried about things becoming all too calculable, do we not need some illuminating signs of calculability to help us on our 'im-possible' way?

While I am sympathetic to calls for a more concrete picture of what a deconstructive practice would involve, I think there are two general points here. Firstly, deconstruction is not a method or theory that exists outside the specific contexts in which it engages. The demand for a general political theory of deconstruction misses this point. Indeed, such a demand would seem to seek an ordeal-free deconstruction, a deconstruction that somehow overcomes the undecidability that it reveals to be the very experience of doing justice to the other. Moreover, any demand that deconstruction set out a positive theory of the good overlooks the negativism of deconstruction. But, and this is the second point, this does not mean that deconstruction does not provide concrete examples of practical engagement.[30] While these examples do not provide a theory for praxis, I hope they at least give some concrete grip to the deconstructive demand to develop 'complex dispositions', to cultivate 'the difference to oneself that constitutes identity', to develop a 'culture of oneself as a culture of the other'.

In light of this, perhaps we have left Derrida a little too soon. Let's return to the scene and listen for a moment. Derrida, recall, was talking about those discourses and systems that open onto no future and close themselves off from the coming of the other:

> Nondemocratic systems are above all systems that *close* and *close themselves off* from this coming of the other. They are systems of homogenization and of integral calculability. In the end and beyond all the classical critiques of fascist, Nazi, and totalitarian violence in general, one can say that they are systems that close the 'to come'. (N, 182)

This is the critique we have already come across regarding systems that close the 'to come' and, in doing so, close off the arriving of the other. Put differently, these systems close off the very space an ethos of interruption seeks to maintain. Here Derrida identifies these systems as 'nondemocratic' and this leaves those of us back in the ethico-political marketplace with a question: does this mean that, for Derrida, maintaining an ethos of interruption points to a democratic politics? Let's listen as Derrida returns to the scene:

> When I spoke a while ago about the opening of . . . the coming of the other . . . that is also an experience of the impossible. It's the sole true provocation to be reflected upon . . . [D]emocracy, for me, is the political experience of the impossible, the political experience of opening to the other as possibility of impossibility. (N, 194)

If we are to flesh out the politics of maintaining an ethos of interruption, then it is to the experience of democracy that we must now turn.

'Democratic politics begins where certainty ends'[31]

We can begin to see why the demand to maintain an ethos of interruption points towards a democratic politics if we look briefly at Claude Lefort's characterisation of the democratic form of society. According to Lefort, before the democratic revolution power was embodied in the body of the monarch, which as both natural and divine represented the unity and order of society. The monarch also figured as the head of the body politic, with the hierarchy of its members, the distinctions between ranks, and the whole network of societal relations resting on an unconditional basis. The democratic revolution, according to Lefort, explodes when the body politic is decapitated. The result of this is that power is no longer embodied in the figure of the monarch. Instead, 'the locus of power becomes an *empty place*'.[32] This process of disincorporation of the body politic not only replaces substantial unity with a fundamental openness, but initiates a more generalised uncertainty with the disentangling of the spheres of power, law and knowledge.

> Democracy is instituted and sustained by the *dissolution of the markers of certainty*. It inaugurates a history in which people experience a fundamental indeterminacy as to the basis of law, power and knowledge, and as to the basis of relations between *self* and *other* at every level of society.[33]

This brings into view three key features of the radical undecidability of democracy. Firstly, democracy is a form of society where power is constantly in search of a basis as law and knowledge are no longer taken to be embodied in the person or group who exercise it.[34] With no substantial foundations but only an 'empty place', democracy is a society of contestation, where the legitimation of social conflict is institutionalised. As such, democracy is, for Lefort, 'a society which, in its very form, welcomes and preserves indeterminacy'.[35] With the dissolution of the markers that determined relations between self and other, new ways of thinking and modes of expression emerge, and multiple perspectives unfold, giving rise to new demands that call into question the formal viewpoint of law.[36] Democracy, on this picture, is an experience of radical uncertainty.

Secondly, democracy is the interminable experience of an interrupted identity:

> There is no law that can be fixed, whose articles cannot be contested, whose foundations are not susceptible or being called in question . . . there is no representation of a centre and of the contours of society: unity cannot efface social division. Democracy inaugurates the experience of an ungraspable, uncontrollable society in which the people will be said to be sovereign . . . but whose identity will constantly be open to question.[37]

With the dissolving of substantial foundations, and the legitimation of social conflict amidst multiple perspectives, modes of thinking and forms of expression, the identity of 'the people' will always be open to contestation and transformation. This gives the democratic form of society an intrinsic plasticity: 'what is instituted never becomes established, the known remains undermined by the unknown, the present proves to be indefinable.'[38]

Thirdly, democracy is defined by an intrinsic historicity. If the identity of the demos is constantly open to contestation, if the contours of a democratic society are in an interminable process of transformation, then democracy 'proves to be the historical society *par excellence*'.[39] In a phrase that captures this form of society, Lefort describes democracy as 'the theatre of an uncontrollable adventure'.[40]

Lefort's account foregrounds the experience of openness set within the very structure of a democratic form of society. This can be seen in the three features just identified: the experience of (1) a radical undecidability, (2) the interminable interruption of identity, and (3) an intrinsic historicity. These features of democracy mark it out — and Lefort (like Derrida) draws our attention to the 'originality', 'singularity', 'unprecedented' nature of democracy — as a society that remains constitutively open to the experience of interruption.[41] Lefort's account suggests that democracy is precisely the maintaining of a space – an empty space – that enables new voices to emerge and new demands to be raised. We might say that democracy is a form of society that maintains a space for the arriving of the incalculable other and, thus, ensures an always interrupted identity. Not only does democracy not close itself off from this interruption, but, as Lefort points out, it 'welcomes and preserves' it. In short, democracy remains structurally 'to come'.

While Derrida may not subscribe to all the particularities of Lefort's narrative, there are striking similarities. Derrida, like Lefort, draws attention to aspects of democracy that mark it out from all other regimes. These include the three features identified above. While these similarities are interesting in themselves, having Lefort's account in the background will hopefully help concretise some of Derrida's more abstract remarks concerning the concept of democracy.

Derrida identifies three key aspects of democracy (I focus on his account in *Rogues*). The first is an emptiness in the very concept 'democracy'. Derrida suggests that there is something about democracy, about the meaning of the democratic, that is 'empty, vacant' (RS, 8), that when we 'try to return to the origin' democracy is not to be found, it 'does not present itself' (RS, 9). Derrida identifies this emptiness as an essential aspect of democracy. Democracy cannot 'gather itself around a presence' (RS, 40) because 'at the very centre of the concept' there is a 'freedom of play, an opening of indetermination and undecidability'. And it is this freedom in the concept and interpretation of the democratic that 'makes its history turn' (RS, 23–5). It does so because the empty place at the very centre of the democratic opens, and leaves democracy open to, the contestation and struggles of conflicting interpretations of what constitutes the democratic. This lack of 'proper meaning', of a meaning that would end the contestation over the democratic, is an essential aspect of democracy. Indeed, it defines democracy: 'what is lacking in democracy is proper meaning . . . Democracy is defined, as is the very ideal, by this lack of the proper and self-same. And so it is defined only by turns, by tropes' (RS, 37). The empty place of democracy is occupied by competing visions and tropes of what is 'properly' democratic, but it is never saturated by any one of them. What is 'proper' to democracy is to remain open to the next turn of the democratic.

The emptiness at the heart of democracy leads to the second key feature of the democratic, namely, its openness to self-critique and transformation. In short, its intrinsic historicity. And again, like Lefort, Derrida will insist that this is 'an essential, original, constitutive, and specific possibility of the democratic, indeed as its very historicity, an intrinsic historicity that it *shares with no other regime*' (RS, 72, my emphasis). This is emphasised again when Derrida describes

> the absolute and intrinsic historicity of the *only* system that welcomes in itself, in its very concept . . . the right to self-critique. Democracy is the *only* system, the *only* constitutional paradigm, in which, in principle, one has or assumes the right to criticize everything publicly, including the idea of democracy, its concept, its history, and its name. Including the constitutional paradigm and the absolute authority of the law . . . whence its chance and fragility. (RS, 86–7, my emphasis; cf. ARSS, 121)[42]

Unlike those nondemocratic systems marked by a movement of closing off and denying historicity ('the already-thought, the already-seen', as Lefort puts it[43]), the features here identified by Derrida as specific to democracy mark democracy out as the only system that welcomes and takes up its own interminable and essential transformation.

These reflections bring us to the third key feature of democracy – the interrupted identity of the demos. Understood in terms of emptiness, interminable self-critique and intrinsic historicity, democratic identity would remain in constant flux, forever on the move and, therefore, forever lacking. The essence of democracy would be to have no essence, no identity. For democracy to be what it most essentially is would require that it 'is never properly what it is, never *itself*' (RS, 37). The very essence of democracy would define democracy as that which defies the proper, the manifestation of an essence, or definitive identity. If this were not the case, if one could point to the identity of democracy, the proper 'it-self' of democracy, one would fill in the very openness of democracy around which its interminable self-critique, and thus historicity, turns (RS, 37). That is to say, the manifestation of the essence of democracy would be the end of democracy. If so, then it would seem that the attempt to grasp the identity of democracy is *a priori* doomed. The heart of democracy that one attempts to grasp remains 'hollowed out at its centre by a vertiginous semantic abyss' (RS, 72).

On the edge of this abyss we begin to feel the dizzying pull of those paradoxical 'X without X' formulations often deployed by Derrida (PF, 42, 80–1): 'For it is perhaps a question here of an essence without an essence . . . of a concept without a concept' (RS, 32), of a 'concept of a democracy without concept' (RS, 37). Once sucked into the whirlpool of these formulations, into the dizzying turns of the 'without', must we not abandon the very attempt to hold on to the concept of democracy? Democracy, as Lefort says, would appear only as ungraspable. We are left, it seems, only with traces of democracy, with democracy 'itself' as a trace (RS, 39):

> Democracy is what it is only in the différance by which it defers itself and differs from itself . . . it is (without being) equal and proper to itself only insofar as it is inadequate and improper, at the same time behind and ahead of itself. (RS, 38)

Understood in these differential terms, democracy always escapes our grasp and any attempt to fix its identity. Interminably open to the interruption of the other, democracy is, in the words of Lefort, the 'experience of an ungraspable, uncontrollable society' whose identity is always in question and whose contours are constantly transformed. Or, put differently, democracy is that form of society which maintains the space for the interruption of an incalculable other.

From this account, we can see why Derridean deconstruction points towards democracy. Democracy is the 'only' regime that is defined by the openness of a radical undecidability, the 'only' regime that welcomes contestability and takes up its own intrinsic historicity, the 'only' regime that calls for its own transformation. It is, in short, the only regime that is constituted by an ethos of interruption.

'Deconstruction is not the only activity needed in town'[44]

Democracy may welcome interruption, but how does it preserve it? Derrida's account of democracy emphasises openness, radical undecidability, interminable self-critique, and intrinsic historicity. This leaves democracy as the site of conflicting interpretations that no essence can arrest. As a result, democracy can only be defined by turns and tropes. But amidst the turns and tropes of competing interpretations, how are we to distinguish between alternative turns that are part of the democratic promise and turns that threaten an alternative to democracy?

> Who, then, can take it upon him- or herself, and with what means, to speak from one side or another of the front, of democracy *itself*, of an *authentic* democracy *properly speaking*, when it is precisely the concept of democracy *itself*, in its univocal and proper meaning, that is presently and forever lacking? When assured of a numerical majority, the worst enemies of democratic freedom can, by a plausible rhetorical simulacrum . . . present themselves as staunch democrats. (RS, 34)

Here one cannot separate the promise from the threat. Indeed, on this account, when it comes to democracy one is forever exposed to the 'threat *in* the promise itself' (RS, 82). If this is so, then how is one to differentiate between those democratic others we would welcome and those ghosts that Derrida insists we must practise recognising?

Derrida is acutely aware of this problem. Indeed, this is something he identifies in his discussion of the autoimmune pervertibility of democracy. From the democratic rise to power of fascist and Nazi totalitarianisms, to the post-September 11 restrictions on democratic freedoms in the name of protecting democracy from its enemies, Derrida points to 'a whole series of examples of an autoimmune pervertibility of democracy'. The suspension of Algerian elections in 1992 is, for Derrida, an 'exemplary' case of this pervertibility, one that is 'typical of all the assaults on democracy in the name of democracy'. The democratically elected government of Algeria suspended democratic elections when it looked as though a party committed to ending democracy and installing a theocratic regime would win the election. This 'sovereign' decision to suspend democracy, 'so as to immunize it against a much worse and very likely assault,' reveals for Derrida the 'autoimmune suicide' at work in democracy. According to Derrida, this autoimmune pervertibility is not a mere empirical going wrong of democracy, but an essential aspect of it. In order to maintain and protect itself, democracy necessarily limits and threatens itself. With no guarantee that the self-limitation of democracy is more democratic than the perceived threat, the suicide of democracy can always be translated into murder (RS, 31–5). This is the reason why Derrida insists that the very promise of democracy 'risks and must always risk being perverted into a threat' (ARSS, 120). With the promise of democracy essentially haunted by this threat, Derrida observes that 'it has always been very difficult, and for essential reasons, to distinguish rigorously between the goods and evils of democracy' (RS, 21).

If deconstruction demands that we maintain an ethos of interruption, then this threat-in-promise pervertibility presents a difficulty. It is a difficulty that has recently been articulated by Hägglund, who refers to this as the 'logic of essential corruptibility' at work in deconstruction.[45] Turning to Hägglund's account will bring out one of the problems with Derrida's theorisation of democracy (and deconstructive accounts inspired by it), and the need for supplementary discourses.

Hägglund argues that this logic of essential corruptibility shows that 'the conceptual borders that serve to distinguish one regime as "democratic" in contradistinction to another are essentially permeable', and thus there will always be 'the threat of democracy becoming totalitarian'.[46] Siding with Laclau against what he sees as Simon Critchley's misguided attempt to secure a distinction between the democratic and nondemocratic, Hägglund argues that 'the deconstructive point is precisely that there is *no such guarantee* for what is democratic and nondemocratic'.[47] From the logic of essential corruptibility, Hägglund maintains that the very attempt to distinguish between democratic and nondemocratic cannot be secured: 'there can be no essential demarcation of democracy from dictatorship.'[48] Needless to say, this puts pressure on the nondemocratic/democratic distinction that was to help us back in the ethico-political marketplace.

I think one of the reasons why we end up in this position is because of the connection that Derrida makes between democracy and *différance*. We saw this at the end of the previous section, and this, I think, prompts Derrida and Hägglund to head in the wrong direction. Similar to his structural reading of ethical claims for deconstruction, Hägglund maintains that what one takes for specific conditions of democracy are in fact the conditions 'for life in general'.[49] That is to say, just as the openness that many see as providing an ethics of deconstruction is in fact a necessary structural feature of any system, so what this thinking of democracy as *différance* suggests is that democracy, like *différance*, is at work in every regime. Hägglund arrives at this conclusion via Derrida's discussion of the 'autoimmune necessity' of *renvoyer* (sending/putting off) inscribed within democracy. For Derrida, this process of *renvoi* operates in terms of, on the one hand, a spatial 'sending off of the other through exclusion' (whether it is sending the other back home, away from the public space or the voting booths, excluding enemies from the democratic process, and so forth) and, on the other hand, the temporal putting off or 'deferral' of democracy (whether it is the postponement of elections, the adjournment of democracy until the next round, or its essential and interminable incompletion (RS, 36–9)). Here both senses of *différance* (to differ and defer) are in operation, leading to Derrida's claim that 'democracy is differential; it is *différance*, *renvoi*, and spacing', and his linking of the thinking of *différance* with a thinking of 'the autoimmune *double bind* of the democratic' (RS, 38, 39). This double bind is precisely the autoimmune logic at work in democracy, a logic whereby democracy, in order to defend and preserve itself, necessarily attacks and limits itself, this double *renvoi* of democracy always being a process of sending/putting off that is carried out in the name of democracy, as precisely a democratic *renvoi* (RS, 36).

It is from this account that Hägglund generalises the problem of democracy to every regime. This would present a problem for the view that I have been outlining, namely, the idea that we can elaborate specific features of democracy that mark it out as the political experience to which deconstruction points. Citing Derrida's claim that concludes this *différance*-based elaboration of democracy – 'there is always some trace of democracy; indeed, every trace is a trace of democracy' (RS, 39) – Hägglund maintains that 'the problem of democracy is at work in every moment and every political regime'. The reason for this is because any exercise of power is necessarily open to 'alteration and critique' insofar as it is subject to the trace structure of time and, consequently, a continual negotiation with a past and future that may overturn that power. This leads Hägglund to conclude not simply that democracy may become totalitarian but, in a surprising reversal, that totalitarianism, indeed 'even the most' totalitarian power, is already and always 'engaged in a "democratic" relation'.[50] Just as there is always a threat *in* the promise of democracy, likewise there is always a 'democratic' relation in totalitarianism.

I say 'reversal' but in Hägglund's argument this identification of a 'democratic' relation in totalitarianism is the first move. Hägglund first identifies this 'democratic' relation and then goes on to argue that '[f]or the same reason, there can be no essential demarcation of democracy from dictatorship'.[51] But what exactly is the reason that accounts for both the 'democratic' relation in totalitarianism and the impossibility of any essential demarcation of democracy from dictatorship? It would seem that it is the necessity of having to 'remain more or less open to alteration and critique', for it is this that imposes the necessity of a continual negotiation with a past and future that may overturn any exercise of power. If one did not have to remain open in this sense, then there would be no necessity of negotiation.

But why describe this having to remain open to alteration and critique as 'democratic'? No doubt this would be a necessity for any democracy, but is this necessity itself democratic? Although Hägglund flanks 'democratic' with quotation marks, it is far from certain that they can carry the burden this passage places on them. If we are to accept that having to 'remain more or less open to alteration and critique' is, itself, a 'democratic' relation, then we would have to conclude that democracy is a general feature of any and every system. There would always have to be a 'democratic' relation, because this openness is a necessary structural feature of any system. This is Hägglund's position and it would seem to follow from Derrida's *différance*-based discussion of democracy, and his claim that 'there is always some trace of democracy' and that 'every trace is a trace of democracy' (RS, 39).[52]

This raises problems. It was precisely because such openness was a necessary structural feature of any system that claims for any ethico-political orientation of deconstruction were ruled out by Hägglund. To recall, the response to those who point to the openness that Derrida continually emphasises as offering a particular ethico-political demand was to say: how could there not be this openness? Such openness is the condition for any change to occur. The absence of such openness would be death. Such structural openness to alteration is, as Hägglund puts it, 'the condition for life in general'. But if this is so, then it is not clear why this should be described as a democratic relation. And if we drop the reference to democratic here, then this would, presumably, also require dropping a key claim of the corruptibility thesis: that there is a democratic relation in every regime. If, however, we hold to the claim that openness to alteration and critique is to be described as a democratic relation, then presumably one should accept that calls for openness to alteration and critique are, indeed, democratic demands.[53] In short, if one holds to the democratic relation claim, then one should accept the democratic demand claim.

If I have understood Hägglund correctly, his reading of deconstruction makes the former claim, but denies the latter claim. Hägglund might avoid the problem I have presented here by suggesting that the notion of a democratic relation is not to be understood in the same way as a democratic orientation or practice. By 'democratic' one would not be referring to democratic practices (institutionalised in, say, rights of freedom of speech, the press, association; the right to assembly, to vote; regular multi-party elections; a vibrant public sphere; separation of powers, to cite just a few of the more familiar markers), but simply to the necessity of remaining open to alteration that results from *différance* and the trace. Hence the quotation marks around 'democratic'. But this is precisely the problem: can these quotation marks maintain their grip on the 'democratic'; can they hold on to the legacy of democracy in this ascent to the rarefied levels of conceptual analysis where mere openness to alteration is itself 'democratic'? Isn't this the kind of formalism that invited complaints from thinkers as different as Critchley and McCarthy?

To describe democracy in differential terms is one thing; to say that democracy 'is' *différance* (assuming that one could talk in this way) is quite another. While the former may open up interesting ways of understanding democracy, the latter seems to withdraw democracy into the movement of the trace, as something we can only speak of in the dissolving terms of the 'without'. Again, this looks like the kind of ineffable gestures that McCarthy warned us about. The problem here is that one is in danger of committing a similar kind of mistake as the overly structural reading of undecidability we discussed in the previous chapter, namely, that the experience of democracy is lost. To talk of democracy in terms of the trace or to describe it 'as' *différance* generalises democracy such that we risk losing any sense of the complex dispositions and concrete practices of democratic engagement. Indeed, it would be hard to see how Derrida could talk of any 'specific possibility of the democratic', or 'intrinsic' possibilities that it 'shares with no other regime', if it 'is' *différance*, as opposed to being differential. This would be less moving upstream (to recall Dews's criticism) than getting out of the stream altogether.

Even if one were to view this identification of democracy 'as' *différance* as an aside aimed at countering the 'ethico-political turn' reading of Derrida's work (this is not the only place where Derrida links *différance* to a thinking of politics (PF, 104–6; N, 93, 182)), something has still gone wrong here. Indeed, I think this points to a more general problem with certain deconstructive approaches to democracy, namely, attention seems to be focused on emphasising the radical undecidability of the regime, its permanent risk or contamination. In the context of Derrida's account, much of this is motivated by the desire to bring out the radical aspects of democracy in order to disturb any neo-liberal good conscience (SM, 83; GD, 86). Now, while this may be needed, an account of how one goes about surrounding that democratic uncertainty 'with the maximum of guarantees, knowledge [and] precautions' (ROD, 34) is also needed. Derrida tells us that ethical and political responsibility implies that we 'try to programme, to anticipate, to define laws and rules' (ROD, 7) and so it seems fair to ask: what would a deconstructive approach to democracy look like?

Without exploring the concrete practices of democracy, this deconstructive account faces a number of potential problems. Firstly, it not only identifies an essential pervertibility in democracy, but seemingly leaves us abandoned to this pervertibility. Here both the 'mere openness' and 'withdrawal' worries return. But even if we cannot eliminate this vulnerability, Derrida's account calls for decisions that would minimise this as much as possible. Those of us back in the ethico-political marketplace need something in addition to the claim that democracy is *différance*. Secondly, it is hard to see how this deconstructive account would actually motivate one to take up the democratic task. If we look at the account so far, democratic engagement is anything but easy. I must consistently engage in decisions all the while haunted by uncertainty and constantly exposing myself to disturbing interruptions that challenge my identity and attachments. This is demanding. If one is to take up this task, then more needs to be said about the possibilities of doing so, and the kind of political practices that would sustain it.

Notes

1. Thomas Fuller, *Gnomologia*, 1732, 374. OED entry for 'conscience'.
2. Murdoch, *The Sovereignty of Good*, 72.
3. AP, 19; DE, 87, 101; FL, 52; GD, 25, 67, 85; N, 99, 103, 138, 179, 232; PF, 42; PM, 139; PS, 286, 287, 361; RDP, 86; ROD, 20; SM, xv, 15, 28, 66, 97, 233; TOH, 41, 45, 81.
4. Wilson, 'That sweet sound sleep that is the lot o' a gude conscience', *Blackwood Magazine*, April 1827, 476.
5. Bohman notes that the increasing deep conflicts that polities face 'make impossible a world without moral loss' (PD, 73).
6. See LI, 138; N, 182, 232; PF, 219; PS, 359, 361; TOH, 41, 45, 81.
7. Kearney, 'Aliens and Others', 260.
8. Wolin, *The Seduction of Unreason*, 223–4.
9. Hägglund, *Radical Atheism*, 187.
10. 'Maintain' suggests both a perilous holding in the face of an interminable threat or danger and a nourishing that sustains such holding.
11. Cf. 'any promise in its very structure requires fulfilment. There is no promise that does not require its fulfilment. Affirmation requires a position. It requires that one move to action . . . even if it is imperfect' (N, 26).
12. Hägglund acknowledges that Derrida suggests an opposition between 'good' systems that are open to the future and 'bad' systems that close down the future. However, Hägglund insists that this opposition is 'untenable given the logic of deconstruction'. There can be no normative claim, because 'openness to the future is unconditional in the

sense that *everything* (including every system or action) is necessarily open to the future' (*Radical Atheism*, 231–2, n. 4). But if this is so, then it is hard to make sense of what Derrida is doing here. I think there is a way of making sense of this. Derrida identifies these systems not in terms of being closed but rather as systems that 'close and close themselves off from' the coming of the other. That is to say, these systems are marked by a general discourse of *closing* off, not a state of *being closed*. That structurally they can never be closed in no way precludes one from speaking of these as systems of closing off. Indeed, it is because of the impossibility of attaining the desired closure of a society that has expunged any trace of contingency or historicity that these systems are systems of incessant closing off. What is crucial here is to appreciate the unavoidable/undeniable layers at work: structurally every system is unavoidably open, but the undeniable layer points to the possibility of systems constructing themselves around denying, suppressing or closing themselves off from this openness. Democratic systems, however imperfect they may be, structure themselves around the institutionalisation of this openness. It is at this level that Derrida's distinction between 'good' and 'bad' systems is operating. Once we take this into account, then there is no reason why structural openness necessarily renders normative claims against systems of closing off a non-starter.
13. FL, 28; FWT, 53; N, 13, 16, 194, 242, 296, 372; PF, 67; PM, 11; PS, 198; RS, 145, 150–1; TOH, 18, 78.
14. Wolin, *The Seduction of Unreason*, 236–8.
15. See Fraser, 'The French Derrideans', 65.
16. Wolin, *The Seduction of Unreason*, 234, 240.
17. Critchley, *The Ethics of Deconstruction*, 200.
18. Cf. 'to allow the coming of the entirely other, passivity . . . is not suitable. Letting the other come is not inertia ready for anything whatever' (PSY, 39).
19. McCarthy criticises Derrida's work for having little to contribute to a 'constructive ethicopolitical task', for having 'no suggestion of . . . alternatives', and for failing to set out 'the evaluative perspective from which he judges those effects [of his deconstructive practice] to be good' (PI, 111, 112).
20. As the 'finally' in this passage indicates, one does not simply decide from a position of ignorance.
21. I draw on the account of negativism developed in Freyenhagen, *Adorno's Practical Philosophy*.
22. Amidst the 'delirious hallucinations' and 'glaring hypocrisy' of the

Fukuyama 'euphoria', Derrida lists ten 'plagues' of the capitalist order, showing that, 'despite the manic disavowal', the 'world is going badly' (SM, 78–85).

23. The law in question made it illegal to open one's home to undocumented immigrants. This speech, delivered by Derrida during a demonstration at the Théâtre des Amandiers, is an example of the Aristotelian approach to rhetoric and public deliberation touched on in Chapter 2. Not only do we see a certain *ethos* emerge in the descriptions of his reactions to the wrongness of the law and, in particular, the phrase that is the focus of the opening, but it is clear that the speech aims to situate the audience within a particular emotional orientation to this issue so that the wrongness of the situation can be recognised. And what ties the *ethos* and *pathos* of the speech together is the *logos* of the speech; that is, the series of arguments that make up the body of Derrida's address. The democratic reason-giving displayed in this speech brings into view for us the kind of relation to rhetoric that the deliberative approaches in Chapter 2 miss. I do not have space to develop the more detailed account of Derrida's relation to Aristotle that is no doubt called for here. Building on this relation to rhetoric, and the account of the undecidable nature of practical judgement developed in the last two chapters, a suggestion from an anonymous reviewer – that we might 'characterise Derrida on judgement in negative Aristotelian terms . . .' – seems the right way to go.

24. Elsewhere, Derrida links the situation of the *sans-papiers*, and the specific law in question, to 'refugees of every kind, immigrants with or without citizenship, exiled or forced from their homes, whether with or without papers, from the heart of Nazi Europe to the former Yugoslavia, from the Middle East to Rwanda, from Zaire all the way to California, from the Church of St. Bernard to the thirteenth arrondissement in Paris . . .'. He goes on to refer to 'the crimes *against* hospitality endured by the guests [*hôtes*] and hostages of our time, incarcerated or deported day after day, from concentration camp to detention camp, from border to border, close to us or far away' (AD, 71, 101).

25. As I write, the Italian government is prosecuting those rescuing migrants at sea, leading to claims that they are 'criminalising solidarity'. See Boffey and Tondo, 'Captain of migrant rescue ship says Italy "criminalising solidarity"', *The Guardian*, 15 June 2019. Recently, the US government tried to convict a teacher of 'harboring migrants' when he provided two immigrants with water, food and lodging. See Associated Press, 'Jurors refuse to convict activist facing 20 years for

helping migrants', *The Guardian*, 12 June 2019. In the UK, laws targeting homeless people left one judge lamenting: 'I will be sending a man to prison for asking for food when he was hungry.' See Greenfield and Marsh, 'Hundreds of homeless people fined and imprisoned in England and Wales', *The Guardian*, 20 May 2019.

26. Derrida expresses this concern when describing a 'remoralization of deconstruction' that 'risks reassuring itself . . . and promoting a new dogmatic slumber'. Acknowledging that in expressing such a concern 'one gives ammunition to the officials of anti-deconstruction', Derrida nevertheless 'prefer[s] that to the constitution of . . . a community of complacent deconstructionists, reassured and reconciled with the world in ethical certainty, good conscience, satisfaction of service rendered, and the consciousness of duty accomplished . . .'. See Derrida, 'Passions', 13–15.
27. Fraser, 'The French Derrideans', 72; Critchley, *The Ethics of Deconstruction*, 200, 215.
28. Wolin complains that 'in lieu of a more concrete specification . . . of how we should open ourselves to the other' and of what this would mean in terms of 'forms of practical life conduct', Derrida's account 'seems more frustrating than illuminating' (*The Seduction of Unreason*, 233). I hope the account outlined so far, and further developed in the following chapter, lessens this frustration.
29. See Bernstein, *The New Constellation*, chapter 6.
30. See the account of the politics of the stage and the work of resistance in Chapter 3 and the empirical work discussed in Chapter 6. See also the example of Derrida's intervention in the immigration debate in France and his account of hospitality (above and Chapter 6).
31. Barber, 'Foundationalism and Democracy', 349.
32. Lefort, *Democracy and Political Theory*, 17.
33. Ibid. 19.
34. The idea of one person or group embodying the law has always remained a political fiction. The very form of law implies a distinction between those who exercise power and that which legitimises that exercise. Democracy does not create that gap; rather, it makes that gap explicit. At times this is lost in the contrast Lefort wants to make between the democratic and nondemocratic.
35. Lefort, *Democracy and Political Theory*, 16.
36. Ibid.
37. Lefort, *The Political Forms of Modern Society*, 303–4.
38. Ibid. 305.
39. Lefort, *Democracy and Political Theory*, 16.

40. Lefort, *The Political Forms of Modern Society*, 305.
41. Lefort, *Democracy and Political Theory*, 24, 34, 16.
42. Derrida refers to the 'essential historicity of democracy', suggesting that 'democracy' is 'the only name of a regime . . . open to its own historical transformation, to taking up its own intrinsic plasticity and its interminable self-criticizability' (RS, 25). Cf. 'the inherited concept of democracy is the only one that welcomes the possibility of being contested, of contesting itself, of criticizing and infinitely improving itself' (ARSS, 121).
43. Lefort, *The Political Forms of Modern Society*, 296.
44. Connolly, *Identity\Difference*, 14.
45. Hägglund, *Radical Atheism*, 177.
46. Ibid.
47. Ibid. 186.
48. Ibid. 177; cf. 172, 186, 188, 202.
49. Ibid. 177.
50. Ibid.
51. Ibid.
52. Lefort again would be instructive here. Discussing the freedoms proclaimed in the French Declaration of the Rights of Man of 1791, Lefort notes: 'where they do not exist, we look in vain for the slightest trace of it [democracy].' He also argues that a totalitarian regime 'implies the ruin of democracy'. See Lefort, *Democracy and Political Theory*, 39, 28. Cf. Derrida, FWT, 82–3.
53. In *calling* for such openness deconstruction would be calling for a 'democratic' relation. Part of the denial of any ethico-political injunction, if I have understood this correctly, is that this is not a unique feature of democratic regimes. But the fact that all systems *contain* this relation does not, in itself, make the *call* for such a relation any less of a democratic call. A key difference here is that while those authoritarian systems may well contain such a relation, as systems they do not call for or welcome that relation. Indeed, quite the opposite. This is a variation of the point made in n. 12 above.

6

The Democratic Venture

Does the deconstructive account of democracy leave any hope for the possibility of realising a just constitutional regime? The account of democratic pervertibility does not seem promising. And as Rawls notes (in an echo of Kant), without this hope one may wonder whether life is worth living.[1] In this final chapter I attempt to avoid that despairing position. I shall do so by discussing deconstructive and deliberative approaches to constitutional democracy, and, in particular, how each addresses its alleged paradoxical nature. I begin by revisiting the deconstructive account of democracy that left us in what seemed like a hopeless position at the end of the last chapter. I argue that Derrida's account of democracy presupposes constitutional safeguards that, in principle, check the pervertibility he identifies. I support this by discussing Derrida's response to what he takes to be an exemplary case of such pervertibility – the cancellation of elections in Algeria in 1992. While pervertibility cannot be eliminated, I argue that deconstruction demands that we pursue the least perverting perversion (see Chapter 5). My second step is to bring the deconstructive and deliberative understandings of constitutional democracy into conversation. Here I identify an area of overlap and a key difference. The former is their shared historical understanding of democratic legitimacy. The latter is their approach to the indeterminacy of democratic constitution-making. Deliberative approaches present a dialectical story of self-correcting learning processes, while the deconstructive approach points to the 'non-dialectizable' indeterminacy of that process. The latter picture emerges from the antinomic understanding of the 'im-possibility' of doing justice to the other developed in Chapters 4 and 5.[2] This is something deliberativists need to consider if they are to avoid slipping into a self-congratulatory narrative. As a final step, I point to glimpses of a less confident, more vigilant, deliberative approach, and the possibility of a deliberative-deconstructive dialogue in terms of their shared hope in the perfectibility of democracy and the promise this contains for doing justice to the other in their otherness. I end the chapter by pointing to current empirical research that not only gives hope for dialogue, but also gives encouragement for praxis.

I. A Discontented and Disconcerting Regime

From its birth democracy has been seen as a discontented regime. That is to say, as a regime that is marked by a lack of content and restraint. Democratic identity emerges, Plato tells us, through the internal conflict between 'the narrow economical way' of the repressed oligarch father, and the 'desires' of the more unrestrained democratic son.[3] It is because of the lack of any authoritative pattern of life that democracy is, according to Plato, constitutively unable to restrain desire and therefore is never assured the peace of mind of consensus. Plato was right to see a certain weakness as constitutive of democracy.[4] For modern democratic theorists, however, this weakness is no reason to reject democracy. While Plato saw in this conflict and discontent a sign of degeneration (557e), modern democratic theorists hold to this as the very promise of the democratic venture. Whether understood in terms of an agonistic clash, a vibrant deliberative exchange, or the perilous openness to the interruption of an incalculable other, democracy is seen as the best wager in the pluralised lifeworlds of modernity.

This openness of democracy to the other is not something that Plato missed. In a democracy, observes Plato, individuals are granted the liberty to arrange their lives as they choose and therefore one finds the 'greatest variety of individual character' there, more than in any other form of society (555c). With the freedom and 'diversity of its characters', democracy, 'like the different colours in a patterned dress', weaves itself into an infinite variety of models and multicoloured patterns, such that 'it contains every possible type [of constitution]' (557c–d). Although Plato describes democracy as a 'form of society', it seems to be defined by a lack of form. Rather than pointing to a particular regime or the contents of a particular paradigm, democracy seems to name a dis-contented opening of a freedom and diversity that contains 'patterns of so many constitutions and ways of life' (561e). This is not simply the freedom *of* democracy, but a freedom *in the concept* of democracy that we saw Derrida emphasise in the previous chapter. Indeed, what Plato seems to be describing is a regime open to the other as other, an unconditional hospitality to any pattern of life. But this is precisely the problem. This freedom and openness would seem to leave us vulnerable to the problems that Plato warns us about. When Plato describes the democrat becoming 'in his waking life what he was only occasionally in his dreams' (575a), the worry is that, without some restraining content, the adventure and freedom of this 'anarchic form' (558b) of society remains vulnerable to the kind of problems so vividly described in Book VIII of *The Republic*. So while democracy may well begin as Lefort's uncontrollable adventure, what's to stop it descending into Plato's all-too-familiar nightmare?

Why does Derrida refer us back to Plato here? Not only does Derrida's account of democracy echo Plato's warnings about democracy's constitutive vulnerability to the threat of 'the worst', but he specifically locates his own account as emerging from a reading of Plato. Plato stresses the lack of form in democracy, and it is this that will make it difficult to protect democracy from the democrat who becomes in his waking life what he was only occasionally in his dreams. And therein lies the greater difficulty: protecting democracy from 'the democrat'. The threats to democracy today are not confined to self-proclaimed opponents of democracy (RS, 28–9). As Derrida's account suggests, with autoimmunity inscribed within democracy itself, the sending off (*renvoi*) of the other is carried out in the name of democracy, as precisely a democratic *renvoi* (RS, 36). A problem of which Plato was well aware:

> Who, then, can take it upon him or herself, and with what means, to speak from one side or another of this front, of democracy itself, of authentic democracy properly speaking, when it

is precisely the concept of democracy itself, in its univocal and proper meaning, that is presently and forever lacking? When assured of a numerical majority, the worst enemies of democratic freedom can, by a plausible rhetorical simulacrum (and even the most fanatical Islamists do this on occasion), present themselves as staunch democrats. That is one of the many perverse and autoimmune effects of the axiomatic developed already in Plato. (RS, 34)[5]

Even if we question the particular account Plato gives of the descent from democracy into tyranny, Plato, on Derrida's reading, is still pointing to something very disconcerting about democracy. The constitutive lack of form means that democracy authorises a multiplicity of interpretations that makes it difficult not only to protect democracy from its enemies, but to identify authoritatively who the enemy may be. The 'democrat' may turn out to be a real rogue. In taking his bearings from this Platonic understanding of democracy, Derrida is attempting to reactivate a more disconcerting aspect of democracy. Recalling the previous chapter, we could see this as an attempt to disturb the self-possession and complacency of the modern-day democrat. That is to say, there can be no democratic good conscience. But having radicalised democracy in this way, is it possible to keep hold of the democratic promise?

'Thus far shalt thou go and no further' – checking pervertibility?[6]

While Derrida's return to Plato in *Rogues* successfully reactivates a disconcerting aspect of democracy, one wonders why he stops short of engaging with contemporary democratic theorists. When he asks 'why are there so few democrat philosophers . . . from Plato to Heidegger?' (RS, 88), one cannot help but think: why stop at Heidegger? While Derrida's discussion of democracy in *Rogues* engages with Jean-Luc Nancy, there is no engagement with contemporary democratic theorists.[7] This is unfortunate because the most obvious response to the problem of the pervertibility of democracy would be to point to the protections and checks afforded by constitutional rights – something that modern democrats would be quick to invoke. As Paul Patton notes:

> Had he [Derrida] taken into account more recent theorists of liberal democracy, he would have confronted a more complex axiomatic . . . For many modern theorists, the value of freedom is considered to set limits to the operation of the democratic principle of equality in number. The freedom of each is of such value that neither individuals nor the numerical majority are allowed to infringe upon it.[8]

For Patton, the lack of engagement with modern democratic theorists is a missed opportunity that leaves Derrida focused on the problem of the tyranny of the majority. But, Patton notes, this is something that modern liberal theorists have long since addressed.

While the element of numerical majority features in Derrida's account of democratic autoimmunity (RS, 34–6), the latter is not reducible to the former. Derrida's exemplary case is the cancellation of elections in Algeria in 1992 because of fears that the majority were about to vote into power a party that would bring an end to democracy. Autoimmunity is located not only in the possibility of a democratic majority putting an end to individual freedom; it is also located in the power of the state to interrupt the democratic self-determination of a people. When Derrida points to the restrictions on democratic freedoms introduced by the US government after 9/11 as another example of the autoimmunity of democracy, the issue is one concerning not the power of the majority, but the power of the state. Having said this, Patton is right to draw attention to the limitations of Derrida's account that result from the lack of engagement with contemporary democratic theorists. Derrida's return to Plato appears to leave us with a picture of democracy as licensing the freedom to do as one pleases.[9] But the principle of the constitutional exercise of power that informs modern democratic societies checks (in principle) this freedom and, presumably, protects against democracy dying at the majority's hands. As Habermas observes, the freedom of democracy does not give citizens a 'carte blanche permission to make whatever decisions they like'. The freedom to do as one pleases 'is the core of private, not public autonomy' (CD, 767). In the public realm, certain fundamental rights act as checks on the pervertibility that Derrida seems to present as going all the way down to the empty core of democracy. The emptiness of democracy that Derrida emphasises is a constitutionally secured emptiness.

Derrida is no doubt aware of this. As we have seen, he emphasises the need to calculate in order to preserve a space for the interruption of the incalculable other. This is what the demand to maintain ethos of interruption requires. It is to prevent the kind of interruption that would put an end to any future arriving that Derrida insists on the need to identify and block the arriving of certain others. And given his insistence that justice demands the continual creation and reformulation of laws and institutions to safeguard the singularity of the other, the blocking of those others who seek to put an end to the very possibility of any future *arrivant* would need to make reference to legally protected basic rights aimed at securing a space for the singular other. Thus Derrida's own answer to the problem of democratic pervertibility points to fundamental rights positively enacted as basic rights. Indeed, one of the key reasons why Derrida privileges democracy (despite his reservations) is because it constitutes itself around certain fundamental rights that seek to protect the promise from the threat (for example, the right of freedom of speech and public criticism,[10] the right to self-critique and perfectibility (RS, 86), and the right 'of political change' (N, 121), to name but a few; see Chapter 5). It is in reference to these rights, constitutionally guaranteed in any democracy, that democracy is privileged: 'Democracy is the *only* system, the *only* constitutional paradigm, in which, in principle, one has or assumes the right to criticize everything publicly, including the idea of democracy, its concept, its history, and its name' (RS, 86–7, my emphasis).

Indeed, the very practice of deconstruction itself points to, and presupposes, a democratic form of society. Without these rights there would be no space for the practice of deconstruction (or the ethos of interruption it calls for). And if, as Derrida insists, democracy is unique in constituting itself around, and guaranteeing, such rights (recall the emphasis on 'only' in passages above and in Chapter 5), then we need to take seriously his telegraphic assertion: 'no deconstruction without democracy' (PF, 105). If we look at the context in which Derrida makes this claim (strangely overlooked by Hägglund and Laclau) this becomes clear: 'One keeps this indefinite right to the question, to criticism, to deconstruction (guaranteed rights, in principle, in any democracy: no deconstruction without democracy . . .)' (PF, 105). Without the constitutionally guaranteed rights of democracy and the spaces they make possible, there would be no practice of deconstruction. Derrida's references to democracy are not simply offering a deconstructive defence of democracy; they are also pointing to the democratic conditions without which there would be no practice of deconstruction.

Derrida's own practice and understanding of deconstruction, then, presupposes these guaranteed rights and spaces afforded by the constitutional paradigm of democracy. Given this, could we not say that, for Derrida, autoimmunity cannot go all the way down? This is not to say that we could eliminate the autoimmune effects within democracy, but it is to suggest that at some level the possibility of perversion must, in principle, be checked. On this view, we would have an answer to the question that Derrida asks when discussing 'the freedom at play in the concept of democracy':

> [M]ust a democracy leave free and in a position to exercise power those who risk mounting an assault on democratic freedoms and putting an end to democratic freedom in the name of democracy and of the majority that they might actually be able to rally round to their cause? (RS, 36)

The answer would be 'no'. As Thomas Paine might have put it, the constitution that guarantees the rights and spaces that make possible democratic life in effect says: 'Thus far shalt thou go and no further.' And Derrida would seem to agree with this.

Taking sides: 'You need me on that wall'[11]

I have argued that Derrida's emphasis on calculation and laws, and his own practice of deconstruction, suggest the need for constitutionally protected, and positively enacted, basic rights guaranteed in a democratic form of society. As we saw in the previous chapter, the ethos of interruption that maintains a space for the arriving of the other must be saved from the interruption of the interruption. That is to say, one must prevent an arriving that would close down any future arriving (N, 194). And this, Derrida insists, means that we 'must practice recognizing' what he calls 'those . . . ghosts' (SM, 16) that bring with them discourses that 'close themselves off from, and close off, the coming of the other' (N, 182). The opening to the incalculable arriving of who or what comes 'must be safeguarded' (N, 195). Given this, doesn't Derridean deconstruction need someone on the wall? Perhaps not a Colonel Jessup with that Hobbesian look in his eye, but perhaps someone more like Michelman's responsive constitutional judge who, in deconstructive terms, seeks to maintain an ethos of interruption, where the incalculable spaces of democratic freedom are surrounded 'with a maximum of guarantees' (ROD, 34).[12] In Michelman's words: 'constitutional law plays a fundamental role in securing political freedom through, amongst other things, its constant reach for inclusion of the other, of the hitherto excluded – which in practice means bringing to legal-doctrinal presence hitherto absent voices.'[13]

I shall explore this further by discussing Derrida's intervention in the 'exemplary' case of Algeria. Derrida's 'Taking Sides for Algeria' (N, 117–24) was delivered at a meeting initiated by CISA and La Ligue des Droites de l'Homme.[14] The meeting was organised around an *Appeal for Civil Peace in Algeria* that was issued in 1994 as the bloody civil war, which had been sparked by the cancellation of a second round of elections in 1992, continued.[15] Derrida begins with some cautionary remarks about the terms of the *Appeal* itself, but it is his comments on political neutrality that are of particular interest here. Derrida argues that the 'apparent arbitral neutrality' of the *Appeal*, while commendable, does not mean that one is held to political neutrality (N, 117). One must take sides, but neither of the two sides of the 'nondemocratic front' in Algeria. Outlining the ways in which one must take sides, Derrida issues a demand for an 'electoral contract'. As part of this contract, he emphasises three key components of what a 'true democracy' would require in its 'minimal definition':

> 1. A calendar, that is, an electoral commitment; 2. Discussion, that is, of public discourse that is armed only with reasoned arguments, for example in a free press; 3. Respect for the electoral verdict and thus a change in political power [*alternance*] in the course of a democratic process, the possibility of which is never interrupted. (N, 121)

If we imagine a case where it is evident that a party committed to denying these minimal requirements is about to get into power, should the democrat hold to the injunction against interruption? Is Derrida saying that the democrat should allow the total perversion of democracy to take place? What happened to talk of 'preventing certain things from coming to pass' (see Chapter 5)? Who is Derrida taking sides for here?

The injunction against the interruption of the democratic process is, Derrida tells us, issued against both sides of this nondemocratic front. On the one hand, the injunction takes sides against state power. The way Derrida expresses this, however, is less than straightforward. Given the injunction against interruption, one might have expected Derrida to take sides against state power for interrupting the electoral process, but this is not what he says. He takes sides against a state power that 'would not do everything immediately to create the necessary conditions, in particular those of appeasement and discussion, to reengage *as quickly as possible* an interrupted electoral process' (N, 121). Derrida does not say that he is against state power for the decision they took to interrupt the elections; it is the state's behaviour after this decision that is the focus. And even here, the opposition is phrased in conditional terms. Derrida takes sides against a state power that 'would' not do everything to get the process running again. If the Algerian state were to do everything it could to create the 'necessary conditions' for the resumption of elections, would Derrida still take sides against the state?[16]

Can we not detect here a reservation about taking sides against the decision to interrupt? And if so, in this reservation do we not encounter a silent acknowledgement of the limits of democratic pervertibility? The observation that the vote is 'certainly not the whole of democracy' but without the calculation of voices 'there would be no democracy' may suggest that Derrida would still be against any interruption. And, a little later, he does say that the reference to democracy means that one is 'logically' against this perversion (N, 121). But this does not touch the political problem. Without state interruption there would no longer be any votes, any democracy. One either watches democracy die a good democratic death, or one intervenes to save the possibility of future political alternations and the arrival of those incalculable others that Derrida insists must be safeguarded. As we will see, it may well be that in such a situation there is no non-perverting option, only lesser or worse perversions.

On the other hand, Derrida's injunction against interruption takes aim at the other side of this nondemocratic front. But here it is noticeable that Derrida is direct and unequivocal in his opposition to this side:

> We also take sides . . . against whoever does not respect electoral arbitration and whoever would tend, directly or indirectly, before, during, or after such elections, to put into question the very principle that will have presided over such a process; that is, democratic life, the state of law, the respect for freedom of speech, the rights of the minority, of political change, of the plurality of languages, customs, beliefs, etc. We are resolutely opposed – and this side we clearly take with all of its consequences – to whoever would claim to profit from democratic procedures without respecting democracy. (N, 121)

The emphasis – 'and this side we clearly take' – suggests that opposition to the other side (an interrupting state power) was not so clearly taken. Given this 'clear' and 'resolute' opposition to this side of democratic pervertibility, one can imagine the state actor responding: 'we're glad to see you clearly taking sides here, but what do you propose we do in the face of the perversion you so clearly and resolutely oppose? You take sides against this perversion "with all its consequences", but one of those consequences may well be that one faces a choice not between a democratic option and a nondemocratic perversion, but between lesser or worse perversions.' It is difficult to see how Derrida could resist this given that it is one of the lessons of Derridean deconstruction. To recall our previous discussion (see Chapter 5), although we always find ourselves within an economy of violence, not all forms are equivalent. Derrida insists that we have to practise 'violence against violence' in order to 'avoid the worst violence'. This would be a 'violence chosen as the least violence' (VM, 146; cf. LI, 112; N, 235–8; RDP, 83). Or, as he puts it elsewhere, 'the only response is *economic*'; that is to say, it 'is necessary to invent the least bad solution' (FWT, 76). In terms of democratic pervertibility, this would require combating one perversion with another perversion so as to arrive at what one judges, in that singular situation, to be the least perverting perversion.

The way that Derrida intervenes against the particular perversions in the Algerian case seems to provide a response to the more general problem of democratic pervertibility. What he seems to point to is something like a 'principle of preservation'.[17] The insistence that one cannot profit from democratic procedures without respecting democracy before, during and after elections operates as a normative principle. Such a principle would be crucial in determining the legitimacy of collective decisions and thereby checking pervertibility. While the initial minimal definition of democracy would give this principle some grip, this would need to be fleshed out in terms of the rights that we have seen Derrida emphasising, and the account of democratic deliberation we discussed in the first two chapters (see point 2 in his minimal definition of democracy). This principle, fleshed out sufficiently, would rule out collective decisions that would threaten the very democratic procedures they rely upon. Such a principle would be in keeping with not merely the account of deconstruction understood as calling for 'openness to the other', but one that demands that we maintain an ethos of interruption so that the other can arrive in their otherness.

While I have not taken into account the empirical difficulties of trying to determine when such a principle would need to be invoked, what I hope to have shown is that, in principle, the emptiness of democracy that Derrida emphasises need not leave us with unchecked pervertibility. The emptiness of democracy requires a principle of preservation. Such a principle would need to be part of a more complex constitutional framework that seeks to secure the very rights that Derrida insists must be safeguarded if we are to maintain a space for the arriving of the other as other. What Derrida's intervention in the Algerian case brings out is the need for a constitutional response to the pervertibility of democratic openness. In taking sides for Algeria, Derrida, it seems, is also taking sides for constitutional democracy.[18]

In search of legitimacy – 'projecting and reflecting!' (LR, 20)

But we are far from any democratic good conscience. A framework of constitutional rights that regulates public autonomy may well check the perversion whereby democratic politics are brought to an end at the hands of the majority, but this still leaves us with the potential threat of another kind of perversion: the coercive imposition of a particular framework of laws lacking democratic legitimacy. Given the openness and freedom in the concept of democracy, how can we be sure that the interruption of a people's democratic self-determination is itself democratically legitimate? As Derrida puts it: how can we be sure that the 'suicide' of democracy (the self-limitation of democracy for the sake of democracy) will not translate into a 'murder' (the unjust sending off of the other (RS, 35))? For those who never make it onto the stage to begin with, the constitution may stipulate rules of the game to be observed, but the question remains: whose game is being reflected in these rules?[19] As Derrida quotes Nelson Mandela in his text 'The Laws of Reflection': 'The credo of the liberal consists in "the use of democratic and constitutional means . . ." This does not have any meaning for those who do not benefit from them' (LR, 19).[20] The struggles of Mandela and Douglass remind us that constitutions, to be deserving of recognition from citizens, require democratic legitimation. Far from being solved, the problem of pervertibility re-emerges in the paradox of constitutional democracy. On the one hand, constitutional rights are invoked to limit the democratic self-determination of a people so as to check pervertibility at the hands of a majority. On the other hand, the constitution can only achieve legitimacy through the democratic will of a people. The constitution that would limit the pervertibility of a majority ending democracy needs, in order to proceed legitimately, the democratic validation of the people. Constitutionalism must be democratically grounded; democracy must be constitutionally protected.[21]

As a way into this paradox, I want to turn briefly to Derrida's 1976 text 'Declarations of Independence' (N, 46–54) and his 1987 text on Nelson Mandela, 'The Laws of Reflection'. What orientates Derrida in 'Declarations of Independence' is what he later describes as the 'very aporia of democracy . . . How is the people . . . born?'

(RS, 48). Derrida begins by asking who the 'we' is that signs the Declaration. The 'we' of the Declaration speaks in the name of 'the people', and it is the latter, through a relay of representatives, who would sign and declare themselves to be free. But does this declaration describe a people that is already free and independent, or does the people come into existence *as* an independent people in the instant of signing? In the undecidability between the constative and performative structure of the declaration, we glimpse the aporia of founding. The people, in whose name the 'we' of the Declaration speaks, does not actually exist prior to the Declaration:

> They do *not* exist as an entity, the entity does *not* exist *before* this declaration, not *as such*. If it gives birth to itself, as free independent subject, as possible signer, this can hold only in the act of the signature. The signature invited the signer. The signer can only authorize him- or herself to sign once he or she has come to the end, if one can say this, of his or her signature, in a sort of fabulous retroactivity. (N, 49)

It is only with the last stroke of the signature that anyone has the legitimacy, the power and ability to sign. Before the text of the declaration there was no signer by right. 'The free and independent people' who sign the declaration are, in this sense, a fable, a fictional entity that paradoxically gives birth to itself in a 'fabulous retroactivity'. The people, not existing before that act of signing, sign, and, in so doing, give themselves the right to sign. The signing of the declaration, then, is recording what *will have been* there – a united and free people with the right to sign and who then do so.

But this fabulous event, this coup de force that brings into being what will have (to have) been there for any signing to legitimately take place, is concealed in the act of founding. For the act that produces that of which it speaks declares itself to be reflecting what is already the case. As Derrida puts it:

> The . . . fiction then consists in bringing to daylight, *in giving birth to*, that which one claims to reflect so as to take note of it, as though it were a matter of recording *what will have been there* . . . while one is in the act of producing the events. (LR, 18)

Given the right conditions, the legitimacy and legality that the signers give to themselves becomes permanently installed as though this 'fabulous' event of founding did not exist (N, 50). As Noah Horwitz puts it: 'The legitimate order gains its legitimacy by retroactively rendering invisible that its legitimacy rests on the aporia of its founding.'[22] Derrida's short text reactivates this paradox and makes this fabulous retroactivity appear.

The implications of this paradox of founding are pursued in Derrida's text on Mandela. The inauguration of a state or first constitution

> cannot presuppose the previously *legitimized* existence of a nation entity . . . The total unity of a nation is not identified for the first time except by a contract . . . which institutes some fundamental law. Now this contract is never actually signed, except by supposed representatives of the nation . . . This fundamental law cannot, either in law or in fact, simply precede that which at once institutes it and nevertheless supposes it: projecting and reflecting! (LR, 20)

Legitimacy comes into being with the signing of the constitution and it is only after this that a democratic people is constituted. While future democratic practices can seek legitimacy in the procedures and rights laid down in the constitution, the democratic legitimacy of the constitution would presumably require a prior set of democratic procedures laid out in a prior contract/law to regulate the process of becoming a people and forming laws. And with this, as Kevin Olsen explains, an infinite regress sets in:

> Any democratic attempt to create a constitution requires a previous constitution that has already established democratic procedures. There is an infinite regress of procedures presupposing procedures, each necessary to form the procedures following it. The founders will be paralyzed in the position of needing a set of procedures that explains how to go about forming procedures.[23]

Hence the fabulous retroactivity required in the paradoxical act of founding.

One might argue that while this problem of fabulous retroactivity is present in the act of founding, it effectively remains there. That is to say, it is a problem only insofar as we are engaged in the act of founding a constitution. By focusing on the paradoxes of the act of constitutional founding, an approach like Derrida's fails to think about these problems historically. As Seyla Benhabib argues in her critique of Derrida: 'democracies have developed a series of institutional mechanisms for controlling and self-correcting the arbitrariness of original positioning of authority.'[24] Constitutions may emerge in the way that Derrida describes, but once a constitution is up and running the paradox between constitutionalism and democracy works itself out through a dynamic process of self-correction: 'it resolves itself in the dimension of historical time', as Habermas puts it (CD, 774). On this dynamic understanding, legitimacy need not be in place at the start. The 'people' that is called into being in the founding act may be a fiction projected by a particular will. But with this fiction at the heart of the original act, a contradiction exists between the historically contingent identity of those who sign the declaration and the normative contents of the declaration itself. As Benhabib observes, 'we, the people' is no longer taken to be 'we white, propertied males' precisely because abolitionists, working-class movements and suffragettes pointed to the contradiction that exists between the limited, historical 'we' who declare a new constitution, and the normative contents of the declaration itself. For Benhabib, with the founding of a constitution 'a tension, a dialectic . . . unfolds', in which, under pressure from social movements, hitherto marginalised groups are included in an ongoing struggle to better realise the normative contents of the constitution.[25] No doubt the unfolding of this dialectic is a battle subject to 'contingent interruptions and historical regressions', as Habermas notes, but, understood as a 'long-term self-correcting process' (CD, 774), it offers a temporal notion of legitimacy that avoids the paradox of founding to which Derrida seems to be pointing. Rather than being sought in the original act of founding, legitimacy is something to be achieved through an ongoing self-correcting learning process, in which we better realise the 'fabulous' declaration of a free, self-determining people, equal under the law.

Derrida's account of the paradox of founding does not rule

out a historical understanding of constitution-making. Democratic legitimacy, for Derrida, is also to be understood dynamically, rather than something to be sought in some original moment of founding. Democratic legitimacy would depend on the extent to which we live up to the 'fabulous we' at the heart of the constitution. We catch a glimpse of this in Derrida's judgement that the coup de force that founded the constitution of the apartheid state of South Africa was a 'bad coup' (LR, 18). Derrida judges this coup to be a bad coup because it 'remained' a coup de force: 'In this case the coup de force remained a coup de force, thus, as a bad coup' (LR, 18). In order to understand what Derrida means here, we need to recall his remarks concerning the event of founding.

As we have seen, for Derrida, 'the people' that is presupposed for the legitimate act of signing does not actually exist prior to the signing – it only comes into existence after the fact. This is the 'fabulous retroactivity' of the event of founding. Here, then, we see the tension in the founding event that Benhabib identifies: the tension between the 'fabulous we' of a free and independent people declared in the constitution, and a 'historical we' who signs and declares itself to be reflecting this 'fabulous we'. Understood dynamically, the legitimacy of constitution-making depends on the extent to which the 'historical we' reflects the 'fabulous we'. Recalling Derrida's remarks about the possibility of the arbitrary origin of a constitution being forgotten and the violence involved in any act of founding being re-covered, we might say that a 'good' coup is one that succeeds in rendering invisible this coup de force.[26] And this rendering invisible is achieved by a constitution-making process that strives to live up to the 'fabulous we' of the constitution. According to Derrida, in the apartheid state of South Africa this rendering invisible never happened because the violence was '*visibly too great* . . . The white community was *too* much in the minority, the disproportion of wealth *too* flagrant. From then on this violence remains . . . lost in its own contradiction' (LR, 18). Because the contradiction between the 'fabulous we' and 'historical we' remained (and here the door is opened to a temporal understanding of legitimacy) so excessive, the original coup de force remained all too visible. This coup remained a bad coup because the 'historical we' in South Africa did not reflect the 'fabulous we' sufficiently. Indeed, there was no attempt to approximate it. And, as Horwitz suggests, 'it is precisely the attempt to better approximate and take seriously this legal fiction that makes it more likely that the . . . event of foundation will become invisible and recede into the past.'[27] In the absence of this attempt, the contradiction between the fabulous and historical 'we' remained too excessive (and therefore too visible). As a result, the legislative apparatus of the apartheid state 'fails to pay back' the coup de force of the original founding (LR, 18).

In emphasising that the bad coup remains unreflective of the 'fabulous we' it projected, Derrida's account suggests a dynamic understanding of democratic legitimacy. There are two things to note here. Firstly, this corrects the view that Derrida's so-called 'obsession' or 'fixation' with paradoxes at the origins of founding acts 'does not allow us to come to grips with political thought in its historical context'.[28] As the account above suggests, it is through striving to better reflect the 'fabulous we' that the coup de force that founds a constitutional state 'pays back'. And the currency of this paying back would seem to be democratic legitimacy. Secondly, while Derrida's understanding of constitutional-making is historical, this should not be understood as a dialectically unfolding self-correcting learning process, as Benhabib and Habermas suggest. Derrida's understanding of constitution-making is one of contingent, historical struggles, in which the 'historical we' is constantly interrupted by the incalculable arriving of the other. This is an interminable process, the direction of which remains, ultimately, incalculable.

Are we in the same boat? And where are we heading?

As we have seen, for Benhabib and Habermas constitution-making is understood as a historical self-correcting learning process. This account avoids the paradox generated by searching for legitimacy in the event of founding by turning our gaze towards the ever-expanding horizon of a more inclusive 'we'. Legitimacy lies ahead of us, not buried behind us. But the dialectical story of an unfolding self-correcting learning process is a little more Janus-faced than this. We head into this future constantly looking over our shoulder. In order for the paradox of constitutional democracy to be resolved in the dimension of historical time, we must see this as an 'ongoing project' that 'continues across generations' (CD, 768). And this is based on the following assumption:

> [T]he interpretation of the constitutional history as a learning process is predicated on the non-trivial assumption that later generations will start with the same standards as did the founders . . . The descendants can learn from past mistakes only if they are in the same boat as their forebears . . . All participants must be able to recognize the project as the same throughout history and to judge it from the same perspective. (CD, 774)

This is a problematic assumption for at least three reasons. Firstly, by presupposing that we are 'in the same boat', Habermas requires something more than a procedural consensus. To be in the same boat as *our* forebears, we must invoke a particular history, values and identity. If the boat of generations is made out of a procedural consensus only, then in what sense would constitutional framers be our constitutional framers?[29] This would suggest that the self-correcting learning process of actualising the 'still-untapped normative substance of the system of rights laid down in the original document' (CD, 774) requires a boat made out of thicker stuff.[30]

Secondly, the initial problem of democratic self-determination reasserts itself. Descendants must approach the constitution with the same standards and same perspective as their forebears. But these are standards and perspectives that are handed down to us, rather than that which we arrive at through autonomous democratic deliberations. We have seen in the case of both Mandela and Douglass that democratic self-determination may in fact require adopting different standards, judgements and perspectives from previous generations.[31] While Habermas seeks to preserve our democratic autonomy by insisting that we still approach the text of the constitution in a critical fashion, this is still premised on the 'unifying bond' of being in the same boat (CD, 775). But this reminds one of the freedom of Beckett's character to crawl east across the deck of a boat sailing west.[32] To insist that one must adopt the perspectives and standards of judgement of one's forebears, to see oneself as being in the same boat, would seem to close off any question about whose tradition is being handed down to us. As Lasse Thomassen persuasively argues, 'the question of whether this tradition is indeed *ours* cannot be raised', and the question of 'whether we belong to the same "we" is bracketed'.[33]

We can see the importance of these concerns in Frederick Douglass's 1852 Fourth of July address. While carrying out the kind of critique of the Declaration that Benhabib and Habermas point to, Douglass refuses to be part of the 'we'. 'The sunlight that brought life and healing to you', Douglass tells his audience, 'brought stripes and death to me. The Fourth of July is *yours*, not mine.' And in the following year's address, Douglass points to the difficulty he confronts: 'She [America] has no scales in which to weigh our wrongs – she has no *standards* by which to measure *our* rights' (my emphasis).[34] What we see in Douglass's 'yours/our' is a rhetorical positioning that seeks to emphasise that he does not take himself to be in the same boat as his audience, nor to be judging by the same standards.

This leads to a third problem. The story of a self-correcting learning process encourages us to look back on the struggles of those who saw themselves, and were seen, as not being in the same boat as their contemporaries, as actually being in the same boat. It is as if political actors are swept up by a process operating behind their backs; what they see as precarious, contingent, historical struggles turn out, 'in the long run' (CD, 774), to be part of our self-correcting learning process. As Habermas writes:

> Once the interpretative battles have subsided, all parties recognize that the reforms are achievements, although they were first sharply contested. In retrospect they agree that, with the inclusion of marginalized groups . . . the hitherto satisfied presuppositions for the legitimacy of existing democratic procedures are better realized. (CD, 774–5)

One of the reasons why we might be led to think in this way is because of the Janus-faced aspect of this dialectical story. While we move forward towards a legitimacy that is uncovered with each expansion of the 'we', part of understanding this as a learning process is to be found in the backward glance to the 'still-untapped normative substance of the system of rights laid down in the original document' (CD, 774). On this account, as formally excluded groups are included in the registers of justice, this is retrospectively seen as a dialectical progression in which we now better realise the normative content of our constitution. But as William Connolly suggests, 'the dialectic understanding always functions best as a retrospective description of movements that have already migrated from a place under justice to a place on the register of justice.' And, for Connolly, this misses the most precarious moment of political struggle, namely, the difficulties and risks involved before one manages to get a foothold in the dialectic.[35]

We can think about this by returning to Douglass. Today we see Douglass as being in the same boat as us, but did his contemporaries? When Douglass rejects the advice to 'argue more and denounce less', when he opts for a 'scorching irony' and a 'fiery stream of biting ridicule', insisting that 'it is not light that is needed, but fire', whose boat would he have been put in?[36] Contemporary deliberativists do recognise the need for non-deliberative means for deliberative ends (see Chapter 2), but in advance of success, how is one to know who is currently in 'our boat'? The emphasis Habermas places on 'could' in the following remark carries the full weight of this problem: 'the democratic project of the realization of equal civil rights actually feeds off the resistance of minorities, which although appearing as enemies of democracy to the majority today, *could* actually turn out to be their authentic friends tomorrow.'[37] Today the fire of Douglass is seen as reasonable, but that specific democratic turn could have turned out differently.[38] This raises the question of how, without occupying this retrospective position, we can be sure that our current practices leave a space for the interruption of those others struggling today outside our registers of justice. What we see as a reasonable demand that is 'in our boat', and what we perceive to be an irrational thrashing around in the waves, is entangled in all sorts of biases set within our practices, perceptions and justifications that not only leave us deaf to those struggling to cross the borders of justice, but contribute to their not being heard at all. The storm blasting Benjamin's angel of history would counsel a more 'pessimistic induction'.[39]

The retrospective viewpoint of a recognised achievement that 'we' enjoy after the interpretative battles have subsided (who determines when 'we' have arrived at this viewpoint and how?) risks silently passing over — and silencing — those who have capsized during the storm of such battles. Who are they? Where are they? Do these lost-at-sea 'others' retrospectively agree? What price will they have to pay to be helped back into 'our' boat? And what price will 'we' pay for granting them the 'freedom' to crawl east across our deck as we celebrate the achievements of our dialectical voyage west?[40] Recall that this process is 'inevitably permeated by ethics':

> Because ethical-political decisions are an unavoidable part of politics, and because their legal regulation expresses the collective identity of a nation of citizens, they can spark battles . . . What sets off the battles is . . . the fact that every legal community and every democratic process for actualizing basic rights is inevitably permeated by ethics. (IO, 218)

While this *seeks* to avoid the 'moralistic misunderstanding of the democratic principle of legitimacy',[41] it returns us to the problems raised in Chapter 1. Given the ethical permeation of 'every' democratic process, it is not clear from where the confidence in arriving at our 'post-battle' perspective emerges. As Cooke observes: 'In democracies in which citizens have different and often conflicting ethical convictions and commitments, it is unlikely that they will ever reach agreement as to the general acceptability of substantive democratic decisions.'[42] Habermas does acknowledge the blindness of the Enlightenment to 'the barbaric reverse side of its own mirror', and the way in which this 'rigidified rationalism has been transformed into the stifling power of a capitalist world civilization, which assimilates alien cultures and abandons its own traditions to oblivion'.[43] But the full existential weight of 'assimilated' and 'oblivion' is in danger of being lost in descriptions of a self-correcting learning process subject to 'interruptions' (CD, 774). By telling ourselves this dialectical story of an unfolding learning process, where 'all parties' recognise post-battle achievements, we risk succumbing to the sirens of self-congratulation that resound from the depths of this dialect.[44]

To warn of these sirens is not to court cynicism about the possibilities of doing justice to the other; it is to remind ourselves of the perilous nature of this passage to and of the other. While we should welcome new voices that manage to make it on board, we should not lose sight of the fact that any movement that succeeds in such a perilous journey 'thereby exposes retrospectively *absences* in a practice of justice'.[45] The various terms that we have seen Derrida use to describe this experience of opening a passage to the other serve as warnings,[46] 'like searchlights without a coast, they sweep across the dark sky . . . and harbour the invisible in their very light'. In the depths of this ordeal, we are not sure of what 'danger or abysses' await us, 'nor even if a destination remains . . . determined' (PF, 80).[47] Perhaps it would be better to think in terms of an incalculable destination, one that takes its bearings from a heading other than that of a self-correcting process, what Derrida calls the 'heading of the other' (TOH, 15; see n. 57 below). This voyage is one that refuses any democratic good conscience, that ventures towards the other with a modesty about our ability to do justice, and maintains a relentless vigilance about the injustices of our present calculations.

The dialectic story, in contrast, seems swept along by a confidence in the justice of our current practices, a confidence based on our anticipated arrival at future ports of inclusion (that is itself based on a backwards glance at our achievements). But given the deliberative account of democratic politics, in which not only is the 'we' of the people 'contested and essentially contestable' but where the very rules which bind the will of the people are 'constantly interpreted, reappropriated and contested', what in this process keeps afloat such confidence about the direction of travel?[48] What gives us the confidence that we are on the way to a more inclusive polity in the future? If the only thing guiding this process is the democratic will of citizens, how can we be sure that we are not blown off course and drifting in the direction of Plato's nightmare voyage, where others are thrown overboard or left unrescued?[49] One does not have to be an advocate of philosopher rulers to appreciate that this is no mere paranoid phantasm; one only has to look around at the contemporary state of politics in Europe and the US.[50] It is thus not clear from what perspective we, postmetaphysical democrats, judge such worrying developments as 'contingent interruptions'

(CD, 774), the temporary pitching and yawing of our dialectical voyage, rather than signs of our foundering. Olsen puts the point well:

> [W]e cannot consider the constitution legitimate *now* if we have no probable basis for expecting it to pursue full inclusion in the future. Unfortunately, we cannot expect this kind of directionality from *within* a self-amending political regime – at least, not when we define it as dynamic and open-ended . . . Political deliberation can produce many different kinds of results: tolerant, inclusive, egalitarian ones as well as xenophobic, exclusionist, and differentiating ones . . . Absent some other influence, there's no reason to suppose that the process of constitutional amendment would promote inclusion over exclusion. We cannot conclude that the progressive development towards full inclusion is any more likely than the myriad other directions that constitutional development could take.[51]

If we take seriously the indeterminate nature of these dynamic democratic processes, then the possibility of our constitution-making practices veering disastrously off course remains ever-present. The dynamic understanding of constitution-making places us in the less than comforting position of reassuring ourselves of the justice of our present practices on the basis of an indeterminate, open-ended process subject to (the possibility of significant) change. While this may avoid the paradox of founding, it leaves us facing 'the paradox of dynamic indeterminacy'.[52]

A 'non-dialectizable antinomy' (OH, 79)

While Derrida shares a dynamic understanding of democratic constitution-making, this is understood in the sense of the 'to come' (see Chapter 5). Confronting the dynamic indeterminacy of constitution-making, we can never be assured that our current practices are just. As the account of the ordeal of undecidability revealed (see Chapters 4, 5), this uncertainty is not an empirical moment that can be overcome. The demand that gives rise to this ordeal – that of having to calculate the incalculable – means that our striving to do justice to the other, of maintaining an ethos of interruption, is forever confronted with the 'im-possible' task of responding to antinomic injunctions. In contrast to an unfolding dialectic, the deconstructive picture is one of a 'non-dialectizable antinomy' (OH, 79).[53] Let me unpack this a little more concretely.

Let's return to Derrida's call for civil disobedience and to change laws in France targeting undocumented immigrants (see Chapter 5). Those resisting the law were struggling for what Derrida described as a 'more generous – and no less calculated – hospitality'. This reference to calculation is explicitly aimed at countering the claim that those resisting the law were irresponsibly demanding that the French state 'open all gates' (FWT, 61). As Derrida put it: 'We were not advocating an unconditional hospitality' (DE, 100). Why not? One might think that unconditional hospitality is precisely what the arriving of an incalculable other calls for. Isn't this part of the ethos of interruption that doing justice to the other demands that we maintain? No, but yes.

When Derrida noted that 'we are not dreamers', he was not simply acknowledging the historical conditions in which 'today no government, no nation state, will simply open its borders' (DE, 101); he was also recognising the necessity of conditional hospitality. 'Pure [unconditional] hospitality', observes Derrida, 'consists in leaving one's house open to the unforeseeable arrival, which can be an intrusion, even a dangerous intrusion.' And given this, 'unconditional hospitality can have perverse effects' (FWT, 59). To call for unconditional hospitality would be to call for an openness to the other that would leave one exposed to any other. Unconditional hospitality, then, 'is not a political or juridical concept' (FWT, 59; N, 101). To point this out is not to give in to those all-too-familiar discourses marked by a 'xenophobic convulsion' and cynical 'mystification' (N, 142). Rather, it is to insist that, in the given situation we find ourselves in, we must calculate as best we can in order to maintain an ethos of interruption, while not leaving ourselves exposed to 'anything whatsoever' (SM, 168; see Chapter 5). These calculations may take the form of resisting certain laws, but they may also take the form of calculating laws in order to prevent the interruption of such an ethos. In the singular situation of undocumented immigrants in France, those resisting the law did so because they judged that, within the laws of conditional hospitality, 'there was much more space to welcome foreigners' (FWT, 59).

While Derrida insisted that those resisting the law were not dreamers, the idea of unconditional hospitality is still something that 'we anxiously dream of and desire' (FWT, 60). We have seen the cause of the anxiety, so why the desire? Derrida's claim is that for conditional laws of hospitality to be hospitable, we need the idea of pure, unconditional hospitality. This seems to be both a conceptual and an ethical claim. In terms of the former, consider the following: 'If we have a concept of conditional hospitality, it is because we also have an idea of a pure hospitality' (DE, 98); without the idea of 'pure hospitality . . . there is no concept of hospitality' (FWT, 60); 'to be what it "must" be, hospitality must not pay a debt or be governed by a duty', it must be offered 'beyond debt and economy' (OH, 82). The idea here is that if I offer hospitality *in order* to conform to a duty or prescription, or if I offer hospitality *on condition* that the other behave in conformity to my rules, so that my welcome is 'backed by certain assurances', this would not be genuine (pure) hospitality (ARSS, 129). Genuine hospitality entails the unconditionality of a 'pure welcoming' of the 'unexpected one who arrives' (DE, 98). As Derrida puts it: unconditional hospitality is 'hospitality *itself*' (ARSS, 129).

This conceptual claim has ethical implications. If I am to understand my practical engagements as seeking more just forms of hospitality, then I can only do so in reference to this idea of pure hospitality, for this is essentially what hospitality is. Ethically speaking, then, '[o]nly an unconditional hospitality can give meaning and practical rationality to a concept of hospitality' (RS, 149). In the absence of this, not only would we lack a concept of hospitality, but we would 'not even be able to determine any rules for conditional hospitality' (ARSS, 129). And so the practical engagements of those resisting the specific immigration law in the name of a more just conditional hospitality were expressive of a desire for unconditional hospitality. From this deconstructive account, the more general claim would be the following: if our laws of conditional hospitality are 'not guided, given inspiration . . . by the law of unconditional hospitality', then they 'cease to be laws of hospitality' (OH, 79).[54]

We can now formalise the antinomy in terms of Derrida's

'heterogeneous but indissociable' thesis (ARSS, 129).[55] On the one hand, hospitality, to be what it most essentially is, must be pure; it must resist all calculations and remain unconditionally open to the arrival of not only an unforeseeable other, but a non-identifiable other.[56] This 'great Law of [unconditional] hospitality' thus remains heterogeneous to the laws of hospitality that are always conditioned by rights, duties, norms and so forth. On the other hand, in order for there to be any practices of hospitality at all, the Law of unconditional hospitality 'needs the laws' of conditional hospitality (OH, 75–81). This is not the ethico-political point about avoiding the danger of opening ourselves up to the 'anything whatsoever'. Rather, it is a 'constitutive' (OH, 79) point about what is required to open ourselves up to the other 'and offer him or her anything whatsoever' (ARSS, 129). Similar to his remarks about the promise of justice requiring effective forms of action and organisation if it is not to remain spiritual or abstract (see Chapter 5), Derrida maintains that without concrete laws of conditional hospitality, unconditional hospitality would 'risk being abstract, utopian, illusory' (OH, 79). We must 're-inscribe the unconditional into certain conditions' so that it becomes determinate, effective; otherwise it 'gives nothing' (ARSS, 130). Here, then, we see that these two orders of hospitality are not only heterogeneous to one another, but, at the very same time, indissociable from one another.

I have focused on the case of undocumented immigrants because in this 'anxious desire' to transform the laws of hospitality we see, in concrete terms, the 'non-dialectizable antinomy' structuring all our strivings to do justice to the other. We see this very same structure, for example, in relation to justice and law:

> The incalculable unconditionality of hospitality . . . exceeds the calculation of conditions, just as justice exceeds law . . . Justice can never be reduced to law . . . to the norms or rules that condition law . . . The interruption of a certain unbinding opens the free space of the relationship to the incalculable singularity of the other. It is there that justice exceeds law but at the same time motivates the movement, [the] history [of law] . . . The heterogeneity between justice and law does not exclude but, on the contrary, calls for their inseparability: there can be no justice

without an appeal to juridical determinations and to the force of law; and there can be no becoming, no transformation, history, or perfectibility of law without an appeal to a justice that will nonetheless always exceed it. (RS, 150)[57]

Returning to the discussion of the dynamic indeterminacy of constitution-making, we can now see that while Derrida shares with deliberativists the desire for a more inclusive polity, and while he understands that desire to be the very thing that inspires our historical struggles for justice, those struggles will always be haunted by the anxious awareness of the 'im-possibility' of doing justice to the other. This anxiety is not only the anxiety haunting the fallibilistic consciousness of the 'unbelieving sons and daughters of modernity';[58] it is an anxiety that emerges from the very ordeal of striving to do justice to the other. But it is precisely here, in this anxiety, that all our responsibilities emerge: 'political, juridical, and ethical responsibilities have their places ... only in this transaction ... between these two hospitalities' (ARSS, 130).[59]

A life worth living

The deconstructive approach avoids the dangers of both self-congratulatory optimism and cynical despair. While Derrida insists that there can be no democratic good conscience, this is not meant 'to cultivate ... depression or the irreducible feeling of guilt'. Neither does it counsel a resigned withdrawal into fatalism or pessimism (ROD, 21–3; PM, 139).[60] That I experience the antinomic injunctions of doing justice to the other as an ordeal does not mean that this is privative (ARSS, 119; DE, 64; N, 343–70; RS, 84). As we have seen, 'im-possibility' names that experience through which the possibility of doing justice is given. Rather than a disabling condition, 'im-possibility' announces the 'affirmative experience of the coming of the other'. That is to say, it is that which 'gives deconstruction its movement' (N, 104), that provokes the desire to create more inventive ways to welcome the other, to maintain an ethos of interruption (FWT, 59; N, 247). Indeed, 'without this experience of the impossible one might as well give up on ... justice' (SM, 65).

When Derrida described justice or hospitality as something 'we anxiously dream of and desire', he may have been getting a little carried away with his own rhetoric. But I think there is precision here. It is this anxiety that accounts for the relentless vigilance of deconstruction, a vigilance that is often mistaken for sceptical demonstrations of impossibility in the privative sense. So, for example, when Derrida insists that '[t]he democracy to come obliges one to challenge instituted law in the name of an indefinitely unsatisfied justice, thereby revealing the injustice of calculating justice' (N, 252), some are likely to be wholly unsatisfied with this 'indefinitely unsatisfied' and see in this 'challenge' the wholesale critique of a defeatist scepticism, rather than an ethically motivated vigilance.[61] As I have attempted to show, this deconstructive 'challenge' can take many forms, whether it's transforming the apparatus of academic discourses, institutions of higher education or the media (Chapter 3); it can also take the form of resisting specific laws, engaging in civil disobedience, defending democracy and international law, and so forth (see above and Chapter 5). But none of this would make sense if we lost sight of the desire that drives such practical engagements, namely, the desire to create and maintain an ethos of interruption so that one does justice to the other in their otherness.

That Derrida often refers to a 'desire', 'experience' (see Chapter 4) or 'promise' is important.[62] The ordeal of undecidability and the negativism of deconstruction (see Chapters 4 and 5) means that the unconditional – whether this is understood in terms of 'justice' or 'pure hospitality' – is not an object of knowledge that we could set out and articulate, such that we could know our destination and chart a safe passage towards it. But this does not mean that we are left helplessly adrift in the violent tides of history. Although Derrida thinks that we are always within an economy of violence (see above and Chapter 5), he nevertheless holds on to the 'irreducible promise of the relation to the other as essentially non-instrumental'. Here's how he describes this promise:

> [It] is not the dream of a beatifically pacific relation, but of a certain experience of friendship . . . This is a friendship, what I sometimes call an *aimance*, that excludes violence; a non-

appropriative relation to the other that occurs without violence and on the basis of which all violence detaches itself and is determined. (RDP, 83)

In this dream of a non-instrumental and non-appropriative relation to the other one can, perhaps, hear a faint echo of 'the idea of an undistorted intersubjectivity' that Habermas insists we 'have no choice but to presuppose'. Habermas describes this idea as 'the formal characterization of the necessary conditions for the forms, not able to be anticipated, of a worthwhile life'. Acknowledging that there is 'no theory' for this, Habermas points to a praxis 'inspired' by our 'intuitive anticipations' of such a life. While historical experience may rob praxis of its confidence, such inspiring intuitions 'can still leave it with some hope'.[63] While Connolly is right to point out that the self-correcting dialect retrospectively reveals absences in practices we took to be just, the very fact that such arrivals have taken place provides some hope for the possibility of future interruptions.

As we have seen, both the deliberative and deconstructive approaches place their hope for such a worthwhile life in democracy, despite the injustices all too evident in contemporary democratic societies. A key reason for this, from a deconstructive perspective, is the 'absolute and intrinsic historicity' of democracy, a historicity that is 'unique among all political systems' (RS, 86–7; see Chapter 5). This radical historicity is what Derrida seeks to remind us of with the formulation 'democracy to come'.[64] It is this 'to come' that gives 'democracy . . . the structure of a promise' (OH, 78; RS, 86). And while this structure means that in our strivings for justice we are denied the assurance of the future perfect, the 'to come' of democracy 'let's resonate . . . an invincible promise' (ARSS, 114), the promise of transforming our current practices so that we 'leave a passage for the other' (PSY, 45). It is this that inspires us, amidst the waves of antinomic injunctions, to struggle for the 'constant . . . renewal of the democratic promise' (N, 180).

Here, then, we approach what might be called a deconstructive faith in the 'im-possibility' of a just regime. For Derrida, the desire for justice, for an unconditional justice that remains transcendent to the conditional laws that it nevertheless requires to arrive, is something we cannot give up on; it is that which we must postulate (and Derrida will emphasise this word), and remain faithful to, in the name of the promise contained within a democracy that is to come, and a history that promises to become otherwise.

> Is not this exigency faithful to one of the two poles of rationality, namely, to this *postulation* of unconditionality? I say *postulation* in order to gesture toward the demand, the desire, the imperative exigency; and I say postulation rather than principle in order to avoid the princely and powerful authority of the first, of the *arkhē* or the *presbeia*. (RS, 142)

The unconditional appears here as a postulate of practical reason, a postulation that gives aspiration to our struggles for justice, but which leaves the sovereign principialities of knowledge. That we leave the terrain of knowledge does not mean that we are without knowledge (see Chapter 5); it means that we are without any assured passage or guaranteed port of arrival. We set out in faith and hope. The whirlpools awaiting us are not simply ones of problematisation, but of aporia. It is within these seas that we must struggle to calculate our passage to 'the least bad conditions . . . the most just legislation' (PM, 67). Whether it is the norms of an institution, discourses in the public sphere, specific laws in our state, or international law, this faith in the possibility of this impossible unconditionality (the 'im-possible') guides us endlessly.

> I am not unaware of the apparently utopic character of the horizon I'm sketching out here . . . [T]hough this . . . is not only *utopic* but *aporetic* . . . I continue to believe that it is faith in the possibility of this impossible . . . that must govern all our decisions. (ARSS, 115)

Do the shores of a realistic (possible) utopia (impossible) come into view here? Perhaps not. But we are heading away from the rocks of cynicism and despair. And although we are breathing the 'air of a faith', this is a faith 'without credulity'. Indeed, Derrida insists that this faith is a way of 'keeping within reason' (RS, 153), what we might call a reasonable faith in the 'im-possibility' of a just regime:

> [T]he *reasonable* would take into account the accounting of juridical *justness* or exactitude . . . but it would also strive, across transactions and aporias, for *justice*. The reasonable, as I understand it . . . would be a rationality that takes account of the incalculable, so as to give an account of it, there where this appears impossible, so as to . . . reckon *with* it, that is to say, with the event of *what* or *who* comes. (RS, 159)

This would be a 'hypercritical faith' that opens up a passage to the incalculable other and demands that we calculate so as to maintain an ethos of interruption (RS, 153). Without the space opened up by the experience of this 'im-possibility' we would be left with 'a poor possible, a futureless possible, a possible already *set aside*, so to speak, life-assured' (ROD, 30). This would be a life where one would 'count on what is coming', where one would 'have the prospect' but would 'no longer invite . . . no longer receive' or 'even think to see . . . coming'. This would not be a life worth living; it would be a life of resignation and cynicism, a life of 'calculation without justice' (SM, 169). The life that Derrida sees as worth living emerges through the affirmation of the 'im-possible'. Such an affirmation is

> attached to life . . . but to a life other than that of the economy of the possible, an im-possible life no doubt . . . the only one that *is worthy* of being lived . . . the only one from which to depart (notice I say from which *to depart*) for a possible thinking of life. (WA, 276)

The parenthetical remark emphasises that the 'im-possibility' of a just regime is not the paralysing end to our struggles for justice, but that which instigates the movement for justice. It is the point of departure. While this may be a departure into that which is perilous, and while it may be one where we are denied any good conscience, it is only in that venture that the promise of doing justice to the other as other is able to breathe. It is what inspires the democratic venture.

Pre-departure possibilities

The dialectical account of the deliberative approach can be very helpful for those who have successfully made it into the registers of justice. But given the retrospective aspect of this account, it says very little about those others who have not succeeded. The dialectical account leaves those border crossings in the dark. The antinomic account of the deconstructive approach, in contrast, situates us in the ordeal of that night. However, both approaches hold to the promise of a more inclusive polity as the very condition of the democratic venture. Without wishing to offer a full itinerary, and without suggesting that both approaches could depart in the same boat, I would like to suggest possible points of departure that could offer encouragement to the democratic venture of each.

Recent empirical work suggests promising areas for future research that could benefit both approaches and open up a productive dialogue. The benefit to the deconstructive approach would be to ground that orientation more concretely. While I have pointed to examples of deconstructive practices that contribute to an ethos of interruption – such as the politics of the stage and work of resistance (see Chapter 3) and acts of civil disobedience in response to immigration law (see Chapter 5 and above) – more empirical work is needed. Such work would give the deconstructive approach more grip and (hopefully) would open it up to other democratic theorists. Deliberativists have recently started engaging in the kind of empirical work that is already reorienting deliberative theory towards a more dissensual conceptualisation of democratic politics and a more fine-grained analysis of the multiple forms of exclusion that take place off-stage. To indicate the possibilities for a future dialogue in this direction, I shall touch briefly on content and methodology.

Let's begin with methodology. From the more deconstructive end, Prentoulis and Thomassen's analysis of the 2011 protests in Greece and Spain seems particularly promising.[65] Noting that a key driver of the protests in both cases was the 'sense of not being heard and not having a voice', the authors seek not only to 'analyse their [the protesters'] discourse', but to 'do justice to it'.[66] By the latter, the authors seek to avoid subjecting the protesters' discourse to any theoretical model, and instead aim to 'let the protesters speak in their own voice'. One cannot help but hear echoes of Derrida's description of justice: 'that I let the other be other' (N, 105). This methodological reflexivity makes explicit the dangers of erasing the singularity of the other in the very movement of trying to give voice to the other. Moreover, the authors recognise that this danger cannot be wholly avoided – there will be an unavoidable appropriation in subjecting those voices to analysis.[67] In recognising this, the analysis seems to be orientated by a methodological injunction to 'betray as little as possible' both the singularity of the voices analysed, and the 'univocal communication' of analysis that is required to give them a hearing (PS, 360; see Chapters 3 and 5). We are not far from the antinomic injunctions of deconstruction.

From the deliberative end of this dialogue, the empirical turn in deliberative theory presents a more complex picture. Since the more recent systemic turn, the empirical turn has itself turned from a focus on measuring the deliberative quality of mini-publics (such as citizen juries and deliberative polls) to investigating the more conflictual aspects of the deliberative system. Deliberativists engaging in this research are adopting an 'interpretative approach'.[68] According to Ercan et al., one of the key virtues of adopting this approach is that it provides in-depth investigations of the 'lived experience' of social actors that can help 'illuminate a phenomenon or experience that is "in the dark"' and, through this, 'assist in bringing excluded or marginalised "voices" into research'.[69] Such empirical investigations would not only inject deliberative theory with a little more 'deconstructive' anxiety about those who do not make it onto the deliberative stage, but they would also provide resources for identifying threats to, and thus contributing to the task of, maintaining an ethos of interruption.

Two subsets of the interpretative approach identified by Ercan et al. – frame analysis and discourse-dramaturgical analysis – can be understood as already contributing to a politics of the stage (see Chapter 3). In the context of recent debates in Germany about immigration and integration, Ercan has deployed frame analysis to show how culture-based and gender-based framing of 'honour killings' produced 'representation[s] of the "other" [that] not only led to the demonization of both men and women in immigrant cultures, but also served to preserve the fiction of German national homogeneity'.[70] This led to the construction of 'us' and 'them' boundaries that immigrants could only cross by adopting the values and practices of the majority culture.[71] These frames ultimately contributed to exclusionary immigration policies and the silencing of alternative discourses in both the public sphere and more formal decision-making forums.[72] Such research not only helps identify forms of exclusion that happen off-stage, but also contributes to highlighting forms of 'internal exclusion' (to recall Iris Young's phrase from Chapter 2) that take place on stage.

In the aftermath of the assassination of Theo van Gogh in Amsterdam in 2004, Hajer and Uitermark used a discourse-dramaturgical approach to provide a fine-grained analysis of the discourses deployed by politicians, the media and prominent actors in the public sphere in struggles to impose a particular frame on that situation. Focusing on specific discursive tactics (such as 'emotive rerouting' and 'bridging and wedging') and the particular staging of discourses (in both the formal and the informal public sphere), their work not only reveals various strategies aimed at excluding certain actors from the public sphere, but also identifies counter-strategies that can contribute to maintaining a more inclusive public sphere.[73]

In both cases we see contemporary deliberative theorists focusing on precisely those silenced voices that the dialectic threatens to leave in the dark. In addition to helping us better understand the mechanisms of that silencing (what Derrida would call the codes or frames), this work also identifies alternative strategies that can help interrupt those frames and thus open a space for the other to appear in their otherness.

The turn of these deliberative theorists to framing and discourse-dramaturgical analysis overlaps with Imogen Tyler's work on social abjection. Drawing on a range of theoretical traditions, Tyler provides detailed empirical analysis of the ways in which the figuration of disenfranchised populations as 'abjects' (through a whole system of mediations) legitimises 'the reproduction and entrenchment of inequalities and injustice'.[74] In doing so, Tyler provides rich resources for deconstructive and deliberative approaches 'to consider states of exclusion from multiple perspectives, including the perspectives of those who are "obligated to inhabit the impossible edges of modernity'".⁷⁵ Tyler's approach incorporates various elements of the interpretative approach and successfully brings marginalised voices into research and their experiences of abjection to light. The various ways Tyler describes her approach – the 'storying of revolts' or 'restaging of protests' – exhibit a methodological reflexivity not only in terms of the 'reframing of events' and the 'mediation of resistance' that one might think any research unavoidably engages in; she also explicitly states that her approach is adopted in order to provide 'counter-mediations' that will help 'reinvent . . . new political idioms' to 'fracture' the current neo-liberal consensus.⁷⁶ In the language of Chapter 3, Tyler's work not only seeks to put on stage the frames and codes of the dominant political and media apparatus; she also seeks to interrupt and transform those codes. In doing so, Tyler's work is a concrete contribution to the ongoing work of maintaining an ethos of interruption.

Unsurprisingly, this discussion of methodology has already spilt over into issues of content. With mention of attempts to fracture the neo-liberal consensus, we touch on an area of research that is emerging as a possible point of departure for future dialogue, namely, research into activism and new forms of social movements. While research into activism has typically highlighted the limitations of the deliberative model, deliberative theory is increasingly engaging in such research to reflect on its own conceptualisation of democratic politics. The deliberative approach of both della Porta's research on the global justice movement in Italy, and Mendonça and Ercan's analysis of the 2013 protests in Turkey and Brazil, overlaps with Prentoulis and Thomassen's analysis of the 2011 protests in Greece and Spain.⁷⁷ There are key areas emerging from this research that promise to open up shared ground for future dialogue that I can only gesture toward here.

Firstly, there is a recognition that emerging social movements are trying to interrupt the existing codes and apparatus that structure the dominant forms of politics. The aim of such interruption is not simply to make the system more accommodating to hitherto excluded voices (although such inclusion is crucial); the aim is to transform the very apparatus or framework of democratic politics. Prentoulis and Thomassen summarise this well:

> The majority of the protesters see what they are doing as a new form of politics . . . raising new demands in a new form, and this is what makes it difficult for them to be heard within the existing political system. The demands are not only demands to the political system . . . but also demands about the political system . . . Seen in this light, the unresponsiveness of the political system to their demands only shows the necessity of changing the system fundamentally.[78]

It is not coincidental that I have introduced this first point in the 'deconstructive' language of the discussion in Chapter 3. What Derrida was engaged in at a more micro level, emerging social movements seem to be attempting at the macro level.

Secondly, this research reveals an emphasis on maintaining heterogeneity within these movements. In the words of one activist: 'it is important and necessary to defend and valorize the multiple beliefs and ideological, political, cultural and religious positions.'[79] This valorisation of heterogeneity is also evident in the importance placed on what activists term 'subjectivity'. As della Porta points out: 'In contrast to the totalizing model of militancy in past movements . . . there is affirmation of the value of individual experiences and capacities.'[80] This valorisation of heterogeneity and individual experience is, in the words of one activist, 'our ideal horizon', a horizon that inspires struggles, here and now, for 'a society in which subjectivities can co-exist, can be rich'. The politics of these activist-movements seeks to build such a society, 'otherwise we would have to be content with the levelling-down model that is imposed on us'. As deliberativists study these movements, their own conceptualisation of deliberative theory will increasingly open up to this emphasis on heterogeneity and the singularity of the other in all their ('rich') otherness.[81]

Thirdly, the ideal horizon of a politics of heterogeneity and singularity is pre-figured and 'defended' in the organisational structures of these movements. The horizontal nature of the assemblies and the reticular relations between the various affinity groups and organisations is a recurring feature identified in this research. While these fluid structures seek to ensure the openness and heterogeneity of the movement, this is maintained by a whole series of procedures that structure the discussions that take place within and between different sites of these movements. Indeed, one sociologist cited by della Porta remarked that 'a 60s activist would be surprised by the procedural machinery that today accompanies the democratic deciding process' within these emerging movements.[82] In this sense, a novel aspect of the organisational structure of these contemporary movements is their deliberative elements – the instituted procedures designed to ensure processes of democratic discussion and decision-making whilst still remaining open to heterogeneity.[83]

All the research cited here highlights a tension within the organisational structure of these contemporary movements. On the one hand, horizontal structures seek to keep movements open to heterogeneity and singularity. On the other hand, vertical structures require representation at various levels of decision-making.[84] The internal dynamics of these movements reflect, in many ways, the tension of doing justice to the other that has been a key theme of this book: how can we ensure the inclusion of the other without erasing their otherness? Recall one way in which Derrida formulates that tension:

> [H]ow is one to, *on the one hand*, reaffirm singularity of the idiom . . . the rights of minorities, linguistic and cultural differences . . . How is one to resist uniformization, homogenization . . .? But, *on the other hand*, how is one to struggle for all that without sacrificing the most univocal communication . . . democratic discussion, and the law of the majority? Each time one must *invent* so as to betray as little as possible both one and the other – *without any prior assurance* of success. (PS, 360)

This is precisely the tension that these social movements are trying to negotiate, not only in terms of the external political structures that they seek to transform, but also in terms of the ideal horizon they themselves seek to practise and pre-figure within their internal structure. While there is no assurance of success, in their striving to invent new forms of engagement such movements provide a concrete example of how to negotiate, in practice, the tensions involved in attempting to include the other in their otherness.

I hope that the contemporary developments touched on here,

and the broader account I have set out in this book, provide encouragement for praxis, and a hopeful point of departure for future dialogue. Let us, then, depart.

Notes

1. Rawls, *Political Liberalism*, lxii, 172; Rawls, *The Law of Peoples*, 128.
2. Although my reading of deconstruction as orientated by the 'impossibility' of doing justice was developed independently of Miriam Bankovsky's *Perfecting Justice in Rawls, Habermas and Honneth: A Deconstructive Perspective*, our approaches overlap. Despite this independent development, I have learnt a great deal from Bankovsky's book. In particular, I am indebted to Bankovsky for the relation between Rawls and Derrida. For the same reason, I am indebted to Johan Van der Walt, 'Rawls and Derrida on the Historicity of Constitutional Democracy and International Justice'.
3. Plato, *The Republic*, 554a–561. All subsequent in-text references are to this text unless otherwise indicated.
4. Derrida tells us that Plato sees democracy as 'weak, asthenic (*asthenēs*)', as having 'little power (*dynamis*) to effect either good or bad because of a polyarchic multiplicity that disperses command' (RS, 76).
5. A few pages later Derrida observes: 'At this point we are simply examining the implications of what Plato says when he speaks of the democratic freedom or license . . . that would authorize every constitution or paradigm and, thus, every interpretation' (RS, 37).
6. Paine, *The Rights of Man*, 210.
7. The discussion of Nancy is something of a 'brotherly spat' (RS, 49) and more of an opportunity for Derrida to stake out his understanding of the autoimmunity of democracy. What Derrida's account of democratic autoimmunity lacks is any detailed engagement with modern democratic theories of constitutionalism. Having said this, one of the things that Derrida increasingly insists on is the need for a more robust international law. We see this, for example, in his discussion of limiting the sovereignty of nation states with reference to the Universal Declaration of Human Rights, and the creation of institutions such as the International Criminal Court (RS, 87). This is even more explicit when Derrida argues for a reformed United Nations (here in particular the veto power wielded by permanent members of the Security Council) with effective force to sanction powerful states as well as an intervening force so that it is no longer dependent on the will of the more powerful states. He goes on to argue for a strengthening of

international institutions of law and an International Court of Justice with their own autonomous force (ARSS, 115). A similar argument is advanced in the paper Derrida delivered to UNESCO in 1999, 'Globalization, Peace and Cosmopolitanism' (N, 371–86).
8. Patton, 'Derrida's Engagement with Political Philosophy', 163.
9. I leave aside the question of how accurate a reading of Plato Derrida gives. Indeed, it seems that this is a self-conscious form of 'active inheritance'. See Derrida's comments about democracy to come belonging to 'at least one of the lines of thought coming out of the Platonic tradition' and how 'this cannot always be said without a bit of duplicity, if not some polemical bad faith'. However, 'it also cannot be said without some verisimilitude' (RS, 26). For more on 'active inheritance' see FWT, 1–19; N, 110; SM, 12–16.
10. Derrida, 'Passions', 23.
11. Colonel Jessup in Rob Reiner's 1992 film *A Few Good Men*.
12. Just as Derrida's emphasis on the incalculable does not dismiss calculation any more than his emphasis on impossibility dismisses possibility, so his emphasis on the risk of democracy does not dismiss the need to minimise that risk as far as possible. One sees this not only in his emphasis on calculation and laws, but also on 'guarantees . . . precautions' (ROD, 34), 'guardrails against the worst' (N, 180), the need for openness to be 'safeguarded' (N, 194), to 'maintain a minimum of security' (N, 17), and 'all possible assurance' (PS, 198).
13. Michelman, 'Law's Republic', 1529; cf. 1496, n. 10.
14. The International Committee for the Support of Algerian Intellectuals and the League for the Rights of Man. The meeting followed the issuing of an *Appeal for Civil Peace in Algeria*, which Derrida participated in preparing.
15. In the first round of elections the Front Islamique du Salut (FIS) party gained a majority of the vote and seemed likely to secure power. Elections were cancelled before the second round because of fears that the FIS would put an end to democracy. As former US diplomat Edward Djerejian expressed this concern more generally: the democratic implications of such electoral victories would be 'one man, one vote, one time'.
16. The notion of 'necessary conditions' is given no elaboration. Derrida mentions 'appeasement' and 'discussion' but this gets us no further. I think here is an example where the insights of deliberativists would help to flesh out these 'necessary conditions'. Bohman's account would be particularly useful here, structured as it is around the modest ideal of 'continued cooperation' (see Chapter 2). This is all the more

important given point 2 in Derrida's minimal definition of a 'true democracy'.
17. Blaug, 'New Theories of Discursive Democracy', 69. In Blaug's insistence that democrats must consent to the 'fairest *unfair* practices' one can hear a Derridean echo of 'least violent violence'.
18. Similarly, Derrida maintains that despite all the de facto betrayals and failures to live up to democracy he 'would take the side of the camp that, in principle, by right of law, leaves a perspective open to perfectibility in the name of . . . democracy, international law . . .' (ARSS, 113–14).
19. See Michelman's account of the potentially 'authoritarian' nature of a 'backward looking jurisprudence' that views 'adjudicative actions as legitimate only insofar as dictated by the prior normative utterance, express or implied, of extra-judicial authority'. By the latter, Michelman means 'the formally enacted preferences of a recent legislative or past constitutional majority, or with the received teaching of a historically dominant, supposedly civic, orthodoxy' ('Law's Republic', 1496).
20. Or consider Douglass's 1853 address: America 'has no scales in which to measure our wrongs . . . no standard by which to measure our rights'. See also his response to Chief Justice Roger B. Taney's infamous 1857 Dred Scott decision. See Frank, 'Staging the Dissensus'.
21. Thomassen has an excellent discussion of this in *Deconstructing Habermas*, chapter 2. For recent discussions of this paradox see Olsen, 'Paradoxes of Constitutional Democracy'; Habermas, 'On Law and Disagreement'; Habermas, 'Constitutional Democracy'; Ferrara, 'Of Boats and Principles'; Honig, 'Dead Rights, Live Futures'; Michelman, 'Morality, Identity and "Constitutional Patriotism"'; Michelman, 'How Can the People Ever Make Laws?'.
22. Horwitz, 'Derrida and the Aporia of the Political', 162.
23. Olsen, 'Paradoxes of Constitutional Democracy', 331; cf. CD, 774.
24. Benhabib, 'Democracy and Difference', 140.
25. Ibid. 137.
26. Horwitz, 'Derrida and the Aporia of the Political', 166–9.
27. Ibid. 169.
28. Benhabib, 'Democracy and Difference', 132ff. Having said this, Benhabib's postscript (ten years after the original text) does seem to reflect a more considered view. While Derrida in the original text is said to view constitutional politics as 'mere humbug, mere routine' and to have no grasp of 'really existing democracies' (140), in the postscript Benhabib 'can now see how deconstruction can be so close

to an ethos of radical democracy'. It is still surprising that Benhabib did not consider Derrida's text on Mandela, published in 1987, especially considering she references Mandela as an example of the kind of politics Derrida misses.
29. Ferrara, 'Of Boats and Principles'.
30. See Michelman, 'Morality, Identity and "Constitutional Patriotism"'.
31. Recall Michelman's worry about the 'authoritarian' possibilities of a 'backward looking jurisprudence' (n. 19 above).
32. Beckett, 'Molloy', in *Molloy, Malone Dies, The Unnameable*, 51.
33. Thomassen, *Deconstructing Habermas*, 53.
34. Cited in Frank, 'Staging the Dissensus', 91.
35. Connolly, *The Ethos of Pluralization*, 187.
36. Cited in Frank, 'Staging the Dissensus', 98.
37. Habermas, 'Fundamentalism and Terror', 42.
38. Despite Lord Byron's defence of the Luddites, the fire of their sense of injustice was (turned out to be?) seen as irrational fury, rather than incandescent justice. 'Luddite' is still used as a pejorative term to suggest backwardness and resistance to change in working practices. This also returns us to the 'no argument' argument discussed in Chapter 3.
39. Allen, *The End of Progress*, 138, 160. One does not need such levels of horror to be pessimistic here, as critics of deliberation have shown (see Chapter 2). Deliberativists are not blind to this. See, for example, Bohman (PD, 114–20).
40. Not only does this account potentially silence those who presently do not see themselves within this 'we', but it 'leaves us unprepared for the appearance of ressentiment' (Honig, 'Dead Rights, Live Futures', 798). Mouffe's account of the re-emergence in contemporary life of what were thought to be archaic passions of a bygone age should give us pause for thought here (see Chapter 1). This is not to say that Habermas does not pause. See, for example, 'Faith and Knowledge', where he refers to 'feelings of humiliation' that result from 'the pain suffered through the disintegration of traditional forms of life' (328). See also his appeal to hope rather than confidence in the face of what 'historical experience teaches' ('Transcendence from Within', 316). I will return to this.
41. Cooke, 'Violating Neutrality?', 269. For the emphasis on 'seeks' see n. 44 below.
42. Cooke, 'Violating Neutrality?', 269.
43. Habermas, *Reason and Rationality*, 130.
44. Cooke argues that Habermas's understanding of democratic legitimacy, like his account of moral validity, postulates 'a possible end

point to the process of historical learning' and, as such, threatens to be 'hubristic' and 'finalist'. See Cooke, 'Violating Neutrality?', 265–8. On the threat of self-congratulation in backward-looking narratives of progress see Allen, *The End of Progress*.
45. Connolly, *The Ethos of Pluralization*, 186.
46. It is an 'anxiety', an interminable 'ordeal', a 'night of non-knowledge'; we are 'haunted' by an 'im-possible' task of responding to 'antinomic injunctions'; we strive for a democracy that is always 'to-come' and subject to all sorts of internal perversions, and so on (see Chapter 4).
47. Although describing the work of others, such a description equally applies to Derrida's own work.
48. Benhabib, 'Democracy and Difference', 137, 141; Habermas also insists that public reason remains 'essentially contested' (*Between Naturalism and Religion*, 145). Allen argues that although Habermas suggests that what counts as a learning process is left open at the level of political theory, it is not left open philosophically. See 'Having One's Cake and Eating It Too', 150–2.
49. Plato, *The Republic*, 489b–e. See also Chapter 5, n. 25.
50. Although made in a different context, Bloch's observation about the re-emergence of the 'old dream' for a captain who 'will captivate' seems worryingly contemporary: 'A helmsman they trust and whose course they trust; the work on board ship is then made easier. The voyage is safer if everyone does not find it necessary to check the direction all the time. All this has been proven in practice, with the best democratic conscience.' Bloch, 'On the Original History of the Third Reich', 35.
51. Olsen, 'Paradoxes of Constitutional Democracy', 331.
52. Ibid. 333.
53. See also Derrida, 'Hospitality', 362–4.
54. Derrida makes an even broader claim: 'a politics that does not maintain a reference to this principle of unconditional hospitality is a politics that loses its reference to justice . . . the right to speak of justice in a credible way' (N, 101).
55. This is a familiar move in Derrida's work, whether he is analysing the concept of 'decision', 'forgiveness' or 'justice'. We have touched on the first and the last of these in the account developed over the last three chapters. In relation to the concept of 'forgiveness' see Gormley, 'The Impossible Demand of Forgiveness'.
56. Here I would give up all mastery of my home, and would have to do so 'without asking questions such as: who are you? what are you coming for? will you work with us?' (DE, 98).

57. While Derrida insists that we must 'stand on the side of human rights', he is just as insistent that in taking up, in 'an affirmative way', the very historicity and perfectibility of those rights, 'we must never prohibit the most radical questioning possible of all the concepts at work here . . . Whence the difficulty of a responsible transaction' (ARSS, 133). This exposes one far more to the dynamic indeterminacy of constitution-making than the dialectical story of a self-correcting learning process. On this deconstructive picture, our passage to the other would be one characterised by what one might call experiences of 'unselfing'. I take the latter term from Murdoch, *Metaphysics as a Guide to Morals*, 17.
58. Habermas, 'Faith and Knowledge', 334.
59. For a detailed discussion of hospitality in Derrida's work see Haddad, *Derrida and the Inheritance of Democracy*, and Still, *Derrida and Hospitality*.
60. Guilt can, of course, be a positive force. Habermas thinks that although the thought of divine deliverance from the guilt for past suffering is no longer thinkable, this need not leave us resigned to current conditions. Instead, 'we must make the consciousness of guilt into something positive, something that spurs us to fight the conditions that have produced the guilt'. See Habermas, 'Transcendence from Within', 312.
61. We saw this with McCarthy's critique (Chapter 4). I think Fraser's claim that a deconstructive approach 'impedes the possibility of political thought' (also Chapter 4) emerges, in part, from a similar underappreciation of the notion of 'im-possibility' driving Derrida's work. This is also the case for criticisms developed in Žižek, 'Melancholy and the Act', and Negri, 'The Spectre's Smile'.
62. For 'desire' see DE, 101; FWT, 60; OH, 147; ROD, 30; RS, 135, 142. For 'promise' see ARSS, 114; N, 180; RS, 86; SM, 59, 89; TOH, 78.
63. Habermas, 'Transcendence from Within', 315–16.
64. 'Democracy to come' is not simply a neutral description of the concept of democracy, it is also 'an imperative injunction' (RS, 91).
65. My use of 'deconstructive' is not meant to suggest that any of the work I include in this section draws on deconstruction. Indeed, it does not. Rather, I mean to suggest that this work overlaps with a number of areas that I have discussed in my account of deconstruction. As such, this is work from which those in the deconstructive tradition can depart (in the sense given to this word in this chapter). As research on contemporary social movements reveals them to have an increasingly reticular structure, perhaps this is one of the things we can learn from those movements.

66. Prentoulis and Thomassen, 'Political Theory in the Square', 168, 166.
67. Ibid. 169.
68. Ercan, Hendriks and Boswell, 'Studying Public Deliberation after the Systemic Turn'.
69. Ibid. 198.
70. Ercan, 'Creating and Sustaining Evidence for "Failed Multiculturalism"', 663.
71. Ibid. 667.
72. Ibid. 671. Ercan goes on to identify key factors that contribute to certain frames gaining dominance.
73. Hajer and Uitermark, 'Performing Authority'.
74. Tyler, *Revolting Subjects*, 8.
75. Ibid. 4.
76. Ibid. 13.
77. Della Porta, 'Deliberation in Movement'; Mendonça and Ercan, 'Deliberation and Protest'.
78. Prentoulis and Thomassen, 'Political Theory in the Square', 173.
79. Cited in della Porta, 'Deliberation in Movement', 341.
80. Ibid. 343.
81. Cited in ibid. The language used here almost echoes Habermas's formulation of a 'non-levelling inclusion of the other in their otherness' and Derrida's 'dream' of another experience of friendship, or perhaps comradeship, in which the other is welcomed and affirmed in their singularity.
82. Della Porta, 'Deliberation in Movement', 346.
83. Mendonça and Ercan, 'Deliberation and Protest', 279. While Mendonça and Ercan point to this novelty, they do so in the context of arguing 'that the adversarial nature of the protests helped to promote, rather than hinder, the prospects of deliberation' (268). Here adversarial relations are seen as a driver of deliberation.
84. See Extinction Rebellion, 'A proposal to grow and decentralise', 22 May 2019.

Bibliography

Abizadeh, Arash, 'Does Collective Identity Presuppose an Other? On the Alleged Incoherence of Global Solidarity', *American Political Science Review*, 99:1 (2005), 45–69.

Abizadeh, Arash, 'The Passions of the Wise: Phronêsis, Rhetoric, and Aristotle's Passionate Practical Deliberation', *The Review of Metaphysics*, 52:2 (2002), 267–96.

Adorno, Theodor, 'A Conversation with Theodor W. Adorno', *Der Spiegel*, trans. Gerhard Richter (1962), <https://cominsitu.wordpress.com/2015/09/01/a-conversation-with-theodor-w-adorno-spiegel-1969/> (last accessed 31 January 2020).

Adorno, Theodor, *Critical Models*, trans. Henry W. Pickford (New York: Columbia University Press, 2005).

Adorno, Theodor, *Negative Dialectics* (London: Routledge, 1973).

Allen, Amy, *The End of Progress: Decolonizing the Normative Foundations of Critical Theory* (New York: Columbia University Press, 2017).

Allen, Amy, 'Having One's Cake and Eating It Too', in Craig Calhoun, Eduardo Mendieta and Jonathan VanAntwerpen (eds), *Habermas and Religion* (Cambridge: Polity Press, 2013), 132–53.

Aristotle, *The Nicomachean Ethics*, trans. J. A. K. Thomson (London: Penguin Books, 1976).

Aristotle, *On Rhetoric: A Theory of Civic Discourse*, trans. George A. Kennedy (Oxford: Oxford University Press, 1991).

Aristotle, *The Politics*, trans. T. A. Sinclair (Harmondsworth: Penguin Books, 1962).

Aristotle, *Rhetoric*, trans. Joe Sachs (Newburyport, MA: Focus Publishing, 2009).

Associated Press, 'Jurors refuse to convict activist facing 20 years for helping migrants', *The Guardian*, 12 June 2019, <https://www.theguardian.com/us-news/2019/jun/11/arizona-activist-migrant-water-scott-daniel-warren-verdict> (last accessed 31 January 2020).

Bankovsky, Miriam, *Perfecting Justice in Rawls, Habermas and Honneth: A Deconstructive Perspective* (London: Bloomsbury, 2013).

Barber, Benjamin, 'Foundationalism and Democracy', in Seyla Benhabib (ed.), *Democracy and Difference* (Princeton: Princeton University Press, 1996), 348–59.

Beardsworth, Richard, *Derrida and the Political* (London: Routledge, 1996).

Beckett, Samuel, 'Molloy', in *Molloy, Malone Dies, The Unnameable* (London: Calder and Boyars, 1959).

Benhabib, Seyla, 'Democracy and Difference: Reflections on the Metapolitics of Lyotard and Derrida', in Lasse Thomassen (ed.), *The Derrida-Habermas Reader* (Edinburgh: Edinburgh University Press, 2006), 128–59.

Benhabib, Seyla, 'Introduction: The Democratic Moment and the Problem of Difference', in Benhabib (ed.), *Democracy and Difference* (Princeton: Princeton University Press, 1996), 3–18.

Benhabib, Seyla, 'Toward a Deliberative Model of Democratic Legitimacy', in Benhabib (ed.), *Democracy and Difference* (Princeton: Princeton University Press, 1996), 67–94.

Benhabib, Seyla and Nancy Fraser (eds), *Pragmatism, Critique, Judgment: Essays for Richard J. Bernstein* (Cambridge, MA: MIT Press, 2004).

Benjamin, Walter, 'The Author as Producer', in *Understanding Brecht*, trans. Anna Bostock (London: Verso, 1998), 85–103.

Bennington, Geoffrey, *Interrupting Derrida* (London: Routledge, 2000).

Bernstein, Richard J., *The New Constellation: The Ethical-Political Horizons of Modernity/Postmodernity* (Cambridge: Polity Press, 1991).

Bessette, Joseph M., 'Deliberative Democracy: The Majority Principle in Republican Government', in R. A. Goldwin and W. A. Schambra (eds), *How Democratic Is the Constitution?*

(Washington: American Enterprise Institute for Public Policy Research, 1980), 102–16.

Blaug, Ricardo, 'New Theories of Discursive Democracy', *Philosophy and Social Criticism*, 22:1 (1996), 49–80.

Bloch, Ernst, 'On the Original History of the Third Reich', in Eduardo Mendieta (ed.), *The Frankfurt School on Religion: Key Writings by the Major Thinkers* (New York: Routledge, 2005), 21–40.

Boffey, Daniel and Lorenzo Tondo, 'Captain of migrant rescue ship says Italy "criminalising solidarity"', *The Guardian*, 15 June 2019, <https://www.theguardian.com/world/2019/jun/15/captain-of-migrant-rescue-ship-says-italy-criminalising-solidarity> (last accessed 31 January 2020).

Bohman, James, 'Deliberative Democracy and Effective Social Freedom: Capabilities, Resources, and Opportunities', in Bohman and William Rehg (eds), *Deliberative Democracy: Essays on Reason and Politics* (Cambridge, MA: MIT Press, 1997), 321–49.

Bohman, James, 'Emancipation and Rhetoric: The Perlocutions and Illocutions of the Social Critic', *Philosophy and Rhetoric*, 21:3 (1988), 185–207.

Bohman, James, 'The Politics of Modern Reason: Politics, Anti-Politics and Norms in Continental Philosophy', *The Monist*, 82:2 (1999), 235–53.

Bohman, James, *Public Deliberation: Pluralism, Complexity, and Democracy* (Cambridge, MA: MIT Press, 1996).

Bohman, James, 'Representation in the Deliberative System', in John Parkinson and Jane Mansbridge (eds), *Deliberative Systems* (Cambridge: Cambridge University Press, 2012), 72–94.

Bohman, James, 'Survey Article: The Coming Age of Deliberative Democracy', *The Journal of Political Philosophy*, 6:4 (1998), 400–25.

Bohman, James, 'Two Versions of the Linguistic Turn: Habermas and Poststructuralism', in Seyla Benhabib and Maurizio Passerin d'Entrèves (eds), *Habermas and the Unfinished Project of Modernity: Critical Essays on The Philosophical Discourse of Modernity* (Cambridge: Polity Press, 1996), 197–220.

Bohman, James, '"When Water Chokes": Ideology, Communication and Practical Rationality', *Constellations*, 7:3 (2000), 382–92.

Bohman, James and William Rehg, 'Introduction', in Bohman and Rehg (eds), *Deliberative Democracy: Essays on Reason and Politics* (Cambridge, MA: MIT Press, 1997), ix–xxx.

Brady, John S., 'No Contest? Assessing the Agonistic Critiques of Jürgen Habermas's Theory of the Public Sphere', *Philosophy and Social Criticism*, 30:3 (2004), 331–54.

Cadwalladr, Carole, 'Robert Mercer: The big data billionaire waging war on mainstream media', *The Guardian*, 26 February 2017, <https://www.theguardian.com/politics/2017/feb/26/robert-mercer-breitbart-war-on-media-steve-bannon-donald-trump-nigel-farage> (last accessed 31 January 2020).

Caputo, John, *Deconstruction in a Nutshell* (New York: Fordham University Press, 1997).

Caputo, John, 'The Economy of Signs in Husserl and Derrida', in John Sallis (ed.), *Deconstruction and Philosophy: The Texts of Jacques Derrida* (Chicago: University of Chicago Press, 1987), 99–113.

Carrabregu, Gent, 'Habermas on Solidarity: An Immanent Critique', *Constellations*, 23:4 (2016), 507–22.

Chambers, Simone, *Reasonable Democracy: Jürgen Habermas and the Politics of Discourse* (New York: Cornell University Press, 1996).

Chambers, Simone, 'Rhetoric and the Public Sphere: Has Deliberative Democracy Abandoned Mass Democracy?', *Political Theory*, 37:3 (2009), 323–50.

Cohen, Jean L., 'Strategy or Identity: New Theoretical Paradigms and Contemporary Social Movements', *Social Research*, 52:4 (1985), 663–716.

Cohen, Joshua, 'Deliberation and Democratic Legitimacy', in James Bohman and William Rehg (eds), *Deliberative Democracy: Essays on Reason and Politics* (Cambridge, MA: MIT Press, 1997), 67–92.

Connolly, William E., *The Ethos of Pluralization* (Minneapolis: University of Minnesota Press, 1995).

Connolly, William E., *Identity\Difference: Democratic Negotiations of Political Paradox* (Ithaca: Cornell University Press, 1991).

Connolly, William E., 'Taylor, Foucault, and Otherness', *Political Theory*, 13:3 (1985), 365–76.

Cooke, Maeve, 'Habermas and Consensus', *European Journal of Philosophy*, 3:1 (1993), 246–67.

Cooke, Maeve, 'Violating Neutrality? Religious Validity Claims and Democratic Legitimacy', in Craig Calhoun, Eduardo Mendieta and Jonathan VanAntwerpen (eds), *Habermas and Religion* (Cambridge: Polity Press, 2013), 249–74.

Cooper, John M., 'Ethical-Political Theory in Aristotle's *Rhetoric*', in David J. Furley and Alexander Nehamas (eds), *Aristotle's 'Rhetoric': Philosophical Essays* (Princeton: Princeton University Press, 1994), 193–210.

Critchley, Simon, *The Ethics of Deconstruction: Derrida and Levinas* (Edinburgh: Edinburgh University Press, 1999).

Dahlberg, Lincoln, 'The Habermasian Public Sphere: Taking Difference Seriously', *Theory and Society*, 34:2 (2005), 111–36.

della Porta, Donatella, 'Deliberation in Movement: Why and How to Study Deliberative Democracy and Social Movements', *Acta Politica*, 40:3 (2005), 336–50.

Derrida, Jacques, *Adieu to Emmanuel Levinas*, trans. Pascale-Anne Brault and Michael Naas (Stanford: Stanford University Press, 1999).

Derrida, Jacques, *Aporias*, trans. Thomas Dutoit (Stanford: Stanford University Press, 1993).

Derrida, Jacques, 'Autoimmunity: Real and Symbolic Suicides', in Giovanni Borradori (ed.), *Philosophy in a Time of Terror* (Chicago: University of Chicago Press, 2003), 85–136.

Derrida, Jacques, *Deconstruction Engaged: The Sydney Seminars*, ed. Paul Patton (Sydney: Power Publications, 2001).

Derrida, Jacques, *Edmund Husserl's Origin of Geometry: An Introduction* (Lincoln: University of Nebraska Press, 1989).

Derrida, Jacques, *Ethics, Institutions, and the Right to Philosophy*, trans. and ed. Peter Pericles Trifonas (Oxford: Rowman & Littlefield Publishers, 2002).

Derrida, Jacques, *Eyes of the University: Right to Philosophy 2*, trans. Jan Plug et al. (Stanford: Stanford University Press, 2004).

Derrida, Jacques, 'Force of Law: The "Mystical Foundation of Authority"', in Drucilla Cornell, Michael Rosenfeld and David Gray Carlson (eds), *Deconstruction and the Possibility of Justice* (London: Routledge, 1992), 3–67.

Derrida, Jacques, *The Gift of Death*, trans. David Wills (Chicago: University of Chicago Press, 1996).

Derrida, Jacques, 'Hospitality', in Gil Anidjar (ed.), *Acts of Religion* (New York: Routledge, 2002), 356–420.
Derrida, Jacques, 'Interview with Alan Montefiore', *Oxford Amnesty Lectures*, 13 February 1992, <http://www.youtube.com/watch?v=0B-gzOQLzJk&feature=related> (last accessed 31 January 2020).
Derrida, Jacques, 'The Laws of Reflection: For Nelson Mandela', in Derrida and Mustapha Tili (eds), *For Nelson Mandela* (New York: Seaver Books, 1987), 13–42.
Derrida, Jacques, *Limited Inc* (Evanston: Northwestern University Press, 1988).
Derrida, Jacques, *Margins of Philosophy*, trans. Alan Bass (Brighton: Harvester Press, 1982).
Derrida, Jacques, 'Marx & Sons', in Michael Sprinker (ed.), *Ghostly Demarcations* (London: Routledge, 1999), 213–69.
Derrida, Jacques, 'Mochlos; or, The Conflict of the Faculties', trans. Richard Rand and Amy Wygant, in Richard Rand (ed.), *Logomachia: The Conflict of the Faculties Today* (Lincoln: University of Nebraska Press, 1992), 1–34.
Derrida, Jacques, *Negotiations: Interventions and Interviews, 1971–2001*, ed. Elizabeth Rottenberg (Stanford: Stanford University Press, 2002).
Derrida, Jacques, *Of Grammatology*, trans. Gayatri Chakravorty Spivak (Baltimore: Johns Hopkins University Press, 1976).
Derrida, Jacques, *Of Hospitality*, trans. Rachel Bowlby (Stanford: Stanford University Press, 2000).
Derrida, Jacques, *Of Spirit*, trans. Geoffrey Bennington and Rachel Bowlby (Chicago: University of Chicago Press, 1987).
Derrida, Jacques, 'Onto-Theology of National Humanism: Prolegomena to a Hypothesis', *Oxford Literary Review*, 14:9 (1992), 3–23.
Derrida, Jacques, *The Other Heading*, trans. Pascale-Anne Brault and Michael Naas (Bloomington: Indiana University Press, 1992).
Derrida, Jacques, *Paper Machine*, trans. Rachel Bowlby (Stanford: Stanford University Press, 2005).
Derrida, Jacques, 'Passions: "An Oblique Offering"', in David Wood (ed.), *Derrida: A Critical Reader* (Oxford: Blackwell, 1992), 5–35.

Derrida, Jacques, *Points . . . Interviews 1974–1994*, ed. Elisabeth Weber (Stanford: Stanford University Press, 1995).
Derrida, Jacques, *Politics of Friendship*, trans. George Collins (London: Verso, 1997).
Derrida, Jacques, *Positions*, trans. Alan Bass (London: Continuum, 1972).
Derrida, Jacques, 'The Principle of Reason: The University in the Eyes of its Pupils', *Diacritics*, 13:3 (1983), 3–20.
Derrida, Jacques, *Psyche: Inventions of the Other, Volume I*, ed. Peggy Kamuf and Elizabeth Rottenberg (Stanford: Stanford University Press, 2007).
Derrida, Jacques, 'Remarks on Deconstruction and Pragmatism', in Chantal Mouffe (ed.), *Deconstruction and Pragmatism* (London: Routledge, 1996), 78–90.
Derrida, Jacques, *Responsibilities of Deconstruction*, ed. Jonathan Dronsfield and Nick Midgley, *PLI: Warwick Journal of Philosophy*, 6 (Summer 1997).
Derrida, Jacques, *Rogues: Two Essays on Reason*, trans. Pascale-Anne Brault and Michael Naas (Stanford: Stanford University Press, 2005).
Derrida, Jacques, *Spectres of Marx*, trans. Peggy Kamuf (London: Routledge, 1994).
Derrida, Jacques, *Speech and Phenomena*, trans. David B. Alison (Evanston: Northwestern University Press, 1973).
Derrida, Jacques, 'The Villanova Roundtable', in John Caputo (ed.), *Deconstruction in a Nutshell* (New York: Fordham University Press, 1997), 3–28.
Derrida, Jacques, *Who's Afraid of Philosophy? Right to Philosophy 1*, trans. Jan Plug (Stanford: Stanford University Press, 2002).
Derrida, Jacques, *Without Alibi*, trans. Peggy Kamuf (Stanford: Stanford University Press, 2002).
Derrida, Jacques, *Writing and Difference*, trans. Alan Bass (London: Routledge, 1978).
Derrida, Jacques and Richard Kearney, 'Deconstruction and the Other', in Kearney (ed.), *Dialogues with Contemporary Continental Thinkers* (Manchester: Manchester University Press, 1984), 105–26.
Derrida, Jacques and Elisabeth Roudinesco, *For What Tomorrow Brings*, trans. Jeff Fort (Stanford: Stanford University Press, 2004).

Deveaux, Monique, 'A Deliberative Approach to Conflicts of Culture', *Political Theory*, 31:6 (2003), 780–807.
Dews, Peter, *Logics of Disintegration: Post-Structuralist Thought and the Claims of Critical Theory* (London: Verso, 1987).
Dooley, Mark, 'The Civic Religion of Social Hope: A Response to Simon Critchley', *Philosophy and Social Criticism*, 27:5 (2001), 35–58.
Dow, Jamie, *Passions and Persuasion in Aristotle's Rhetoric* (Oxford: Oxford University Press, 2015).
Dreyer Hansen, Allan and André Sonnichsen, 'Radical Democracy, Agonism and the Limits of Pluralism: An Interview with Chantal Mouffe', *Distinktion: Journal of Social Theory*, 15:3 (2014), 263–70.
Dryzek, John S., *Deliberative Democracy and Beyond: Liberals, Critics, Contestations* (Oxford: Oxford University Press, 2002).
Dryzek, John S., 'Rhetoric in Democracy: A Systematic Appreciation', *Political Theory*, 38:3 (2010), 319–39.
Eagleton, Terry, 'Don't deride Derrida', *The Guardian*, 15 October 2004, <http://www.guardian.co.uk/education/2004/oct/15/highereducation.news> (last accessed 31 January 2020).
Eagleton, Terry, 'Marxism without Marxism', in Michael Sprinker (ed.), *Ghostly Demarcations: A Symposium on Jacques Derrida's Spectres of Marx* (London: Verso, 1999), 83–7.
Elliot, Anthony, *Social Theory and Psychoanalysis in Transition* (Oxford: Blackwell, 1992).
Elster, Jon, 'Introduction', in Elster (ed.), *Deliberative Democracy* (Cambridge: Cambridge University Press, 1998), 1–18.
Elster, Jon, 'The Market and the Forum: Three Varieties of Political Theory', in James Bohman and William Rehg (eds), *Deliberative Democracy* (Cambridge, MA: MIT Press, 1997), 3–34.
Elstub, Stephen, Selen Ercan and Ricardo Fabrino, 'Editorial Introduction: The Fourth Generation of Deliberative Democracy', *Critical Policy Studies*, 10:2 (2016), 139–51.
Engberg-Pedersen, Troels, 'Is There an Ethical Dimension to Aristotelian Rhetoric?', in Amélie Oksenberg Rorty (ed.), *Essay on Aristotle's Rhetoric* (Berkeley: University of California Press, 1996), 116–41.
Engel, Pascal, 'Richard Rorty', *Notre Dame Philosophical Reviews*,

January 2004, <http://ndpr.nd.edu/review.cfm?id=1015> (last accessed 31 January 2020).

Ercan, Selen A., 'Creating and Sustaining Evidence for "Failed Multiculturalism": The Case of "Honor Killing" in Germany', *American Behavioural Scientist*, 59:5 (2015), 658–97.

Ercan, Selen A., Carolyn M. Hendriks and John Boswell, 'Studying Public Deliberation after the Systemic Turn: The Crucial Role for Interpretive Research', *Policy & Politics*, 45:2 (2017), 195–212.

Erman, Eva, 'What Is Wrong with Agonistic Pluralism? Reflections on Conflict in Democratic Theory', *Philosophy and Social Criticism*, 35:9 (2009), 1039–62.

d'Etrèves, Maurizio (ed.), *Democracy as Public Deliberation* (Manchester: Manchester University Press, 2002).

Extinction Rebellion, 'A proposal to grow and decentralise', Extinction Rebellion Social Media, 22 May 2019, <https://www.youtube.com/watch?v=4A9DxCVSHCY> (last accessed 31 January 2020).

Ferrara, Alessandro, 'Of Boats and Principles: Reflections on Habermas's "Constitutional Democracy"', *Political Theory*, 29:6 (2001), 782–91.

Fontana, Benedetto, 'Rhetoric and the Roots of Democratic Politics', in Fontana, Cary J. Nederman and Gary Remer (eds), *Talking Democracy: Historical Perspectives on Rhetoric and Democracy* (University Park: Pennsylvania State University Press, 2005), 27–56.

Fossen, Thomas, 'Agonistic Critiques of Liberalism: Perfection and Emancipation', *Contemporary Political Theory*, 7:4 (2008), 376–94.

Frank, Jason, 'Staging the Dissensus: Frederick Douglass and "We, the People"', in Andrew Schaap (ed.), *Law and Agonistic Politics* (Farnham: Ashgate Publishing, 2009), 87–104.

Fraser, Nancy, 'The Force of Law: Metaphysical or Political?', *Cardozo Law Review*, 13 (1991), 1325–31.

Fraser, Nancy, 'The French Derrideans: Politicizing Deconstruction or Deconstructing the Political?', in Gary B. Madison (ed.), *Working Through Derrida* (Evanston: Northwestern University Press, 1993), 51–76.

Freyenhagen, Fabian, *Adorno's Practical Philosophy: Living Less Wrongly* (Cambridge: Cambridge University Press, 2013).

Fritsch, Matthias, 'Antagonism and Democratic Citizenship (Schmitt, Mouffe, Derrida)', *Research in Phenomenology*, 38:2 (2008), 174–97.
Fritsch, Matthias, 'Derrida's Democracy to Come', *Constellations*, 9:4 (2002), 574–97.
Fritsch, Matthias, 'Equality and Singularity in Justification and Application Discourses', *European Journal of Political Theory*, 9:3 (2010), 328–46.
Fung, Archon, 'Deliberation before the Revolution: Towards an Ethics of Deliberative Democracy in an Unjust World', *Political Theory*, 33:3 (2005), 397–419.
Gagné, Patricia Lorraine, 'The Battered Women's Movement in the "Post-Feminist Era": New Social Movement Strategies and the Celeste Clemencies', PhD manuscript, <https://etd.ohiolink.edu/!etd.send_file?accession=osu1239972311&disposition=inline> (last accessed 31 January 2020).
Garsten, Bryan, *Saving Persuasion: A Defense of Rhetoric and Judgment* (Cambridge, MA: Harvard University Press, 2006).
Garver, Eugene, *Aristotle's Rhetoric: An Art of Character* (Chicago: University of Chicago Press, 1994).
Gasché, Rodolphe, *The Tain of the Mirror: Derrida and the Philosophy of Reflection* (Cambridge, MA: Harvard University Press, 1998).
Gentleman, Amelia, 'Revealed: Depth of Home Office failures on Windrush', *The Guardian*, 18 July 2018, <https://www.theguardian.com/uk-news/2018/jul/18/revealed-depth-of-home-office-failures-on-windrush> (last accessed 31 January 2020).
Gentleman, Amelia, 'Sajid Javid urged to act in immigration scandal "bigger than Windrush"', *The Guardian*, 23 April 2019, <https://www.theguardian.com/uk-news/2019/apr/23/toeic-english-test-sajid-javid-urged-to-act-in-immigration-scandal-bigger-than-windrush> (last accessed 31 January 2020).
Glover, R. W., 'Games without Frontiers? Democratic Engagement, Agonistic Pluralism and the Question of Exclusion', *Philosophy and Social Criticism*, 38:1 (2012), 81–104.
Gorgias, 'Encomium of Helen', in *On Rhetoric: A Theory of Civic Discourse*, trans. and ed. George A. Kennedy (Oxford: Oxford University Press, 1991).
Gormley, Steven, 'Deliberation, Unjust Exclusion, and the

Rhetorical Turn', *Contemporary Political Philosophy*, 18:2 (2019), 202–26.
Gormley, Steven, 'The Impossible Demand of Forgiveness', *International Journal of Philosophical Studies*, 22:1 (2014), 27–48.
Greenfield, Patrick and Sarah Marsh, 'Hundreds of homeless people fined and imprisoned in England and Wales', *The Guardian*, 20 May 2019, <https://www.theguardian.com/society/2018/may/20/homeless-people-fined-imprisoned-pspo-england-wales> (last accessed 31 January 2020).
Guignon, Charles and David R. Hiley (eds), *Richard Rorty* (Cambridge: Cambridge University Press, 2003).
Gürsözlü, Fuat, 'Agonism and Deliberation – Recognizing the Difference', *The Journal of Political Philosophy*, 17:3 (2009), 356–68.
Gutmann, Amy, 'Introduction', in Gutmann (ed.), *Multiculturalism: Examining the Politics of Recognition* (Princeton: Princeton University Press, 1994), 18–21.
Gutmann, Amy and Dennis Thompson, *Democracy and Disagreement* (Cambridge, MA: Harvard University Press, 1996).
Gutmann, Amy and Dennis Thompson, *Why Deliberative Democracy?* (Princeton: Princeton University Press, 2004).
Habermas, Jürgen, *Between Facts and Norms: A Contribution to a Discourse Theory of Law and Democracy*, trans. William Rehg (Cambridge: Polity Press, 1996).
Habermas, Jürgen, *Between Naturalism and Religion*, trans. Ciaran Cronin (Cambridge: Polity Press, 2008).
Habermas, Jürgen, *Communication and the Evolution of Society*, trans. Thomas McCarthy (London: Heinemann, 1979).
Habermas, Jürgen, 'Constitutional Democracy: A Paradoxical Union of Contradictory Principles?', *Political Theory*, 29:6 (2001), 766–81.
Habermas, Jürgen, *Europe: The Faltering Project*, trans. Ciaran Cronin (Cambridge: Polity Press, 2009).
Habermas, Jürgen, 'Faith and Knowledge', in Eduardo Mendieta (ed.), *The Frankfurt School on Religion: Key Writings by the Major Thinkers* (New York: Routledge, 2005), 327–38.
Habermas, Jürgen, 'From Kant's "Ideas" of Pure Reason to the "Idealizing" Presuppositions of Communicative Action:

Reflections on the Detranscendentalized "Use of Reason"', in William Rehg and James Bohman (eds), *Pluralism and the Pragmatic Turn: The Transformation of Critical Theory: Essays in Honor of Thomas McCarthy* (Cambridge, MA: MIT Press, 2001), 11–39.

Habermas, Jürgen, 'Fundamentalism and Terror: A Dialogue with Jürgen Habermas', in Giovanna Borradori (ed.), *Philosophy in a Time of Terror: Dialogues with Jürgen Habermas and Jacques Derrida* (Chicago: University of Chicago Press, 2003), 25–44.

Habermas, Jürgen, *The Future of Human Nature* (Cambridge: Polity Press, 2003).

Habermas, Jürgen, *The Inclusion of the Other: Studies in Political Theory*, trans. Ciaran Cronin (Cambridge, MA: MIT Press, 1999).

Habermas, Jürgen, *Justification and Application*, trans. Ciaran P. Cronin (Cambridge, MA: MIT Press, 1993).

Habermas, Jürgen, *Moral Consciousness and Communicative Action*, trans. Christian Lenhardt and Shierry Weber Nicholsen (Cambridge, MA: MIT Press, 1990).

Habermas, Jürgen, 'On Law and Disagreement: Some Comments on "Interpretative Pluralism"', *Ratio Juris*, 16:2 (2003), 187–94.

Habermas, Jürgen, *The Philosophical Discourse of Modernity*, trans. Frederick Lawrence (Cambridge: Polity Press, 1985).

Habermas, Jürgen, 'Popular Sovereignty as Procedure', in James Bohman and William Rehg (eds), *Deliberative Democracy: Essays on Reason and Politics* (Cambridge, MA: MIT Press, 1997), 35–66.

Habermas, Jürgen, *Postmetaphysical Thinking*, trans. William Mark Hohengarten (Cambridge: Polity Press, 1992).

Habermas, Jürgen, *Reason and Rationality: Essays on Reason, God, and Modernity*, ed. Eduardo Mendieta (Cambridge: Polity Press, 2002).

Habermas, Jürgen, 'Religious Tolerance: The Peacemaker for Cultural Rights', *Philosophy*, 79:307 (2004), 5–18.

Habermas, Jürgen, 'A Reply to my Critics', in John B. Thompson and David Held (eds), *Habermas: Critical Debates* (London: Macmillan Press, 1982), 219–317.

Habermas, Jürgen, 'A Reply to Symposium Participants', *Cardozo Law Review*, 17 (1996), 1477–558.

Habermas, Jürgen, 'Richard Rorty's Pragmatic Turn', in Robert B. Brandom (ed.), *Rorty and his Critics* (Oxford: Blackwell, 2000), 31–55.

Habermas, Jürgen, 'Struggles for Recognition in the Democratic Constitutional State', in Amy Gutmann (ed.), *Multiculturalism: Examining the Politics of Recognition* (Princeton: Princeton University Press, 1994), 107–48.

Habermas, Jürgen, 'Three Normative Models of Democracy', in Seyla Benhabib (ed.), *Democracy and Difference* (Princeton: Princeton University Press, 1996), 21–30.

Habermas, Jürgen, 'Transcendence from Within, Transcendence in this World', in Eduardo Mendieta (ed.), *The Frankfurt School on Religion: Key Writings by the Major Thinkers* (New York: Routledge, 2005), 303–74.

Haddad, Samir, 'Derrida and Democracy at Risk', *Contretemps*, 4 (2004), 29–44.

Haddad, Samir, *Derrida and the Inheritance of Democracy* (Bloomington: Indiana University Press, 2013).

Hägglund, Martin, *Radical Atheism: Derrida and the Time of Life* (Stanford: Stanford University Press, 2008).

Hajer, Maarten and Justus Uitermark, 'Performing Authority: Discursive Politics after the Assassination of Theo Van Gogh', *Public Administration*, 86:1 (2008), 5–19.

Hamacher, Hertz and Thomas Keenan (eds), *Responses: On Paul de Man's Wartime Journalism* (Lincoln: University of Nebraska Press, 1989).

Held, David, *Models of Democracy* (Cambridge: Polity Press, 2000).

Hirschkop, Ken, 'Justice and Drama: On Bakhtin as a Complement to Habermas', *The Sociological Review*, 52:1 (2004), 49–66.

Home Office, *Hate Crime, England and Wales, 2017–18*, <https://assets.publishing.service.gov.uk/government/uploads/system/uploads/attachment_data/file/748598/hate-crime-1718-hosb20 18.pdf> (last accessed 31 January 2020).

Honig, Bonnie, 'Between Decision and Deliberation: Paradox in Political Theory', *The American Political Science Review*, 101:1 (2007), 1–17.

Honig, Bonnie, 'Dead Rights, Live Futures: A Reply to Habermas's

"Constitutional Democracy"', *Political Theory* 29:6 (2001), 792–805.

Honig, Bonnie, 'Difference, Dilemmas, and the Politics of Home', in Seyla Benhabib (ed.), *Democracy and Difference* (Princeton: Princeton University Press, 1996), 257–77.

Honig, Bonnie, *Political Theory and the Displacement of Politics* (Ithaca: Cornell University Press, 1993).

Honig, Bonnie, 'The Politics of Agonism', *Political Theory*, 21:3 (1993), 528–33.

Honig, Bonnie, '"[Un]Dazzled by the Ideal?": Tully's Politics and Humanism in Tragic Perspective', *Political Theory*, 39:1 (2011), 138–44.

Horwitz, Noah, 'Derrida and the Aporia of the Political, or the Theologico-Political Dimension of Deconstruction', *Research in Phenomenology*, 32:1 (2002), 157–76.

Howarth, David, 'Ethos, Agonism and Populism: William Connolly and the Case for Radical Democracy', *British Journal of Politics and International Relations*, 10:2 (2008), 171–93.

Hoy, David Couzens and Thomas McCarthy, *Critical Theory* (Oxford: Blackwell, 1994).

Husserl, Edmund, *Ideas: General Introduction to Pure Phenomenology*, trans. W. R. Boyce Gibson (New York: Collier Books, 1962).

Irwin, T. H., 'Ethics in the *Rhetoric* and in the *Ethics*', in Amélie Oksenberg Rorty (ed.), *Essay on Aristotle's Rhetoric* (Berkeley: University of California Press, 1996), 142–74.

Jewell, John, 'Katie Hopkins and *The Sun*: When the unreadable prints the unspeakable', *The Conversation*, 20 April 2015, <https://theconversation.com/katie-hopkins-and-the-sun-when-the-unreadable-prints-the-unspeakable-40505> (last accessed 31 January 2020).

Kandell, Jonathan, 'Jacques Derrida, abstruse theorist, dies at 74', *New York Times*, 10 October 2004, <http://www.nytimes.com/2004/10/10/obituaries/10derrida.html> (last accessed 31 January 2020).

Kant, Immanuel, *The Critique of Judgement*, trans. J. C. Meredith (Oxford: Oxford University Press, 1953).

Kapoor, Ilan, 'Deliberative Democracy or Agonistic Pluralism? The Relevance of the Habermas-Mouffe Debate for Third

World Politics', *Alternatives: Global, Local, Political*, 27:4 (2002), 459–87.

Karagiannis, N. and Peter Wagner, 'Varieties of Agonism: Conflict, the Common Good, and the Need for Synagonism', *Journal of Social and Political Thought*, 39:3 (2008), 323–33.

Kearney, Richard, 'Aliens and Others: Between Girard and Derrida', *Cultural Values*, 3:3 (1999), 251–62.

Kearney, Richard, *Dialogues with Contemporary Continental Thinkers* (Manchester: Manchester University Press, 1984).

Khan, Gulshan, 'Critical Republicanism: Jürgen Habermas and Chantal Mouffe', *Contemporary Political Theory*, 12:4 (2013), 318–37.

Kierkegaard, Søren, *Concluding Unscientific Postscript*, trans. David F. Swenson and Walter Lowrie (Princeton: Princeton University Press, 1974).

Kirkup, James and Robert Winnett, 'Theresa May Interview', *The Telegraph*, 25 May 2012, <https://www.telegraph.co.uk/news/uknews/immigration/9291483/Theresa-May-interview-Were-going-to-give-illegal-migrants-a-really-hostile-reception.html> (last accessed 31 January 2020).

Knight, Jack and James Johnson, 'What Sort of Equality Does Deliberative Democracy Require?', in James Bohman and William Rehg (eds), *Deliberative Democracy: Essays on Reason and Politics* (Cambridge, MA: MIT Press, 1997), 279–320.

Knops, Andrew, 'Debate: Agonism as Deliberation – On Mouffe's Theory of Democracy', *The Journal of Political Philosophy*, 15:1 (2007), 115–26.

Laclau, Ernesto, 'Deconstruction, Pragmatism, Hegemony', in Chantal Mouffe (ed.), *Deconstruction and Pragmatism* (London: Routledge, 1996), 47–68.

Laclau, Ernesto, *Emancipation(s)* (London: Verso, 1996).

Lawlor, Leonard, *Derrida and Husserl: The Basic Problems of Phenomenology* (Bloomington: Indiana University Press, 2002).

Lefort, Claude, *Democracy and Political Theory*, ed. David Macey (Minneapolis: University of Minnesota Press, 1988).

Lefort, Claude, *The Political Forms of Modern Society: Bureaucracy, Democracy, Totalitarianism*, ed. John B. Thompson (Cambridge: Polity Press, 1986).

Leiter, Brian, 'The Derrida Industry', <http://leiterreports.typepad.com/blog/2004/10/the_derrida_ind.html> (last accessed 31 January 2020).

Little, Adrian, 'Between Disagreement and Consensus: Unravelling the Democratic Paradox', *Australian Journal of Political Science*, 42:1 (2007), 143–59.

Lyotard, François, *The Postmodern Condition: A Report on Knowledge*, trans. G. Bennington and B. Massumi (Manchester: Manchester University Press, 1991).

McCarthy, Thomas, *Ideals and Illusions: On Reconstruction and Deconstruction in Critical Theory* (Cambridge, MA: MIT Press, 1991).

McCarthy, Thomas, 'Legitimacy and Diversity: A Dialectical Reflection on Analytic Distinctions', *Cardozo Law Review*, 17 (1995), 1082–125.

McCarthy, Thomas, 'Reason in a Postmetaphysical Age', in McCarthy and David C. Hoy, *Critical Theory* (Cambridge, MA: Blackwell, 1994), 31–62.

McKenna, W. and Claude J. Evans (eds), *Derrida and Phenomenology* (Dordrecht: Kluwer Academic Press, 1995).

Manin, Bernard, 'On Legitimacy and Political Deliberation', *Political Theory*, 15:3 (1987), 338–68.

Mansbridge, Jane, 'Everyday Talk in the Deliberative System', in Stephen Macedo (ed.), *Deliberative Politics: Essays on Democracy and Disagreement* (Oxford: Oxford University Press, 1999), 211–39.

Mansbridge, Jane, James Bohman, Simone Chambers, Thomas Christiano, Archon Fung, John Parkinson, Denis F. Thompson and Mark E. Warren, 'A Systemic Approach to Deliberative Democracy', in Parkinson and Mansbridge (eds), *Deliberative Systems* (Cambridge: Cambridge University Press, 2010), 1–26.

Markell, Patchen, 'Contesting Consensus: Reading Habermas on the Public Sphere', *Constellations*, 3:3 (1997), 377–400.

Markell, Patchen, 'Making Affect Safe for Democracy?', *Political Theory*, 28:1 (2000), 38–63.

Marsh, Sarah and Patrick Greenfield, 'Recognise attacks on rough sleepers as hate crimes, say experts', *The Guardian*, 19 December 2018, <https://www.theguardian.com/society/2018/dec/19/homeless-attacks-rough-sleepers-hate-crimes> (last accessed 31 January 2020).

Mendonça, Ricardo Fabrino and Selen A. Ercan, 'Deliberation and Protest: Strange Bedfellows? Revealing the Deliberative Potential of 2013 Protests in Turkey and Brazil', *Policy Studies*, 36:3 (2015), 267–82.
Michelman, Frank I., 'How Can the People Ever Make Laws? A Critique of Deliberative Democracy', in James Bohman and William Rehg (eds), *Deliberative Democracy: Essays on Reason and Politics* (Cambridge, MA: MIT Press, 1997), 145–71.
Michelman, Frank I., 'Law's Republic', *Yale Law Review*, 97:8 (1988), 1493–537.
Michelman, Frank I., 'Morality, Identity and "Constitutional Patriotism"', *Ratio Juris*, 14:3 (2001), 253–71.
Mill, John Stuart, 'Considerations on Representative Government', in *Essays on Politics and Society*, ed. J. M. Robson (Toronto: University of Toronto Press, 1977), 371–578.
Mooney, Timothy, 'How to Read Once Again: Derrida on Husserl', *Philosophy Today*, 47:3 (2003), 305–21.
Moore, Alfred, 'Deliberative Elitism? Distributed Deliberation and the Organization of Epistemic Inequality', *Critical Policy Studies*, 10:2 (2016), 191–208.
Morris, Martin, 'Deliberation and Deconstruction: Two Versions of a Post-National Democracy', *Canadian Journal of Political Science*, 34:4 (2001), 763–90.
Mouffe, Chantal, *Agonistics: Thinking the World Politically* (London: Verso, 2013).
Mouffe, Chantal, 'Carl Schmitt and the Paradox of Liberal Democracy', in Mouffe (ed.), *The Challenge of Carl Schmitt* (London: Verso, 1999), 38–54.
Mouffe, Chantal, 'Decision, Deliberation, and Democratic Ethos', *Philosophy Today*, 41:1 (1997), 24–30.
Mouffe, Chantal (ed.), *Deconstruction and Pragmatism* (London: Routledge, 1996).
Mouffe, Chantal, 'Deliberative Democracy or Agonistic Pluralism', *Social Research*, 66:3 (1999), 745–58.
Mouffe, Chantal, 'Democracy, Power, and the "Political"', in Seyla Benhabib (ed.), *Democracy and Difference* (Princeton: Princeton University Press, 1996), 245–66.
Mouffe, Chantal, *The Democratic Paradox* (London: Verso, 2000).

Mouffe, Chantal, 'For an Agonistic Public Sphere', in Lars Tønder and Lasse Thomassen (eds), *Radical Democracy: Politics between Abundance and Lack* (Manchester: Manchester University Press, 2005), 123–33.
Mouffe, Chantal, 'Introduction: Schmitt's Challenge', in Mouffe (ed.), *The Challenge of Carl Schmitt* (London: Verso, 1999), 1–6.
Mouffe, Chantal, *On the Political* (Oxford: Routledge, 2005).
Mouffe, Chantal, 'Politics and Passions: Introduction', *Philosophy and Social Criticism*, 28:6 (2002), 615–16.
Mouffe, Chantal, *The Return of the Political* (London: Verso, 1998).
Mouffe, Chantal and Elke Wagner, 'Interview with Chantal Mouffe', in Mouffe, *Agonistics* (London: Verso, 2018), 271–305.
Mulligan, Kevin, 'How Not to Read: Derrida on Husserl', *Topoi*, 10:2 (1991), 199–208.
Murdoch, Iris, *Fire and the Sun* (Oxford: Clarendon, 1977).
Murdoch, Iris, *Metaphysics as a Guide to Morals* (London: Penguin Books, 1992).
Murdoch, Iris, *The Sovereignty of Good* (Boston: Ark, 1985).
Naas, Michael, '"One Nation . . . Indivisible": Jacques Derrida and the Autoimmunity of Democracy and the Sovereignty of God', *Research in Phenomenology*, 36:1 (2006), 15–44.
Negri, Antonio, 'The Spectre's Smile', in Michael Sprinker (ed.), *Ghostly Demarcations* (London: Verso, 1999), 5–16.
Nietzsche, Friedrich, *Beyond Good and Evil: Prelude to a Philosophy of the Future*, trans. R. J. Hollingdale (London: Penguin, 1990).
Nietzsche, Friedrich, *The Gay Science: With a Prelude in Rhymes and an Appendix of Songs*, trans. Walter Kaufmann (New York: Random House, 1974).
Norris, Christopher, 'Analytic Philosophy in Another Key: Derrida on Language, Truth and Logic', in Madeleine Fagan, Ludovic Glorieux, Indira Hasimbegovic and Marie Suetsugu (eds), *Derrida: Negotiating the Legacy* (Edinburgh: Edinburgh University Press, 2007), 23–44.
Norris, Christopher, *Contest of Faculties: Philosophy after Theory and Deconstruction* (London: Methuen, 1985).
Norris, Christopher, 'Deconstruction, Postmodernism and Philosophy: Habermas and Derrida', in David Wood (ed.), *Derrida: A Critical Reader* (Blackwell, 1992), 167–93.

Norris, Christopher, *Derrida* (Cambridge, MA: Harvard University Press, 1987).

Norval, Aletta, *Aversive Democracy: Inheritance and Originality in the Democratic Tradition* (Cambridge: Cambridge University Press, 2007).

Norval, Aletta, 'Hegemony after Deconstruction: The Consequences of Undecidability', *Journal of Political Ideologies*, 9:2 (2004), 139–57.

Nussbaum, Martha C., *Love's Knowledge: Essays on Philosophy and Literature* (Oxford: Oxford University Press, 1990).

O'Carroll, Lisa, 'EU citizens in UK at risk of Windrush-style catastrophe, say MPs', *The Guardian*, 30 May 2019, <https://www.theguardian.com/uk-news/2019/may/30/eu-citizens-in-uk-at-risk-of-windrush-style-catastrophe-say-mps> (last accessed 31 January 2020).

Olsen, Kevin, 'Paradoxes of Constitutional Democracy', *American Journal of Political Science*, 51:2 (2007), 330–43.

Owen, David, 'Genealogy as Perspicuous Representation', in Cressida J. Heyes (ed.), *The Grammar of Politics: Wittgenstein and Political Philosophy* (Ithaca: Cornell University Press, 2003), 82–96.

Owen, David and Graham Smith, 'Survey Article: Deliberation, Democracy, and the Systemic Turn', *The Journal of Political Philosophy*, 23:2 (2015), 213–34.

Paine, Thomas, *The Rights of Man* (London: Penguin, 1985).

Parkinson, John, *Deliberating in the Real World: Problems of Legitimacy in Deliberative Democracy* (Oxford: Oxford University Press, 2006).

Patton, Paul, 'Derrida's Engagement with Political Philosophy', in Mark Bevir, Jill Hargis and Sara Rushing (eds), *Histories of Postmodernism* (New York: Routledge, 2007), 149–69.

Peeters, Benoît, *Derrida: A Biography*, trans. Andrew Brown (Cambridge: Polity Press, 2013).

Pierce, Andrew J., 'Justice without Solidarity? Collective Identity and the Fate of the "Ethical" in Habermas' Recent Political Theory', *European Journal of Philosophy*, 26:1 (2018), 546–68.

Plato, *The Republic*, trans. Desmond Lee (London: Penguin, 1987).

Prentoulis, Marina and Lasse Thomassen, 'Political Theory in the Square: Protest, Representation and Subjectification', *Contemporary Political Theory*, 12:3 (2013), 166–84.

Rawls, John, *The Law of Peoples* (Cambridge, MA: Harvard University Press, 1999).

Rawls, John, *Political Liberalism* (New York: Columbia University Press, 1996).

Reeve, C. D. C., 'Philosophy, Politics, and Rhetoric in Aristotle', in Amélie Oksenberg Rorty (ed.), *Essays on Aristotle's Rhetoric* (Berkeley: University of California Press, 1996), 191–205.

Rehg, William and James Bohman (eds), *Pluralism and the Pragmatic Turn: The Transformation of Critical Theory: Essays in Honor of Thomas McCarthy* (Cambridge, MA: MIT Press, 2001).

Ricoeur, Paul, *The Rule of Metaphor: The Creation of Meaning in Language*, trans. R. Czerny, K. McLaughlin and J. Costello (London: Routledge, 2003).

Rorty, Richard, *Achieving our Country: Leftist Thought in Twentieth-Century America* (Cambridge, MA: Harvard University Press, 1998).

Rorty, Richard, *Consequences of Pragmatism* (Brighton: Harvester Press, 1982).

Rorty, Richard, *Contingency, Irony, Solidarity* (Cambridge: Cambridge University Press, 1989).

Rorty, Richard, *Essays on Heidegger and Others: Philosophical Papers, Volume 2* (Cambridge: Cambridge University Press, 1991).

Rorty, Richard, 'Habermas, Derrida and the Functions of Philosophy', in Lasse Thomassen (ed.), *The Derrida-Habermas Reader* (Edinburgh: Edinburgh University Press, 2006), 46–99.

Rorty, Richard, 'Is Derrida a Transcendental Philosopher?', in Gary B. Madison (ed.), *Working Through Derrida* (Evanston: Northwestern University Press, 1993), 137–46.

Rorty, Richard, *Objectivity, Relativism, and Truth: Philosophical Papers, Volume 1* (Cambridge: Cambridge University Press, 1991).

Rorty, Richard, *Philosophy and Social Hope* (London: Penguin, 1999).

Rorty, Richard, 'Remarks on Deconstruction and Pragmatism', in Chantal Mouffe (ed.), *Deconstruction and Pragmatism* (London: Routledge, 1996), 13–18.

Richard Rorty, 'Response to Ernesto Laclau', in Chantal Mouffe (ed.), *Deconstruction and Pragmatism* (London: Routledge, 1996), 69–76.

Rorty, Richard, 'Response to Simon Critchley', in Chantal Mouffe (ed.), *Deconstruction and Pragmatism* (London: Routledge, 1996), 41–6.

Rorty, Richard, 'Towards a Postmetaphysical Culture', in Eduardo Mendieta (ed.), *Take Care of Freedom and Truth Will Take Care of Itself: Interviews with Richard Rorty* (Stanford: Stanford University Press, 2006), 46–55.

Rorty, Richard, *Truth and Progress: Philosophical Papers, Volume 3* (Cambridge: Cambridge University Press, 1998).

Rorty, Richard, 'Universality and Truth', in Robert B. Brandom (ed.), *Rorty and his Critics* (Oxford: Blackwell, 2000), 1–30.

Rostbøll, Christian F., *Deliberative Freedom: Deliberative Democracy as Critical Theory* (Albany: State University of New York Press, 2008).

Rummens, Stefan, 'Democracy as a Non-Hegemonic Struggle? Disambiguating Chantal Mouffe's Agonistic Model of Politics', *Constellations*, 16:3 (2009), 377–91.

Sachs, Joe, *Plato* Gorgias *and* Aristotle *Rhetoric* (Newburyport, MA: Focus Publishing, 2009).

Sanders, Lynn, 'Against Deliberation', *Political Theory*, 25:3 (1997), 347–76.

Sartre, Jean Paul, 'Discussion', in *Existentialism and Humanism*, trans. Philip Mairet (London: Methuen, 1989), 57–70.

Schaap, Andrew, 'Agonism in Divided Societies', *Philosophy and Social Criticism*, 32:2 (2007), 255–77.

Schaap, Andrew (ed.), *Law and Agonistic Politics* (Farnham: Ashgate Publishing, 2009).

Schaap, Andrew, 'Political Theory and the Agony of Politics', *Political Studies Review*, 5:1 (2008), 171–93.

Schmitt, Carl, *The Concept of the Political*, trans. George Schwab (Chicago: University of Chicago Press, 1996).

Schumpeter, Joseph, *Capitalism, Socialism and Democracy* (London: Allen & Unwin, 1976).

Schwab, Martin, 'The Fate of Phenomenology in Deconstruction: Derrida and Husserl', *Inquiry*, 49:4 (2006), 353–79.

Scruton, Roger, 'Upon Nothing', *Philosophical Investigations*, 17:3 (1994), 481–506.
Smith, Anna Maria, *Laclau and Mouffe: The Radical Democratic Imaginary* (London: Routledge, 1998).
Smith, Barry and Jeffrey Sims, 'Revisiting the Derrida Affair', *Sophia*, 38:2 (1999), 142–69.
Snow, David A., E. Burke Rochford Jr, Steven K. Worden and Robert D. Benford, 'Frame Alignment Processes, Micromobilization, and Movement Participation', *American Sociological Review*, 51:4 (1986), 464–81.
Staten, Henry, *Wittgenstein and Derrida* (Lincoln: University of Nebraska Press, 1984).
Still, Judith, *Derrida and Hospitality: Theory and Practice* (Edinburgh: Edinburgh University Press, 2010).
Taylor, Matthew, '"White Europe": 60,000 nationalists march on Poland's independence day', *The Guardian*, 12 November 2017, <https://www.theguardian.com/world/2017/nov/12/white-europe-60000-nationalists-march-on-polands-independence-day> (last accessed 31 January 2020).
Taylor, Verta, 'Social Movement Continuity: The Women's Movement in Abeyance', *American Sociological Review*, 54:5 (1989), 761–75.
Thomassen, Lasse, *Deconstructing Habermas* (London: Routledge, 2008).
Thomassen, Lasse (ed.), *The Derrida-Habermas Reader* (Edinburgh: Edinburgh University Press, 2006).
Thompson, John B. and David Held, *Habermas: Critical Debates* (London: Macmillan Press, 1982).
Thomson, Alex, 'What's to Become of "Democracy to Come"?', *Postmodern Culture*, 15:3 (2005).
Thucydides, *The War of the Peloponnesians and Athenians*, trans. James Mynott (Cambridge: Cambridge University Press, 2013).
Tierney, Kathleen J., 'The Battered Women Movement and the Creation of the Wife Beating Problem', *Social Problems*, 29:3 (1982), 207–20.
Tully, James, 'The Democratic Paradox by Chantal Mouffe', *Political Theory*, 30:6 (2002), 862–4.
Tully, James, 'Dialogue', *Political Theory*, 39:1 (2011), 145–60.

Tully, James, *Strange Multiplicity: Constitutionalism in an Age of Diversity* (Cambridge: Cambridge University Press, 1995).

Tully, James, 'The Unfreedom of the Moderns in Comparison to their Ideals of Constitutional Democracy', *The Modern Law Review*, 65:2 (2002), 204–28.

Tyler, Imogen, *Revolting Subjects: Social Abjection and Resistance in Neoliberal Britain* (London: Zed Books, 2013).

Van der Walt, Johan, 'Rawls and Derrida on the Historicity of Constitutional Democracy and International Justice', *Constellations*, 16:1 (2009), 24–43.

Velleman, David, 'Love as Moral Emotions', *Ethics*, 10:9 (1999), 338–74.

Wardy, Robert, 'Mighty Is the Truth and It Shall Prevail', in Amélie Oksenberg Rorty (ed.), *Essays on Aristotle's Rhetoric* (Berkeley: University of California Press, 1996), 56–87.

Waters, Lindsay and Wlad Godzich (eds), *Reading de Man Reading* (Minneapolis: University of Minnesota Press, 1989).

Wenman, Mark, *Agonistic Democracy: Constitutive Power in the Era of Globalisation* (Cambridge: Cambridge University Press, 2013).

White, Stephen K., 'After Critique: Affirming Subjectivity in Contemporary Political Theory', *European Journal of Political Theory*, 2:2 (2003), 209–26.

White, Stephen K., *Postmodernism and Political Theory* (Cambridge: Cambridge University Press, 1996).

White, Stephen K., *Sustaining Affirmation: The Strengths of Weak Ontology in Political Theory* (Princeton: Princeton University Press, 2000).

Wilson, J., 'That sweet sound sleep that is the lot o' a gude conscience', *Blackwood Magazine*, April 1827, 476.

Wingenbach, Ed, *Institutionalizing Agonistic Democracy: Post-Foundationalism and Political Liberalism* (Farnham: Ashgate Publishing, 2011).

Wintour, Patrick and Hatty Collier, 'Nigel Farage launches UKIP campaign amid criticism of "racist" rhetoric', *The Guardian*, 22 April 2014, <http://www.theguardian.com/politics/2014/apr/22/nigel-farage-ukip-european-elections-campaign> (last accessed 31 January 2020).

Wolin, Richard, 'Deconstruction at Auschwitz: Heidegger, de

Man, and the New Revisionism', *South Central Review*, 11:1 (1994), 2–22.

Wolin, Richard, *The Seduction of Unreason: The Intellectual Romance with Fascism from Nietzsche to Postmodernism* (Princeton: Princeton University Press, 2004).

Wolin, Sheldon, 'Fugitive Democracy', in Seyla Benhabib (ed.), *Democracy and Difference* (Princeton: Princeton University Press, 1996), 31–45.

Wood, David, 'The Experience of the Ethical', in Richard Kearney and Mark Dooley (eds), *Questioning Ethics* (London: Routledge, 1999), 105–19.

Wood, David, 'Responsibility Reinscribed (and How)', in Jacques Derrida, *Responsibilities of Deconstruction*, ed. Jonathan Dronsfield and Nick Midgley, *PLI: Warwick Journal of Philosophy*, 6 (Summer 1997), 103–13.

Wood, David and Robert Bernasconi, *Derrida and Différance* (Warwick: Parousa Press, 1985).

Young, Iris Marion, 'Activist Challenges to Deliberative Democracy', *Political Theory*, 29:5 (2001), 670–90.

Young, Iris Marion, 'Communication and the Other: Beyond Deliberative Democracy', in Seyla Benhabib (ed.), *Democracy and Difference* (Princeton: Princeton University Press, 1996), 120–35.

Young, Iris Marion, 'Difference as a Resource for Democratic Communication', in James Bohman and William Rehg (eds), *Deliberative Democracy: Essays on Reason and Politics* (Cambridge, MA: MIT Press, 1997), 383–406.

Young, Iris Marion, *Inclusion and Democracy* (Oxford: Oxford University Press, 2000).

Young, Iris Marion, *Justice and the Politics of Difference* (Princeton: Princeton University Press, 1990).

Žižek, Slavoj, *Did Somebody Say Totalitarianism? Five Interventions in the (Mis)Use of a Notion* (London: Verso, 2001).

Žižek, Slavoj, 'Melancholy and the Act', *Critical Inquiry*, 26:4 (2000), 657–81.

Index

Abizadeh, Arash, 47, 80
Adorno, Theodor W., 8, 31–2, 133, 142n
agonism *see* Mouffe, Chantal: on agonism
Allen, Amy, 272n
antagonism *see* Mouffe, Chantal: on antagonism
aporia, 3, 168, 178–9, 196–7, 242–3, 260
Aristotle, 15, 101n
  on rhetoric, 7, 63, 77–80, 85–92, 98n, 99n, 100n, 120n, 228n; *see also* manipulation; rhetoric

Beardsworth, Richard, 149, 183
Beckett, Samuel, 248
Benhabib, Seyla, 245–7, 249, 270n, 271n
Benjamin, Walter, 141n, 150
Bernstein, Richard J., 11n, 140n, 153
Blaug, Ricardo, 49, 101n, 270n
Bohman, James, 7, 25, 50, 65, 71–7, 94–6, 96n, 97n, 98n, 101n, 112–13, 119, 121, 125–6, 129, 140n, 141, 226n, 269n, 271n
Brady, John, 49–50

Caputo, John, 166
Chambers, Simone, 50
Cicero, 78
Cohen, Jean L., 33–4, 36, 57n, 58n

collective identification, 35
  Habermas, Jürgen, on, 6, 13, 26, 32–8, 48, 56n; *see also* exclusion; Habermas, Jürgen: and passions
  Mouffe, Chantal, on, 6, 13, 17–21, 29–33, 38–52, 57n; *see also* Mouffe, Chantal: friend/enemy distinction; Schmitt, Carl
Connolly, William E., 53, 113, 127, 250, 259
consensus, 4, 6, 12–16, 18, 20–3, 29, 31, 36–40, 48–51, 53, 62, 64, 66, 72–3, 107–8, 110, 122, 131, 138n, 232, 248, 251, 265; *see also* democratic deliberation: and reasoned argument; Habermas, Jürgen: on reasoned argument
Cooke, Maeve, 58n, 251, 271n
Critchley, Simon, 146, 204, 212, 221, 224

deconstruction *see* Derrida, Jacques
deliberative freedom, 7, 74, 93–4
deliberative standing, 4–5, 7, 63, 84, 92–4, 101n, 263
della Porta, Donatela, 265–7
democracy
  agonistic *see* Mouffe, Chantal: on agonism
  and autoimmunity, 9, 59n, 220–2, 231, 233–42, 268n

democracy (*cont.*)
　constitutional, 5, 9, 16, 46, 51,
　　56n, 218, 231–50, 253, 257,
　　268n, 270n, 273n
　and deconstruction *see* Derrida,
　　Jacques: and democracy
　deliberative, 5, 12–14, 16, 20,
　　24–5, 29, 31, 47, 49–51, 53,
　　62, 68–70, 73–4, 83–4, 93–5,
　　97n, 101n, 231–2, 241, 252,
　　259, 262, 265, 267
　and difference, 1, 4–5, 21, 37–8,
　　42–3, 50, 53, 63, 66, 68–71,
　　94, 135, 211, 232, 267
　and equality, 3, 7, 16, 18–19, 23,
　　34, 37, 64, 74–6, 83–4, 92–4,
　　113, 235, 245, 250
　and freedom, 92–3, 217, 220,
　　224, 230n, 232–8, 240, 242–3,
　　246, 268n
　and hope, 10, 57n, 220, 231–2,
　　259–61, 266, 268
　legitimacy of, 3–4, 7, 9, 12,
　　18, 36–8, 50–3, 62, 75–6,
　　83, 229n, 231, 241–9, 251,
　　271n
　liberal, 2, 16, 19, 44–5
　two-track model *see* Habermas,
　　Jürgen: two-track model of
　　democracy
democracy to-come, 139n, 157–8,
　　165, 198, 198–200, 214, 217,
　　226n, 232, 253, 258–62, 269n,
　　272n, 273n; *see also* Derrida,
　　Jacques: and democracy
democratic deliberation
　expansive conception of, 4–6,
　　50, 62–3, 65–9, 72, 76, 78, 82,
　　85–6, 95, 104, 116, 125, 127,
　　144
　and reasoned argument, 4, 8, 15,
　　37–8, 49–50, 62–5, 66–73,
　　75–6, 78, 80–1, 83–5, 88–9,
　　94–6, 98n, 104, 117–29,
　　140n, 141n, 249–50; *see
　　also* consensus; exclusion;
　　Habermas, Jürgen: and reasoned
　　argument; rhetoric
　supplementing approach, 7, 63,
　　65–71, 76–8, 80–6, 89, 95,
　　97n, 98n
　systemic approach, 7, 63, 81–6,
　　89, 92, 95, 96n, 98n, 99n, 127,
　　263
　unjust exclusion, 7, 62–8, 74–8,
　　81–5, 92, 95–6, 97n, 104
Derrida Jacques, 2, 3
　and argumentation, 4–5, 7, 60n,
　　95–6, 103–15, 115–26, 129,
　　133, 136, 139n, 140n, 203, 238
　and calculation, 8, 153–4, 174–5,
　　177–81, 186n, 187n, 188n,
　　190, 192–5, 200, 202–8,
　　210–14, 236–40, 252–8, 260–1,
　　269n; *see also* democracy:
　　constitutional
　on the concept of experience,
　　157, 159–81, 196, 201–2
　and democracy, 5, 9, 102–4, 136,
　　141, 156–9, 165, 185n, 190,
　　198, 202, 214–15, 227n, 228n,
　　231–46, 258–62, 268n, 269n,
　　270n, 271n
　on hospitality, 97n, 210, 228n,
　　233, 254–8, 272n
　and incalculability, 177–81, 192,
　　194, 196, 198–9, 202–3, 205–6,
　　208, 213, 217, 219, 232, 236,
　　238, 240, 247, 252–4, 256, 261,
　　265, 269n
　and normativity, 4–5, 8–9,
　　103–4, 131–6, 137n, 143n,
　　145, 155–9, 177–81, 185n,
　　189–202, 206–15, 221, 224–6,
　　227n, 230–1, 236, 238–9, 241,
　　250, 253–4, 258–61, 263, 266,
　　272n, 273n; *see also* ethos of
　　interruption; Laclau, Ernesto
　and politics, 4–5, 7–9, 38–41, 96,
　　102–4, 108–10, 119, 122–36,
　　140n, 141n, 142n, 143n,
　　144–8, 151–9, 174, 177–81,
　　184n, 185n, 186n, 194–207,
　　212–19, 220–6, 226n, 227n,
　　228n, 229n, 230n, 231–42,
　　245–6, 252–62, 266, 273n
　on Schmitt, 38–41
　and the transcendental, 5, 8, 103,

105–6, 109, 116–17, 138n,
144–50, 154, 161–2, 165–7,
169, 181, 182n, 183n, 184n
and undecidability, 8, 103, 143n,
144–5, 156–60, 168, 173–81,
186n, 187n, 189, 191–204, 206,
213–14, 216–17, 219–20, 225,
228n, 243, 253, 258
Dews, Peter, 8, 146–7, 149, 182n,
225
différance, 9, 105, 114, 138n, 161,
163, 167–9, 219, 221–6
Dooley, Mark, 106
Dryzek, John, 4, 50, 66–72, 76–7,
81–2, 85, 95, 96n, 97n, 99n,
119

Eagleton, Terry, 102, 127
Engel, Pascal, 105
Ercan, Selen, 263, 265, 274n
ethos of interruption, 5, 8–9,
168–74, 180–1, 190, 197–202,
212–15, 220–1, 236–8, 241,
254, 257–8, 261–3, 265; *see also*
Derrida, Jacques: and normativity
event, 108, 113, 168, 170–2, 183n,
198–9, 243–4, 246–7, 261
exclusion, 4–8, 12–13, 16–17,
19–23, 28–9, 31–2, 35, 38–48,
51, 59n, 62–9, 74–6, 82–5, 92–3,
97n, 104, 109, 118, 126, 128–9,
131–3, 135–6, 140n, 142n, 144,
222, 238, 245, 249–50, 252–3,
262–5; *see also* Habermas, Jürgen:
on reasoned argument; Mouffe,
Chantal: friend/enemy distinction;
poverty, political; Schmitt, Carl

Foucault, Michel, 110, 127
Fraser, Nancy, 8, 117–19, 122, 124,
138n, 148, 158, 185n, 212, 273n
Freud, Sigmund, 12, 17–18, 29
Freyenhagen, Fabian, 8, 227n
friend/enemy distinction *see* Mouffe,
Chantal: friend/enemy distinction;
Schmitt, Carl

Gagné, Patricia Lorraine, 35
Garsten, Bryan, 89

Garver, Eugene, 86, 88, 90–1
Gorgias, 85
Gutmann, Amy, 66, 97n, 117–18,
123–4, 139n

Habermas, Jürgen, 2, 3, 12, 259,
271n, 273n, 274n
on collective identification *see*
collective identification
on ethical discourse, 34, 36, 37,
251
identification, Habermas on *see*
exclusion
and impartiality, 4, 6, 13, 16,
18, 21, 23, 27, 34, 36–7, 40,
48–51, 62, 64, 72–3
on the lifeworld, 15–16, 26, 33,
71, 232
and passions, 6, 12–13, 17–18,
20–9, 47, 63
on practical discourse, 6, 13, 16,
21–5, 36–7
public sphere, 6, 24–8, 32–6, 53;
see also public sphere
on reasoned argument, 4, 7, 8,
15–16, 18–28, 31, 36, 40, 46,
50, 62–4, 80, 120, 140n, 250–1;
see also consensus; democratic
deliberation: and reasoned
argument; exclusion
two-track model of democracy, 6,
13, 24–5, 47, 51, 56n
Hägglund, Martin, 8, 156, 196–7,
221–4, 226n, 227n, 236
Hajer, Maarten, 264
Halin, Daniel, 24
Hegel, Georg Wilhelm Friedrich,
23, 106, 108, 110, 121, 146
Heidegger, Martin, 104–8, 137n,
154, 170, 234
Honig, Bonnie, 53–4, 271n
Horwitz, Noah, 244, 247
Howarth, David, 52
Husserl, Edmund, 146, 149, 161–2,
164–6, 170

immigration/ immigrants, 1–2, 10n,
57n, 83, 124, 142n, 155, 209,
228n, 229n, 254–6, 262–4

inclusion, 1, 3–4, 7, 13, 19–21, 23, 26, 34, 44, 46, 56n, 65, 67–71, 74–6, 94, 125, 129, 136, 140n, 238, 247, 249, 252–3, 257, 262, 264–5, 267, 274n

justice, 1–5, 8, 10, 12, 16, 34, 37, 49, 55n, 65, 72, 74–5, 83–4, 95–7, 103, 108–9, 118, 125, 127, 130, 135–6, 140n, 144–5, 155, 157, 174–5, 177–81, 186n, 188n, 189, 190–204, 206, 208, 212–14, 232–3, 236–8, 240–2, 247, 249–50, 252–4, 256–66, 268n, 271n, 272n, 274n

Kant, Immanuel, 14–15, 23, 31, 40, 85, 99n, 105–6, 231
Kapoor, Ilan, 52
Kearney, Richard, 195
Kierkegaard, Søren, 105, 178, 187n

Laclau, Ernesto, 8, 60n, 103, 138n, 144–5, 156–60, 170, 173, 175–7, 179, 195, 221, 236
Lawlor, Leonard, 165
Lefort, Claude, 14, 215–19, 229n, 230n, 233
Lévinas, Emmanuel, 205–6, 210
liberalism, 16–17, 19–20, 29, 44–6, 48, 55n, 225, 235, 242, 265
Lyotard, François, 108

manipulation, 14, 66, 81, 85–92, 101n; *see also* Aristotle: on rhetoric; rhetoric
Markell, Patchen, 24
McCarthy, Thomas, 8, 15, 36–8, 71, 138n, 146–8, 152–4, 156, 158, 182n, 185n, 212–13, 224–5, 227n, 273n
Mendonça, Ricardo Fabrino, 265, 274n
Michelman, Frank, 238, 270n, 271n
Mouffe, Chantal
on agonism, 6, 12–13, 17–18, 39–40, 48–9, 51–4, 55n, 57n, 60n

on antagonism, 6, 12–13, 17–21, 29–32, 38–48, 51–4, 59n, 232
on constitutive outside, 13, 32, 39–42, 47–8, 59n
on fantasy/ phantasy, 6, 13, 18, 29–31, 48
friend/enemy distinction, 12, 17, 19–20, 29, 38–41, 47–8, 51–2; *see also* collective identification
on the passions, 6, 12–13, 17–18, 20–31, 48, 51–3, 271n
on rationalism, 17–18, 20–5, 27–8, 31, 39, 46, 51, 55n, 63, 73
Murdoch, Iris, 172, 190, 213, 273n

Nietzsche, Friedrich, 10, 107, 124, 137n, 213
Norris, Christopher, 105–6

Olsen, Kevin, 244, 253, 270n
Owen, David, 84, 93, 99n, 101n, 124n, 127n

Patton, Paul, 234–5
Plato, 31, 107–8, 121, 232–5, 252, 268n, 269n
pluralism, 7, 13, 16–17, 36–7, 40, 48, 50–3, 57n, 63–5, 68–9, 71–2, 95, 125–6, 128–9, 131, 136, 232, 240; *see also* collective identification: Habermas, Jürgen on; collective identification: Mouffe, Chantal on
politics of the stage, 8, 104, 118, 122, 126–36, 144, 148, 189, 197, 242, 262–5
poverty, political, 74–5, 83–5, 92–4, 101n, 113, 140n
public deliberation, 3, 7, 12, 14, 50–1, 63–7, 71–2, 75–7, 80–2, 85, 93–5, 113, 129, 228n; *see also* inclusion
public reason, 7, 50, 62, 64, 72–4, 95, 125–6, 126, 129, 272n
public sphere, 66, 70, 74, 76, 82, 134, 140n, 224, 260, 264; *see also* Habermas, Jürgen: public sphere

Rawls, John, 82, 231, 268n
rhetoric, 7, 50, 63, 65–71, 76–8, 80–5, 89–92, 95, 98n, 101n, 104, 120, 126, 138n, 249–50, 265; *see also* Aristotle: on rhetoric; manipulation
Rorty, Richard, 7, 103–19, 129–30, 132, 137n, 138n, 144, 156, 158; *see also* Derrida, Jacques: and normativity
Rostbøll, Christian F., 93

Sanders, Lynn, 75
Schmitt, Carl, 12–13, 17, 19–20, 29, 31, 38–42, 48, 51; *see also* Mouffe, Chantal: constitutive outside; Mouffe, Chantal: friend/enemy distinction
Schumpeter, Joseph, 14, 31, 57n
Scruton, Roger, 102, 129, 145–6, 182n
social movements, 26, 33–5, 58n, 76, 245, 265, 267, 273

Thomassen, Lasse, 139n, 249, 262, 265, 270n
Thompson, Denis, 66, 97
Tully, James, 49, 53–4, 60n, 64–5, 74, 119, 129
Tyler, Imogen, 83, 264–5

Uitermark, Justus, 264
undecidability *see* Derrida, Jacques: and undecidability
universalism, universality, 3, 6, 13–15, 23, 34, 36, 47–8, 56n, 64

Velleman, David, 171–2

Weber, Max, 14
Wenman, Mark, 49
Wolin, Richard, 138n, 195, 229n
Wood, David, 170, 173, 197, 202

Young, Iris Marion, 31, 64–5, 68–71, 74, 76, 81, 119, 129, 264

EU representative:
Easy Access System Europe
Mustamäe tee 50, 10621 Tallinn, Estonia
Gpsr.requests@easproject.com

www.ingramcontent.com/pod-product-compliance
Lightning Source LLC
Chambersburg PA
CBHW050203240426
43671CB00013B/2236